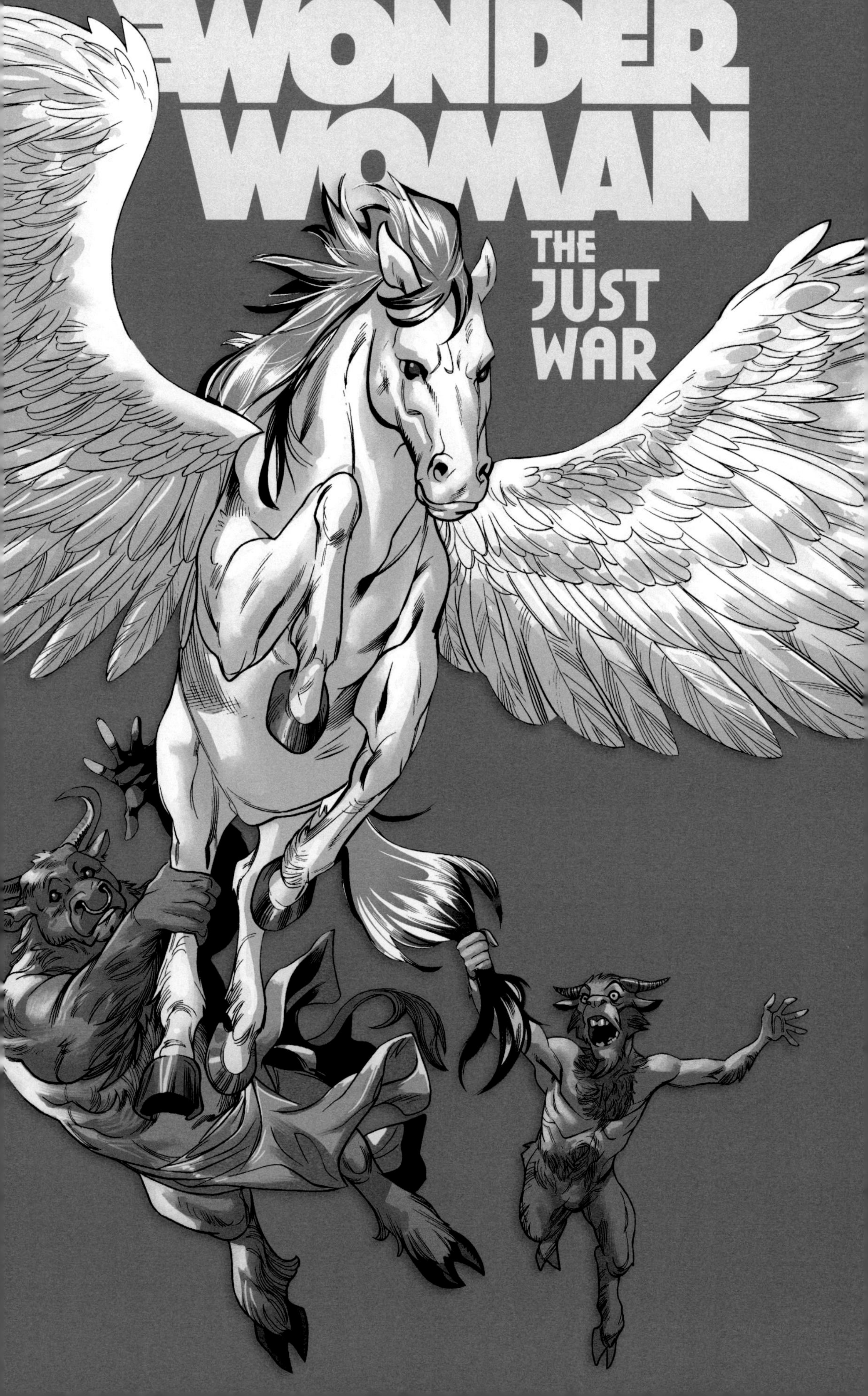
WONDER WOMAN
THE JUST WAR

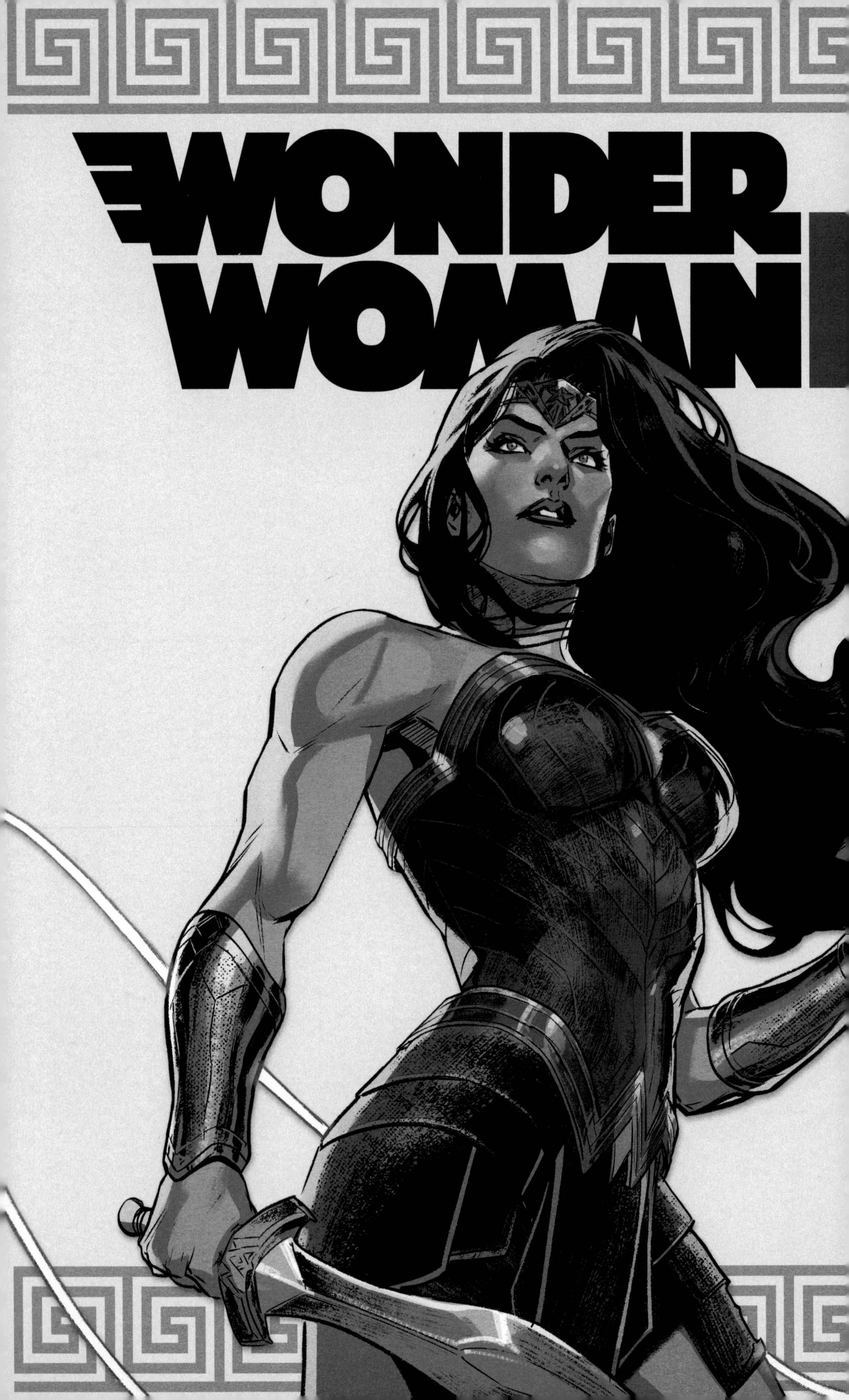
WONDER WOMAN

THE JUST WAR

G. WILLOW WILSON
WRITER

CARY NORD
XERMANICO
JESUS MERINO
EMANUELA LUPACCHINO
PENCILLERS

MICK GRAY
XERMANICO
ANDY OWENS
RAY McCARTHY
INKERS

ROMULO FAJARDO JR.
COLORIST

PAT BROSSEAU
LETTERER

TERRY DODSON & RACHEL DODSON
COLLECTION COVER ARTISTS

WONDER WOMAN CREATED BY WILLIAM MOULTON MARSTON

CHRIS CONROY
Editor – Original Series

DAVE WIELGOSZ
Assistant Editor – Original Series

JEB WOODARD
Group Editor – Collected Editions

ROBIN WILDMAN
Editor – Collected Edition

STEVE COOK
Design Director – Books

MEGEN BELLERSEN
Publication Design

DANIELLE DIGRADO
Publication Production

BOB HARRAS
Senior VP – Editor-in-Chief, DC Comics

PAT McCALLUM
Executive Editor, DC Comics

DAN DiDIO
Publisher

JIM LEE
Publisher & Chief Creative Officer

BOBBIE CHASE
VP – New Publishing Initiatives & Talent Development

DON FALLETTI
VP – Manufacturing Operations & Workflow Management

LAWRENCE GANEM
VP – Talent Services

ALISON GILL
Senior VP – Manufacturing & Operations

HANK KANALZ
Senior VP – Publishing Strategy & Support Services

DAN MIRON
VP – Publishing Operations

NICK J. NAPOLITANO
VP – Manufacturing Administration & Design

NANCY SPEARS
VP – Sales

MICHELE R. WELLS
VP & Executive Editor, Young Reader

WONDER WOMAN VOL. 1: THE JUST WAR

Published by DC Comics. Compilation and all new material Copyright © 2019 DC Comics. All Rights Reserved.
Originally published in single magazine form in WONDER WOMAN 58-65. Copyright © 2019 DC Comics. All
Rights Reserved. All characters, their distinctive likenesses and related elements featured in this publication
are trademarks of DC Comics. The stories, characters and incidents featured in this publication are entirely
fictional. DC Comics does not read or accept unsolicited submissions of ideas, stories or artwork.
DC – a WarnerMedia Company.

PEFC Certified

This product is from
sustainably managed
forests and controlled
sources

PEFC/29-31-337   www.pefc.org

DC Comics, 2900 West Alameda Ave., Burbank, CA 91505
Printed by LSC Communications, Kendallville, IN, USA. 9/20/19. First Printing.
ISBN: 978-1-77950-166-0

Library of Congress Cataloging-in-Publication Data is available.

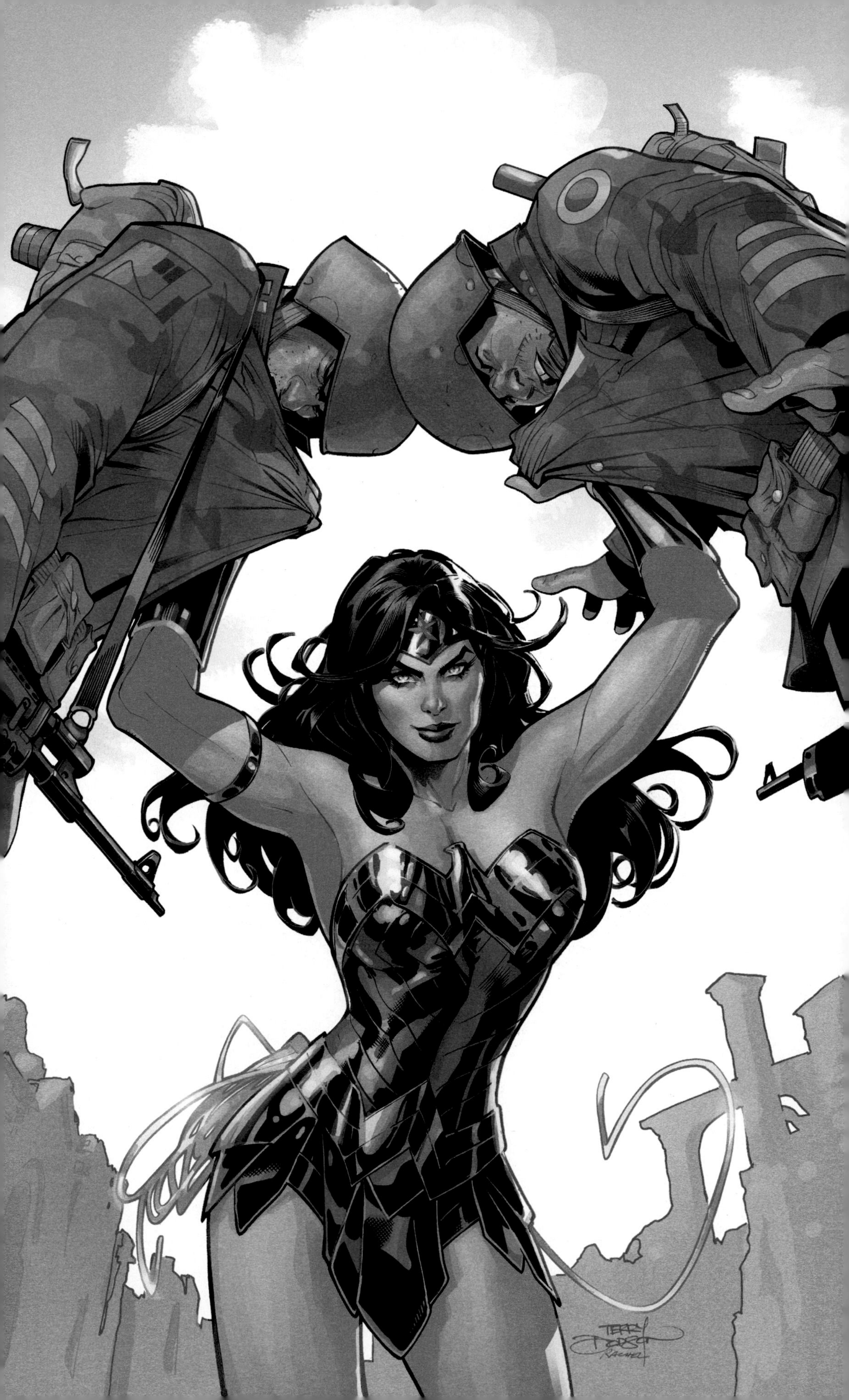
TERRY
DODSON
RACHEL

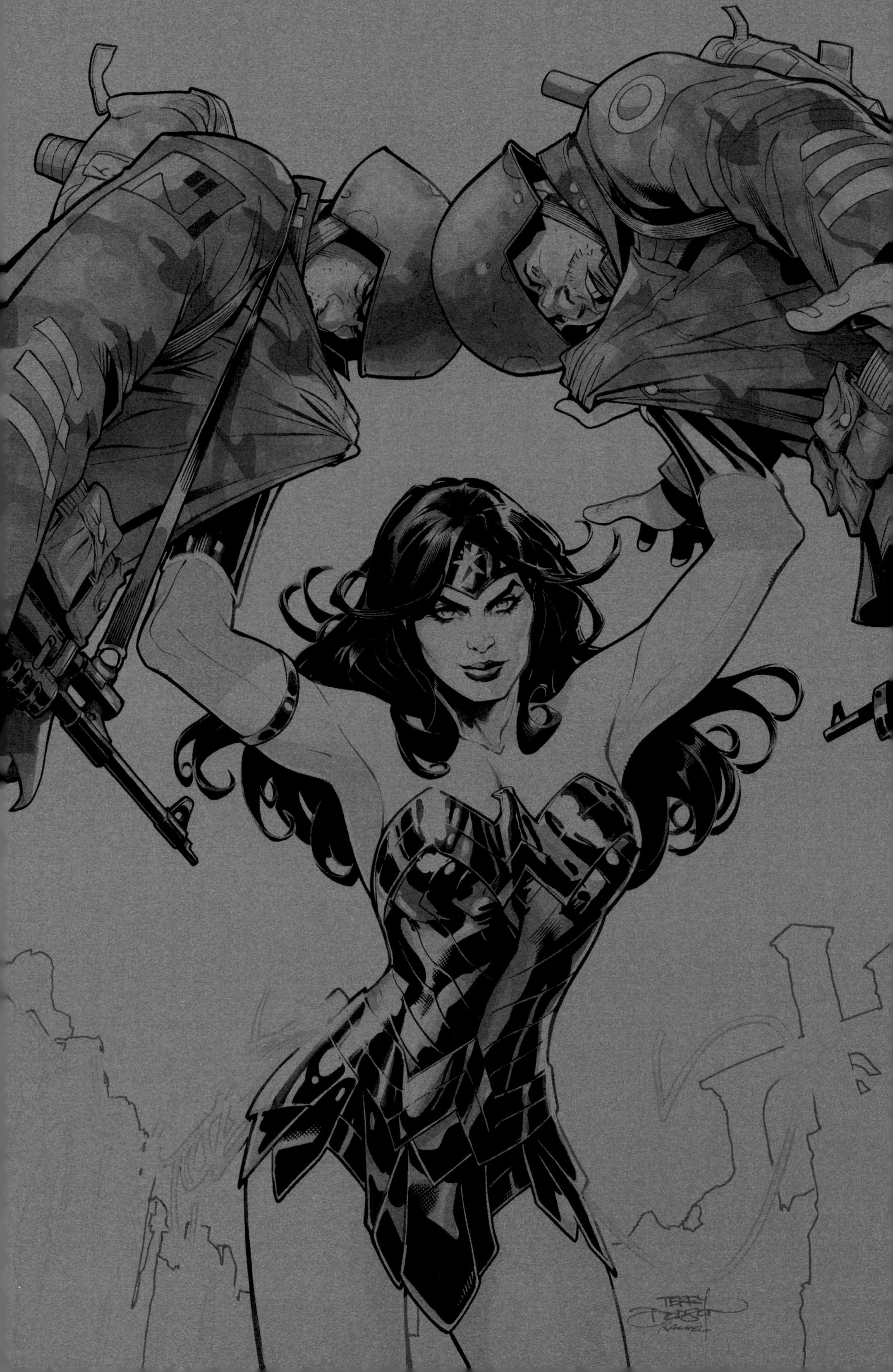

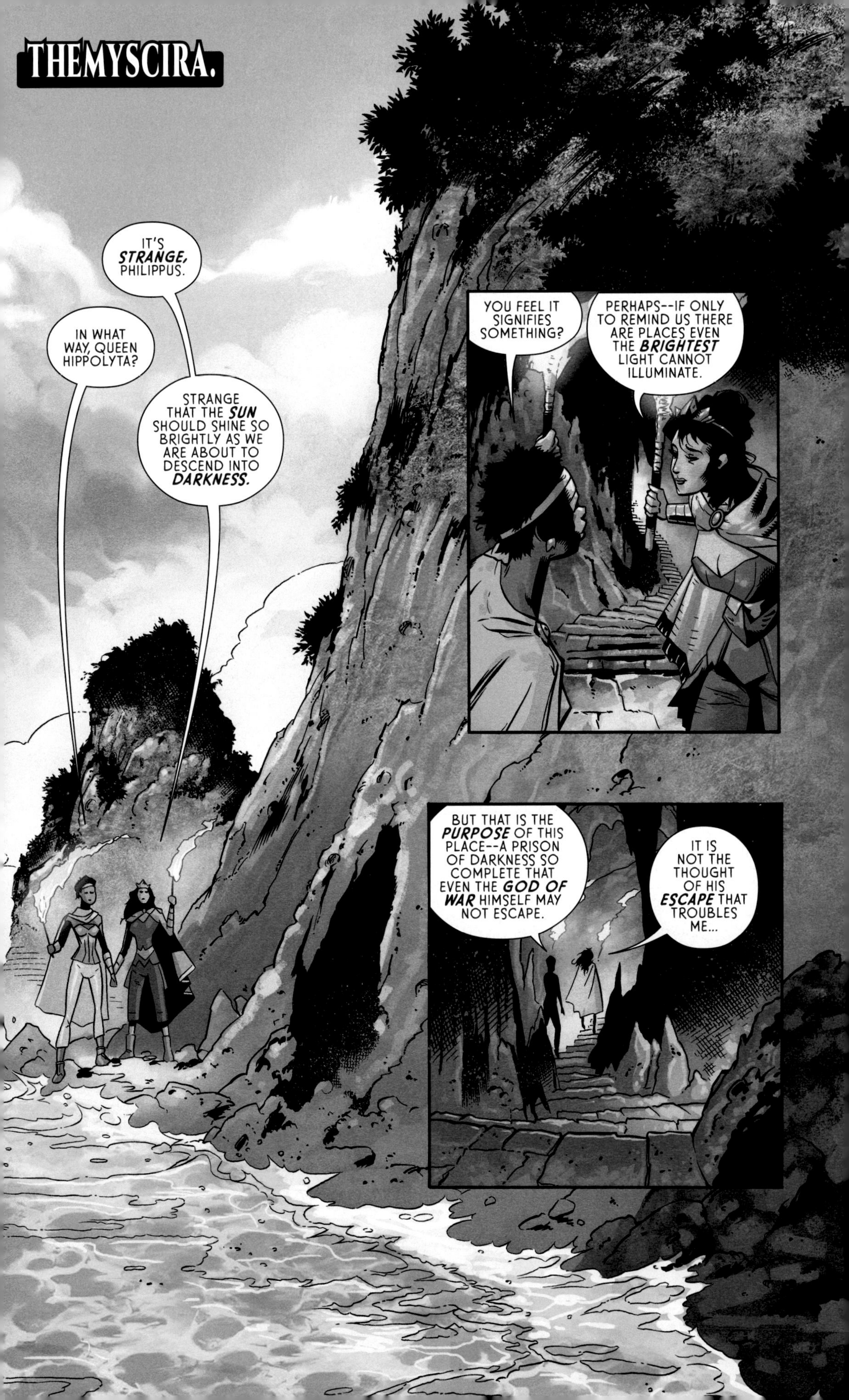
THEMYSCIRA.
IT'S STRANGE, PHILIPPUS.
IN WHAT WAY, QUEEN HIPPOLYTA?
STRANGE THAT THE SUN SHOULD SHINE SO BRIGHTLY AS WE ARE ABOUT TO DESCEND INTO DARKNESS.
YOU FEEL IT SIGNIFIES SOMETHING?
PERHAPS--IF ONLY TO REMIND US THERE ARE PLACES EVEN THE BRIGHTEST LIGHT CANNOT ILLUMINATE.
BUT THAT IS THE PURPOSE OF THIS PLACE--A PRISON OF DARKNESS SO COMPLETE THAT EVEN THE GOD OF WAR HIMSELF MAY NOT ESCAPE.
IT IS NOT THE THOUGHT OF HIS ESCAPE THAT TROUBLES ME...

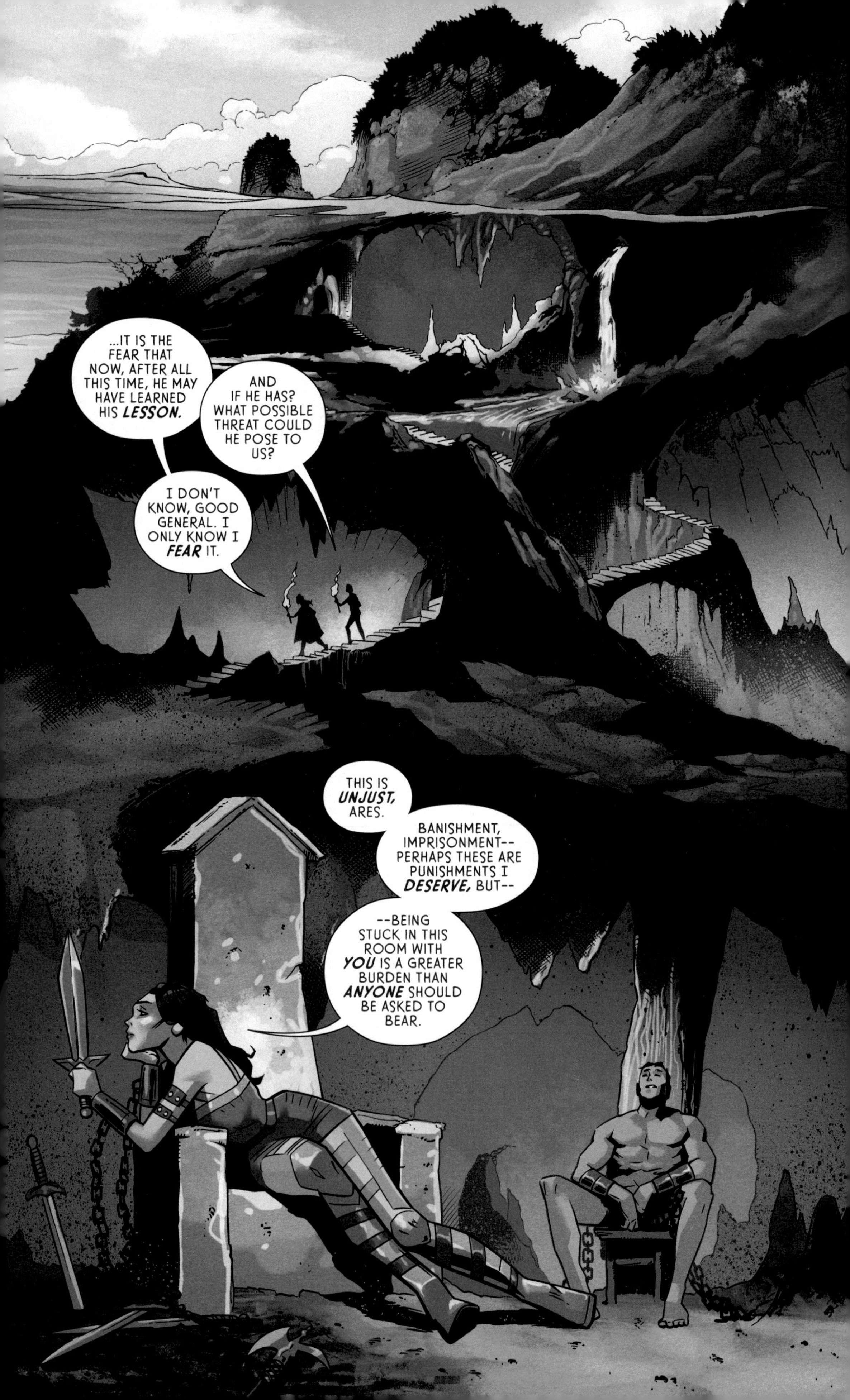
...IT IS THE FEAR THAT NOW, AFTER ALL THIS TIME, HE MAY HAVE LEARNED HIS **LESSON.**
AND IF HE HAS? WHAT POSSIBLE THREAT COULD HE POSE TO US?
I DON'T KNOW, GOOD GENERAL. I ONLY KNOW I **FEAR** IT.
THIS IS **UNJUST,** ARES.
BANISHMENT, IMPRISONMENT--PERHAPS THESE ARE PUNISHMENTS I **DESERVE,** BUT--
--BEING STUCK IN THIS ROOM WITH **YOU** IS A GREATER BURDEN THAN **ANYONE** SHOULD BE ASKED TO BEAR.

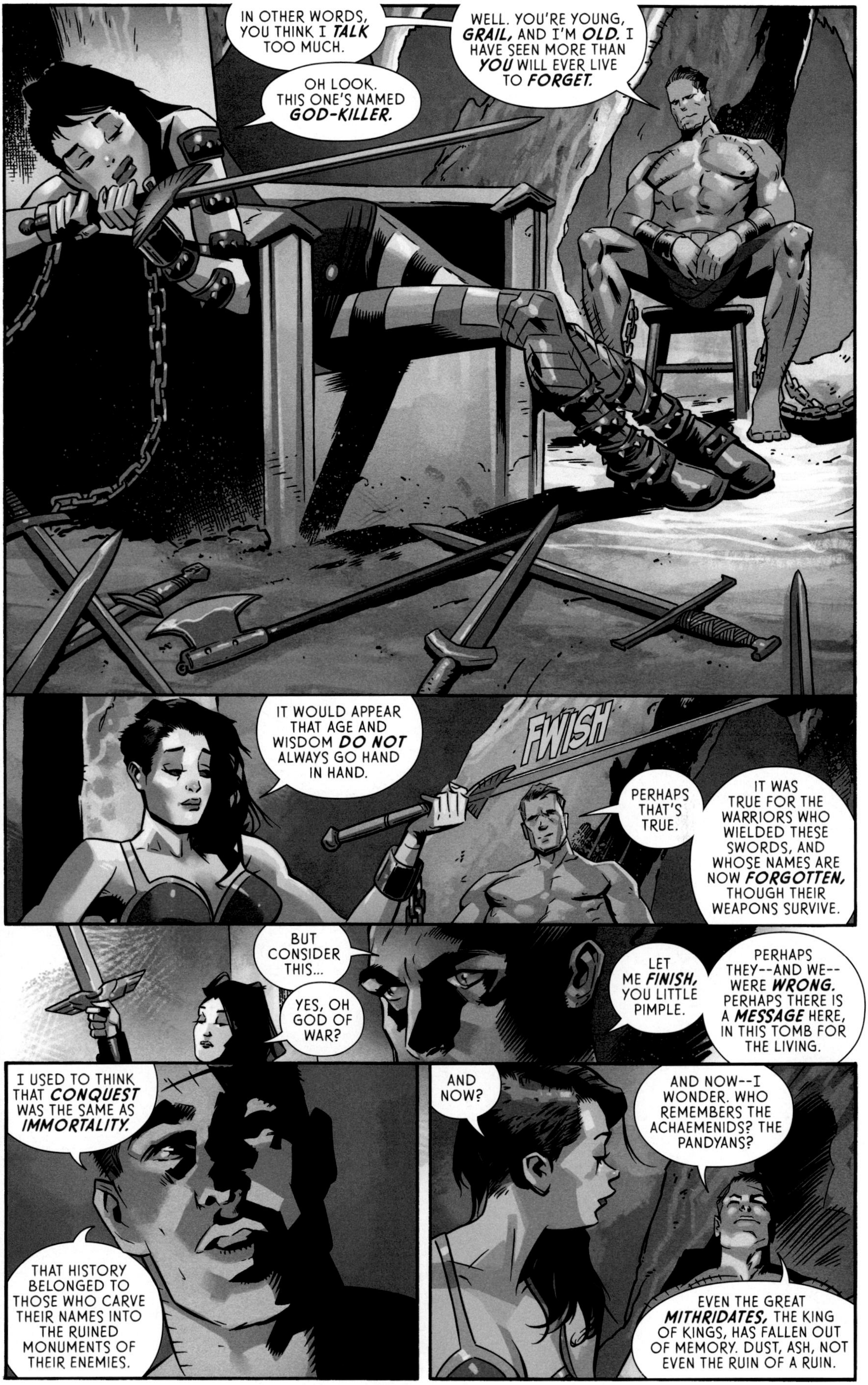
IN OTHER WORDS, YOU THINK I TALK TOO MUCH.
OH LOOK. THIS ONE'S NAMED GOD-KILLER.
WELL. YOU'RE YOUNG, GRAIL, AND I'M OLD. I HAVE SEEN MORE THAN YOU WILL EVER LIVE TO FORGET.
IT WOULD APPEAR THAT AGE AND WISDOM DO NOT ALWAYS GO HAND IN HAND.
FWISH
PERHAPS THAT'S TRUE.
IT WAS TRUE FOR THE WARRIORS WHO WIELDED THESE SWORDS, AND WHOSE NAMES ARE NOW FORGOTTEN, THOUGH THEIR WEAPONS SURVIVE.
BUT CONSIDER THIS...
YES, OH GOD OF WAR?
LET ME FINISH, YOU LITTLE PIMPLE.
PERHAPS THEY--AND WE--WERE WRONG. PERHAPS THERE IS A MESSAGE HERE, IN THIS TOMB FOR THE LIVING.
I USED TO THINK THAT CONQUEST WAS THE SAME AS IMMORTALITY.
THAT HISTORY BELONGED TO THOSE WHO CARVE THEIR NAMES INTO THE RUINED MONUMENTS OF THEIR ENEMIES.
AND NOW?
AND NOW--I WONDER. WHO REMEMBERS THE ACHAEMENIDS? THE PANDYANS?
EVEN THE GREAT MITHRIDATES, THE KING OF KINGS, HAS FALLEN OUT OF MEMORY. DUST, ASH, NOT EVEN THE RUIN OF A RUIN.

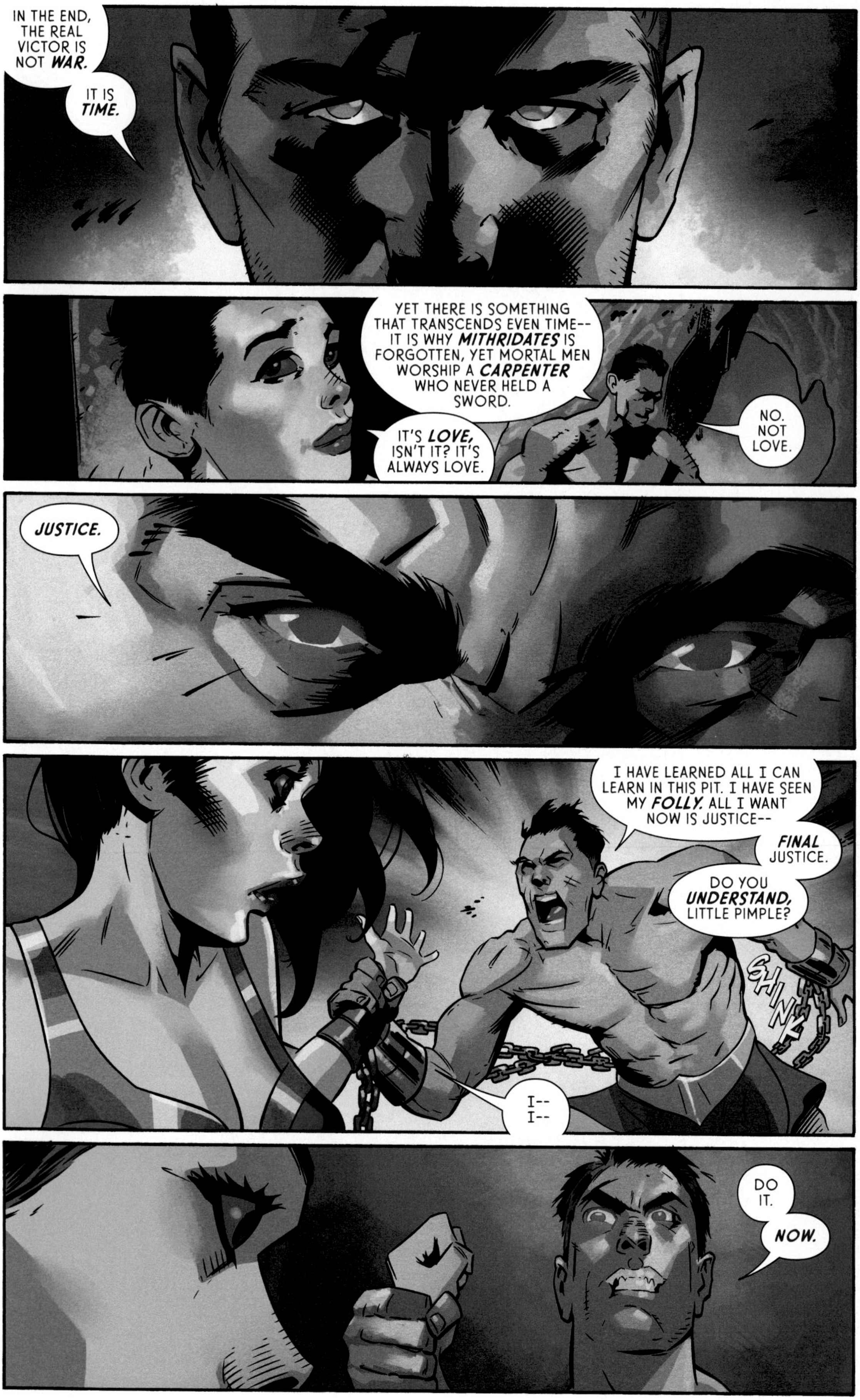
IN THE END, THE REAL VICTOR IS NOT WAR.
IT IS TIME.
YET THERE IS SOMETHING THAT TRANSCENDS EVEN TIME-- IT IS WHY MITHRIDATES IS FORGOTTEN, YET MORTAL MEN WORSHIP A CARPENTER WHO NEVER HELD A SWORD.
IT'S LOVE, ISN'T IT? IT'S ALWAYS LOVE.
NO. NOT LOVE.
JUSTICE.
I HAVE LEARNED ALL I CAN LEARN IN THIS PIT. I HAVE SEEN MY FOLLY. ALL I WANT NOW IS JUSTICE--
FINAL JUSTICE.
DO YOU UNDERSTAND, LITTLE PIMPLE?
SHINK
I-- I--
DO IT.
NOW.

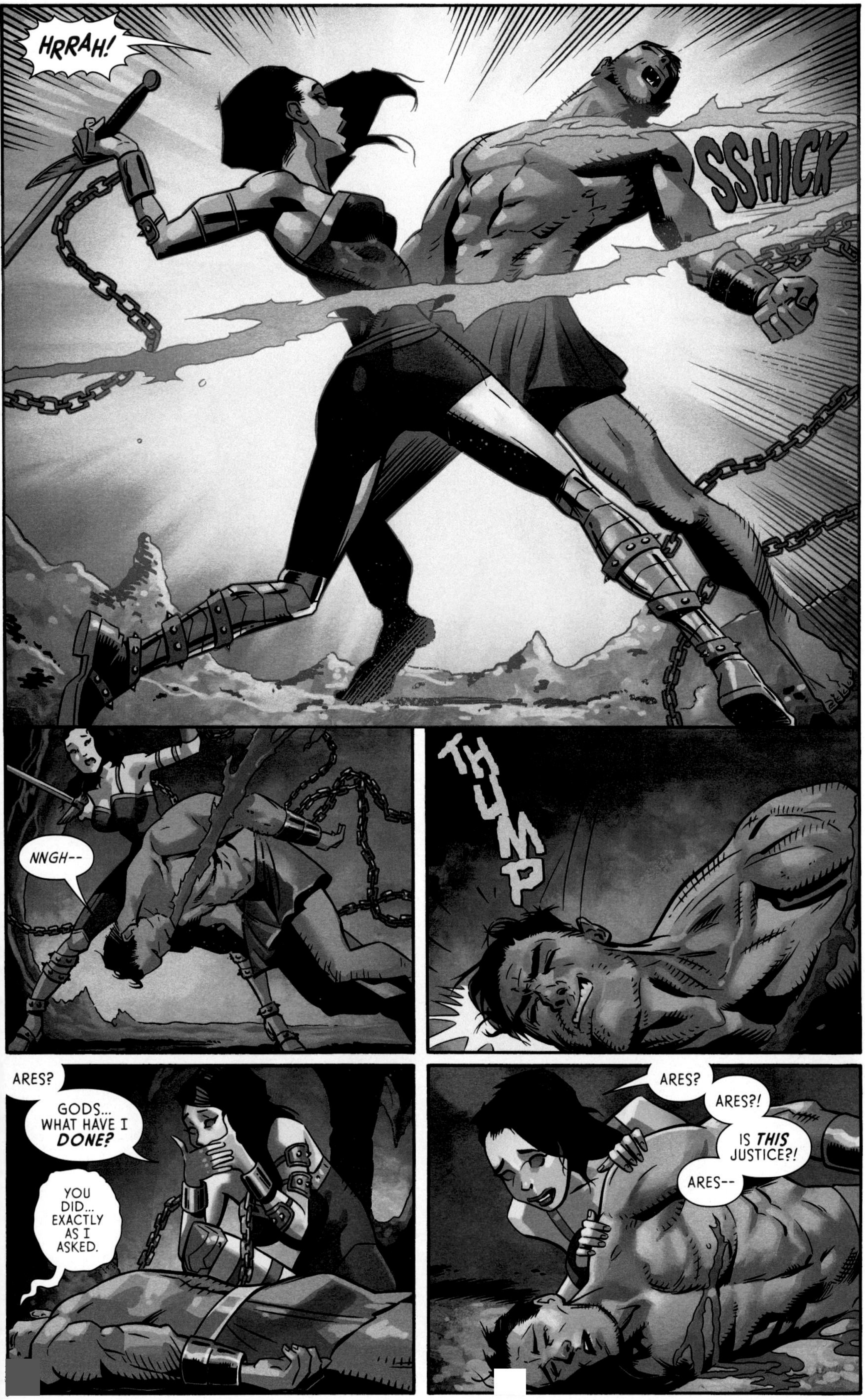
HRRAH!
SSHICK
NNGH--
THUMP
ARES?
GODS... WHAT HAVE I DONE?
YOU DID... EXACTLY AS I ASKED.
ARES?
ARES?!
IS THIS JUSTICE?!
ARES--

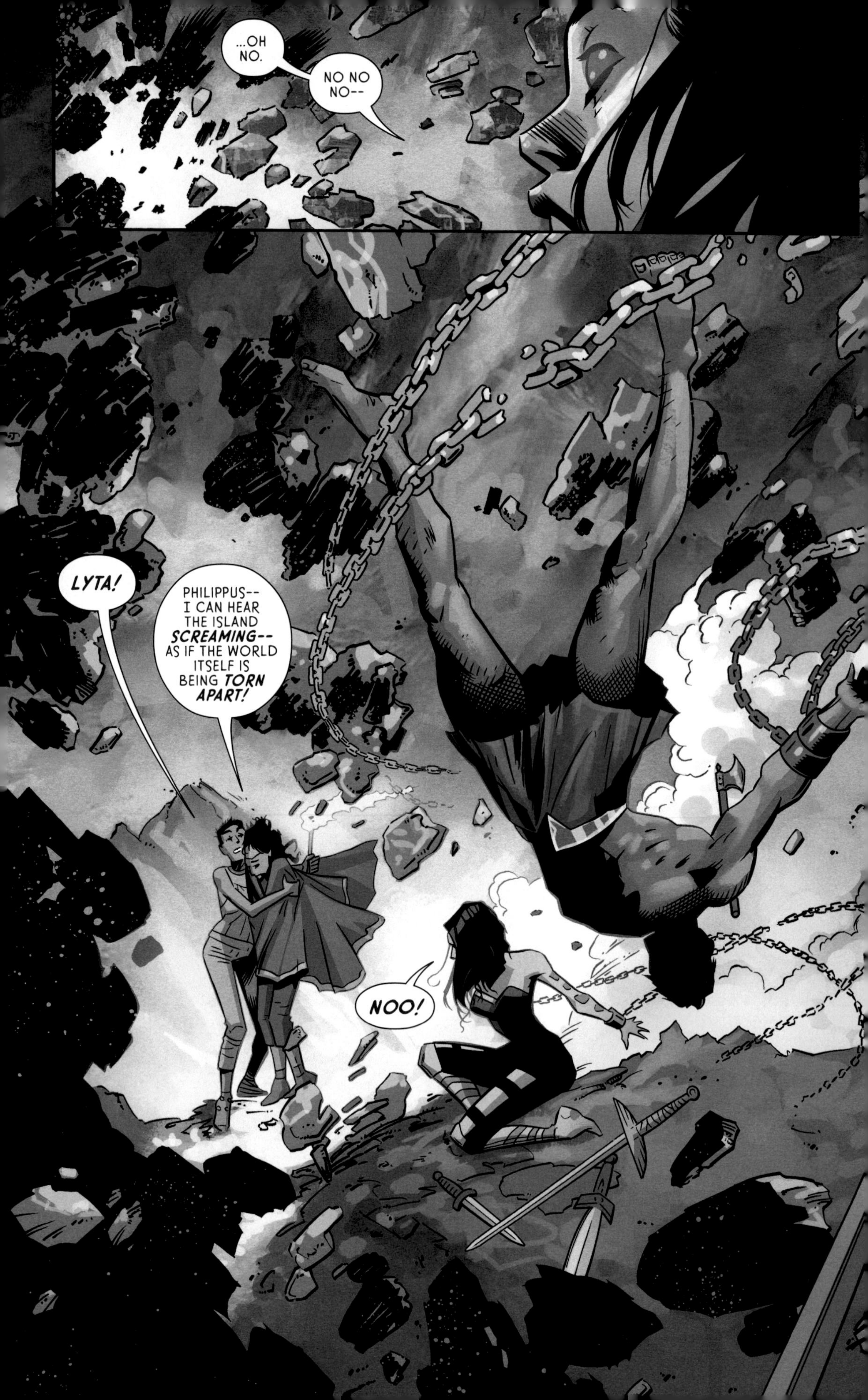
...OH NO.
NO NO NO--
LYTA!
PHILIPPUS-- I CAN HEAR THE ISLAND SCREAMING-- AS IF THE WORLD ITSELF IS BEING TORN APART!
NOO!

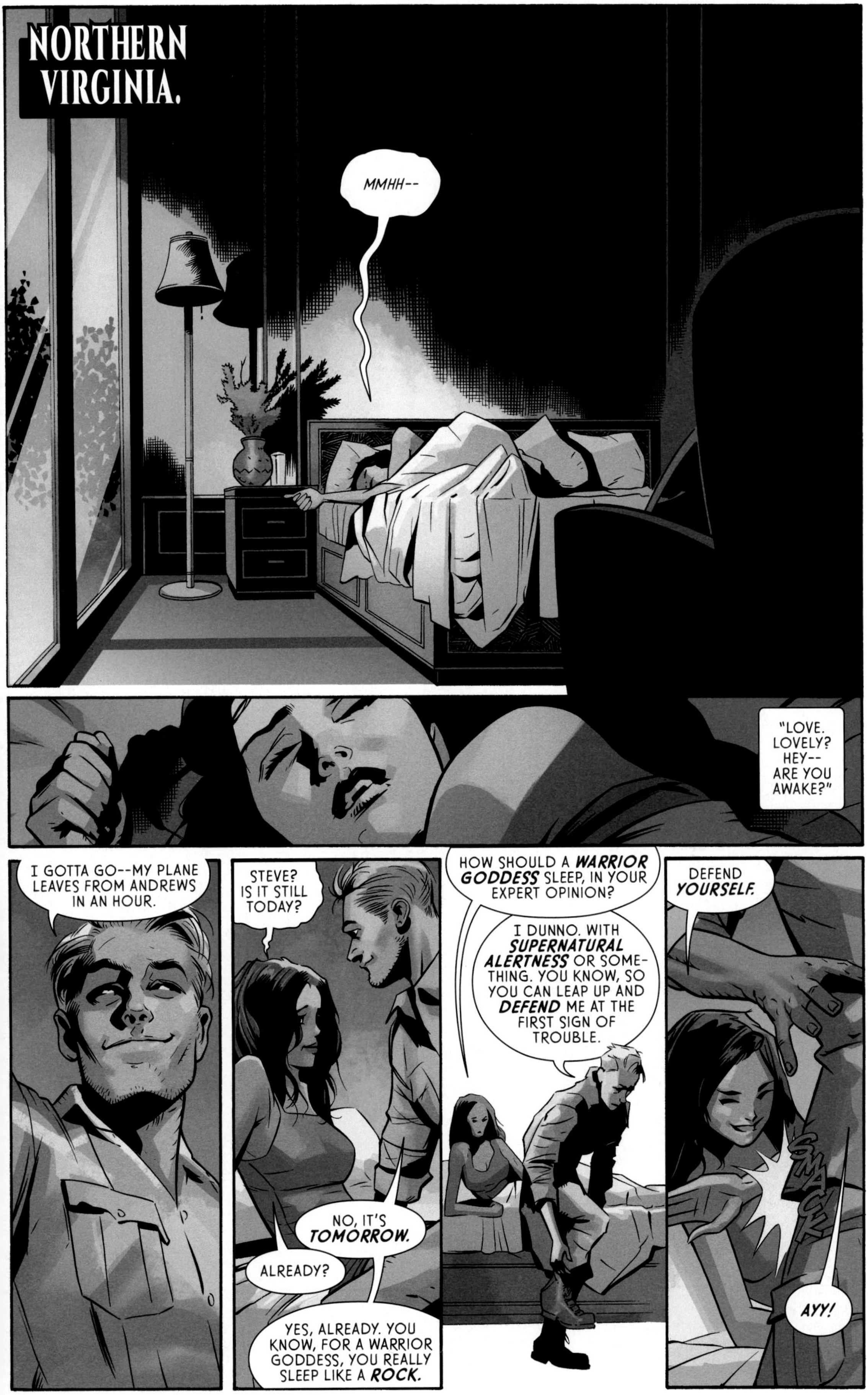
NORTHERN VIRGINIA.
MMHH--
"LOVE. LOVELY? HEY-- ARE YOU AWAKE?"
I GOTTA GO--MY PLANE LEAVES FROM ANDREWS IN AN HOUR.
STEVE? IS IT STILL TODAY?
NO, IT'S TOMORROW.
ALREADY?
YES, ALREADY. YOU KNOW, FOR A WARRIOR GODDESS, YOU REALLY SLEEP LIKE A ROCK.
HOW SHOULD A WARRIOR GODDESS SLEEP, IN YOUR EXPERT OPINION?
I DUNNO. WITH SUPERNATURAL ALERTNESS OR SOME-THING. YOU KNOW, SO YOU CAN LEAP UP AND DEFEND ME AT THE FIRST SIGN OF TROUBLE.
DEFEND YOURSELF.
SMACK
AYY!

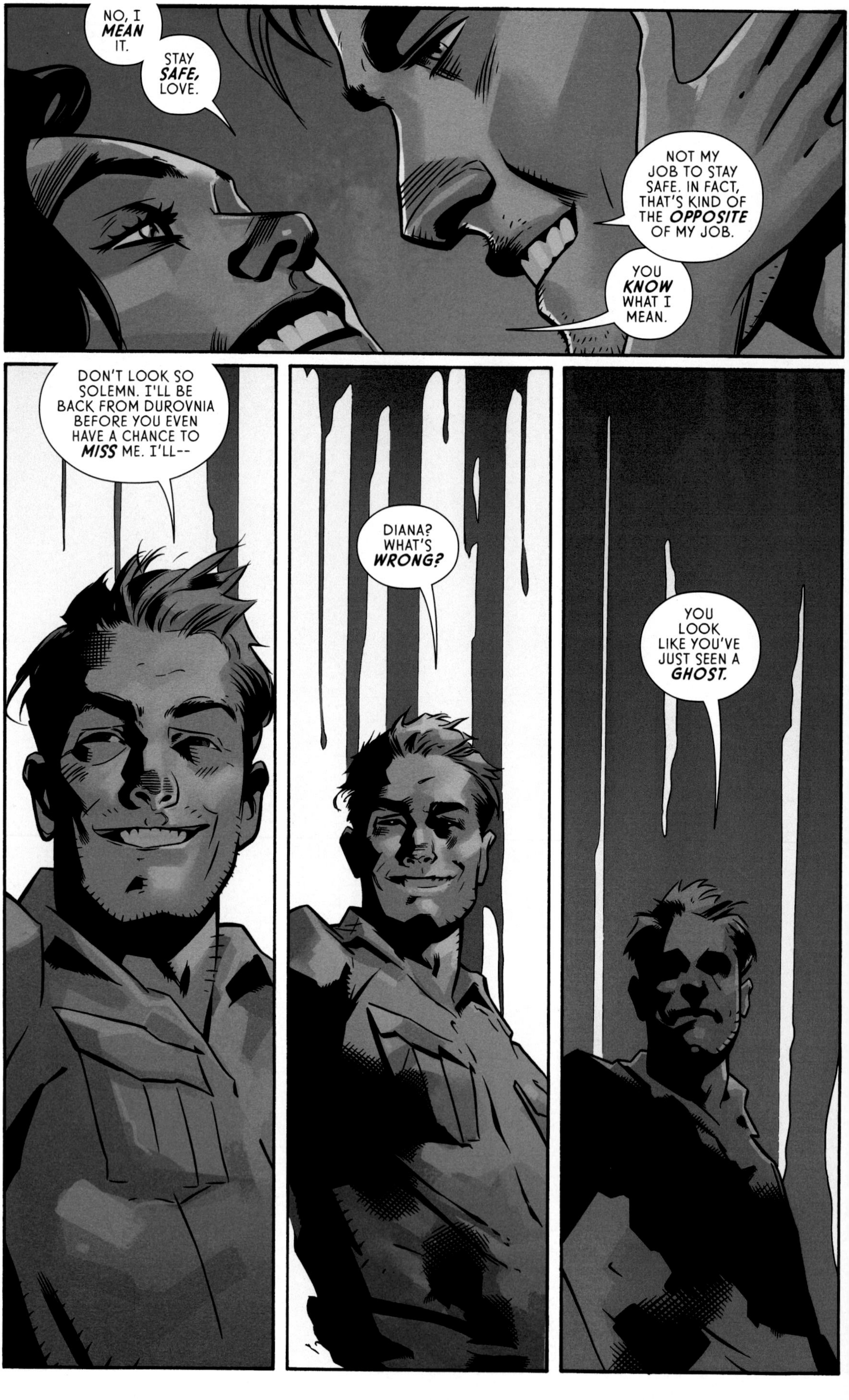
NO, I MEAN IT.
STAY SAFE, LOVE.
NOT MY JOB TO STAY SAFE. IN FACT, THAT'S KIND OF THE OPPOSITE OF MY JOB.
YOU KNOW WHAT I MEAN.
DON'T LOOK SO SOLEMN. I'LL BE BACK FROM DUROVNIA BEFORE YOU EVEN HAVE A CHANCE TO MISS ME. I'LL--
DIANA? WHAT'S WRONG?
YOU LOOK LIKE YOU'VE JUST SEEN A GHOST.

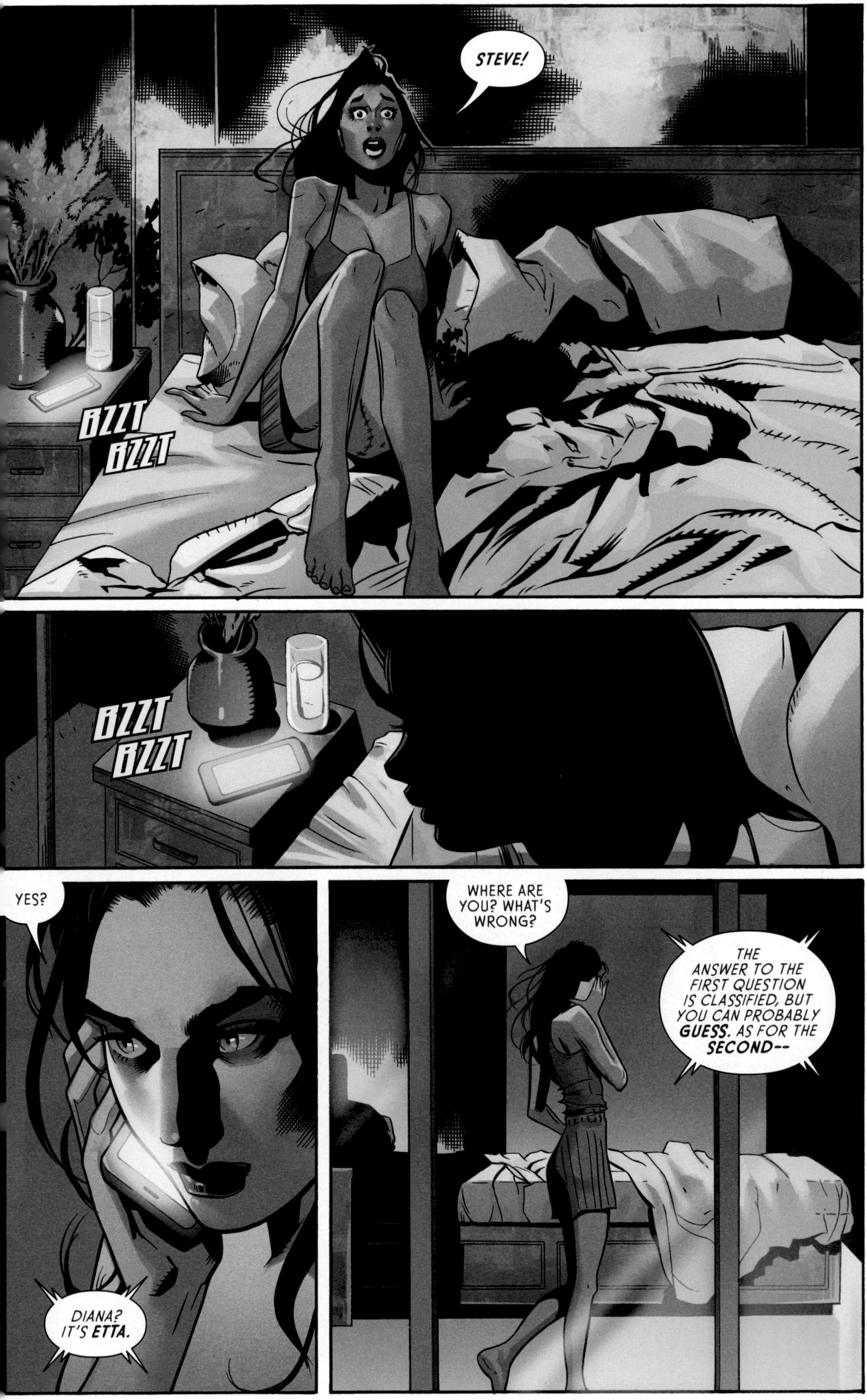
STEVE!
BZZT
BZZT
BZZT
BZZT
YES?
DIANA? IT'S **ETTA.**
WHERE ARE YOU? WHAT'S WRONG?
THE ANSWER TO THE FIRST QUESTION IS CLASSIFIED, BUT YOU CAN PROBABLY **GUESS.** AS FOR THE **SECOND--**

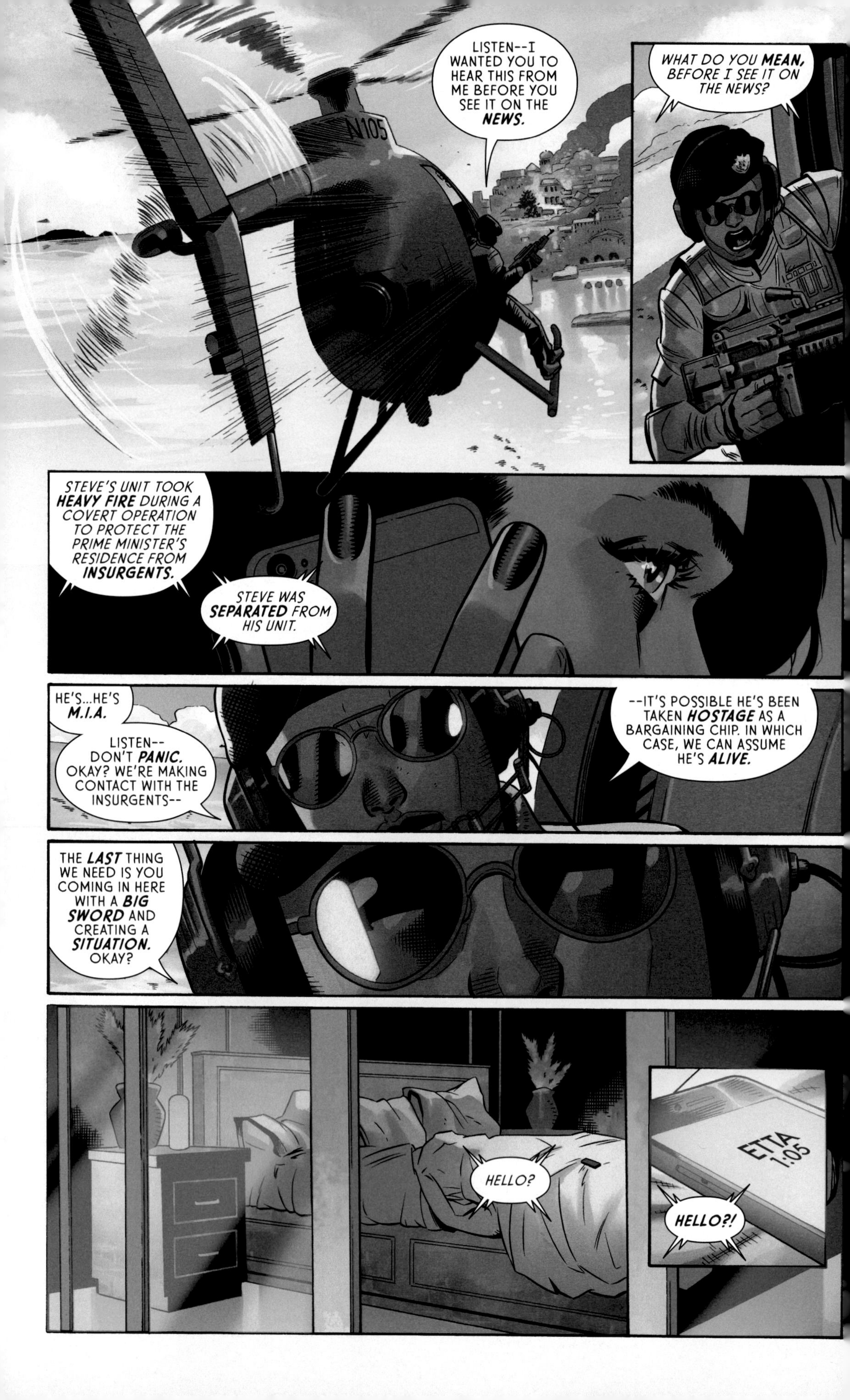
N105
LISTEN--I WANTED YOU TO HEAR THIS FROM ME BEFORE YOU SEE IT ON THE NEWS.
WHAT DO YOU MEAN, BEFORE I SEE IT ON THE NEWS?
STEVE'S UNIT TOOK HEAVY FIRE DURING A COVERT OPERATION TO PROTECT THE PRIME MINISTER'S RESIDENCE FROM INSURGENTS.
STEVE WAS SEPARATED FROM HIS UNIT.
HE'S...HE'S M.I.A.
LISTEN-- DON'T PANIC. OKAY? WE'RE MAKING CONTACT WITH THE INSURGENTS--
--IT'S POSSIBLE HE'S BEEN TAKEN HOSTAGE AS A BARGAINING CHIP. IN WHICH CASE, WE CAN ASSUME HE'S ALIVE.
THE LAST THING WE NEED IS YOU COMING IN HERE WITH A BIG SWORD AND CREATING A SITUATION. OKAY?
HELLO?
ETTA 1:05
HELLO?!

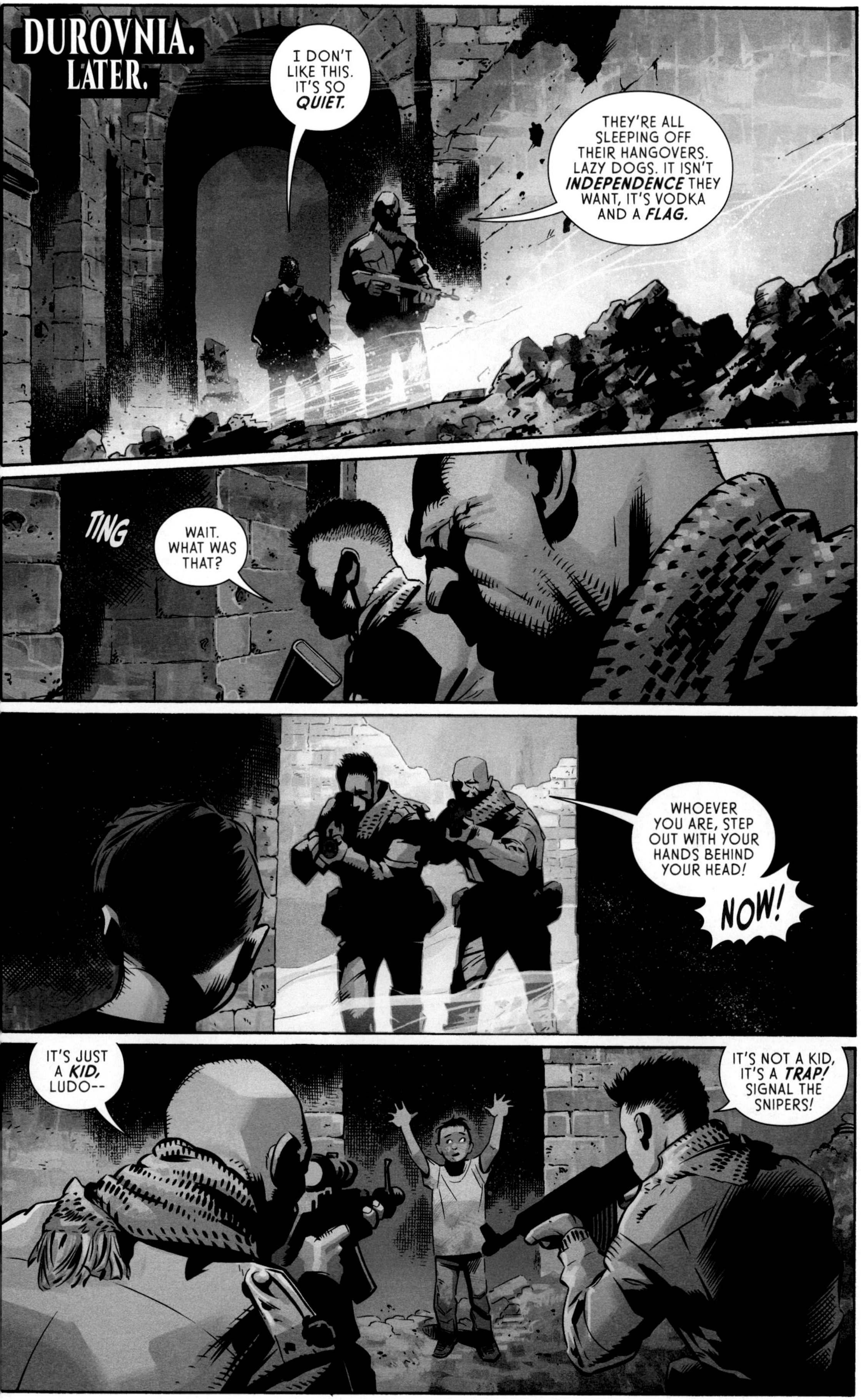
DUROVNIA. LATER.
I DON'T LIKE THIS. IT'S SO QUIET.
THEY'RE ALL SLEEPING OFF THEIR HANGOVERS. LAZY DOGS. IT ISN'T INDEPENDENCE THEY WANT, IT'S VODKA AND A FLAG.
TING
WAIT. WHAT WAS THAT?
WHOEVER YOU ARE, STEP OUT WITH YOUR HANDS BEHIND YOUR HEAD!
NOW!
IT'S JUST A KID, LUDO--
IT'S NOT A KID, IT'S A TRAP! SIGNAL THE SNIPERS!

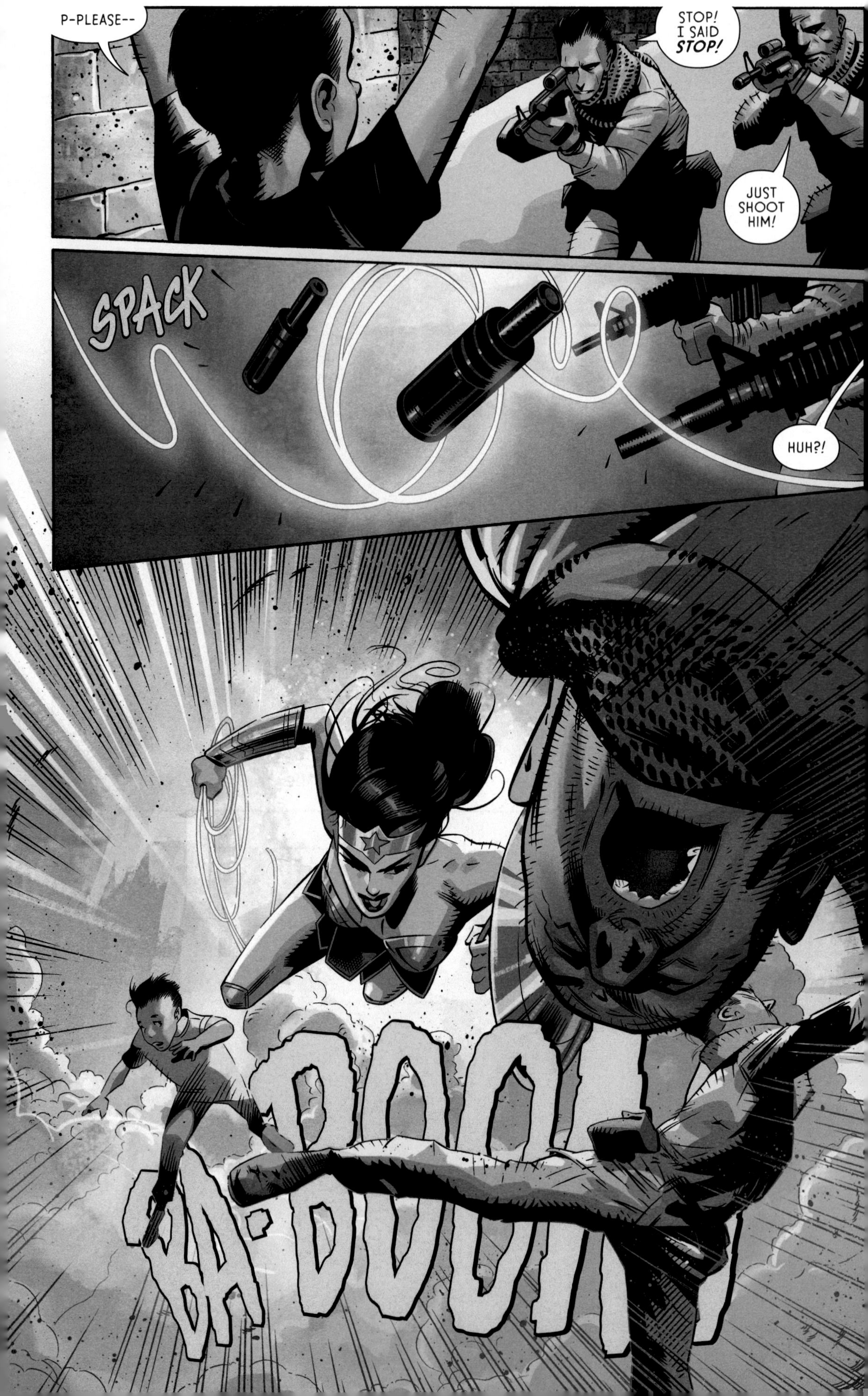
P-PLEASE--
STOP! I SAID STOP!
JUST SHOOT HIM!
SPACK
HUH?!
BA-DOOM

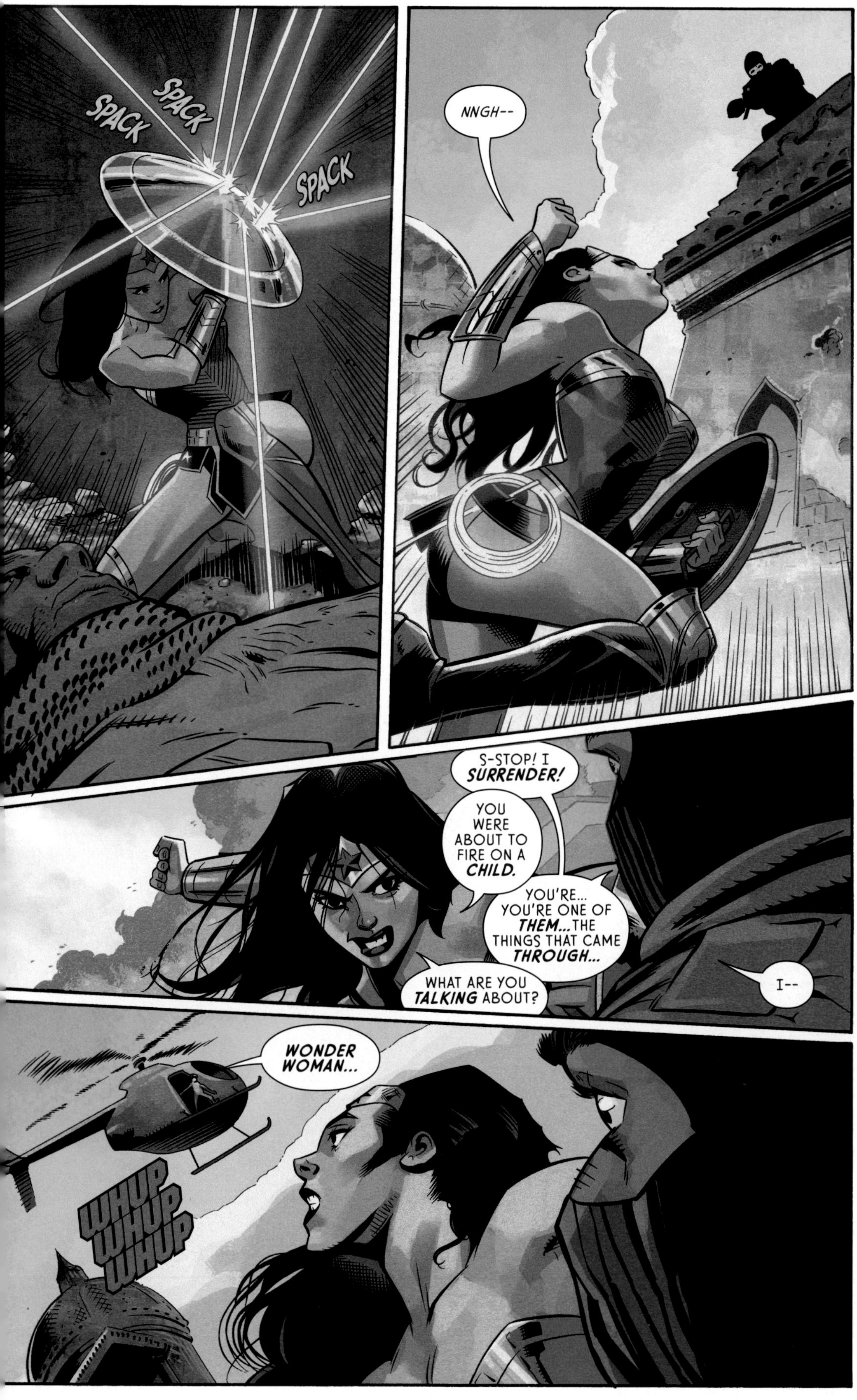
SPACK
SPACK
SPACK
NNGH--
S-STOP! I SURRENDER!
YOU WERE ABOUT TO FIRE ON A CHILD.
YOU'RE... YOU'RE ONE OF THEM... THE THINGS THAT CAME THROUGH...
WHAT ARE YOU TALKING ABOUT?
I--
WONDER WOMAN...
WHUP WHUP WHUP

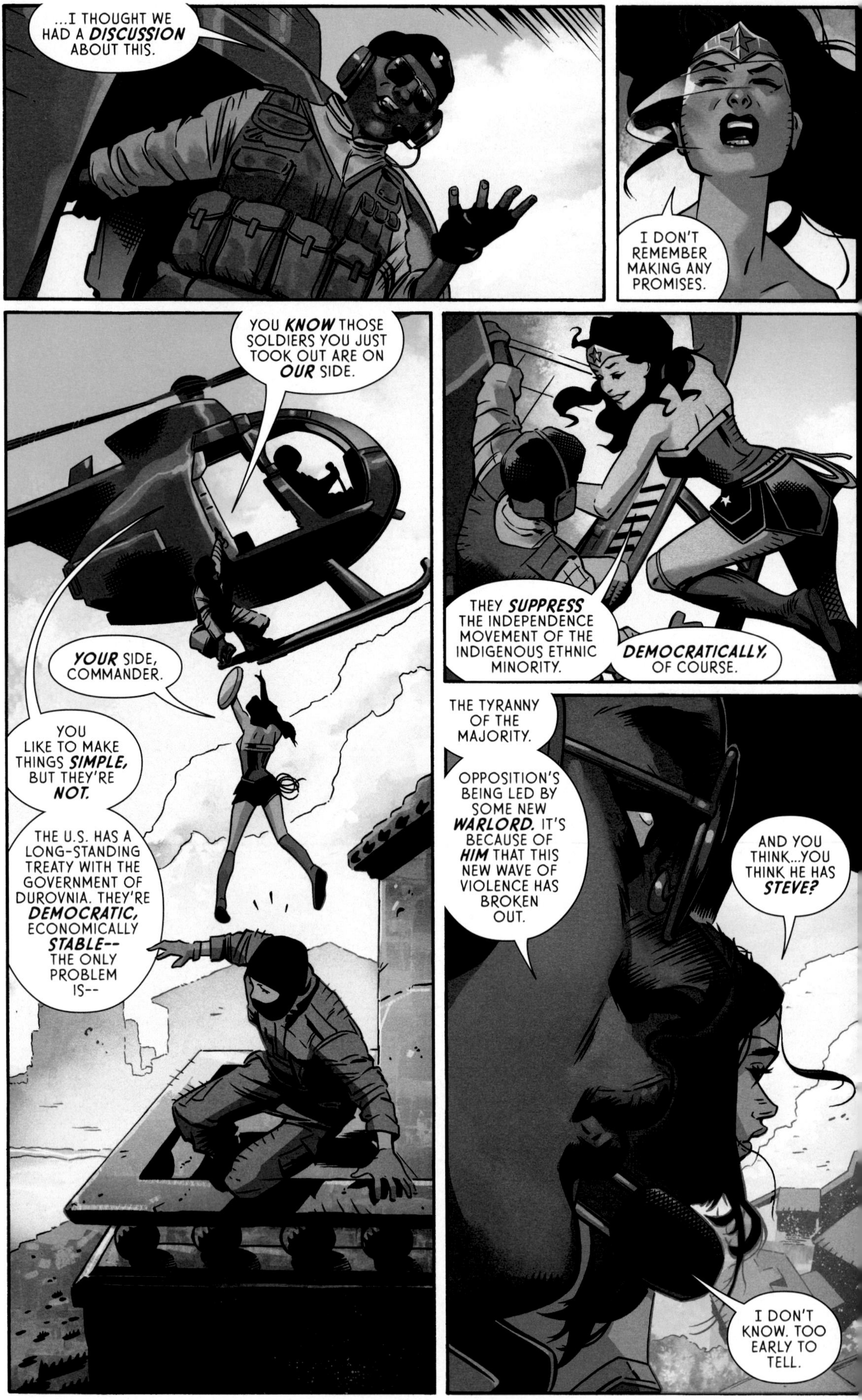
...I THOUGHT WE HAD A DISCUSSION ABOUT THIS.
I DON'T REMEMBER MAKING ANY PROMISES.
YOU KNOW THOSE SOLDIERS YOU JUST TOOK OUT ARE ON OUR SIDE.
YOUR SIDE, COMMANDER.
YOU LIKE TO MAKE THINGS SIMPLE, BUT THEY'RE NOT.
THE U.S. HAS A LONG-STANDING TREATY WITH THE GOVERNMENT OF DUROVNIA. THEY'RE DEMOCRATIC, ECONOMICALLY STABLE-- THE ONLY PROBLEM IS--
THEY SUPPRESS THE INDEPENDENCE MOVEMENT OF THE INDIGENOUS ETHNIC MINORITY.
DEMOCRATICALLY, OF COURSE.
THE TYRANNY OF THE MAJORITY.
OPPOSITION'S BEING LED BY SOME NEW WARLORD. IT'S BECAUSE OF HIM THAT THIS NEW WAVE OF VIOLENCE HAS BROKEN OUT.
AND YOU THINK...YOU THINK HE HAS STEVE?
I DON'T KNOW. TOO EARLY TO TELL.

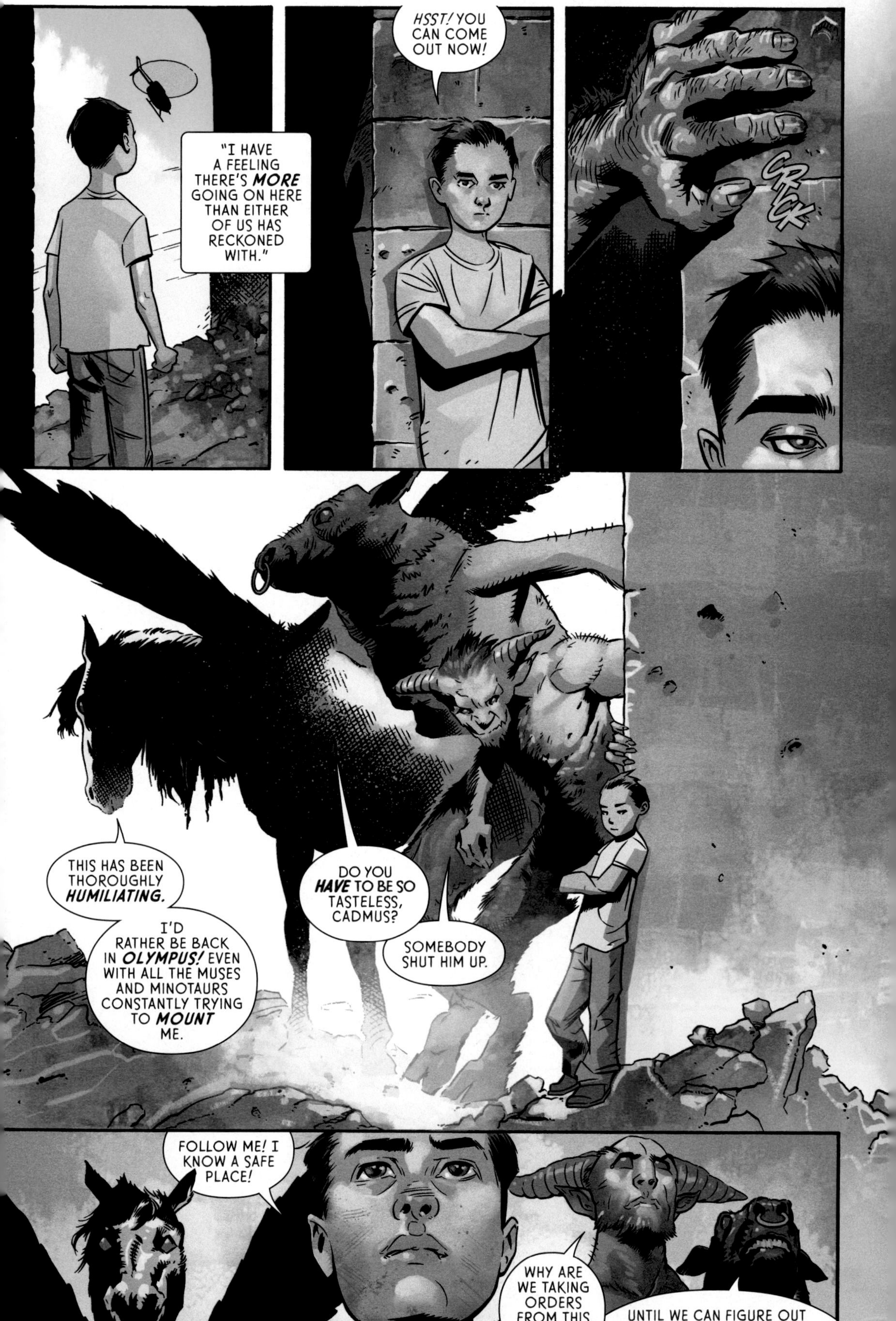
"I HAVE A FEELING THERE'S MORE GOING ON HERE THAN EITHER OF US HAS RECKONED WITH."
HSST! YOU CAN COME OUT NOW!
CRICK
THIS HAS BEEN THOROUGHLY HUMILIATING.
I'D RATHER BE BACK IN OLYMPUS! EVEN WITH ALL THE MUSES AND MINOTAURS CONSTANTLY TRYING TO MOUNT ME.
DO YOU HAVE TO BE SO TASTELESS, CADMUS?
SOMEBODY SHUT HIM UP.
FOLLOW ME! I KNOW A SAFE PLACE!
WHY ARE WE TAKING ORDERS FROM THIS CHILD, EIRENE?
UNTIL WE CAN FIGURE OUT HOW WE GOT HERE, AND WHAT'S HAPPENED TO OUR HOME, WE DON'T HAVE MUCH OF A CHOICE.

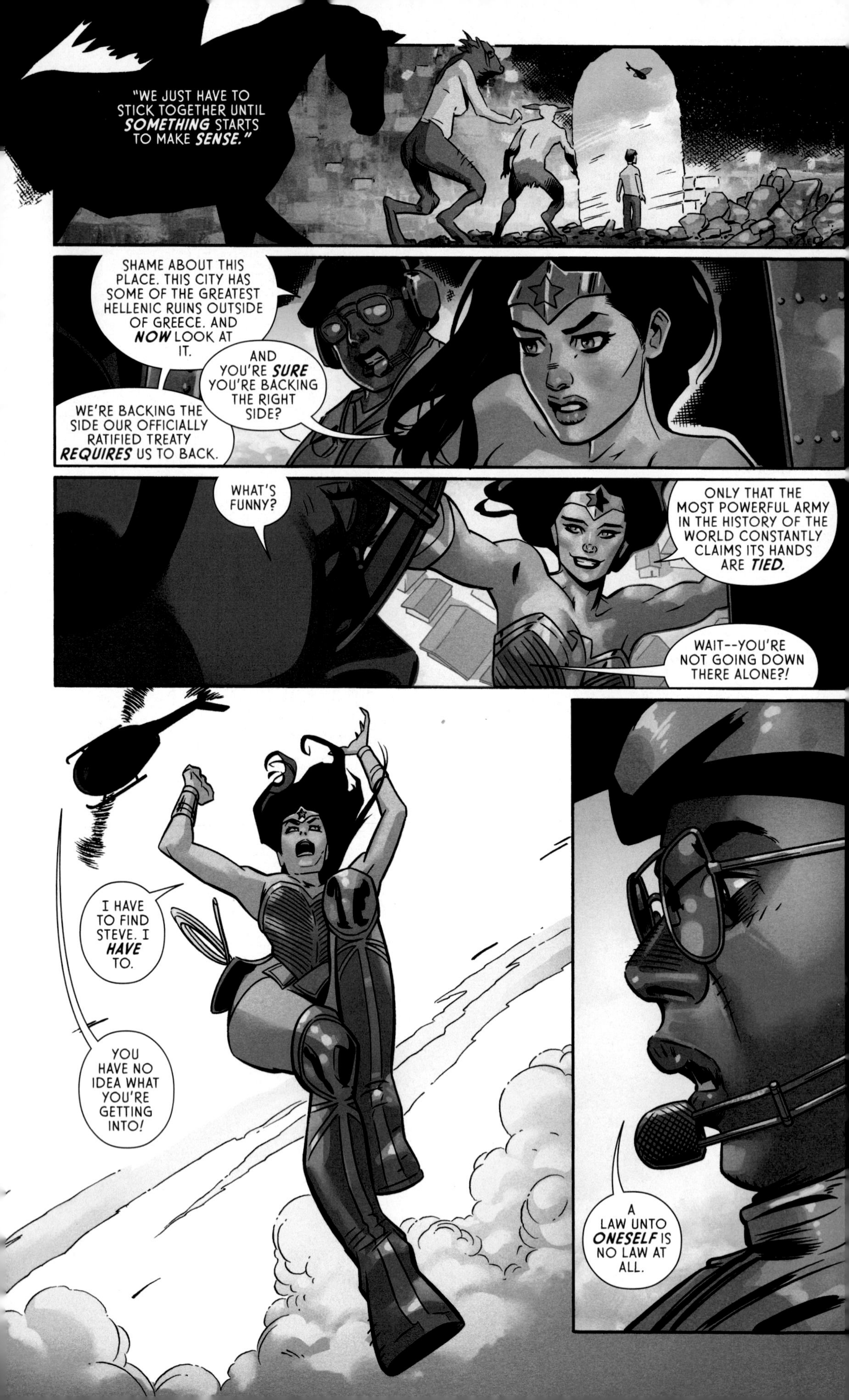
"WE JUST HAVE TO STICK TOGETHER UNTIL SOMETHING STARTS TO MAKE SENSE."
SHAME ABOUT THIS PLACE. THIS CITY HAS SOME OF THE GREATEST HELLENIC RUINS OUTSIDE OF GREECE. AND NOW LOOK AT IT.
AND YOU'RE SURE YOU'RE BACKING THE RIGHT SIDE?
WE'RE BACKING THE SIDE OUR OFFICIALLY RATIFIED TREATY REQUIRES US TO BACK.
WHAT'S FUNNY?
ONLY THAT THE MOST POWERFUL ARMY IN THE HISTORY OF THE WORLD CONSTANTLY CLAIMS ITS HANDS ARE TIED.
WAIT--YOU'RE NOT GOING DOWN THERE ALONE?!
I HAVE TO FIND STEVE. I HAVE TO.
YOU HAVE NO IDEA WHAT YOU'RE GETTING INTO!
A LAW UNTO ONESELF IS NO LAW AT ALL.

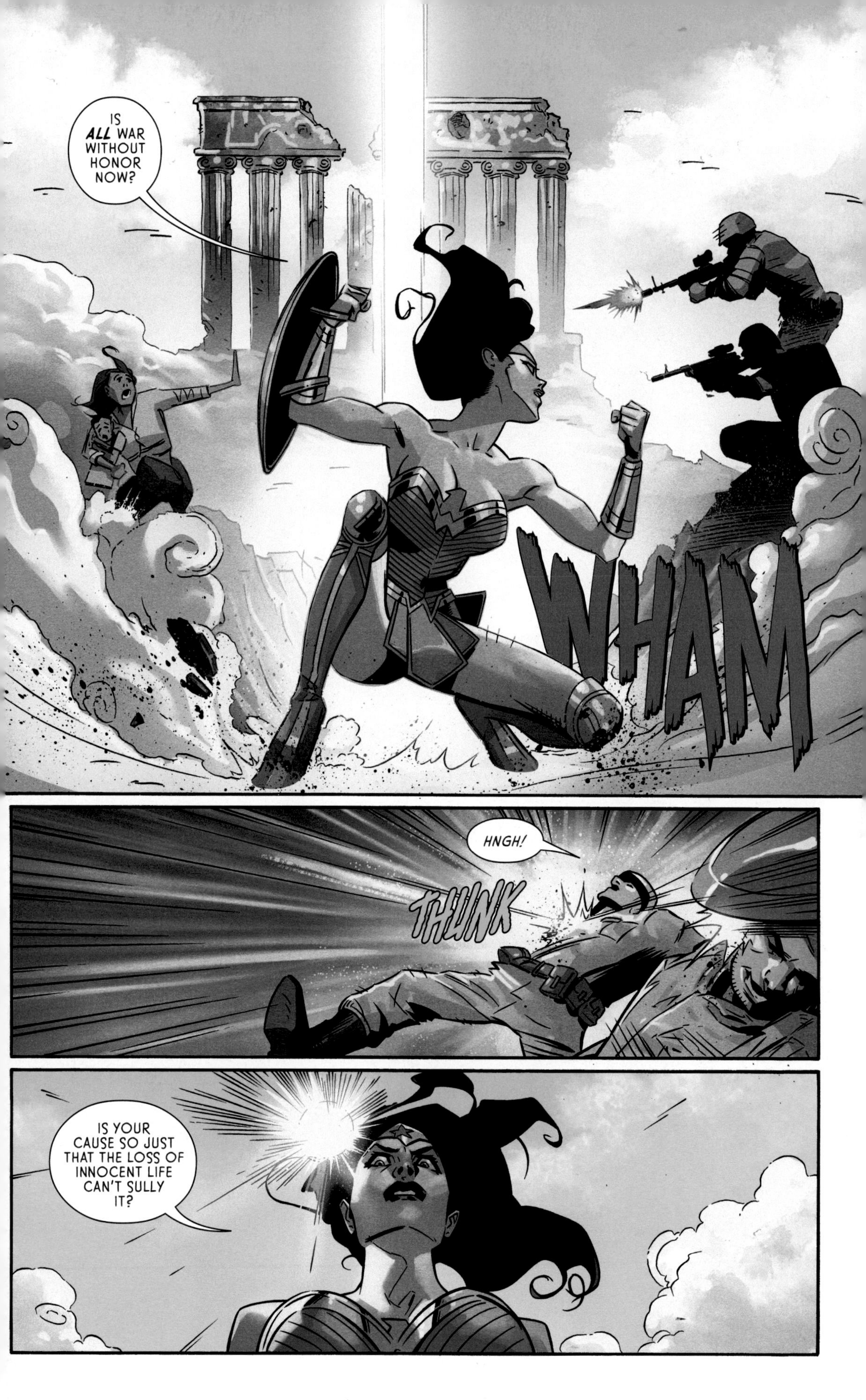
IS ALL WAR WITHOUT HONOR NOW?
WHAM
HNGH!
THUNK
IS YOUR CAUSE SO JUST THAT THE LOSS OF INNOCENT LIFE CAN'T SULLY IT?

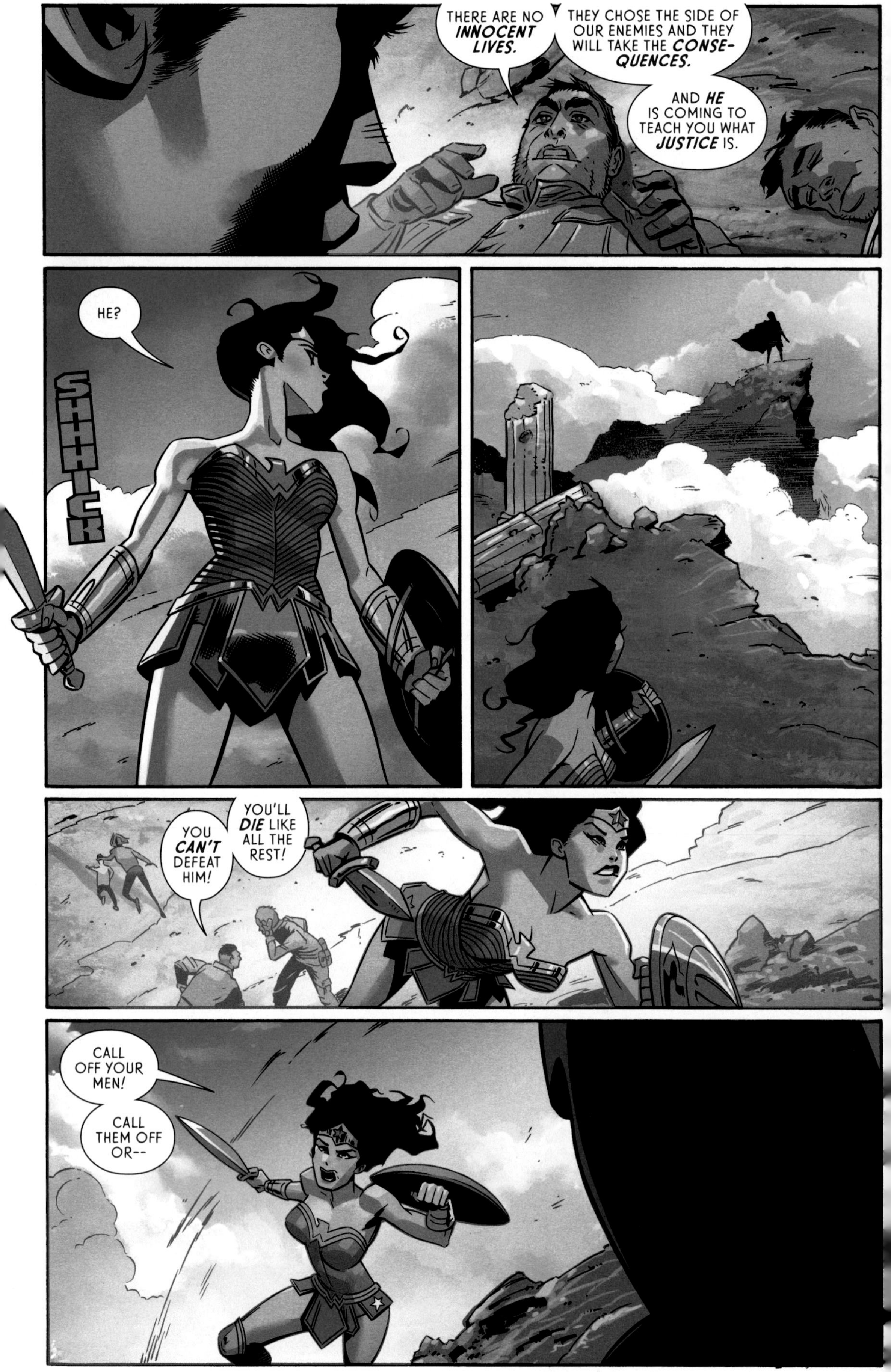
THERE ARE NO INNOCENT LIVES.
THEY CHOSE THE SIDE OF OUR ENEMIES AND THEY WILL TAKE THE CONSE-QUENCES.
AND HE IS COMING TO TEACH YOU WHAT JUSTICE IS.
HE?
SHHHICK
YOU CAN'T DEFEAT HIM!
YOU'LL DIE LIKE ALL THE REST!
CALL OFF YOUR MEN!
CALL THEM OFF OR--

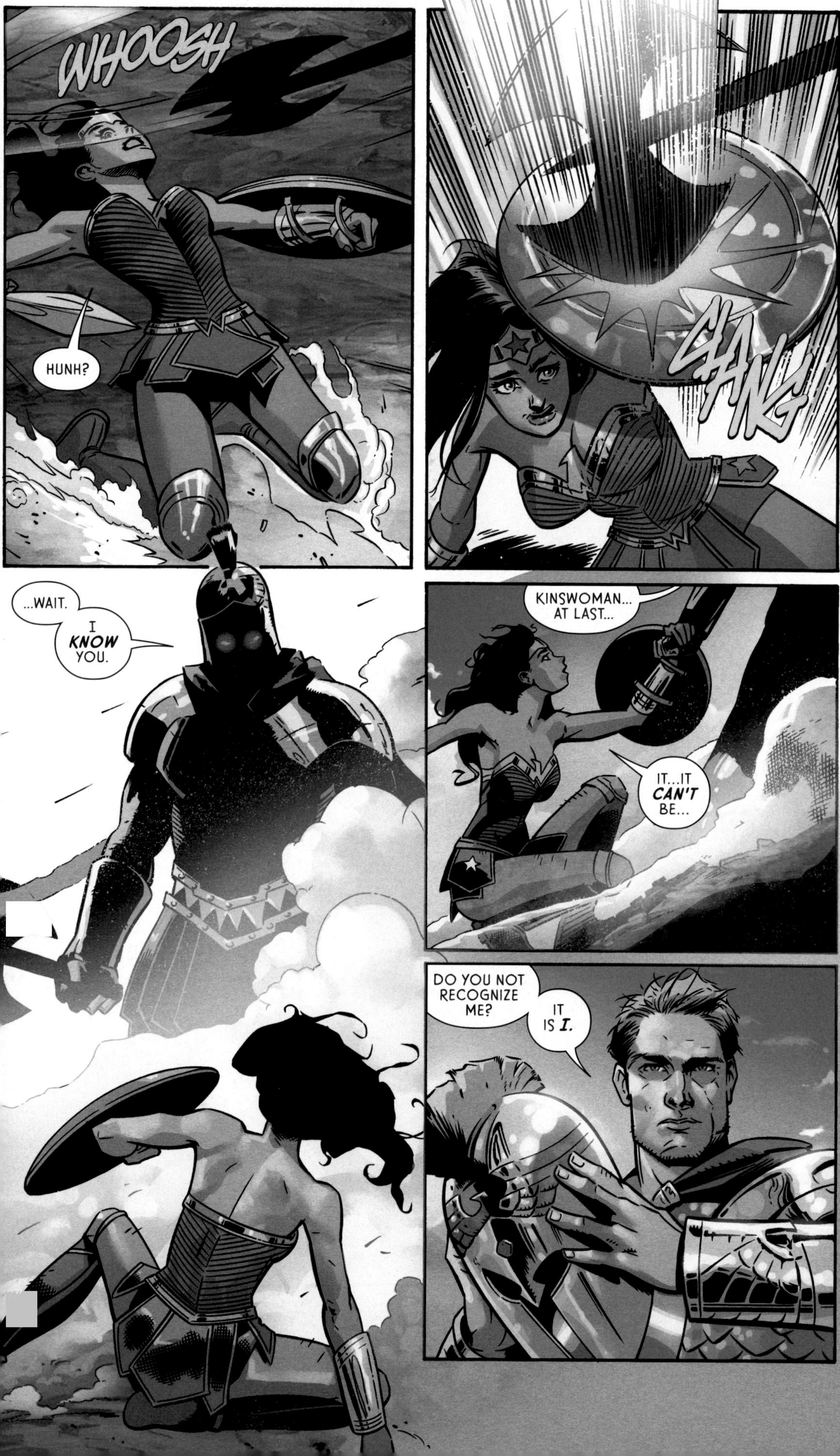
WHOOSH
HUNH?
CHANG
...WAIT.
I KNOW YOU.
KINSWOMAN... AT LAST...
IT...IT CAN'T BE...
DO YOU NOT RECOGNIZE ME?
IT IS I.

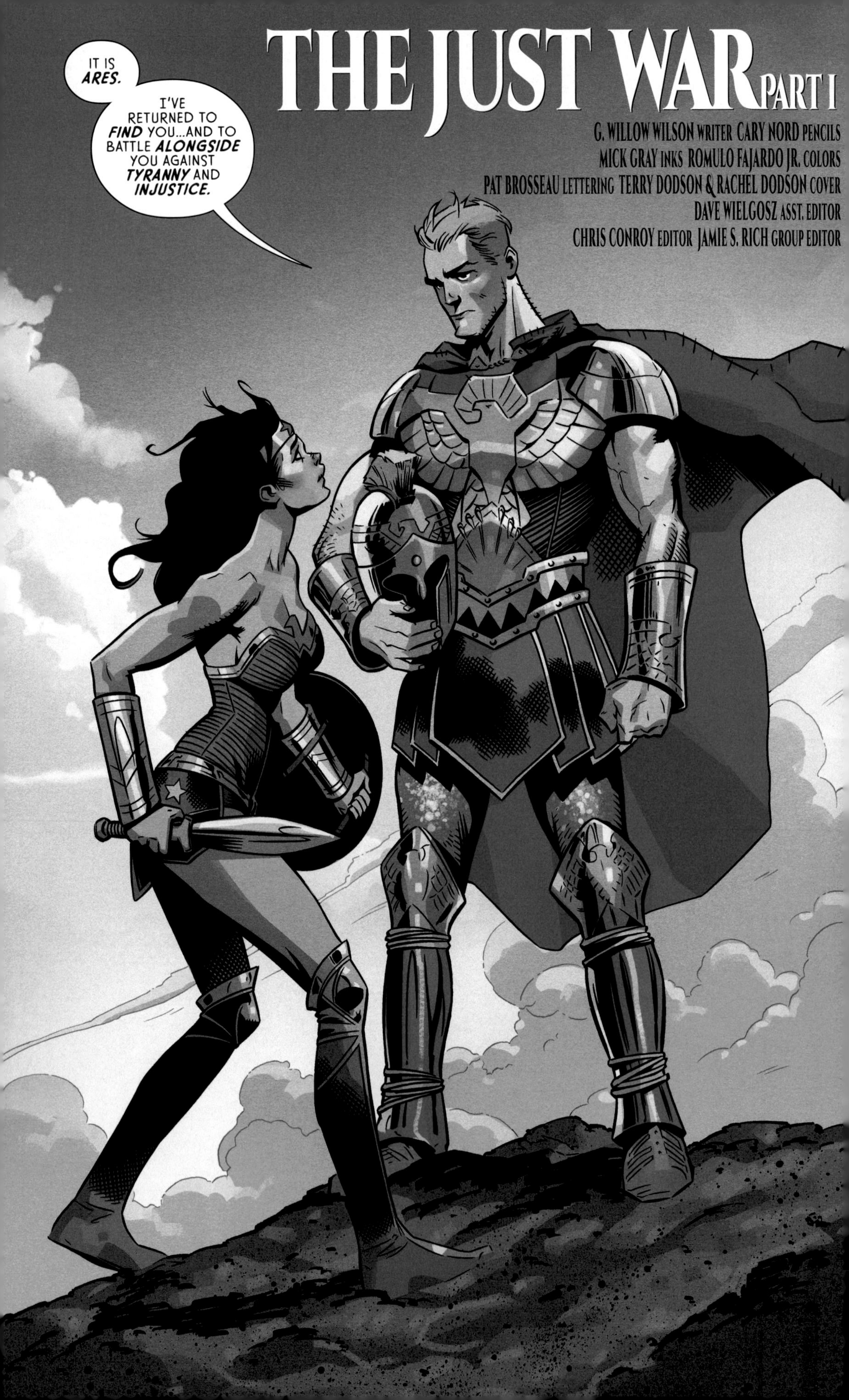
IT IS ARES.
I'VE RETURNED TO FIND YOU...AND TO BATTLE ALONGSIDE YOU AGAINST TYRANNY AND INJUSTICE.
THE JUST WAR PART I
G. WILLOW WILSON WRITER CARY NORD PENCILS
MICK GRAY INKS ROMULO FAJARDO JR. COLORS
PAT BROSSEAU LETTERING TERRY DODSON & RACHEL DODSON COVER
DAVE WIELGOSZ ASST. EDITOR
CHRIS CONROY EDITOR JAMIE S. RICH GROUP EDITOR

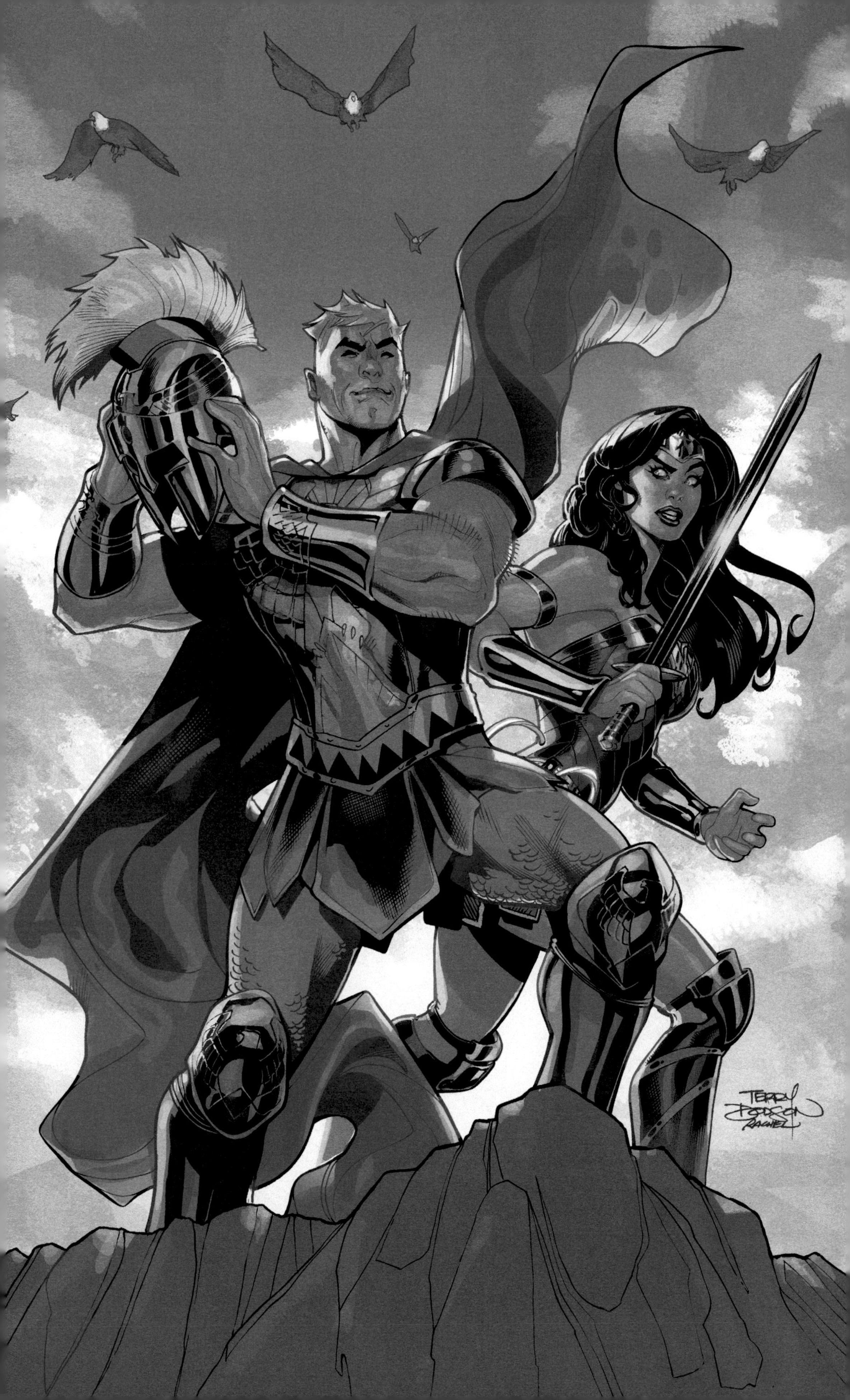
TERRY
DODSON
RACHEL

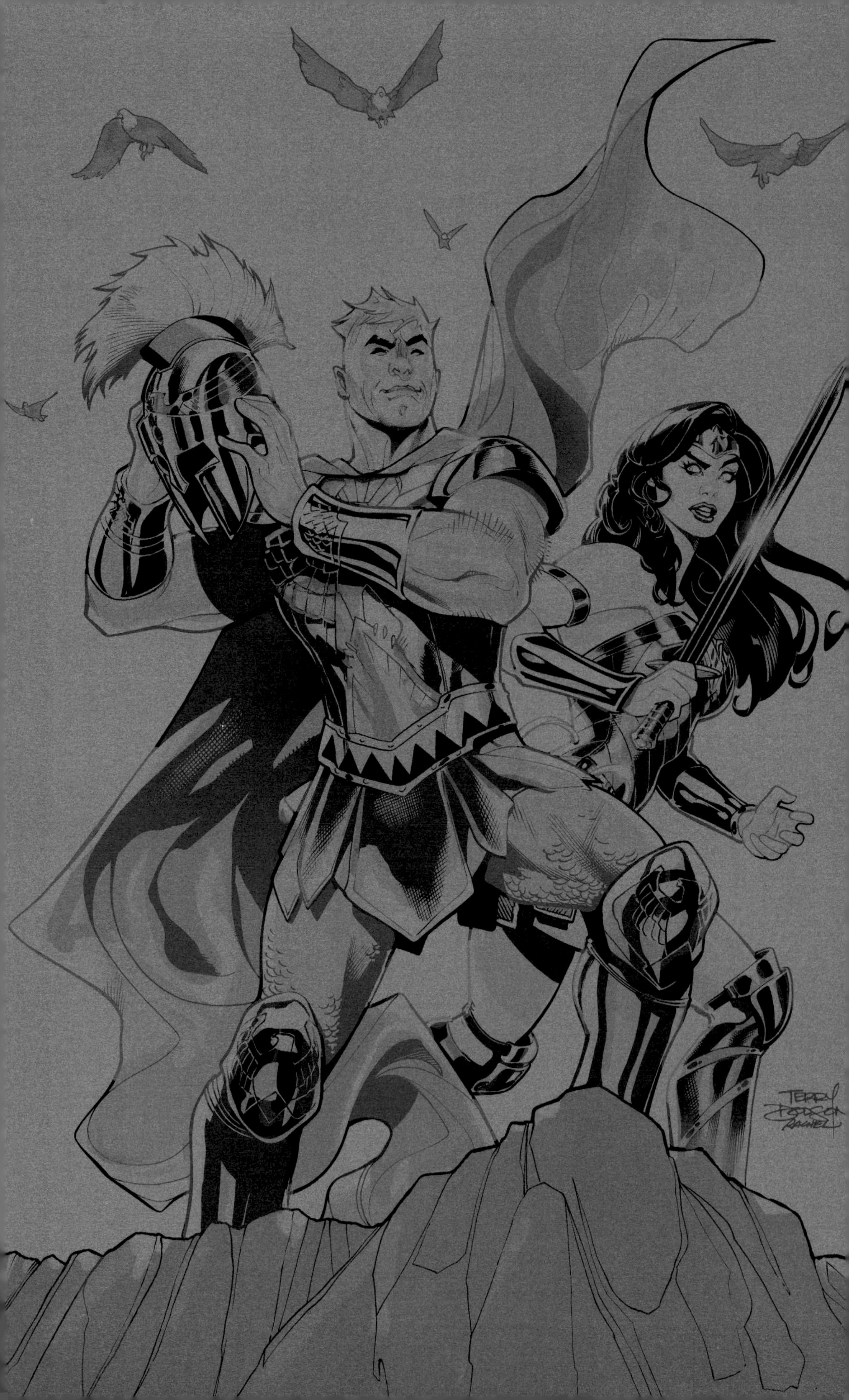
TERRY
DODSON
RACHEL

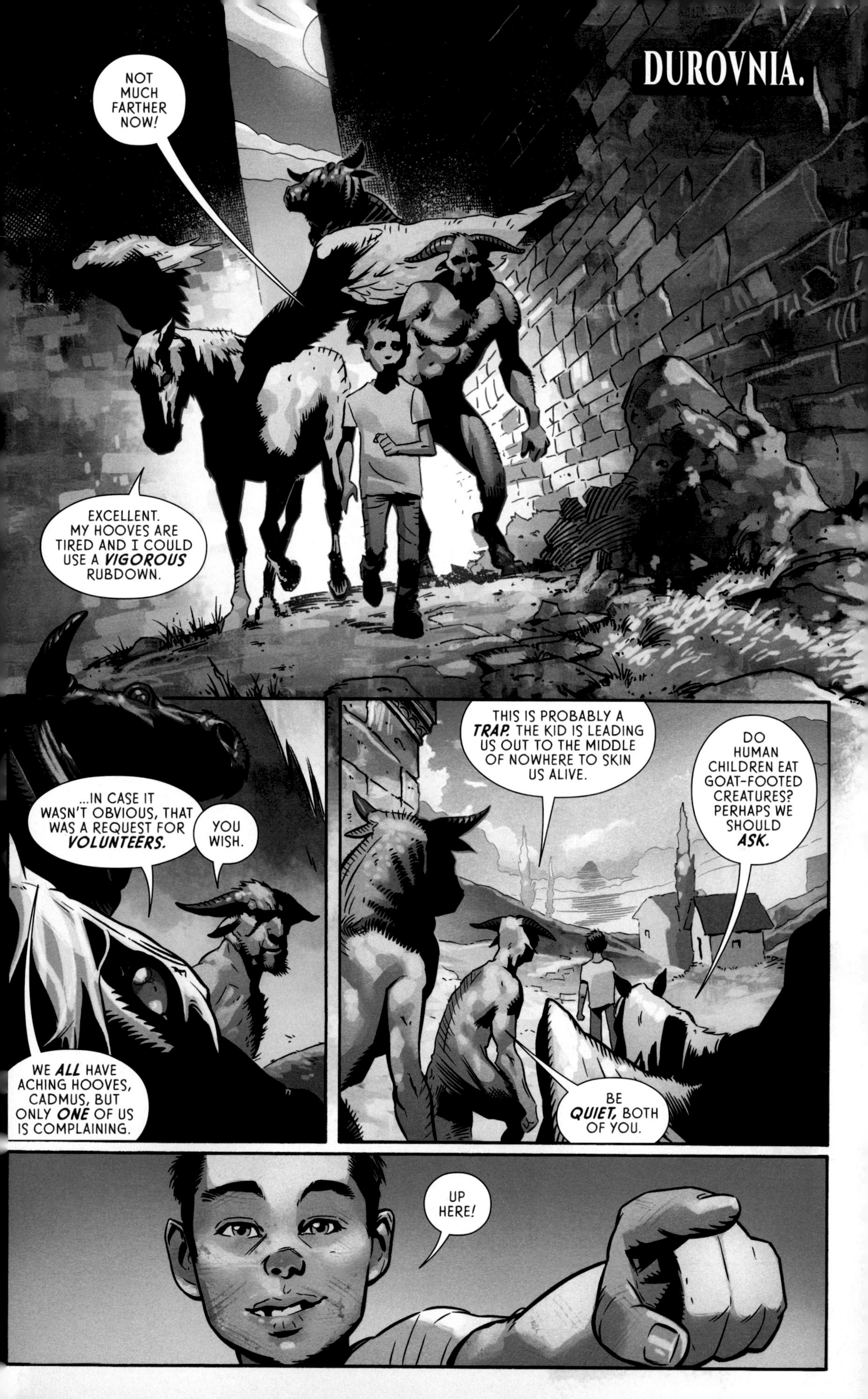
DUROVNIA.
NOT MUCH FARTHER NOW!
EXCELLENT. MY HOOVES ARE TIRED AND I COULD USE A VIGOROUS RUBDOWN.
...IN CASE IT WASN'T OBVIOUS, THAT WAS A REQUEST FOR VOLUNTEERS.
YOU WISH.
WE ALL HAVE ACHING HOOVES, CADMUS, BUT ONLY ONE OF US IS COMPLAINING.
THIS IS PROBABLY A TRAP. THE KID IS LEADING US OUT TO THE MIDDLE OF NOWHERE TO SKIN US ALIVE.
DO HUMAN CHILDREN EAT GOAT-FOOTED CREATURES? PERHAPS WE SHOULD ASK.
BE QUIET, BOTH OF YOU.
UP HERE!

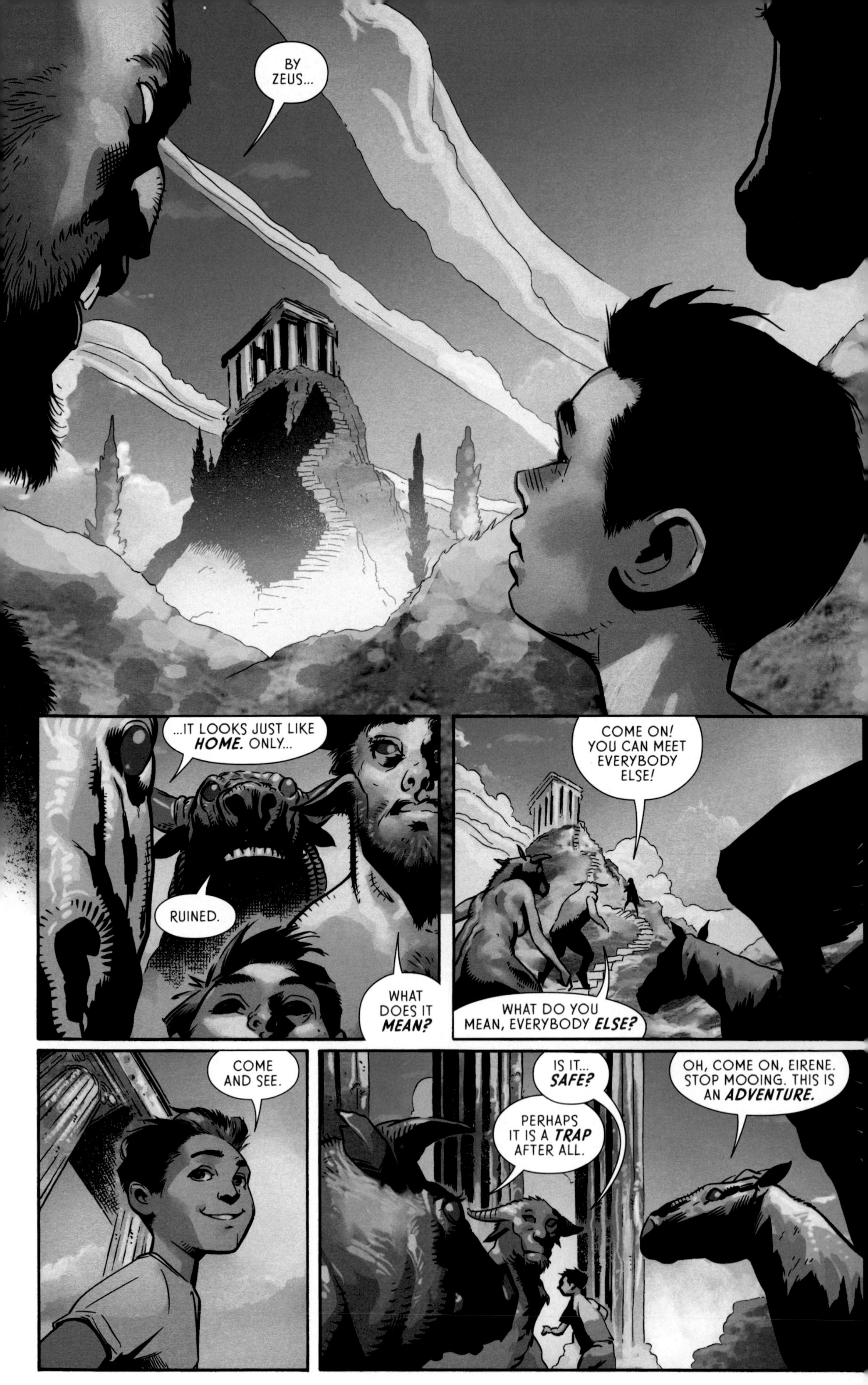

BY ZEUS...
...IT LOOKS JUST LIKE *HOME.* ONLY...
RUINED.
WHAT DOES IT *MEAN?*
COME ON! YOU CAN MEET EVERYBODY ELSE!
WHAT DO YOU MEAN, EVERYBODY *ELSE?*
COME AND SEE.
IS IT... *SAFE?*
PERHAPS IT IS A *TRAP* AFTER ALL.
OH, COME ON, EIRENE. STOP MOOING. THIS IS AN *ADVENTURE.*

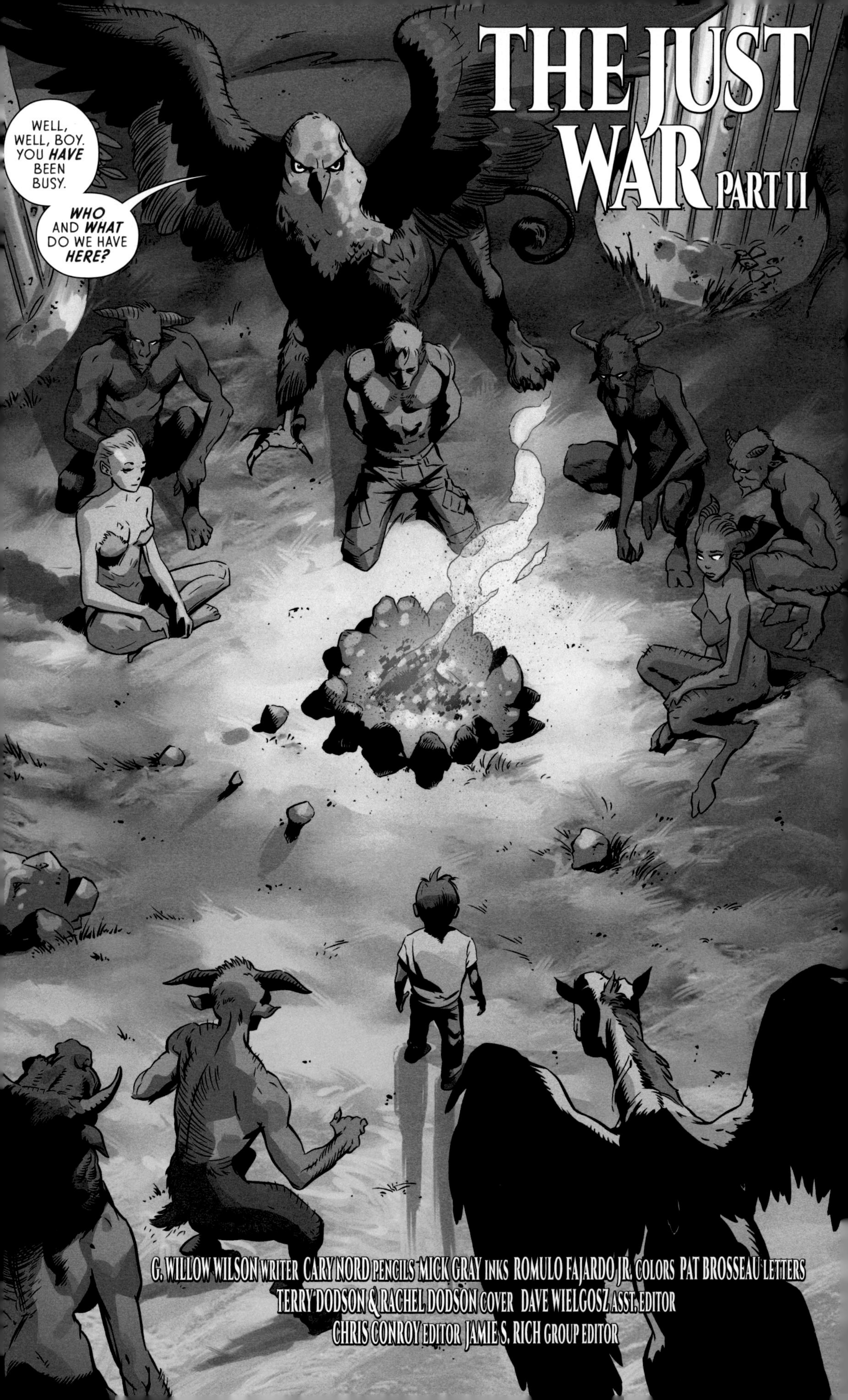
THE JUST WAR PART II
WELL, WELL, BOY. YOU HAVE BEEN BUSY.
WHO AND WHAT DO WE HAVE HERE?
G. WILLOW WILSON WRITER CARY NORD PENCILS MICK GRAY INKS ROMULO FAJARDO JR. COLORS PAT BROSSEAU LETTERS
TERRY DODSON & RACHEL DODSON COVER DAVE WIELGOSZ ASST. EDITOR
CHRIS CONROY EDITOR JAMIE S. RICH GROUP EDITOR

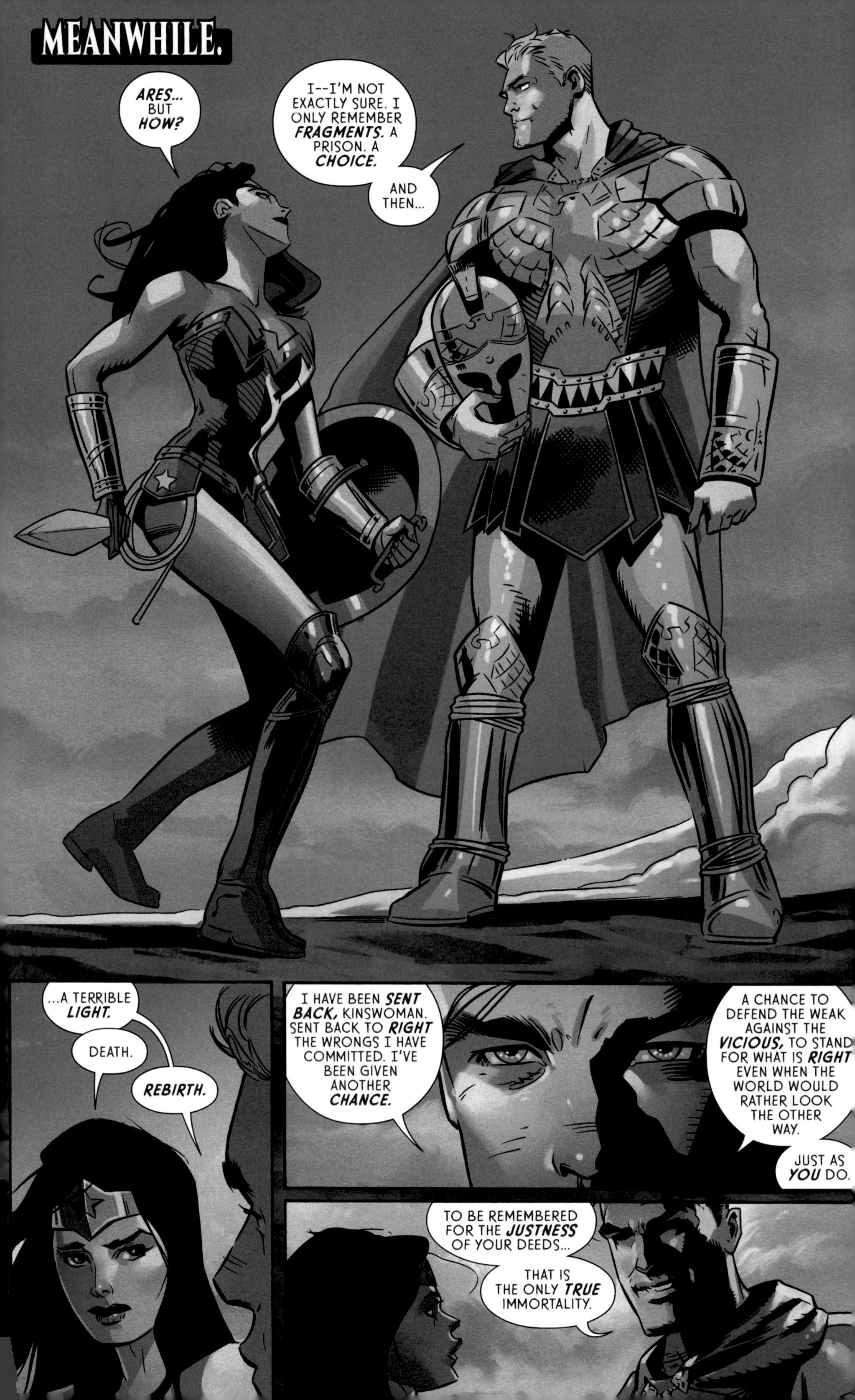
MEANWHILE.
ARES... BUT HOW?
I--I'M NOT EXACTLY SURE. I ONLY REMEMBER FRAGMENTS. A PRISON. A CHOICE.
AND THEN...
...A TERRIBLE LIGHT.
DEATH.
REBIRTH.
I HAVE BEEN SENT BACK, KINSWOMAN. SENT BACK TO RIGHT THE WRONGS I HAVE COMMITTED. I'VE BEEN GIVEN ANOTHER CHANCE.
A CHANCE TO DEFEND THE WEAK AGAINST THE VICIOUS, TO STAND FOR WHAT IS RIGHT EVEN WHEN THE WORLD WOULD RATHER LOOK THE OTHER WAY.
JUST AS YOU DO.
TO BE REMEMBERED FOR THE JUSTNESS OF YOUR DEEDS...
THAT IS THE ONLY TRUE IMMORTALITY.

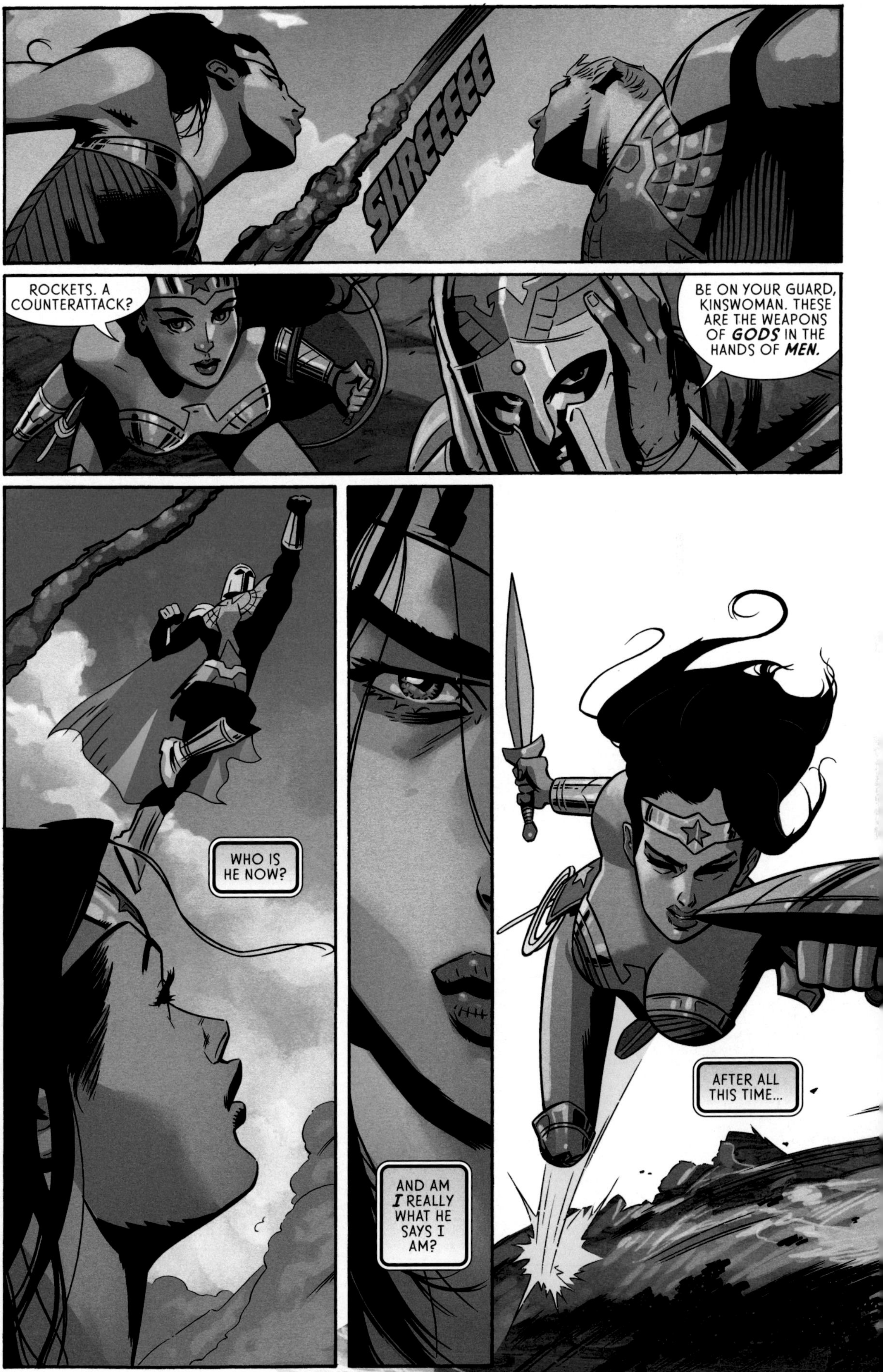
SKREEEEE
ROCKETS. A COUNTERATTACK?
BE ON YOUR GUARD, KINSWOMAN. THESE ARE THE WEAPONS OF **GODS** IN THE HANDS OF **MEN.**
WHO IS HE NOW?
AND AM **I** REALLY WHAT HE SAYS I AM?
AFTER ALL THIS TIME...

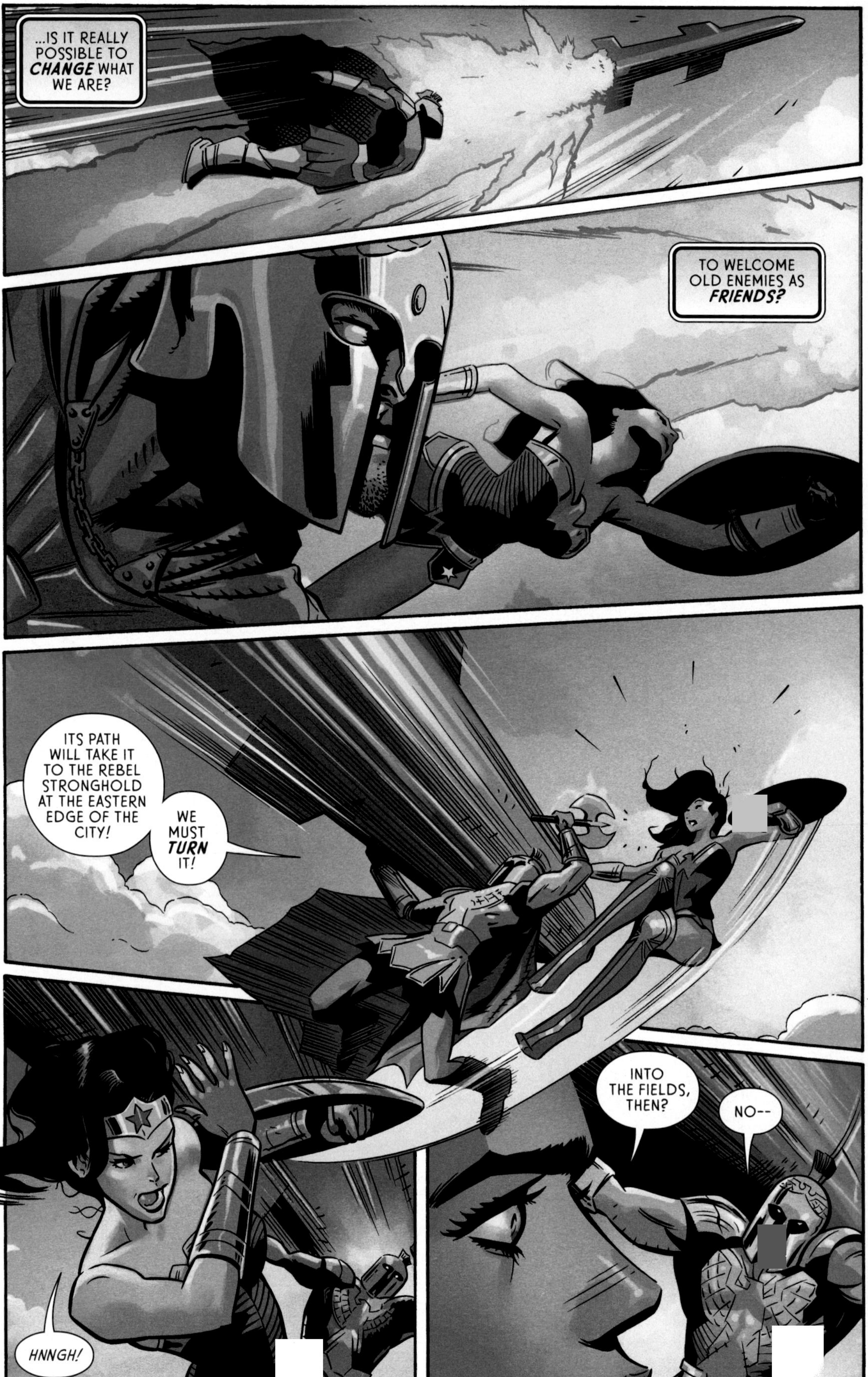
...IS IT REALLY POSSIBLE TO CHANGE WHAT WE ARE?
TO WELCOME OLD ENEMIES AS FRIENDS?
ITS PATH WILL TAKE IT TO THE REBEL STRONGHOLD AT THE EASTERN EDGE OF THE CITY!
WE MUST TURN IT!
HNNGH!
INTO THE FIELDS, THEN?
NO--

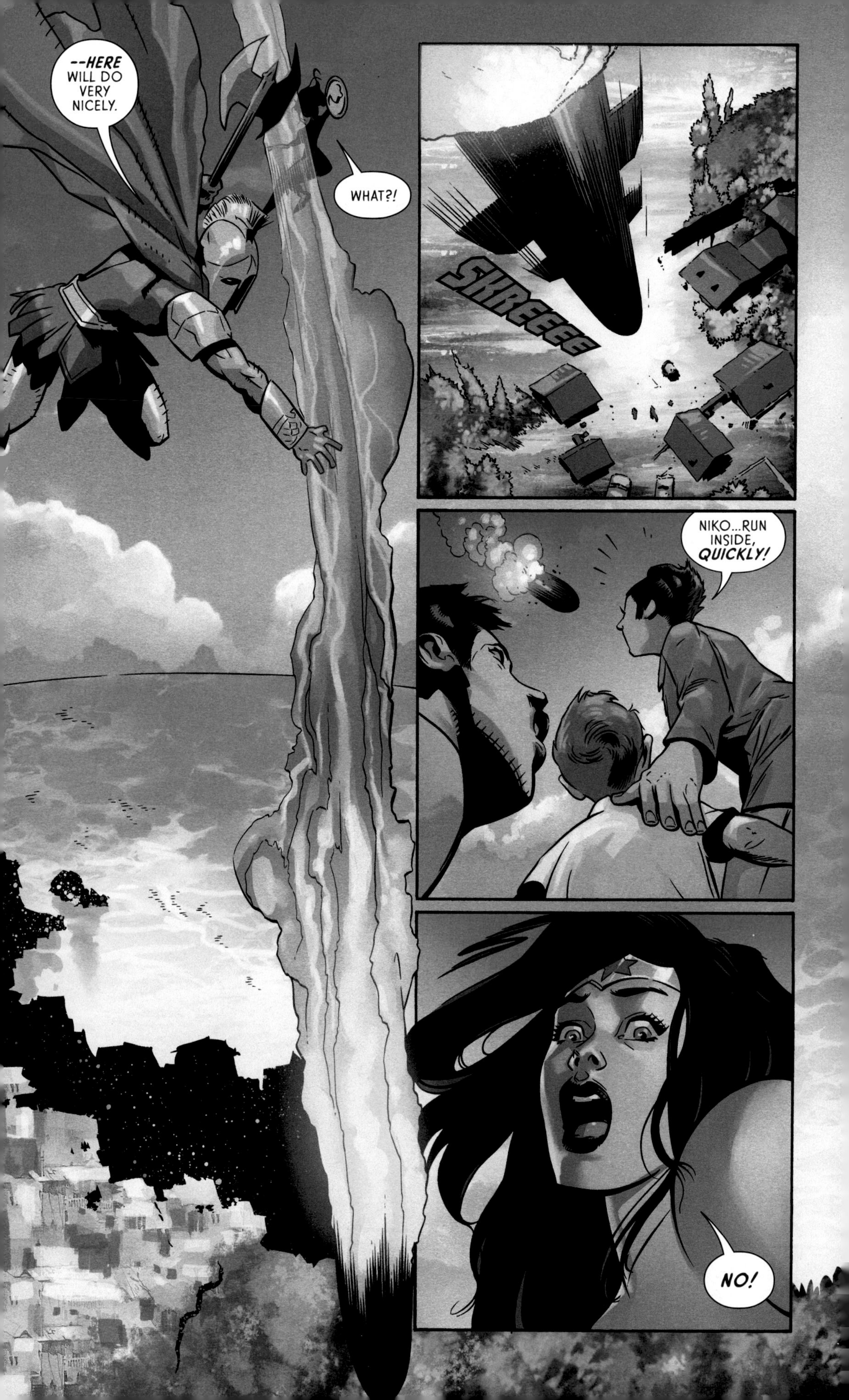
--HERE WILL DO VERY NICELY.
WHAT?!
SKREEEEE
NIKO...RUN INSIDE, QUICKLY!
NO!

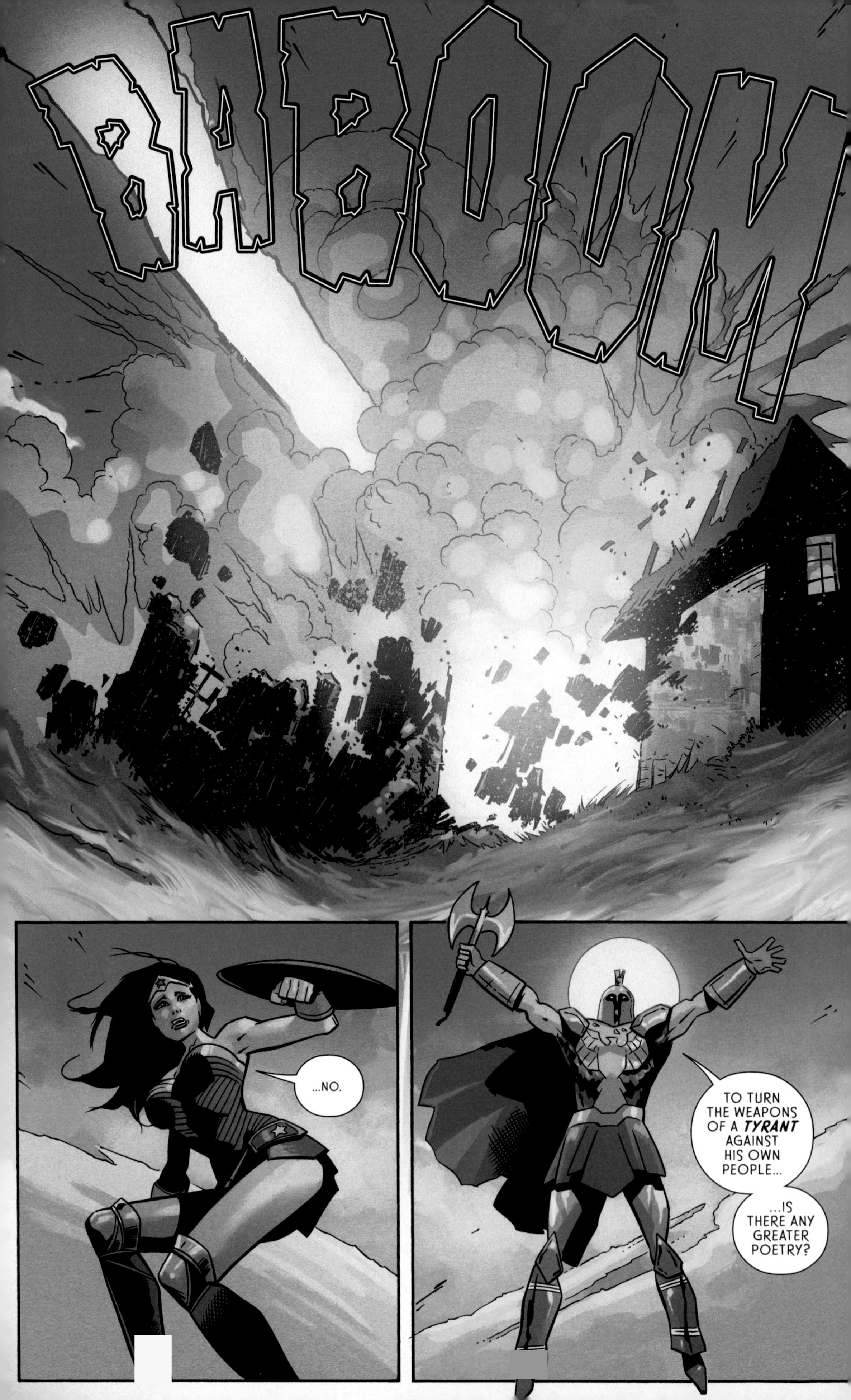
BABOOM
...NO.
TO TURN THE WEAPONS OF A *TYRANT* AGAINST HIS OWN PEOPLE...
...IS THERE ANY GREATER POETRY?

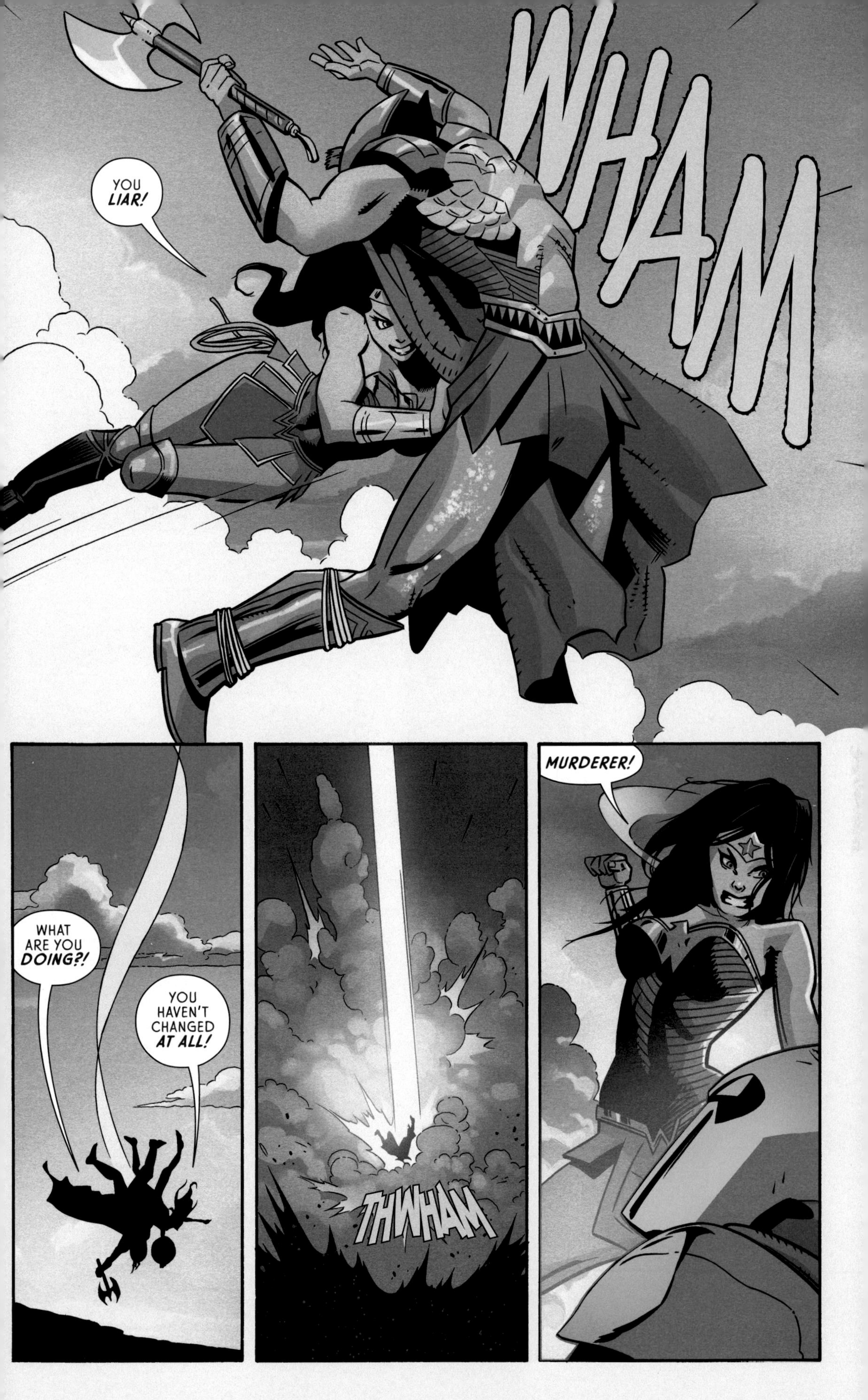
WHAM
YOU LIAR!
WHAT ARE YOU DOING?!
YOU HAVEN'T CHANGED AT ALL!
THWHAM
MURDERER!

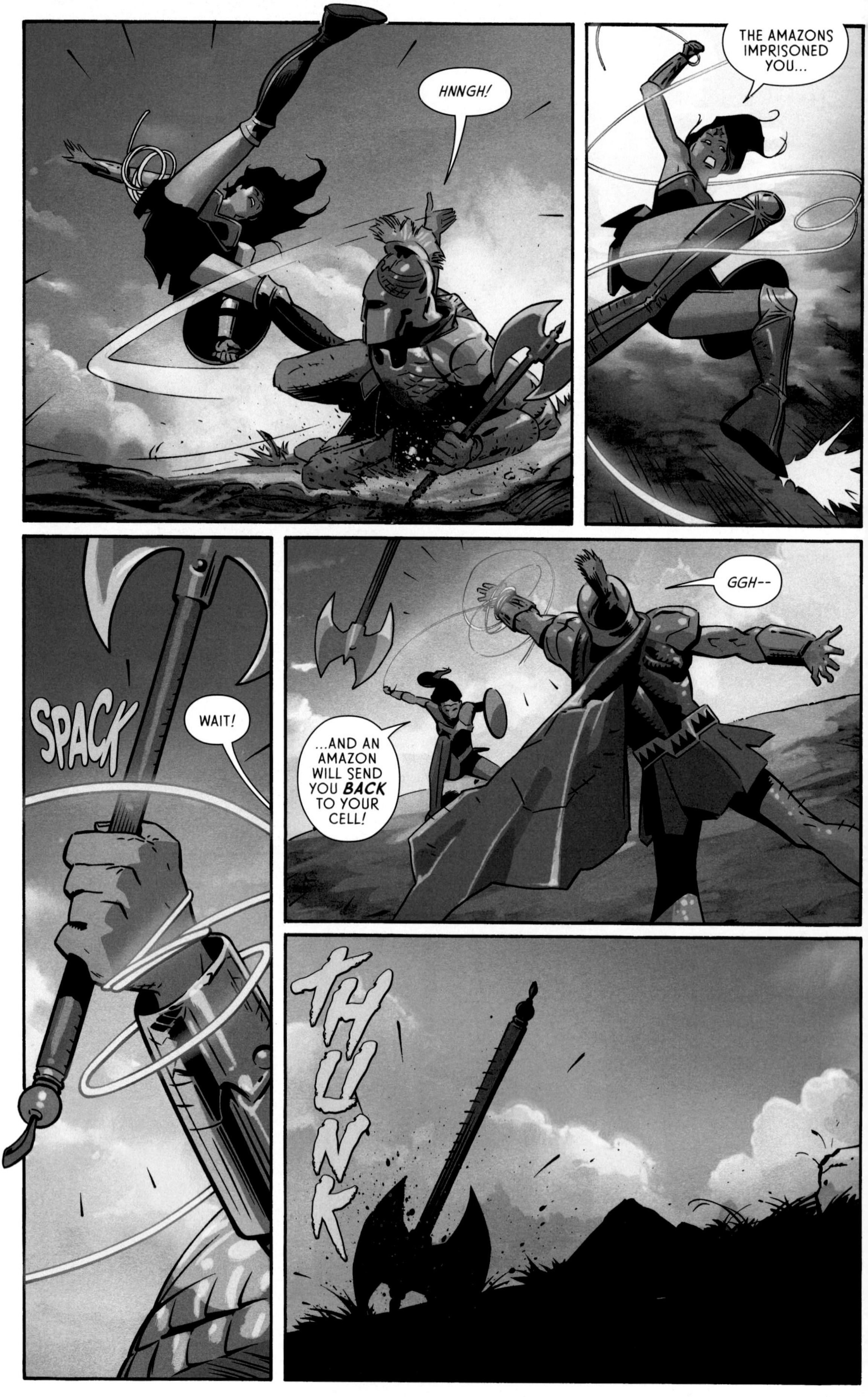
HNNGH!
THE AMAZONS IMPRISONED YOU...
SPACK
WAIT!
GGH--
...AND AN AMAZON WILL SEND YOU BACK TO YOUR CELL!
THUNK

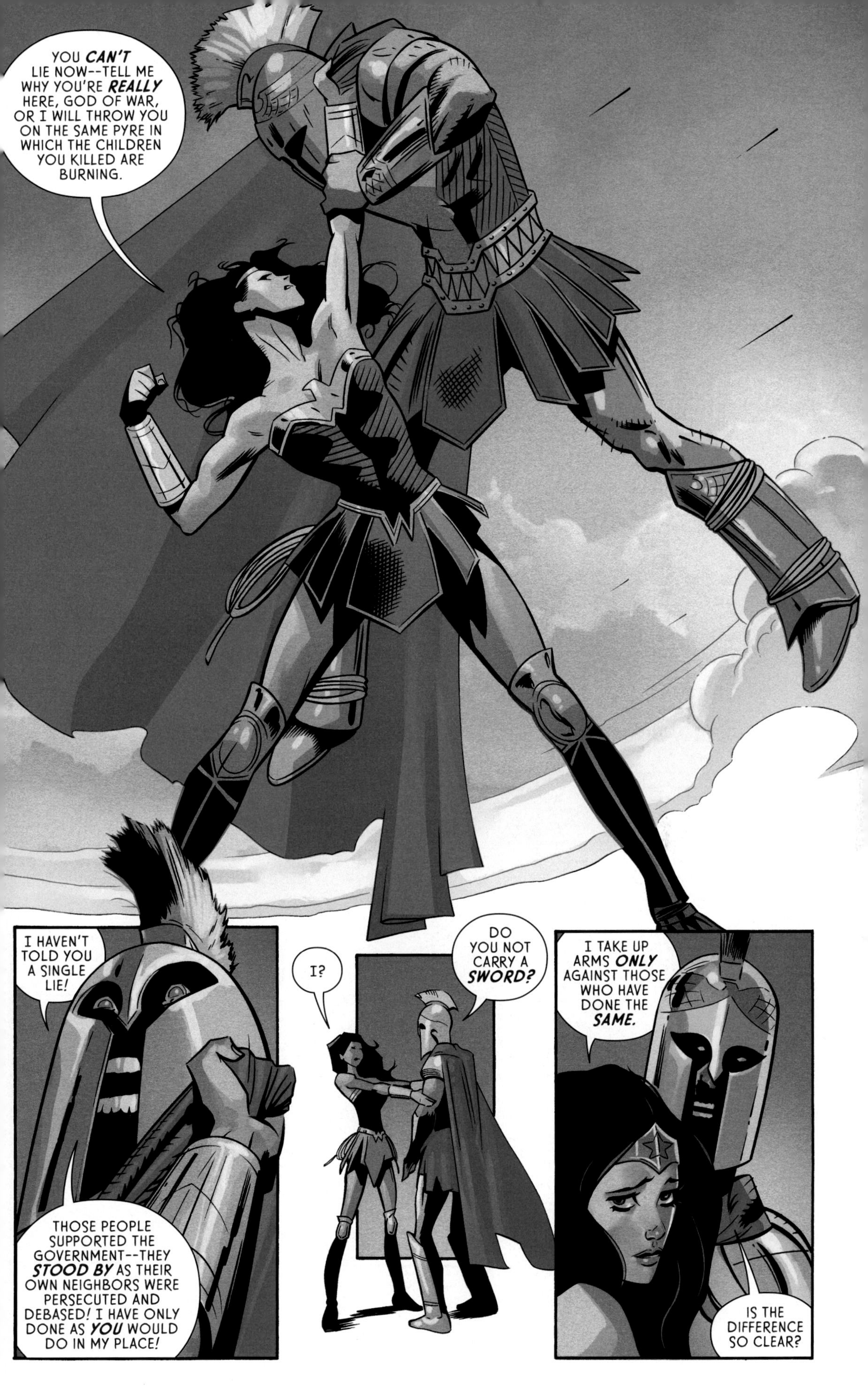

YOU CAN'T LIE NOW--TELL ME WHY YOU'RE REALLY HERE, GOD OF WAR, OR I WILL THROW YOU ON THE SAME PYRE IN WHICH THE CHILDREN YOU KILLED ARE BURNING.
I HAVEN'T TOLD YOU A SINGLE LIE!
THOSE PEOPLE SUPPORTED THE GOVERNMENT--THEY STOOD BY AS THEIR OWN NEIGHBORS WERE PERSECUTED AND DEBASED! I HAVE ONLY DONE AS YOU WOULD DO IN MY PLACE!
I?
DO YOU NOT CARRY A SWORD?
I TAKE UP ARMS ONLY AGAINST THOSE WHO HAVE DONE THE SAME.
IS THE DIFFERENCE SO CLEAR?

RRRRRR--

WHAT IS THAT?

YOUR *FRIENDS* HAVE BROUGHT THEIR WAR-CHARIOTS TO AID THEIR BLOODIED ALLIES.

SHOOM

BUT THEY WILL *NOT* SUCCEED TODAY.

STOP! ARES--

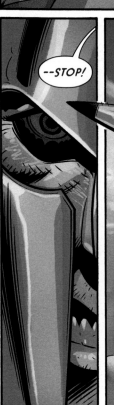

--STOP!

CRUNCH

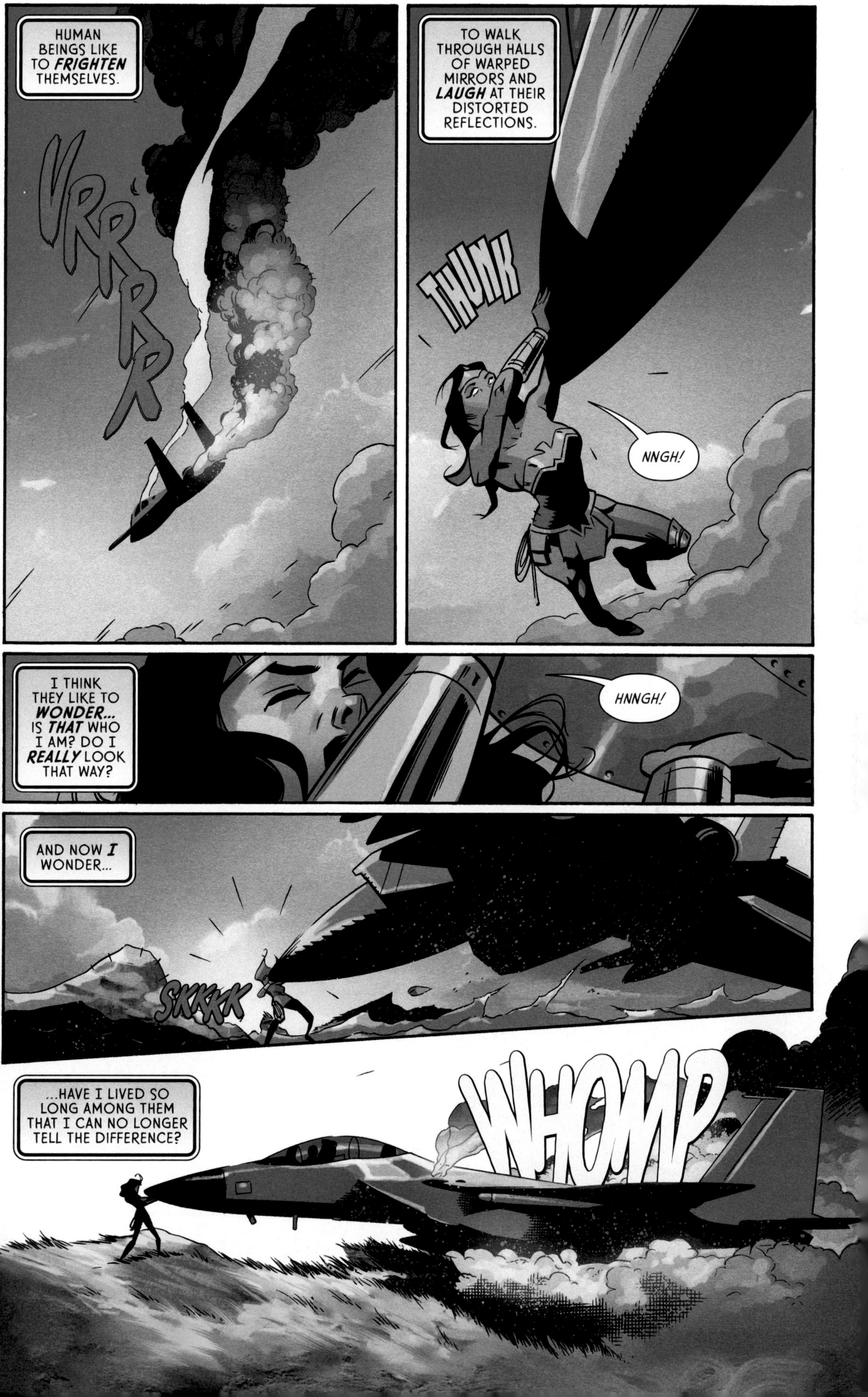
HUMAN BEINGS LIKE TO FRIGHTEN THEMSELVES.
URRRR
TO WALK THROUGH HALLS OF WARPED MIRRORS AND LAUGH AT THEIR DISTORTED REFLECTIONS.
THUNK
NNGH!
I THINK THEY LIKE TO WONDER... IS THAT WHO I AM? DO I REALLY LOOK THAT WAY?
HNNGH!
AND NOW I WONDER...
SKKKK
...HAVE I LIVED SO LONG AMONG THEM THAT I CAN NO LONGER TELL THE DIFFERENCE?
WHOMP

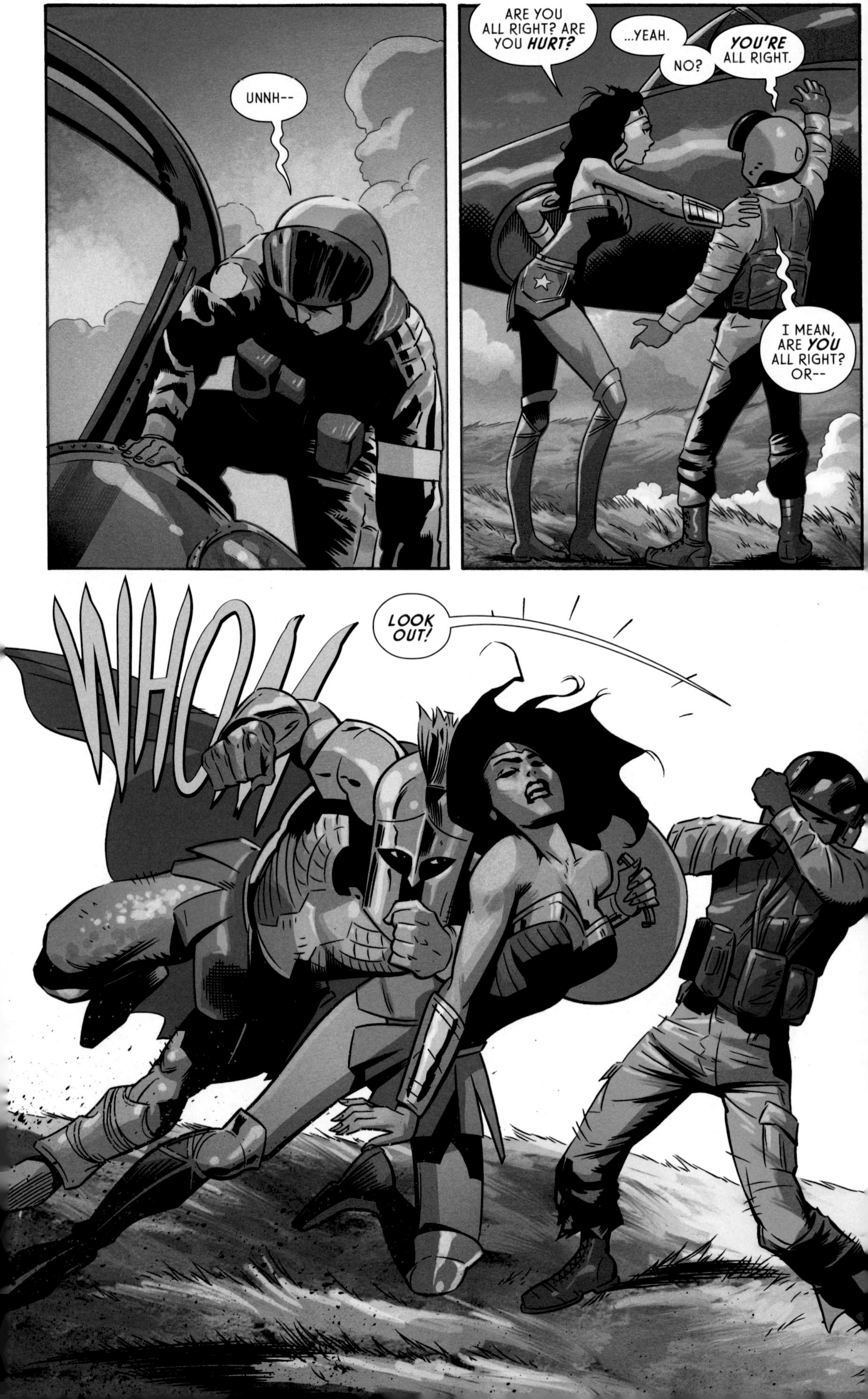
UNNH--
ARE YOU ALL RIGHT? ARE YOU **HURT?**
...YEAH.
NO?
YOU'RE ALL RIGHT.
I MEAN, ARE **YOU** ALL RIGHT? OR--
WHO
LOOK OUT!

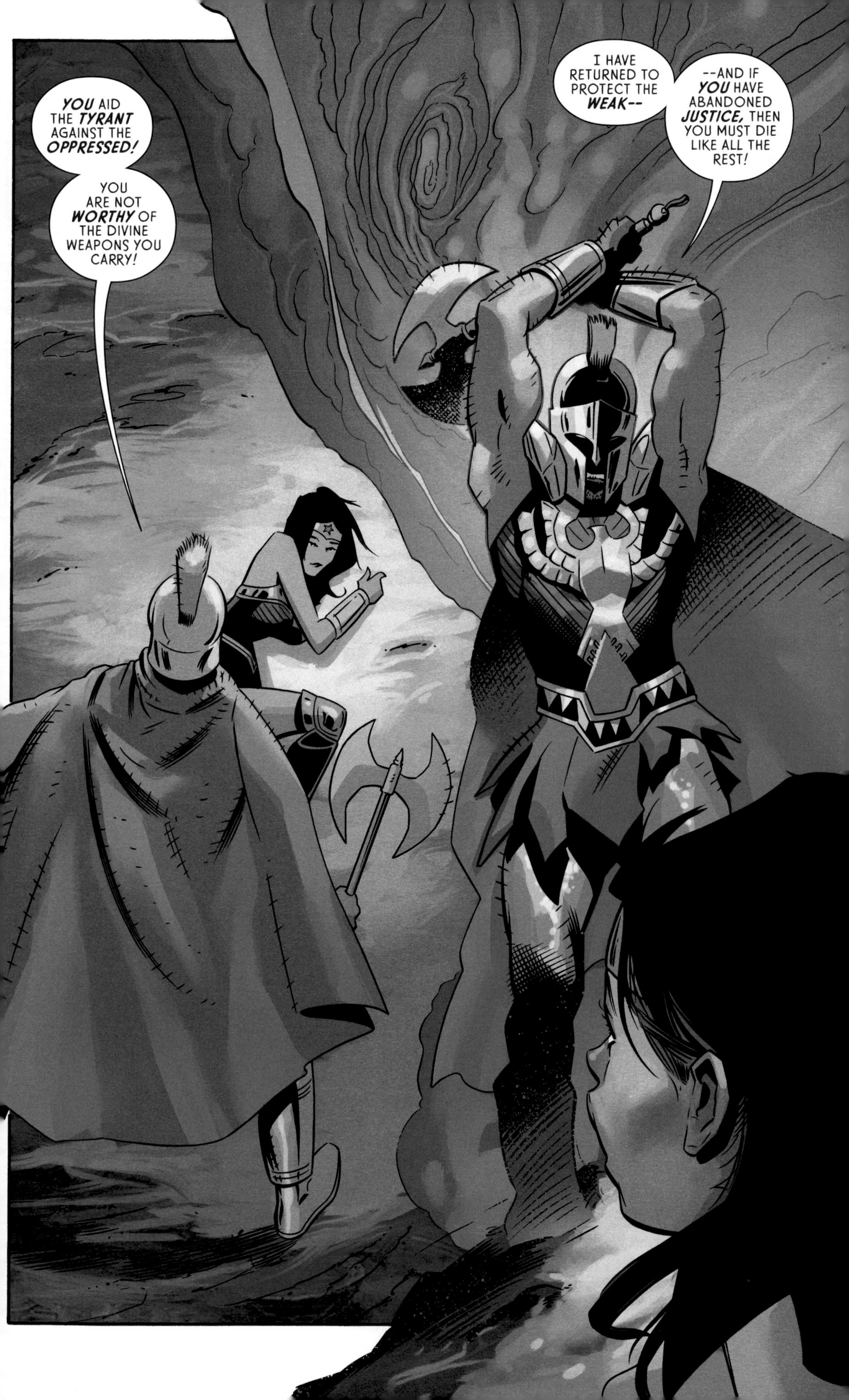

YOU AID THE *TYRANT* AGAINST THE *OPPRESSED!*
YOU ARE NOT *WORTHY* OF THE DIVINE WEAPONS YOU CARRY!
I HAVE RETURNED TO PROTECT THE *WEAK*--
--AND IF *YOU* HAVE ABANDONED *JUSTICE,* THEN YOU MUST DIE LIKE ALL THE REST!

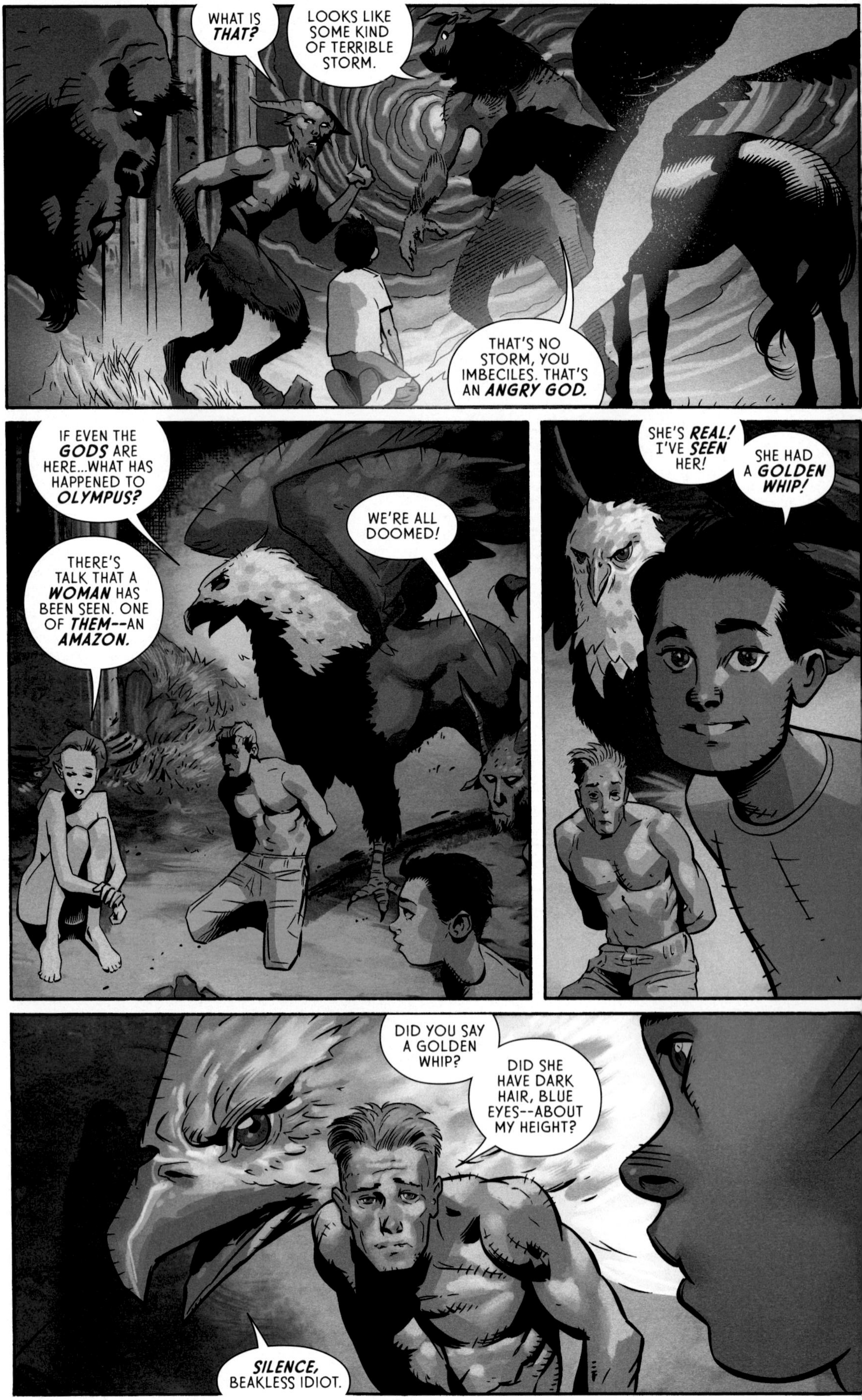
WHAT IS *THAT?*
LOOKS LIKE SOME KIND OF TERRIBLE STORM.
THAT'S NO STORM, YOU IMBECILES. THAT'S AN *ANGRY GOD.*
IF EVEN THE *GODS* ARE HERE...WHAT HAS HAPPENED TO *OLYMPUS?*
THERE'S TALK THAT A *WOMAN* HAS BEEN SEEN. ONE OF *THEM*--AN *AMAZON.*
WE'RE ALL DOOMED!
SHE'S *REAL!* I'VE *SEEN* HER!
SHE HAD A *GOLDEN WHIP!*
DID YOU SAY A GOLDEN WHIP?
DID SHE HAVE DARK HAIR, BLUE EYES--ABOUT MY HEIGHT?
SILENCE, BEAKLESS IDIOT.

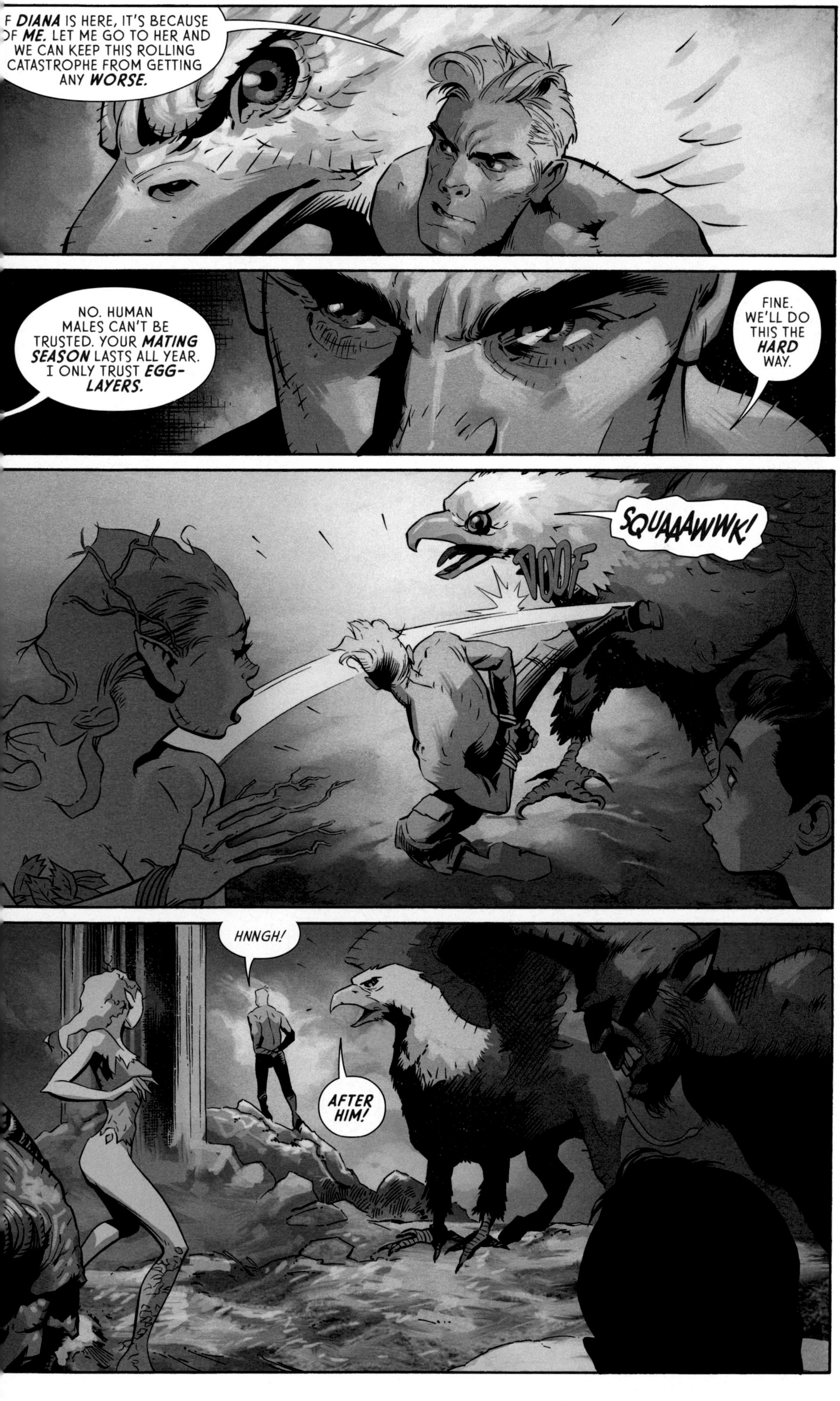
F DIANA IS HERE, IT'S BECAUSE OF ME. LET ME GO TO HER AND WE CAN KEEP THIS ROLLING CATASTROPHE FROM GETTING ANY WORSE.
NO. HUMAN MALES CAN'T BE TRUSTED. YOUR MATING SEASON LASTS ALL YEAR. I ONLY TRUST EGG-LAYERS.
FINE. WE'LL DO THIS THE HARD WAY.
SQUAAAWWK!
DOOF
HNNGH!
AFTER HIM!

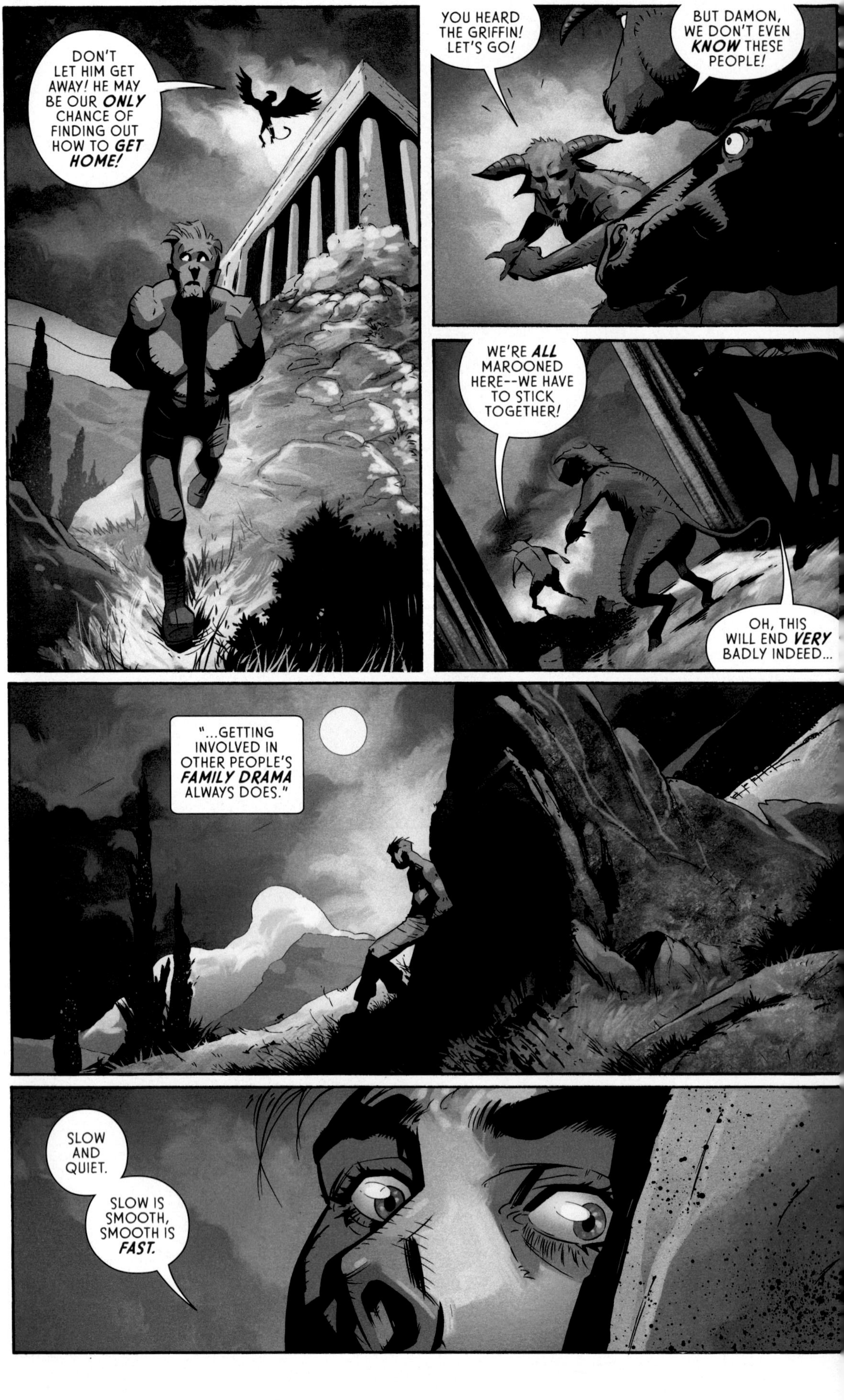
DON'T LET HIM GET AWAY! HE MAY BE OUR ONLY CHANCE OF FINDING OUT HOW TO GET HOME!
YOU HEARD THE GRIFFIN! LET'S GO!
BUT DAMON, WE DON'T EVEN KNOW THESE PEOPLE!
WE'RE ALL MAROONED HERE--WE HAVE TO STICK TOGETHER!
OH, THIS WILL END VERY BADLY INDEED...
"...GETTING INVOLVED IN OTHER PEOPLE'S FAMILY DRAMA ALWAYS DOES."
SLOW AND QUIET.
SLOW IS SMOOTH, SMOOTH IS FAST.

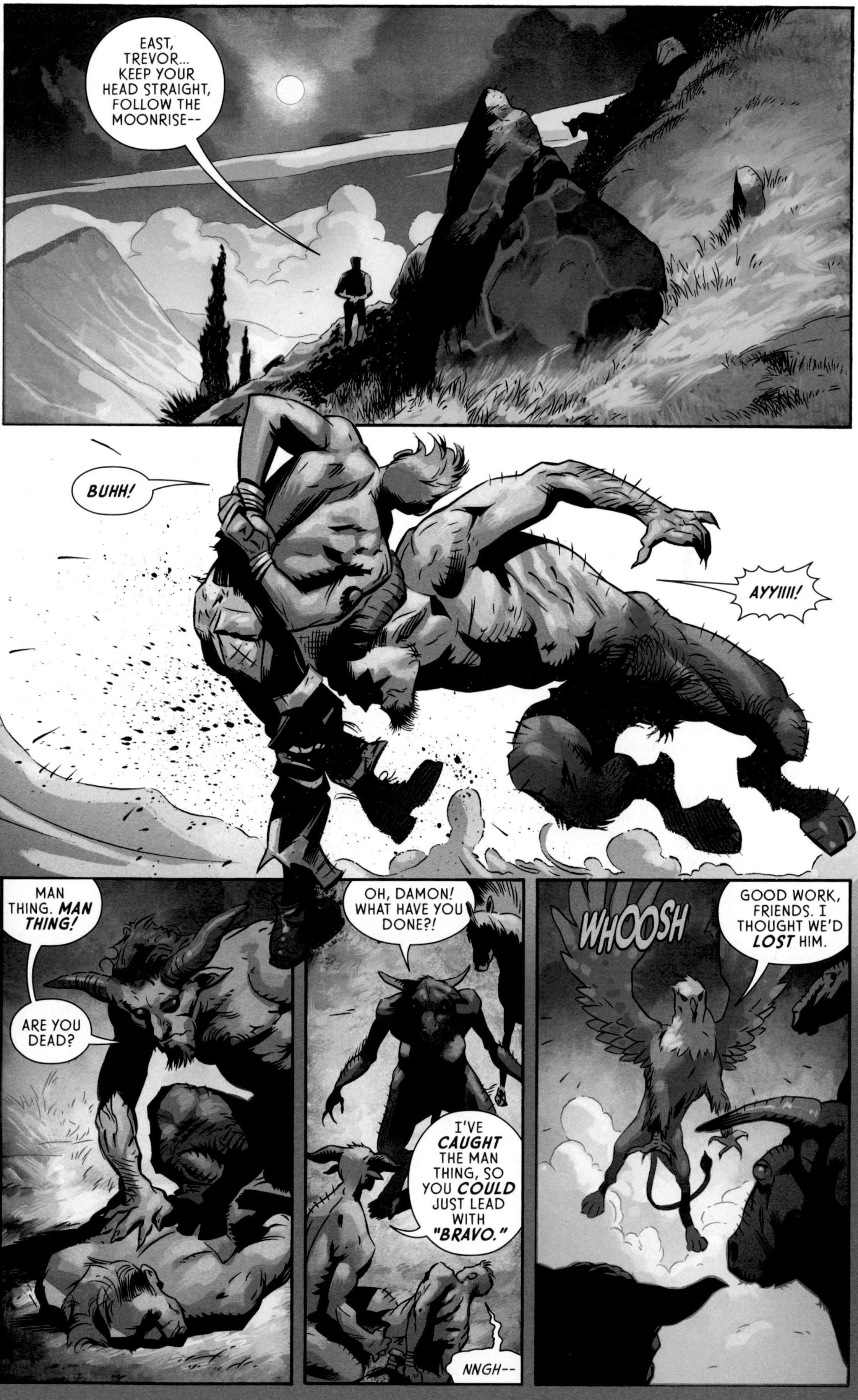
EAST, TREVOR... KEEP YOUR HEAD STRAIGHT, FOLLOW THE MOONRISE--
BUHH!
AYYIIII!
MAN THING. MAN THING!
ARE YOU DEAD?
OH, DAMON! WHAT HAVE YOU DONE?!
I'VE CAUGHT THE MAN THING, SO YOU COULD JUST LEAD WITH "BRAVO."
NNGH--
WHOOSH
GOOD WORK, FRIENDS. I THOUGHT WE'D LOST HIM.

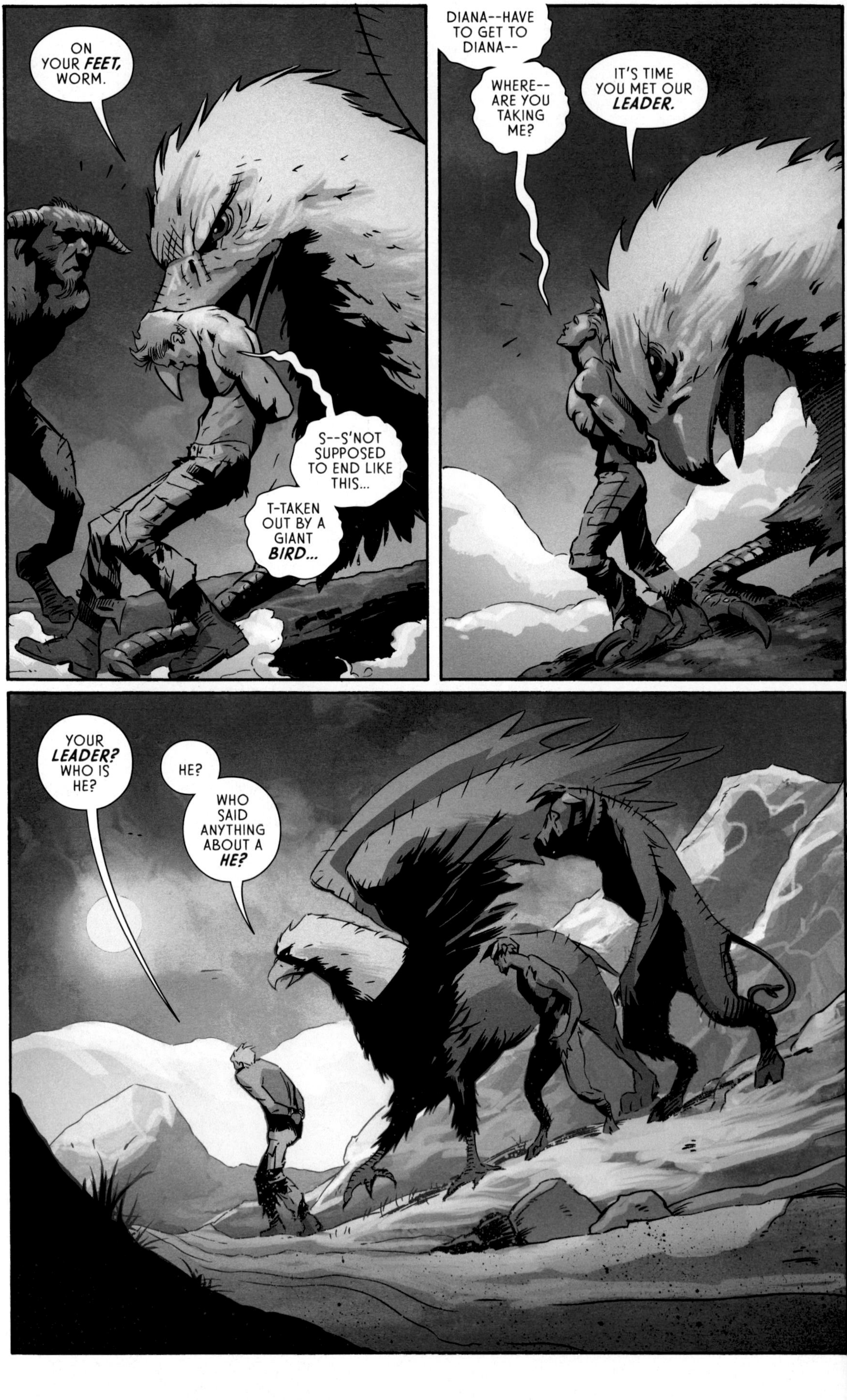
ON YOUR *FEET,* WORM.
S--S'NOT SUPPOSED TO END LIKE THIS...
T-TAKEN OUT BY A GIANT *BIRD...*
DIANA--HAVE TO GET TO DIANA--
WHERE--ARE YOU TAKING ME?
IT'S TIME YOU MET OUR *LEADER.*
YOUR *LEADER?* WHO IS HE?
HE?
WHO SAID ANYTHING ABOUT A *HE?*

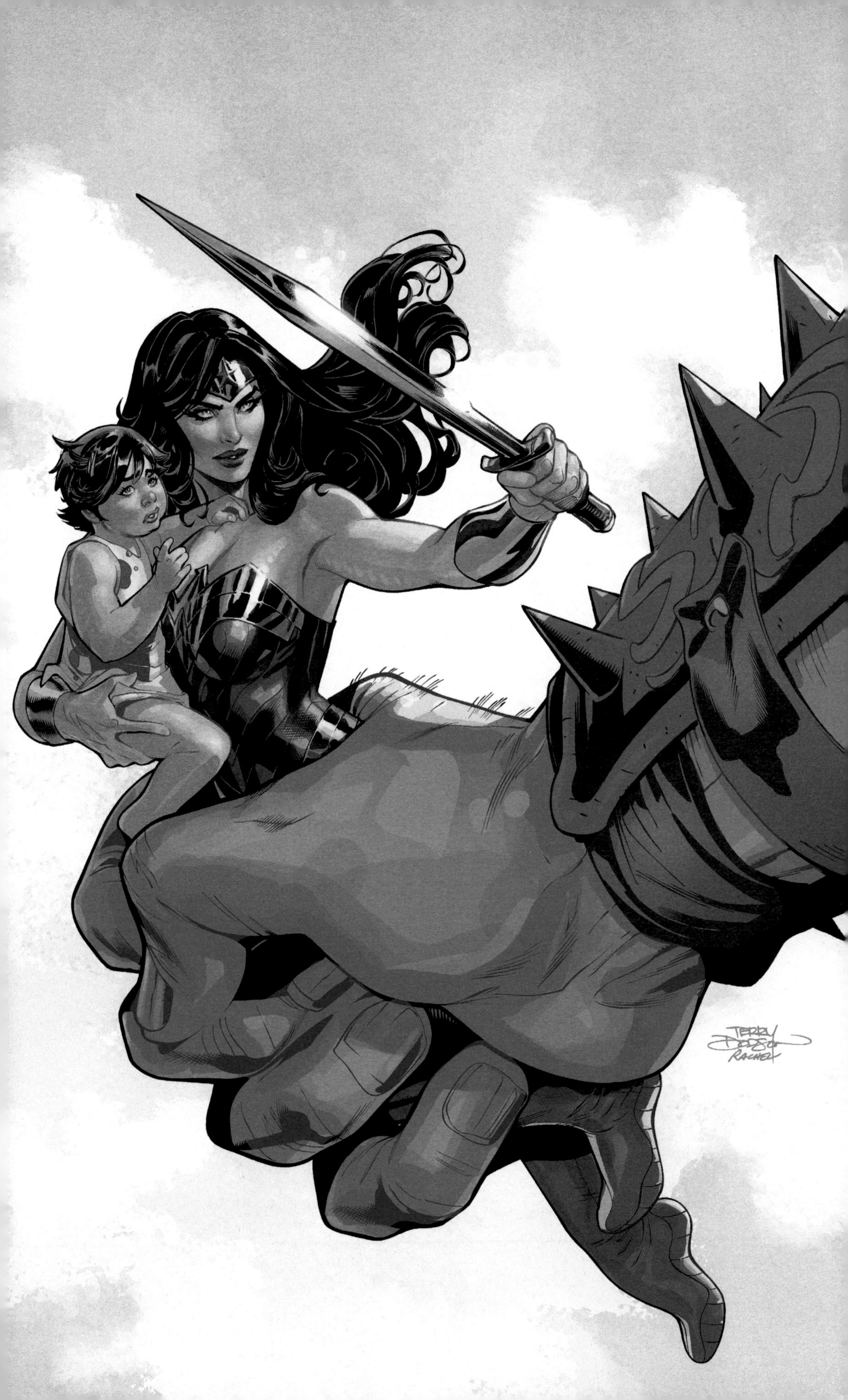
TERRY
DODSON
RACHEL

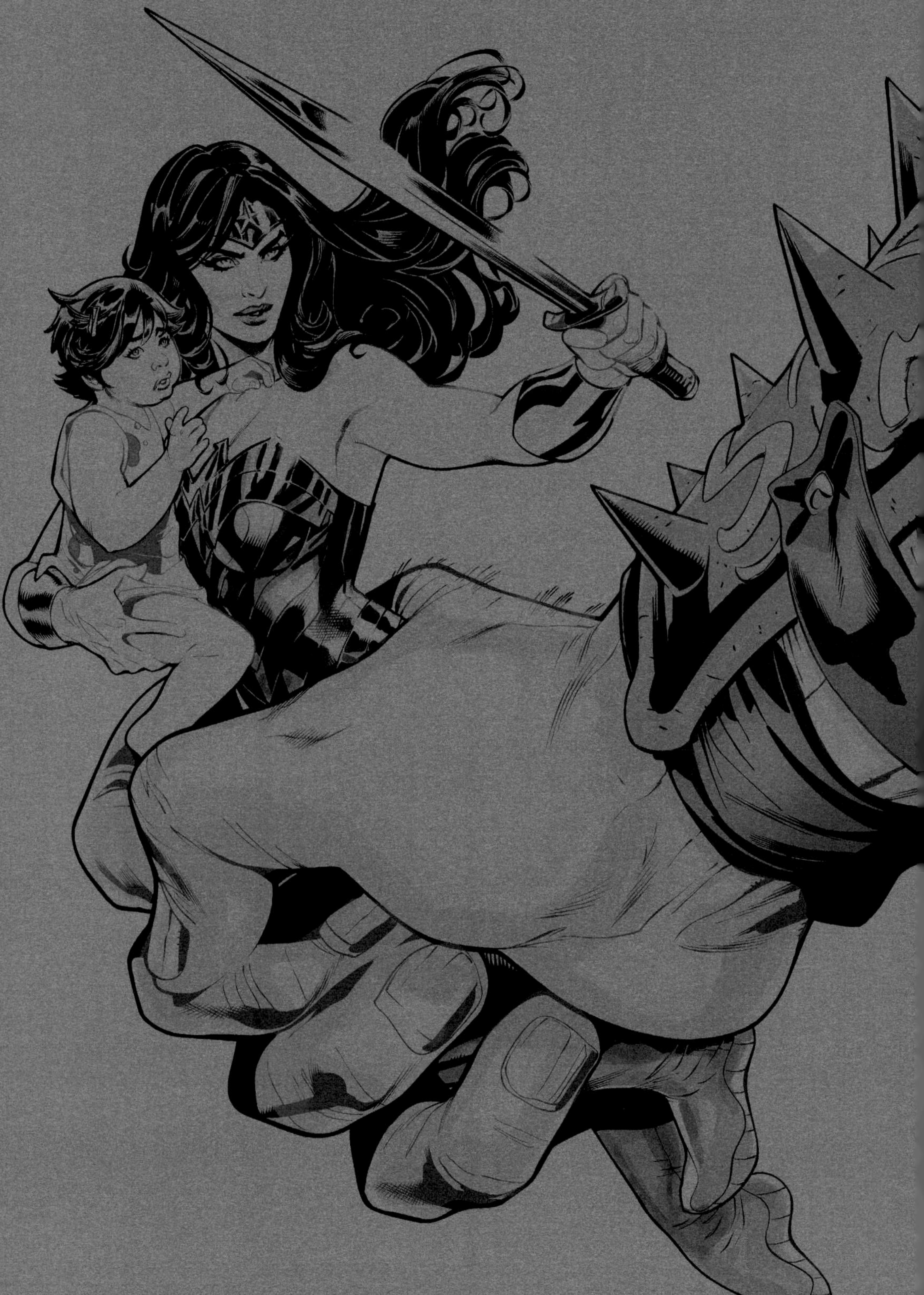

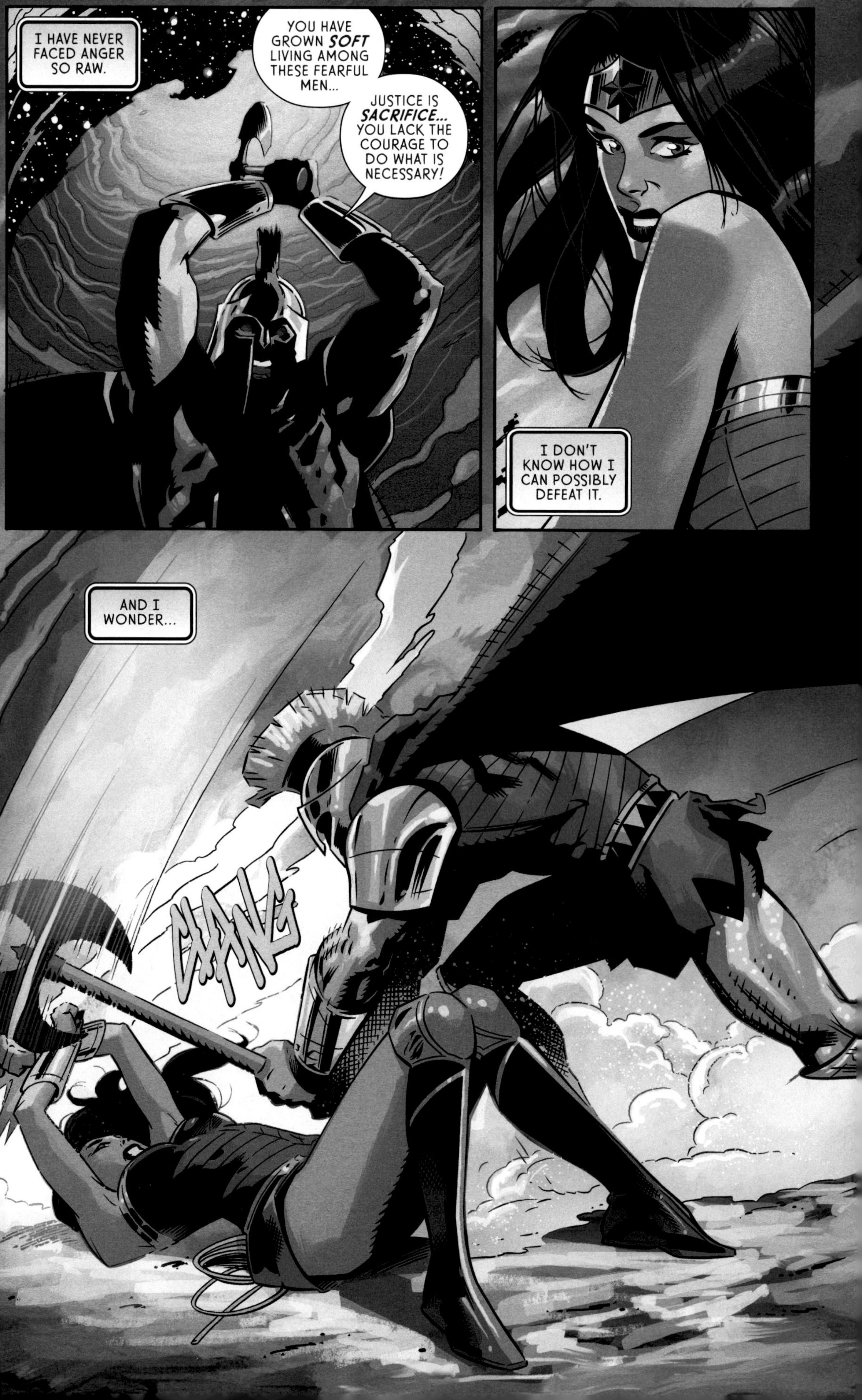

I HAVE NEVER FACED ANGER SO RAW.
YOU HAVE GROWN SOFT LIVING AMONG THESE FEARFUL MEN...
JUSTICE IS SACRIFICE... YOU LACK THE COURAGE TO DO WHAT IS NECESSARY!
I DON'T KNOW HOW I CAN POSSIBLY DEFEAT IT.
AND I WONDER...
CHANG

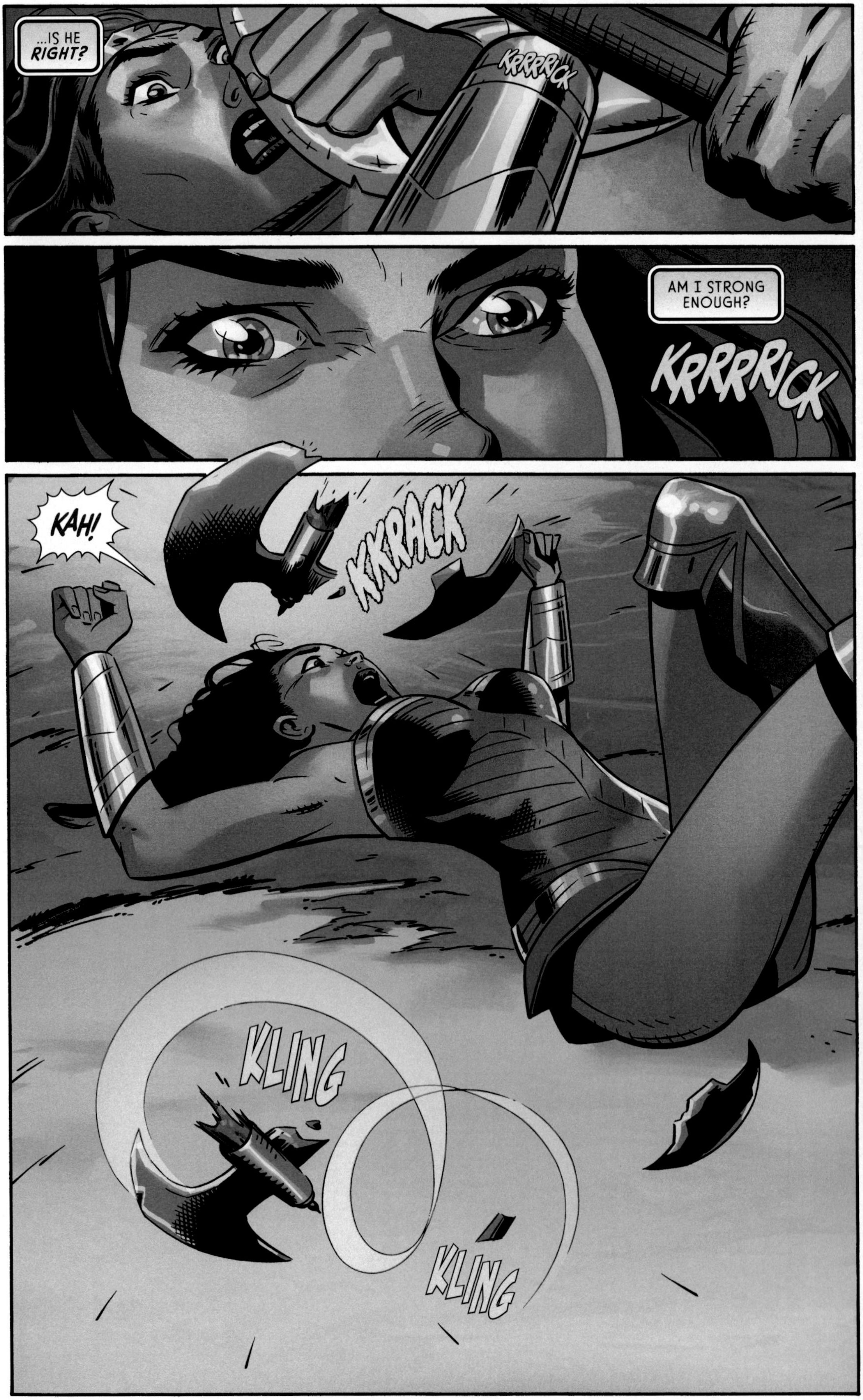

...IS HE RIGHT?
KRRRRICK
AM I STRONG ENOUGH?
KRRRRICK
KAH!
KKRACK
KLING
KLING

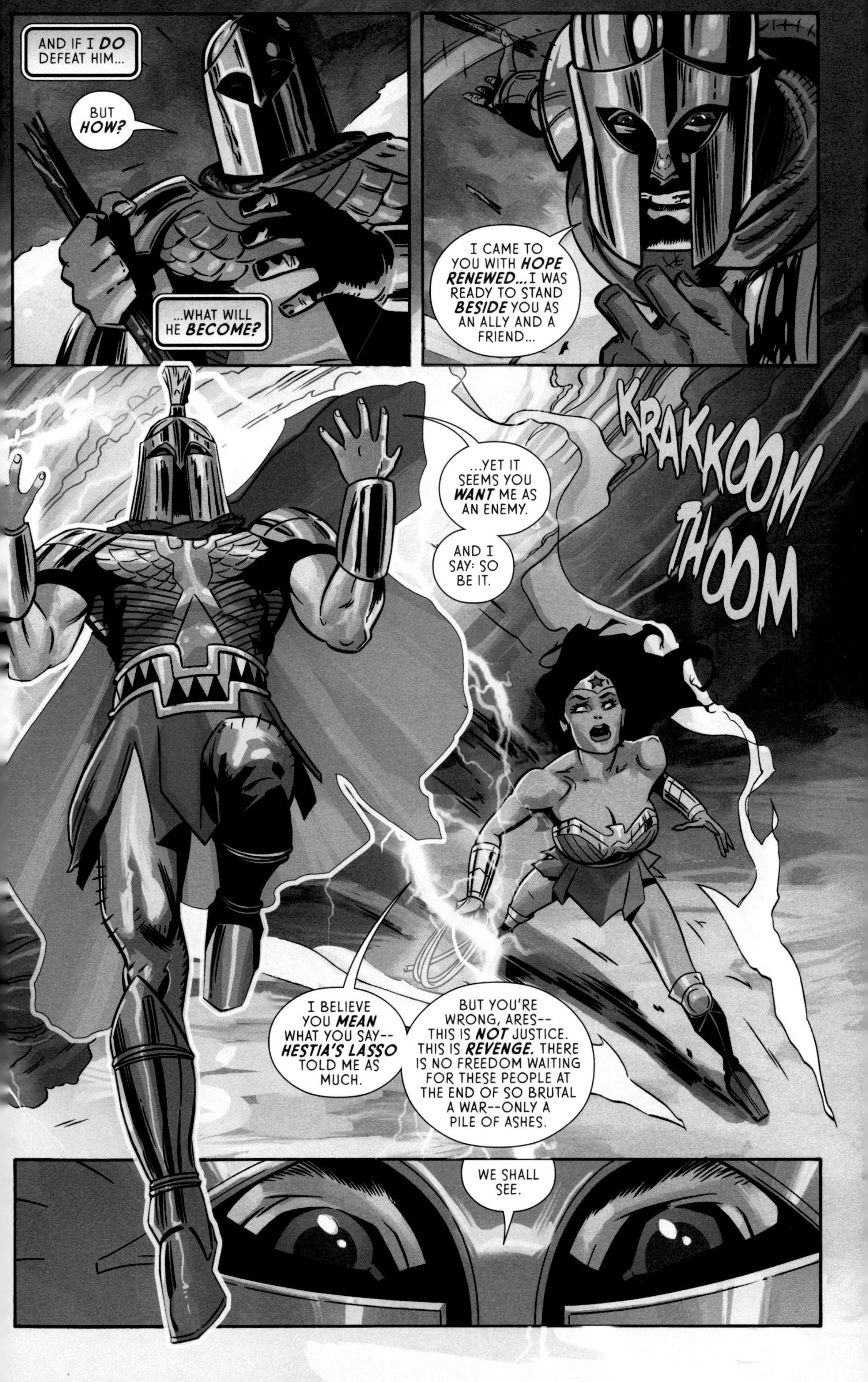
AND IF I DO DEFEAT HIM...
BUT HOW?
...WHAT WILL HE BECOME?
I CAME TO YOU WITH HOPE RENEWED...I WAS READY TO STAND BESIDE YOU AS AN ALLY AND A FRIEND...
KRAKKOOM
THOOM
...YET IT SEEMS YOU WANT ME AS AN ENEMY.
AND I SAY: SO BE IT.
I BELIEVE YOU MEAN WHAT YOU SAY-- HESTIA'S LASSO TOLD ME AS MUCH.
BUT YOU'RE WRONG, ARES-- THIS IS NOT JUSTICE. THIS IS REVENGE. THERE IS NO FREEDOM WAITING FOR THESE PEOPLE AT THE END OF SO BRUTAL A WAR--ONLY A PILE OF ASHES.
WE SHALL SEE.

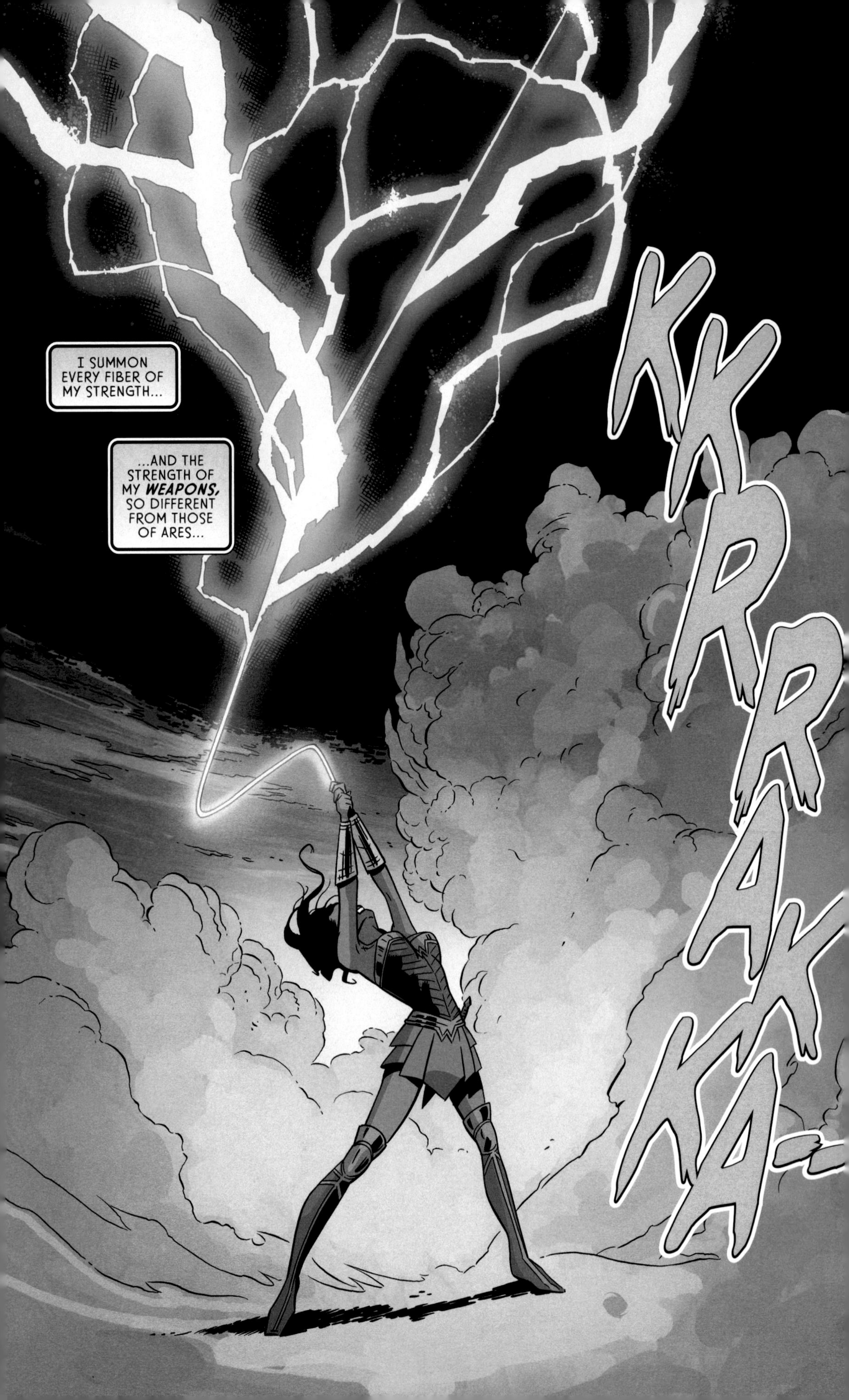
I SUMMON EVERY FIBER OF MY STRENGTH...
...AND THE STRENGTH OF MY *WEAPONS,* SO DIFFERENT FROM THOSE OF ARES...
KKRRAKKA-

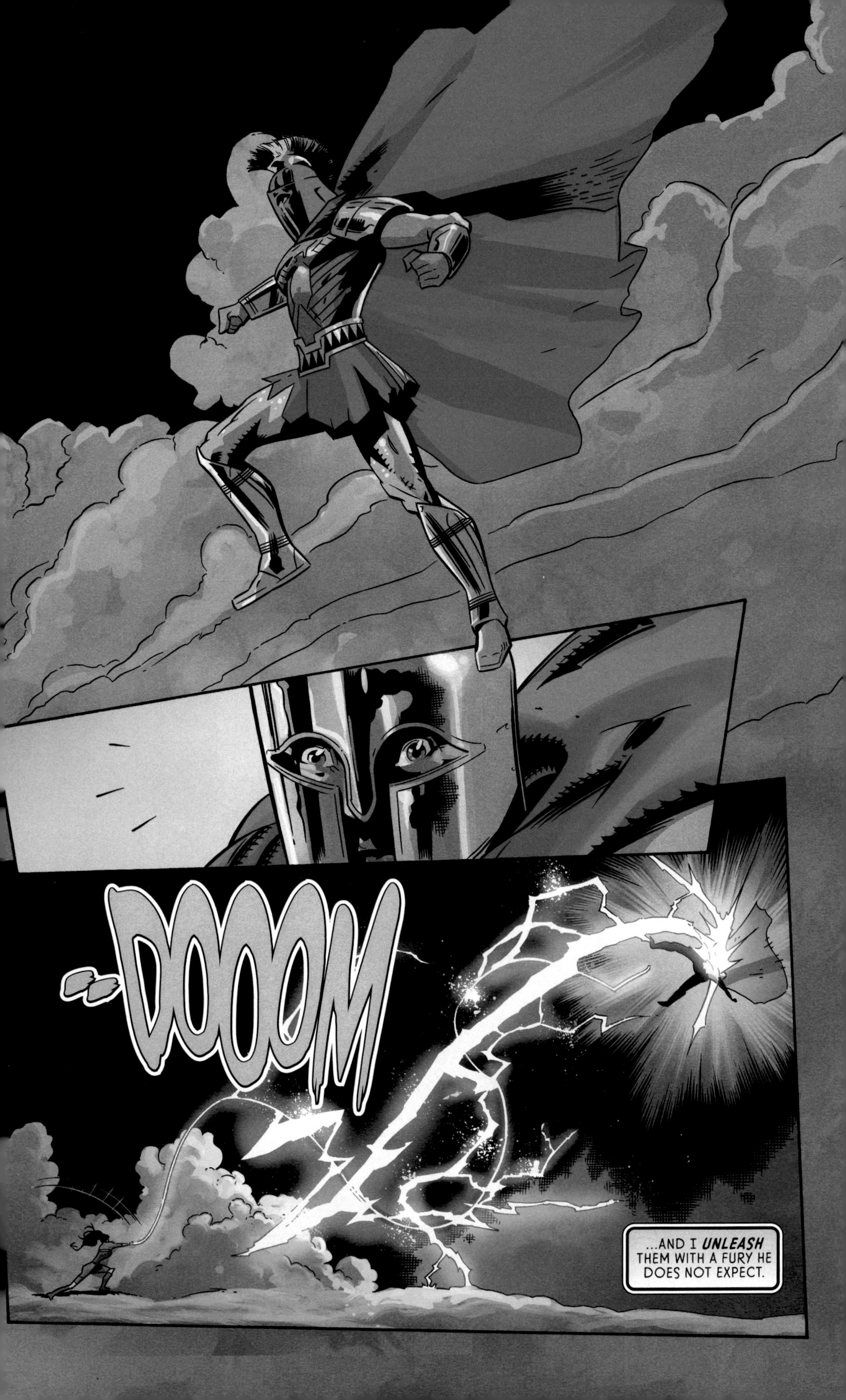

--DOOOM
...AND I UNLEASH
THEM WITH A FURY HE
DOES NOT EXPECT.

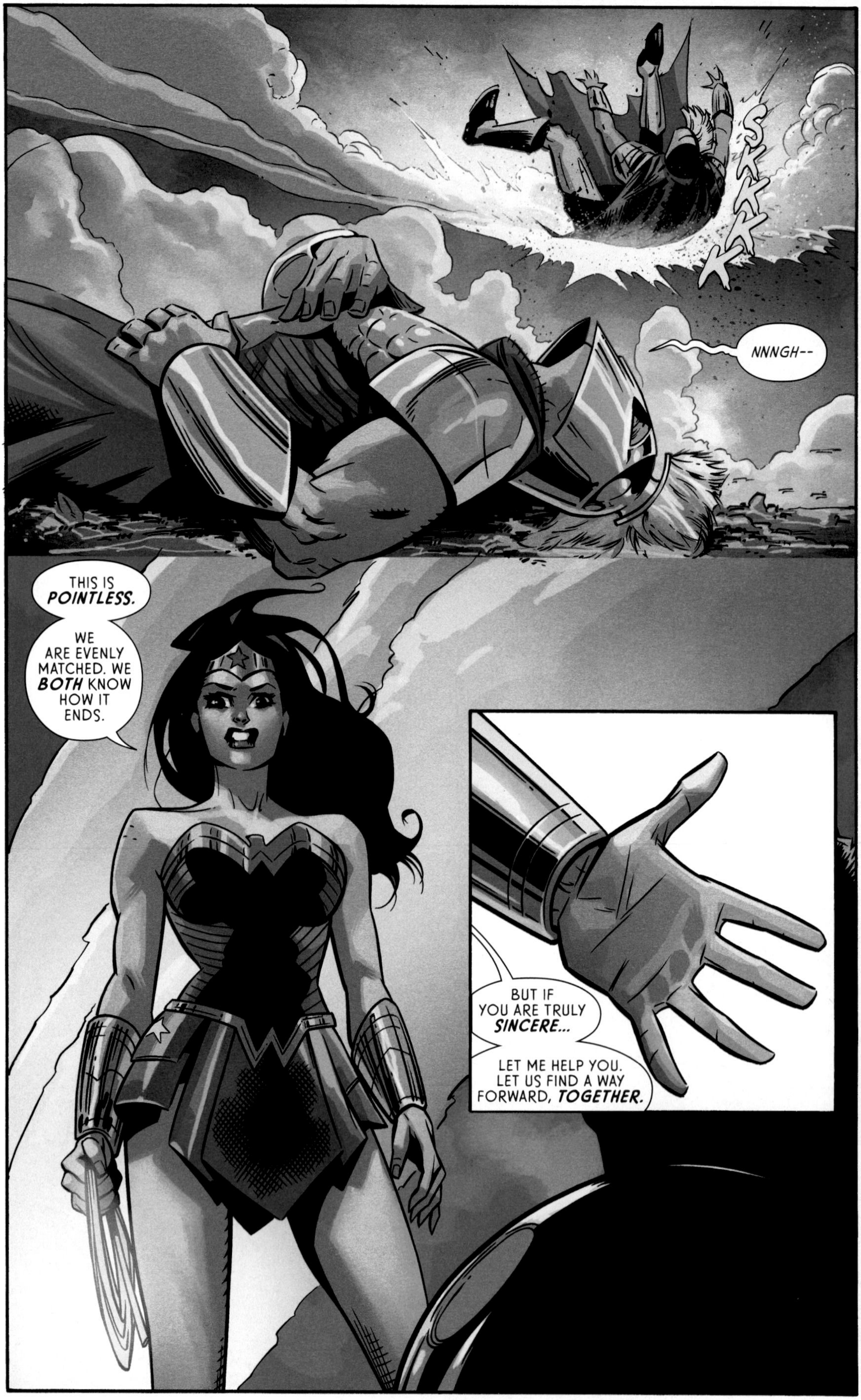
SKKKK
NNNGH--
THIS IS POINTLESS.
WE ARE EVENLY MATCHED. WE BOTH KNOW HOW IT ENDS.
BUT IF YOU ARE TRULY SINCERE...
LET ME HELP YOU. LET US FIND A WAY FORWARD, TOGETHER.

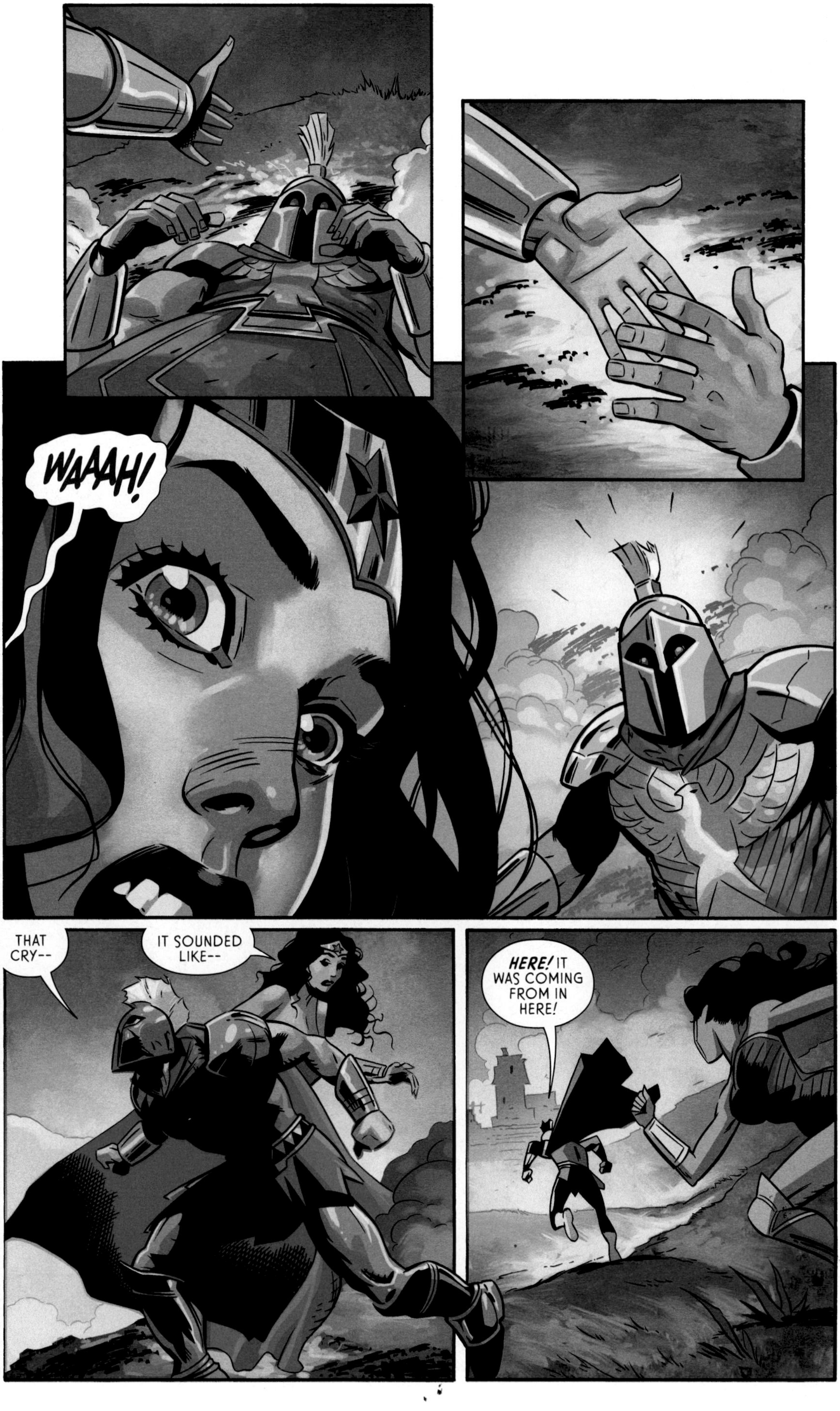
WAAAH!
THAT CRY--
IT SOUNDED LIKE--
HERE! IT WAS COMING FROM IN HERE!

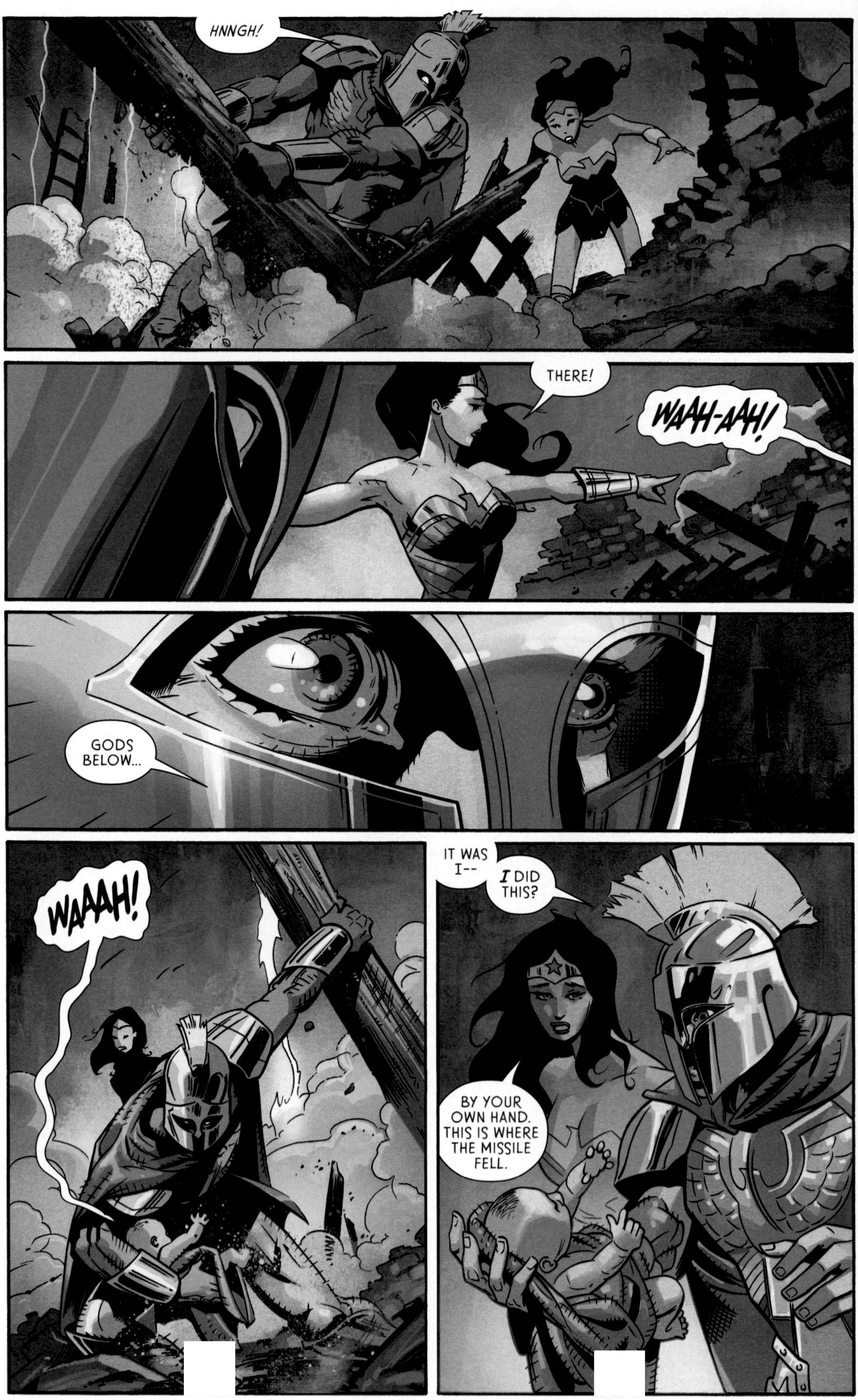
HNNGH!
THERE!
WAAH-AAH!
GODS BELOW...
WAAAH!
IT WAS I--
I DID THIS?
BY YOUR OWN HAND. THIS IS WHERE THE MISSILE FELL.

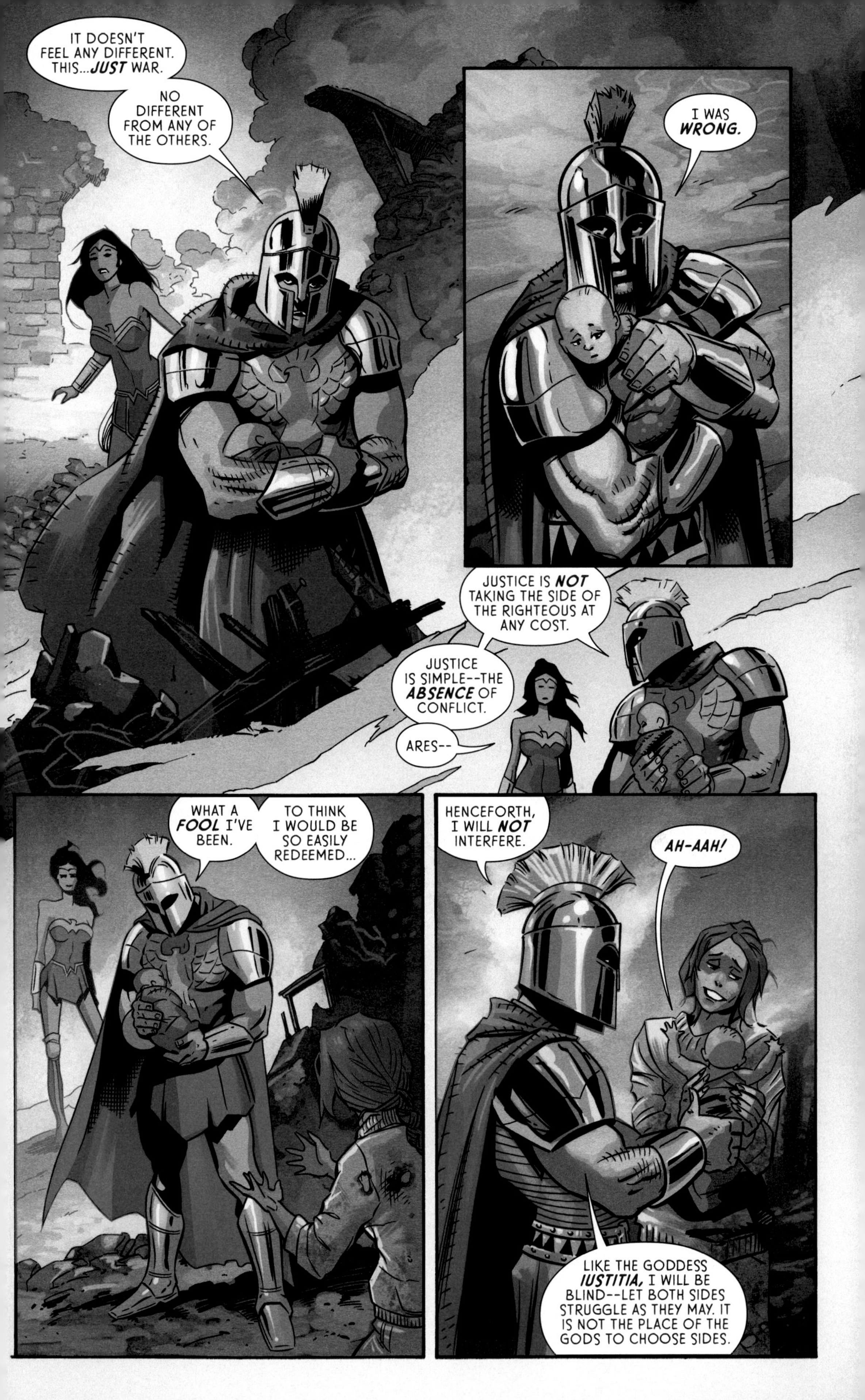
IT DOESN'T FEEL ANY DIFFERENT. THIS...JUST WAR.
NO DIFFERENT FROM ANY OF THE OTHERS.
I WAS WRONG.
JUSTICE IS NOT TAKING THE SIDE OF THE RIGHTEOUS AT ANY COST.
JUSTICE IS SIMPLE--THE ABSENCE OF CONFLICT.
ARES--
WHAT A FOOL I'VE BEEN.
TO THINK I WOULD BE SO EASILY REDEEMED...
HENCEFORTH, I WILL NOT INTERFERE.
AH-AAH!
LIKE THE GODDESS IUSTITIA, I WILL BE BLIND--LET BOTH SIDES STRUGGLE AS THEY MAY. IT IS NOT THE PLACE OF THE GODS TO CHOOSE SIDES.

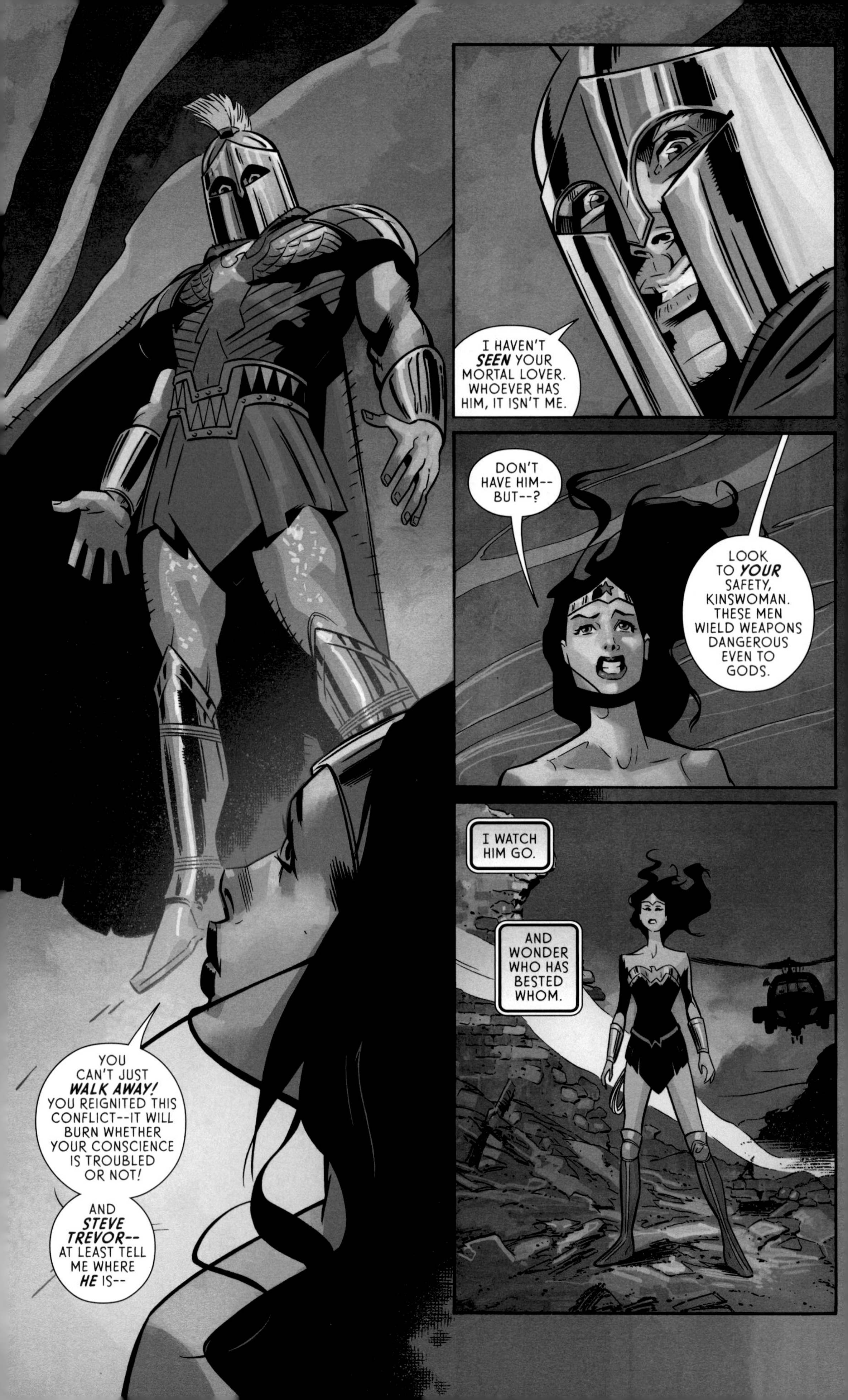
YOU CAN'T JUST WALK AWAY! YOU REIGNITED THIS CONFLICT--IT WILL BURN WHETHER YOUR CONSCIENCE IS TROUBLED OR NOT!
AND STEVE TREVOR-- AT LEAST TELL ME WHERE HE IS--
I HAVEN'T SEEN YOUR MORTAL LOVER. WHOEVER HAS HIM, IT ISN'T ME.
DON'T HAVE HIM-- BUT--?
LOOK TO YOUR SAFETY, KINSWOMAN. THESE MEN WIELD WEAPONS DANGEROUS EVEN TO GODS.
I WATCH HIM GO.
AND WONDER WHO HAS BESTED WHOM.

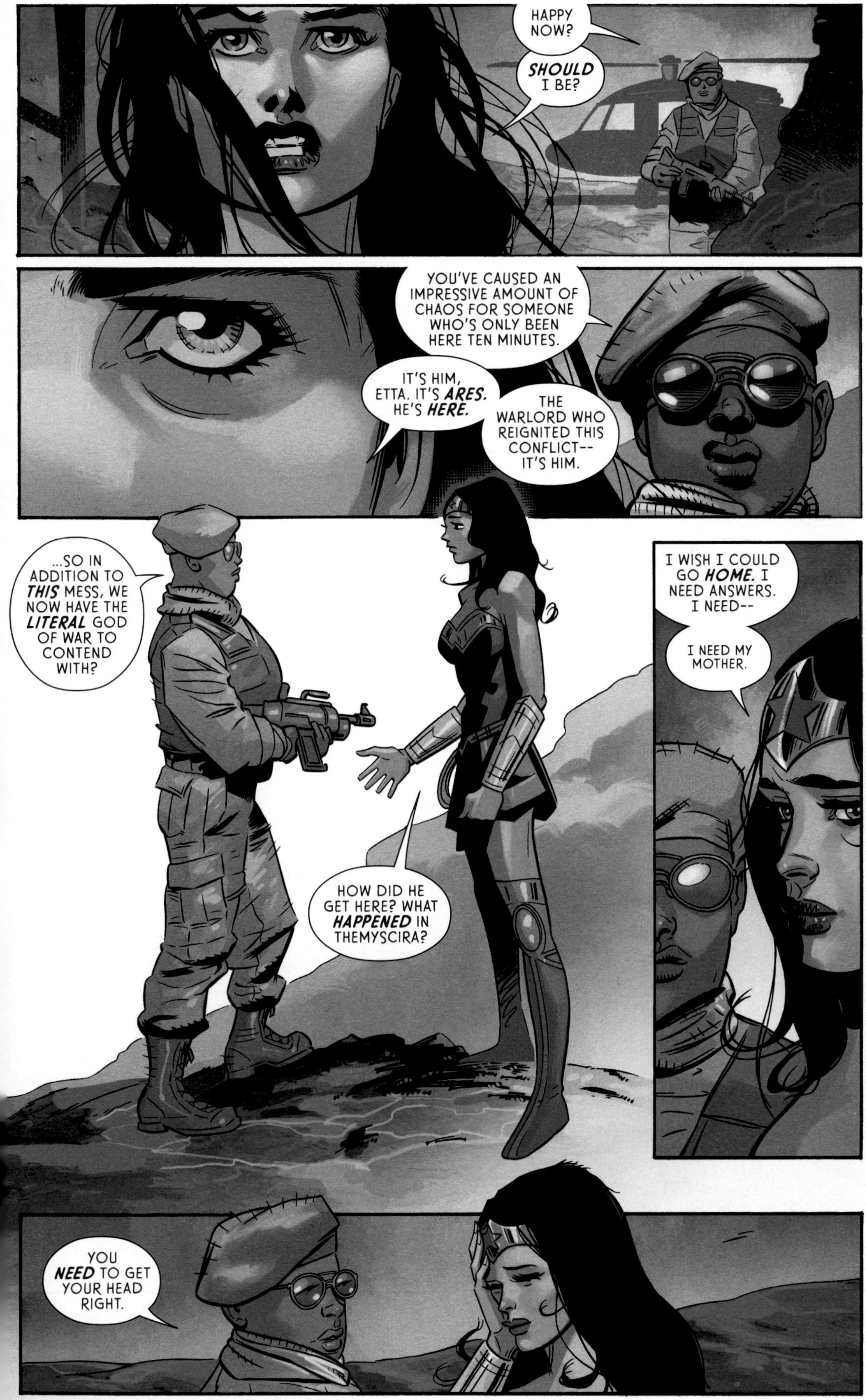
HAPPY NOW?
SHOULD I BE?
YOU'VE CAUSED AN IMPRESSIVE AMOUNT OF CHAOS FOR SOMEONE WHO'S ONLY BEEN HERE TEN MINUTES.
IT'S HIM, ETTA. IT'S ARES. HE'S HERE.
THE WARLORD WHO REIGNITED THIS CONFLICT-- IT'S HIM.
...SO IN ADDITION TO THIS MESS, WE NOW HAVE THE LITERAL GOD OF WAR TO CONTEND WITH?
HOW DID HE GET HERE? WHAT HAPPENED IN THEMYSCIRA?
I WISH I COULD GO HOME. I NEED ANSWERS. I NEED--
I NEED MY MOTHER.
YOU NEED TO GET YOUR HEAD RIGHT.

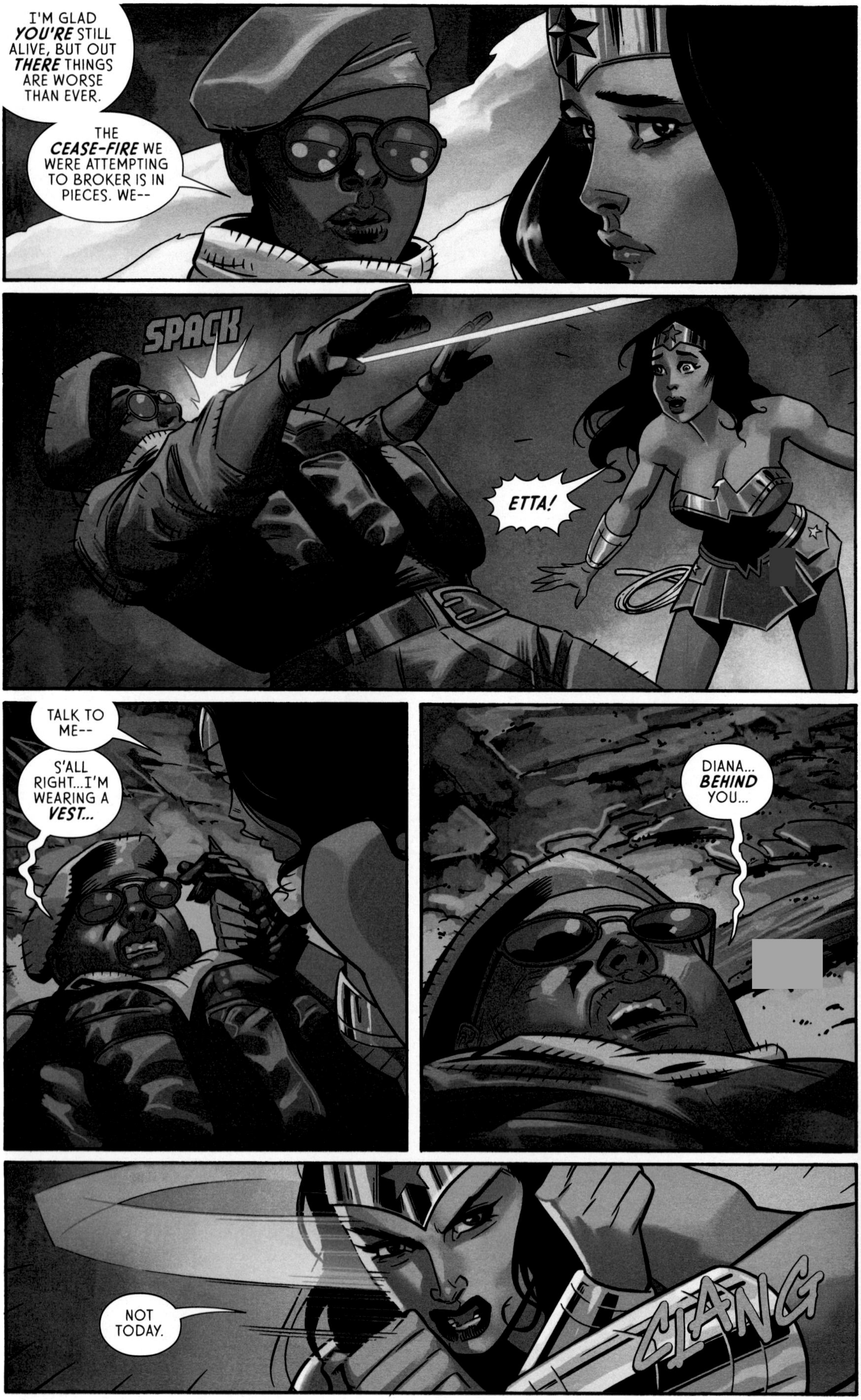
I'M GLAD YOU'RE STILL ALIVE, BUT OUT THERE THINGS ARE WORSE THAN EVER.
THE CEASE-FIRE WE WERE ATTEMPTING TO BROKER IS IN PIECES. WE--
SPACK
ETTA!
TALK TO ME--
S'ALL RIGHT...I'M WEARING A VEST...
DIANA... BEHIND YOU...
NOT TODAY.
CLANG

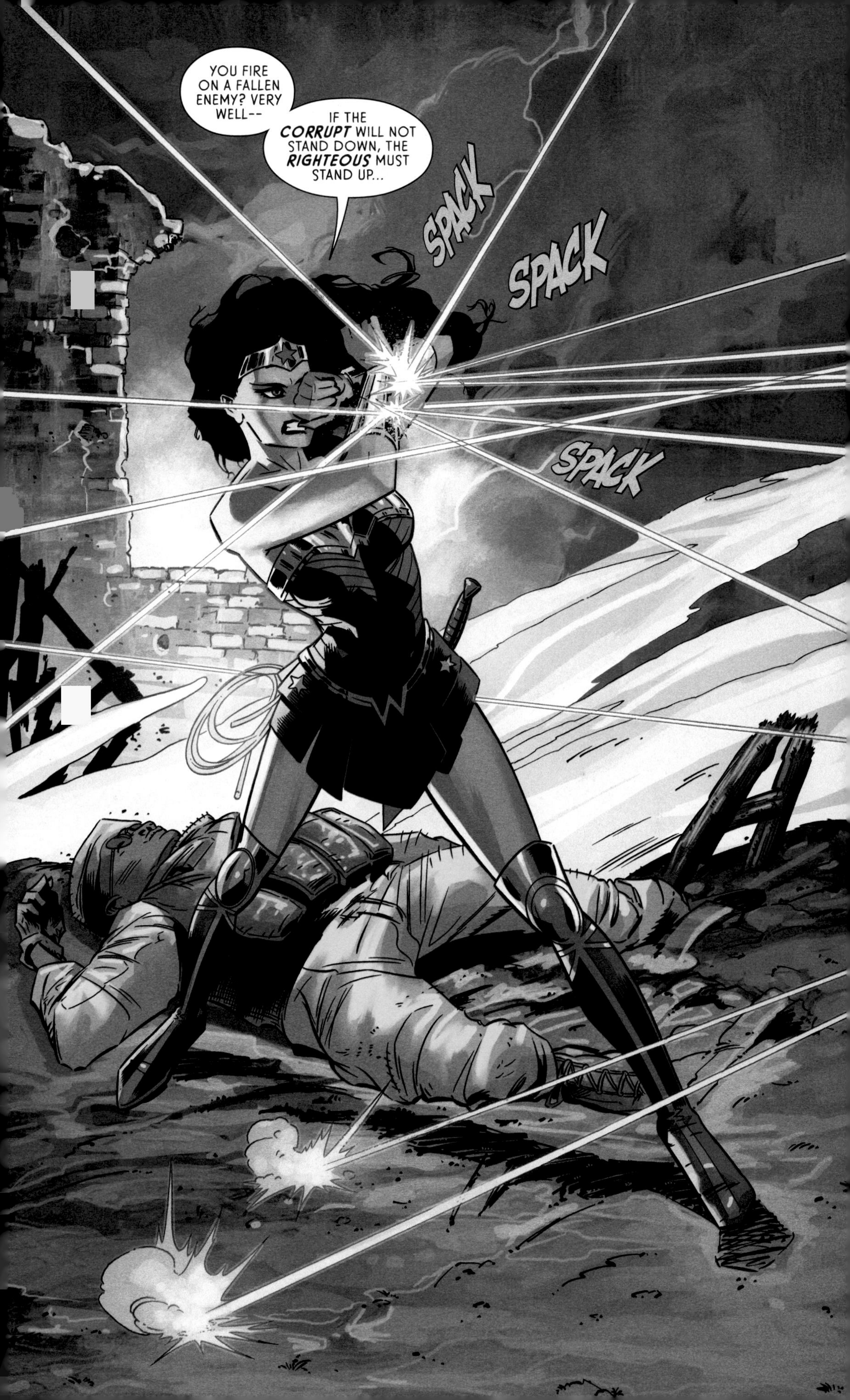
YOU FIRE ON A FALLEN ENEMY? VERY WELL--
IF THE **CORRUPT** WILL NOT STAND DOWN, THE **RIGHTEOUS** MUST STAND UP...
SPACK
SPACK
SPACK

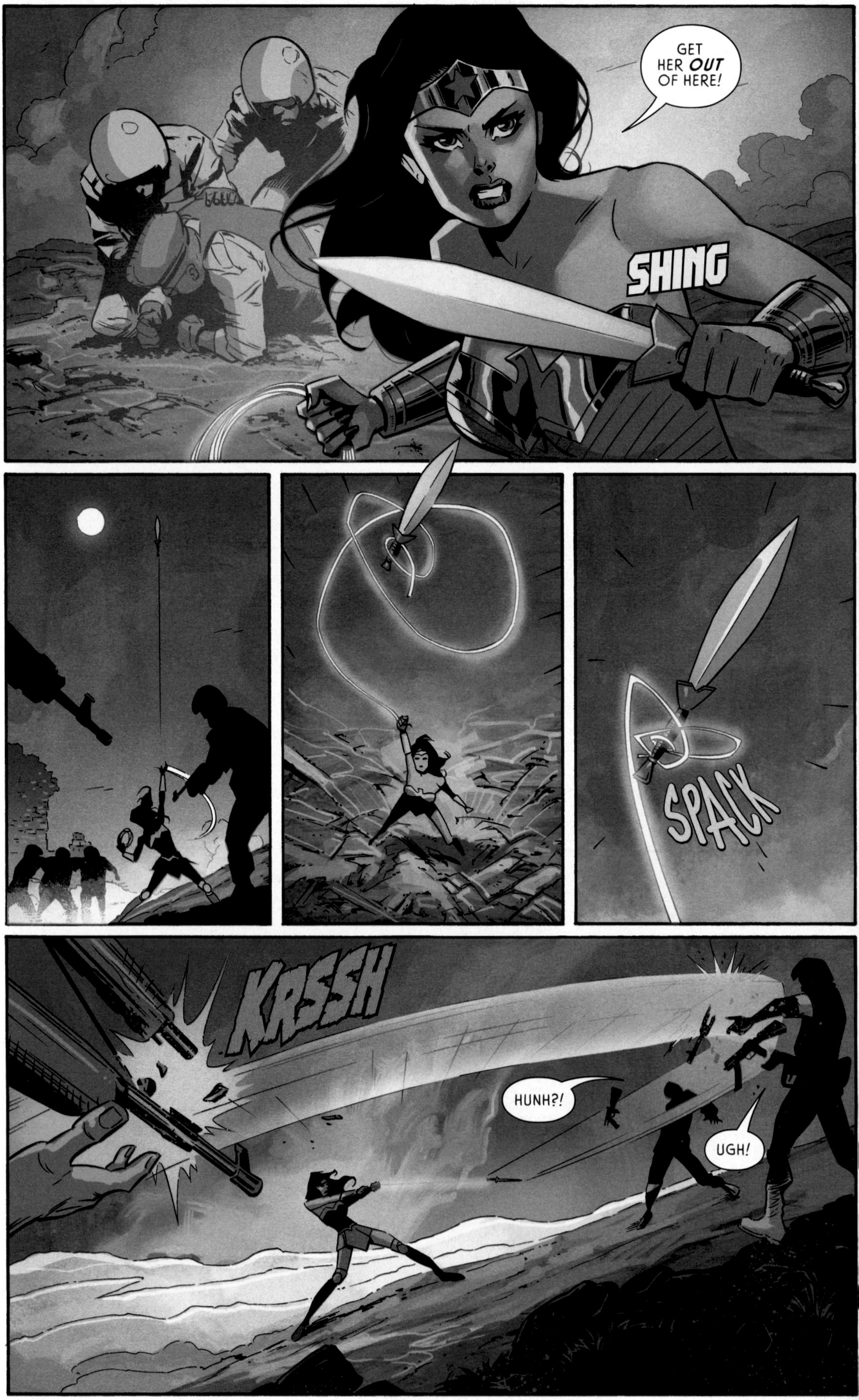
GET HER *OUT* OF HERE!
SHING
SPACK
KRSSH
HUNH?!
UGH!

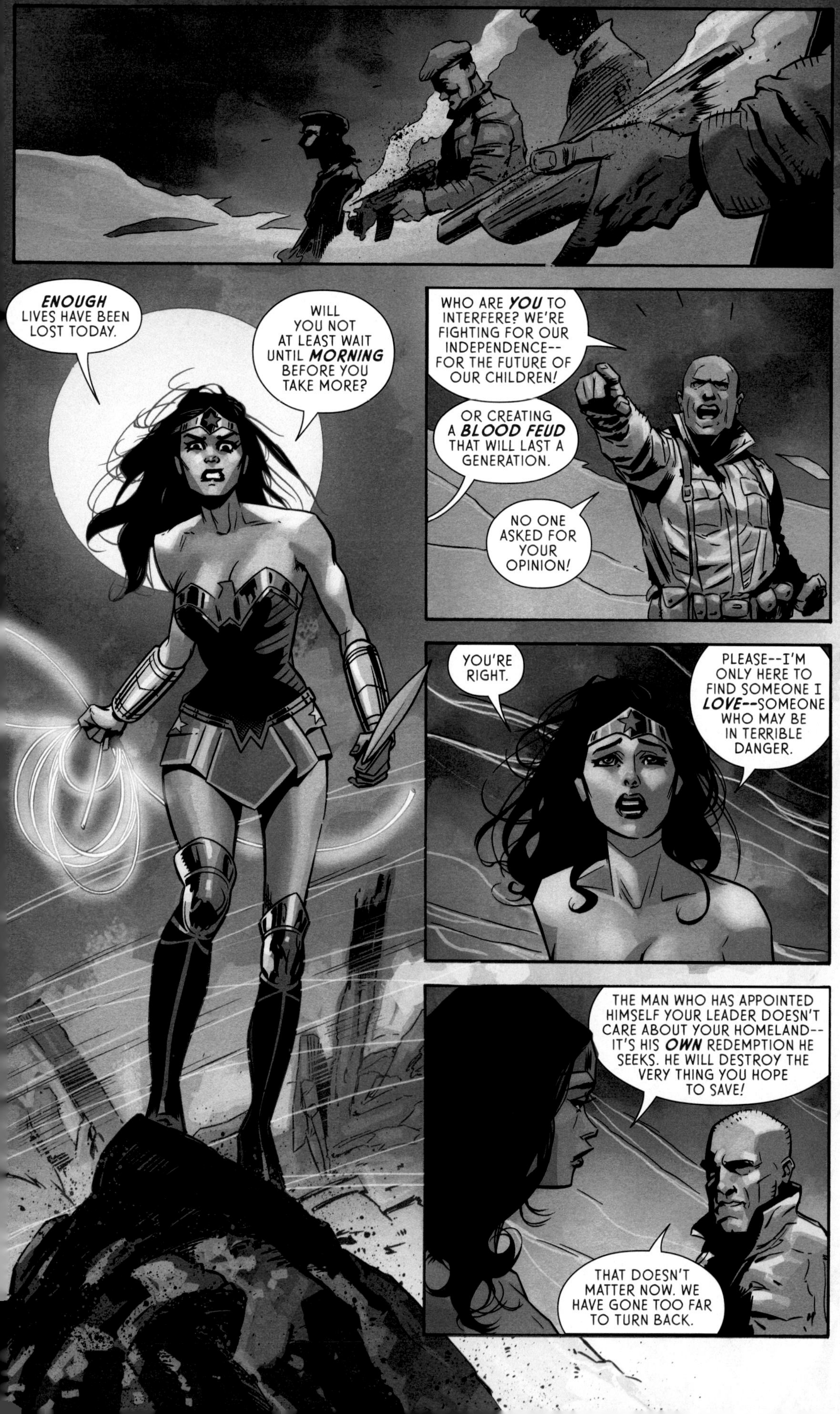
ENOUGH LIVES HAVE BEEN LOST TODAY.
WILL YOU NOT AT LEAST WAIT UNTIL MORNING BEFORE YOU TAKE MORE?
WHO ARE YOU TO INTERFERE? WE'RE FIGHTING FOR OUR INDEPENDENCE-- FOR THE FUTURE OF OUR CHILDREN!
OR CREATING A BLOOD FEUD THAT WILL LAST A GENERATION.
NO ONE ASKED FOR YOUR OPINION!
YOU'RE RIGHT.
PLEASE--I'M ONLY HERE TO FIND SOMEONE I LOVE--SOMEONE WHO MAY BE IN TERRIBLE DANGER.
THE MAN WHO HAS APPOINTED HIMSELF YOUR LEADER DOESN'T CARE ABOUT YOUR HOMELAND-- IT'S HIS OWN REDEMPTION HE SEEKS. HE WILL DESTROY THE VERY THING YOU HOPE TO SAVE!
THAT DOESN'T MATTER NOW. WE HAVE GONE TOO FAR TO TURN BACK.

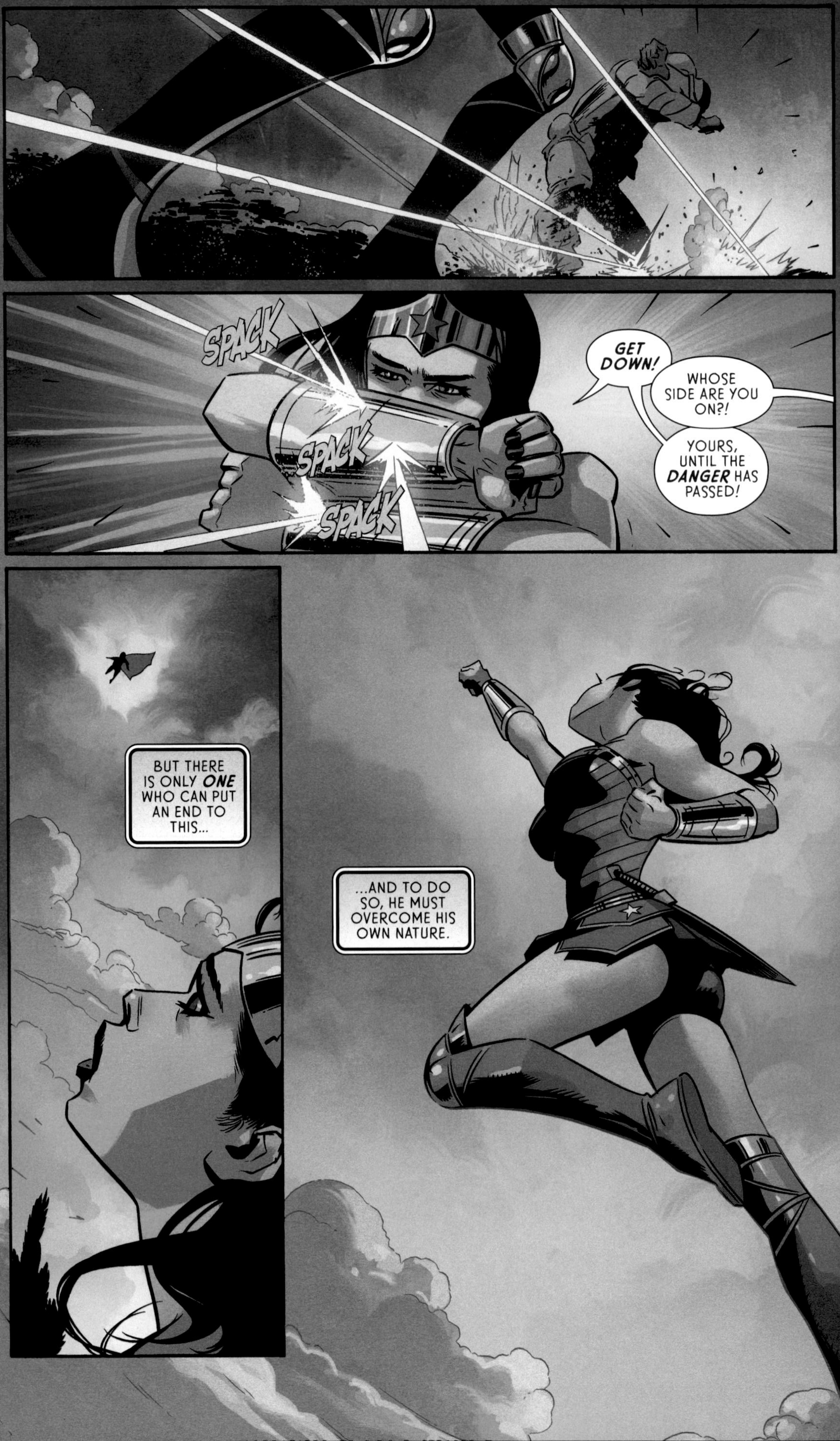
SPACK
SPACK
SPACK
GET DOWN!
WHOSE SIDE ARE YOU ON?!
YOURS, UNTIL THE DANGER HAS PASSED!
BUT THERE IS ONLY ONE WHO CAN PUT AN END TO THIS...
...AND TO DO SO, HE MUST OVERCOME HIS OWN NATURE.

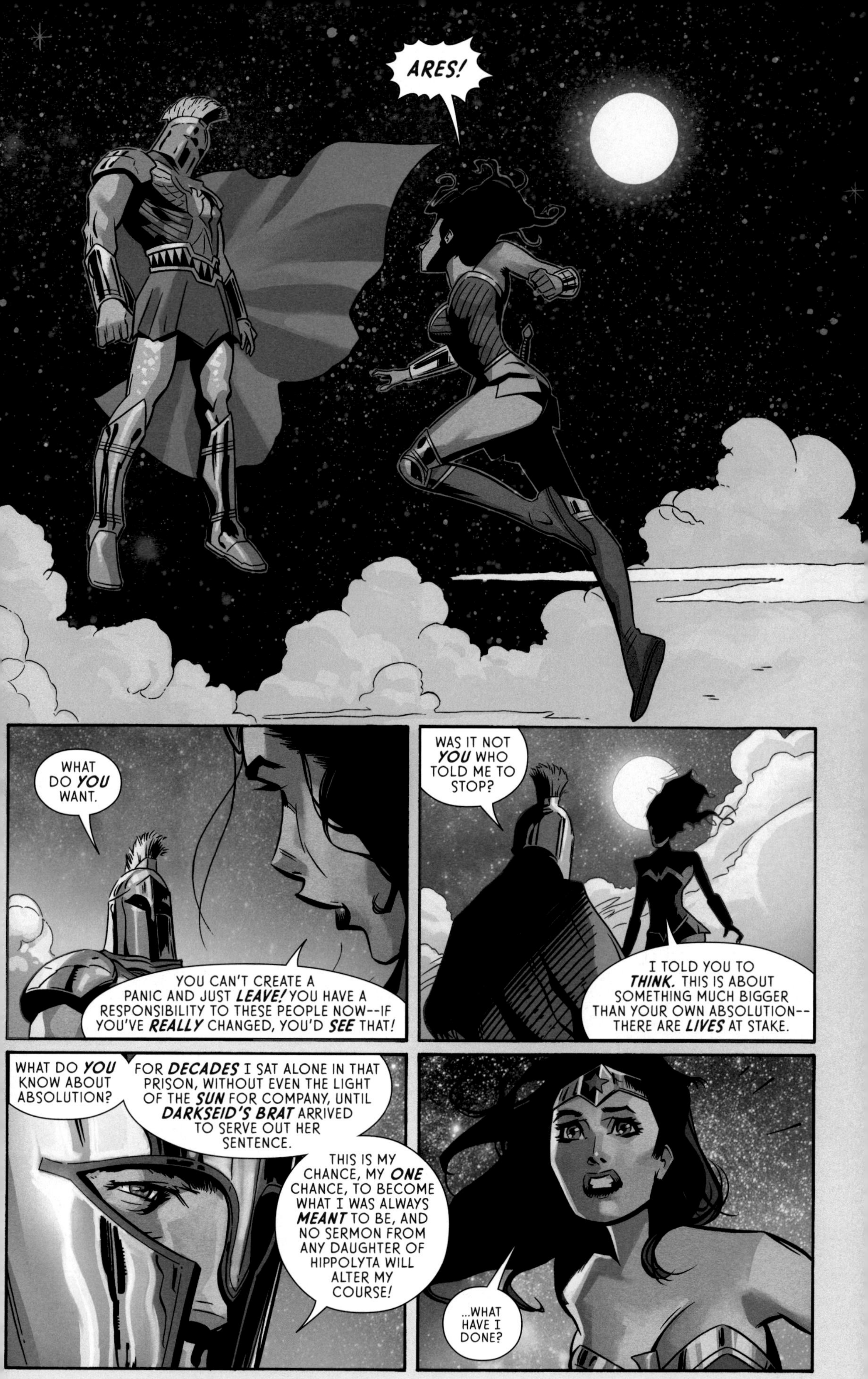
ARES!
WHAT DO YOU WANT.
YOU CAN'T CREATE A PANIC AND JUST LEAVE! YOU HAVE A RESPONSIBILITY TO THESE PEOPLE NOW--IF YOU'VE REALLY CHANGED, YOU'D SEE THAT!
WAS IT NOT YOU WHO TOLD ME TO STOP?
I TOLD YOU TO THINK. THIS IS ABOUT SOMETHING MUCH BIGGER THAN YOUR OWN ABSOLUTION--THERE ARE LIVES AT STAKE.
WHAT DO YOU KNOW ABOUT ABSOLUTION?
FOR DECADES I SAT ALONE IN THAT PRISON, WITHOUT EVEN THE LIGHT OF THE SUN FOR COMPANY, UNTIL DARKSEID'S BRAT ARRIVED TO SERVE OUT HER SENTENCE.
THIS IS MY CHANCE, MY ONE CHANCE, TO BECOME WHAT I WAS ALWAYS MEANT TO BE, AND NO SERMON FROM ANY DAUGHTER OF HIPPOLYTA WILL ALTER MY COURSE!
...WHAT HAVE I DONE?

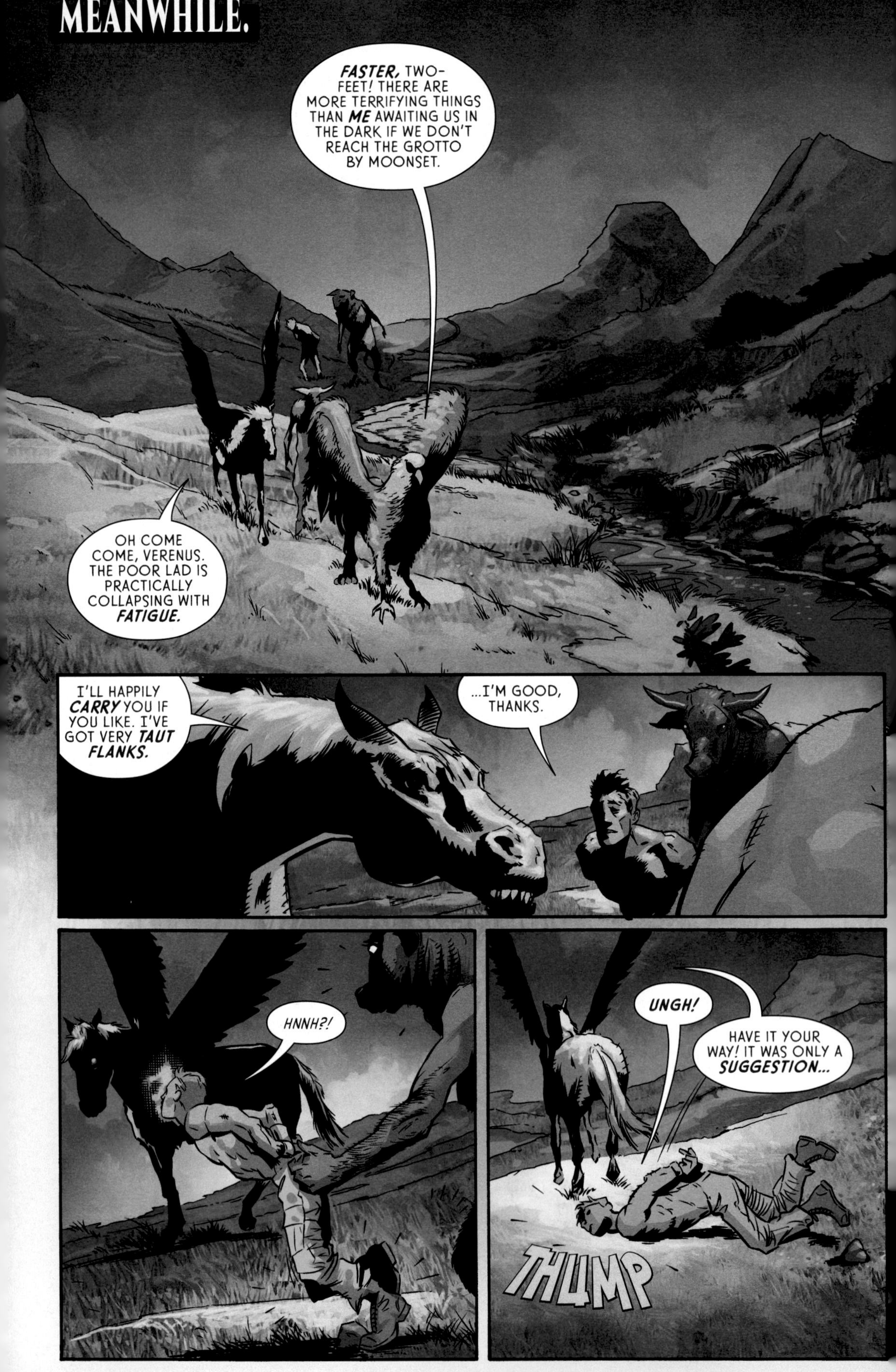
MEANWHILE.
FASTER, TWO-FEET! THERE ARE MORE TERRIFYING THINGS THAN ME AWAITING US IN THE DARK IF WE DON'T REACH THE GROTTO BY MOONSET.
OH COME COME, VERENUS. THE POOR LAD IS PRACTICALLY COLLAPSING WITH FATIGUE.
I'LL HAPPILY CARRY YOU IF YOU LIKE. I'VE GOT VERY TAUT FLANKS.
...I'M GOOD, THANKS.
HNNH?!
UNGH!
HAVE IT YOUR WAY! IT WAS ONLY A SUGGESTION...
THUMP

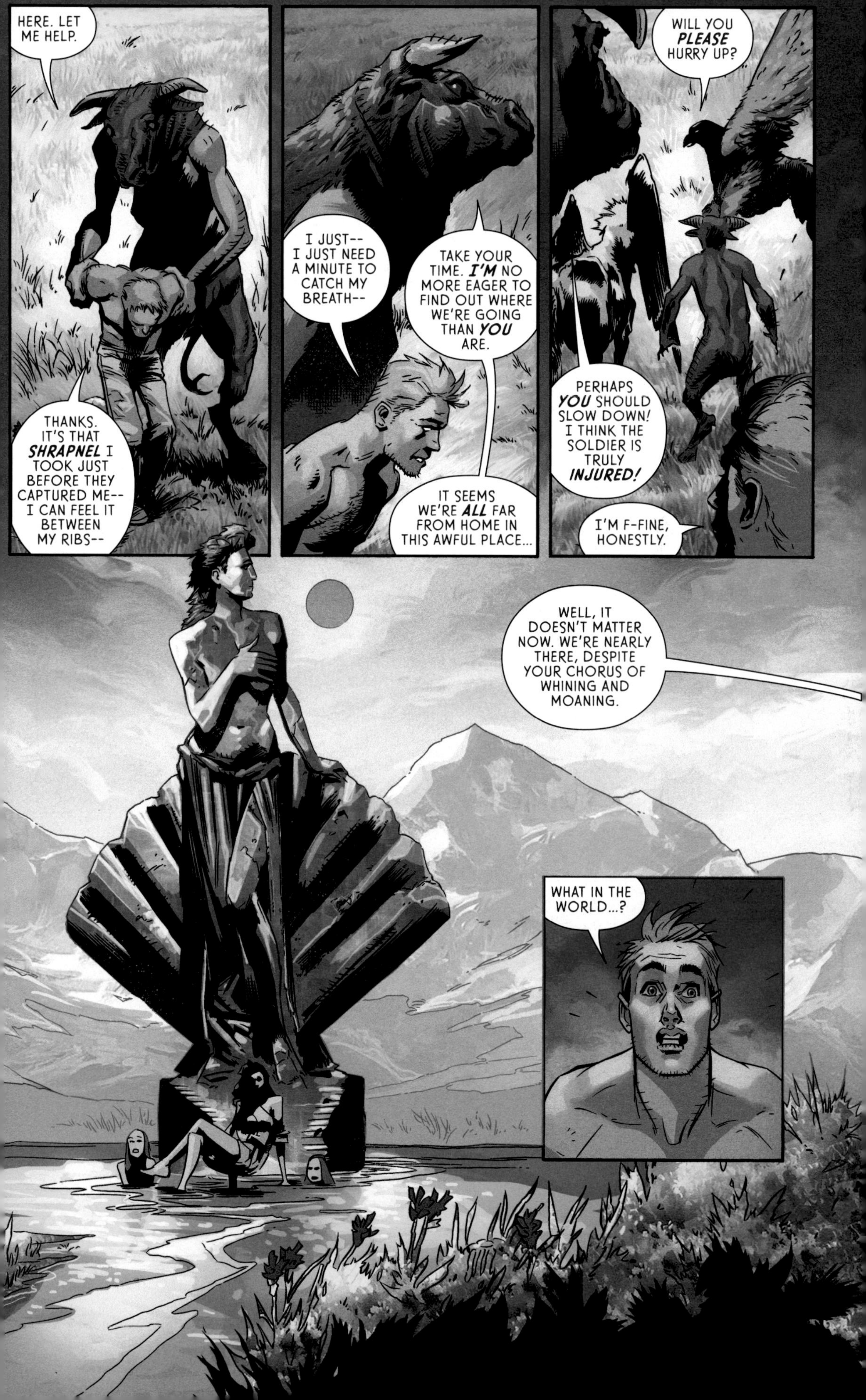
HERE. LET ME HELP.
THANKS. IT'S THAT SHRAPNEL I TOOK JUST BEFORE THEY CAPTURED ME-- I CAN FEEL IT BETWEEN MY RIBS--
I JUST-- I JUST NEED A MINUTE TO CATCH MY BREATH--
TAKE YOUR TIME. I'M NO MORE EAGER TO FIND OUT WHERE WE'RE GOING THAN YOU ARE.
IT SEEMS WE'RE ALL FAR FROM HOME IN THIS AWFUL PLACE...
WILL YOU PLEASE HURRY UP?
PERHAPS YOU SHOULD SLOW DOWN! I THINK THE SOLDIER IS TRULY INJURED!
I'M F-FINE, HONESTLY.
WELL, IT DOESN'T MATTER NOW. WE'RE NEARLY THERE, DESPITE YOUR CHORUS OF WHINING AND MOANING.
WHAT IN THE WORLD...?

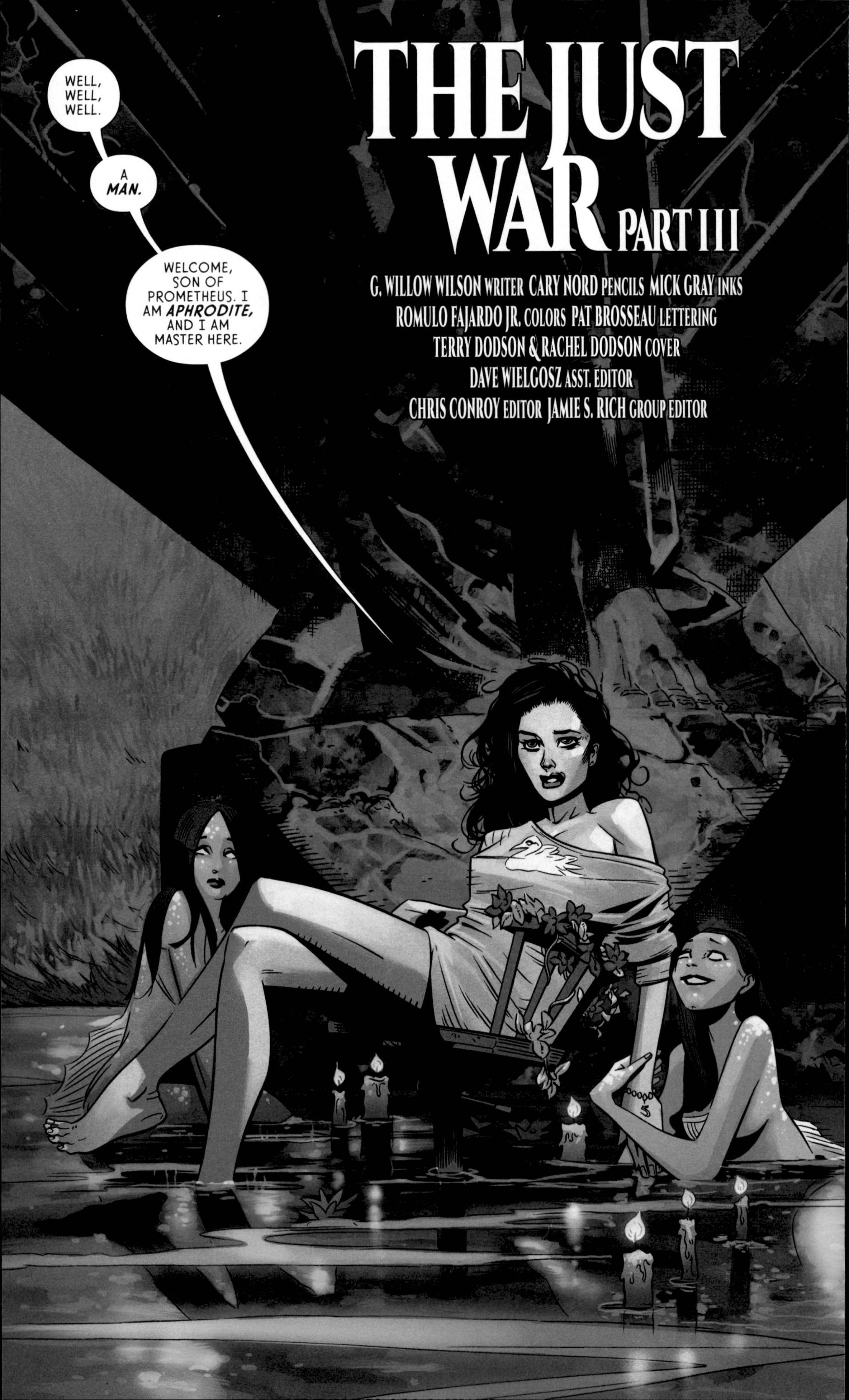
WELL, WELL, WELL.
A MAN.
WELCOME, SON OF PROMETHEUS. I AM APHRODITE, AND I AM MASTER HERE.
THE JUST WAR PART III
G. WILLOW WILSON WRITER CARY NORD PENCILS MICK GRAY INKS
ROMULO FAJARDO JR. COLORS PAT BROSSEAU LETTERING
TERRY DODSON & RACHEL DODSON COVER
DAVE WIELGOSZ ASST. EDITOR
CHRIS CONROY EDITOR JAMIE S. RICH GROUP EDITOR

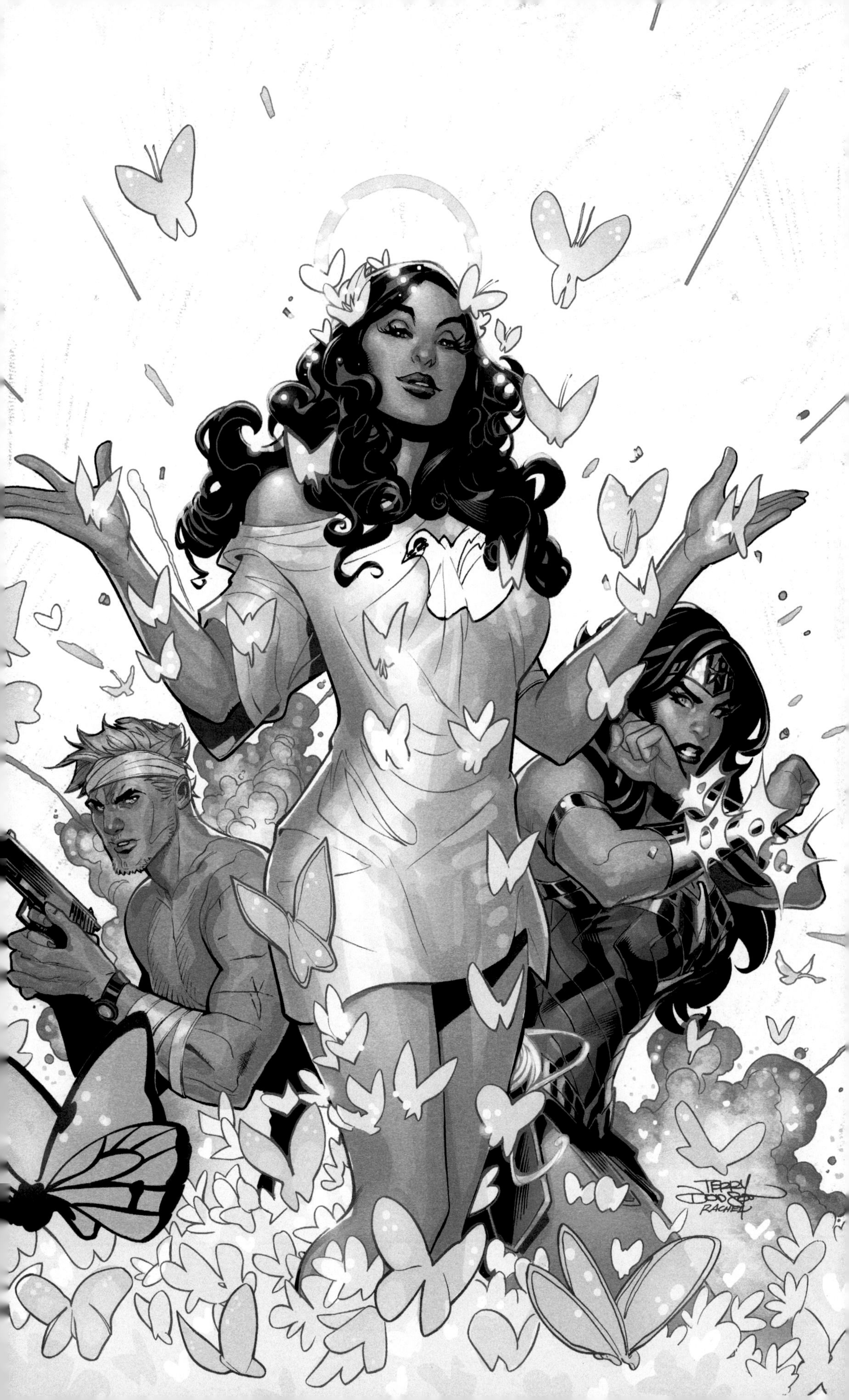

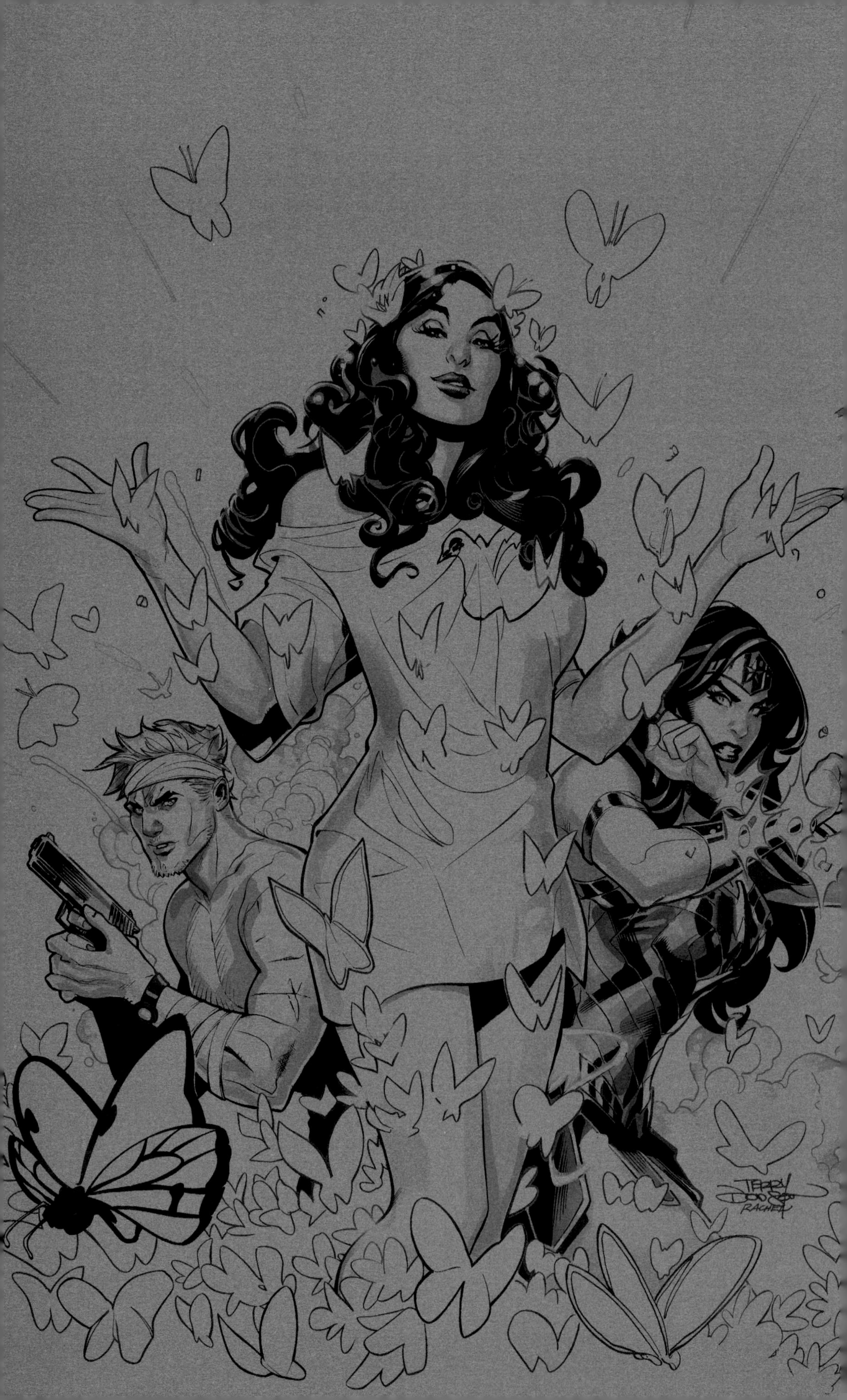

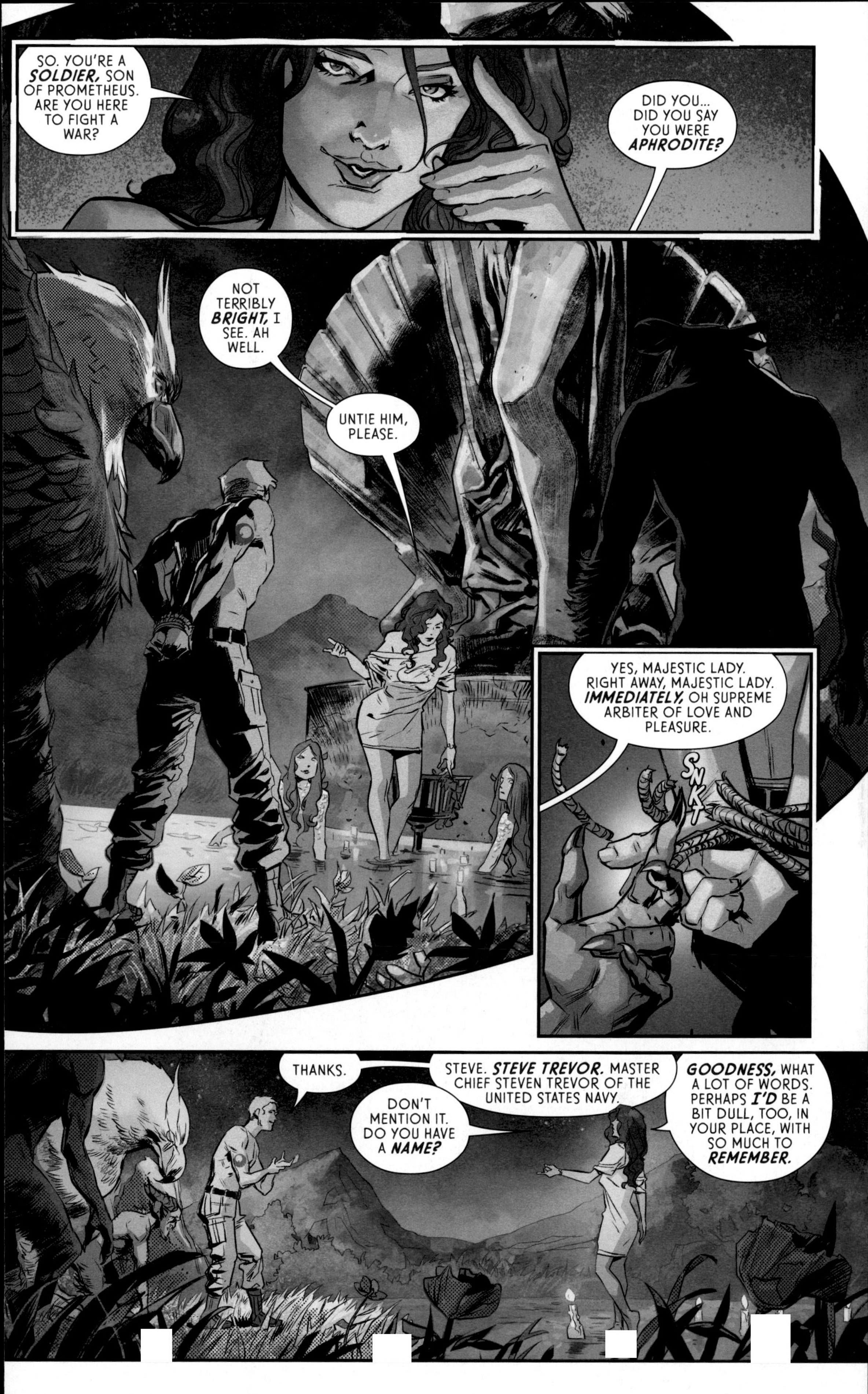
SO. YOU'RE A SOLDIER, SON OF PROMETHEUS. ARE YOU HERE TO FIGHT A WAR?
DID YOU... DID YOU SAY YOU WERE APHRODITE?
NOT TERRIBLY BRIGHT, I SEE. AH WELL.
UNTIE HIM, PLEASE.
YES, MAJESTIC LADY. RIGHT AWAY, MAJESTIC LADY. IMMEDIATELY, OH SUPREME ARBITER OF LOVE AND PLEASURE.
SNKT
THANKS.
DON'T MENTION IT. DO YOU HAVE A NAME?
STEVE. STEVE TREVOR. MASTER CHIEF STEVEN TREVOR OF THE UNITED STATES NAVY.
GOODNESS, WHAT A LOT OF WORDS. PERHAPS I'D BE A BIT DULL, TOO, IN YOUR PLACE, WITH SO MUCH TO REMEMBER.

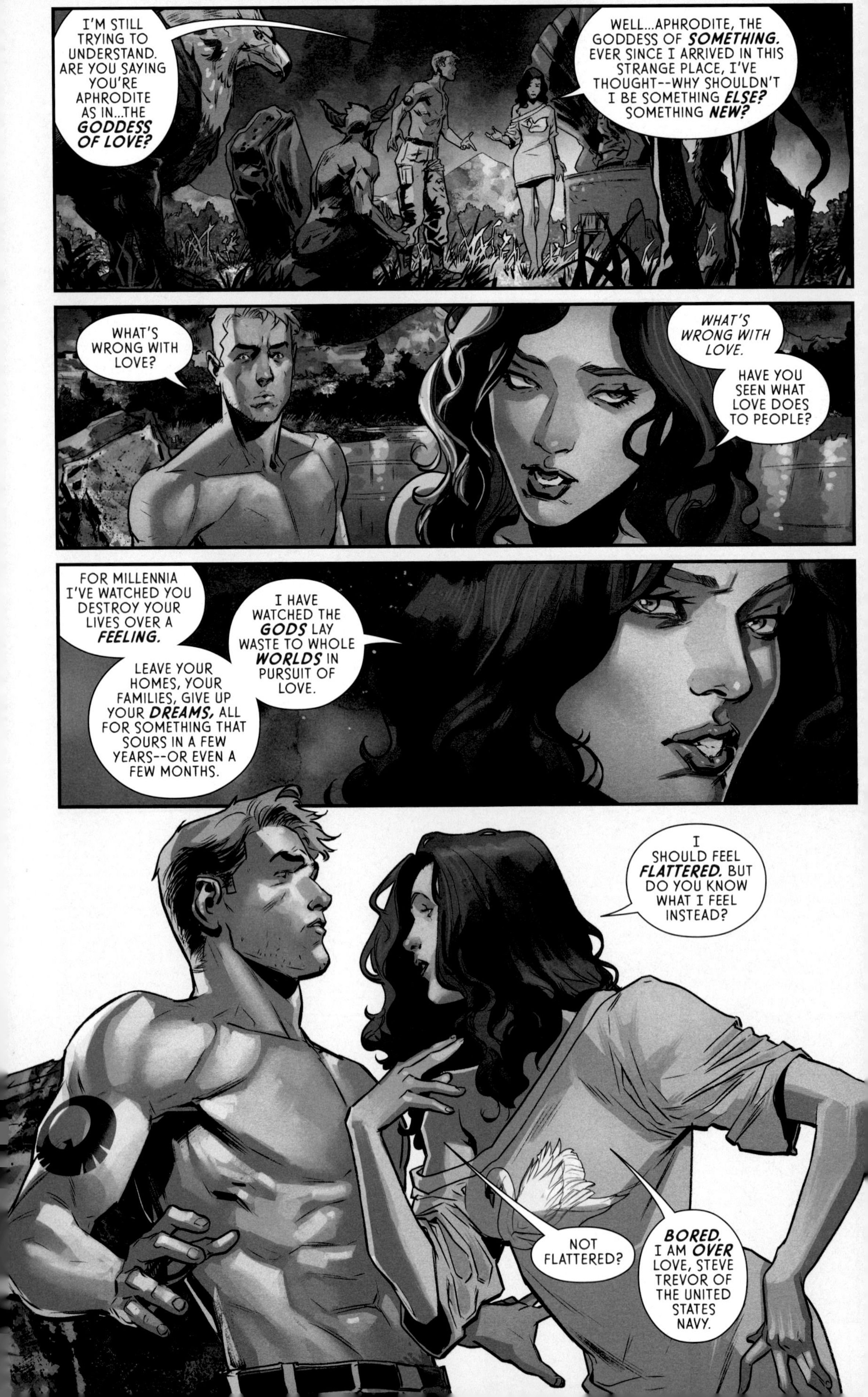
I'M STILL TRYING TO UNDERSTAND. ARE YOU SAYING YOU'RE APHRODITE AS IN...THE GODDESS OF LOVE?
WELL...APHRODITE, THE GODDESS OF SOMETHING. EVER SINCE I ARRIVED IN THIS STRANGE PLACE, I'VE THOUGHT--WHY SHOULDN'T I BE SOMETHING ELSE? SOMETHING NEW?
WHAT'S WRONG WITH LOVE?
WHAT'S WRONG WITH LOVE.
HAVE YOU SEEN WHAT LOVE DOES TO PEOPLE?
FOR MILLENNIA I'VE WATCHED YOU DESTROY YOUR LIVES OVER A FEELING.
LEAVE YOUR HOMES, YOUR FAMILIES, GIVE UP YOUR DREAMS, ALL FOR SOMETHING THAT SOURS IN A FEW YEARS--OR EVEN A FEW MONTHS.
I HAVE WATCHED THE GODS LAY WASTE TO WHOLE WORLDS IN PURSUIT OF LOVE.
I SHOULD FEEL FLATTERED. BUT DO YOU KNOW WHAT I FEEL INSTEAD?
NOT FLATTERED?
BORED. I AM OVER LOVE, STEVE TREVOR OF THE UNITED STATES NAVY.

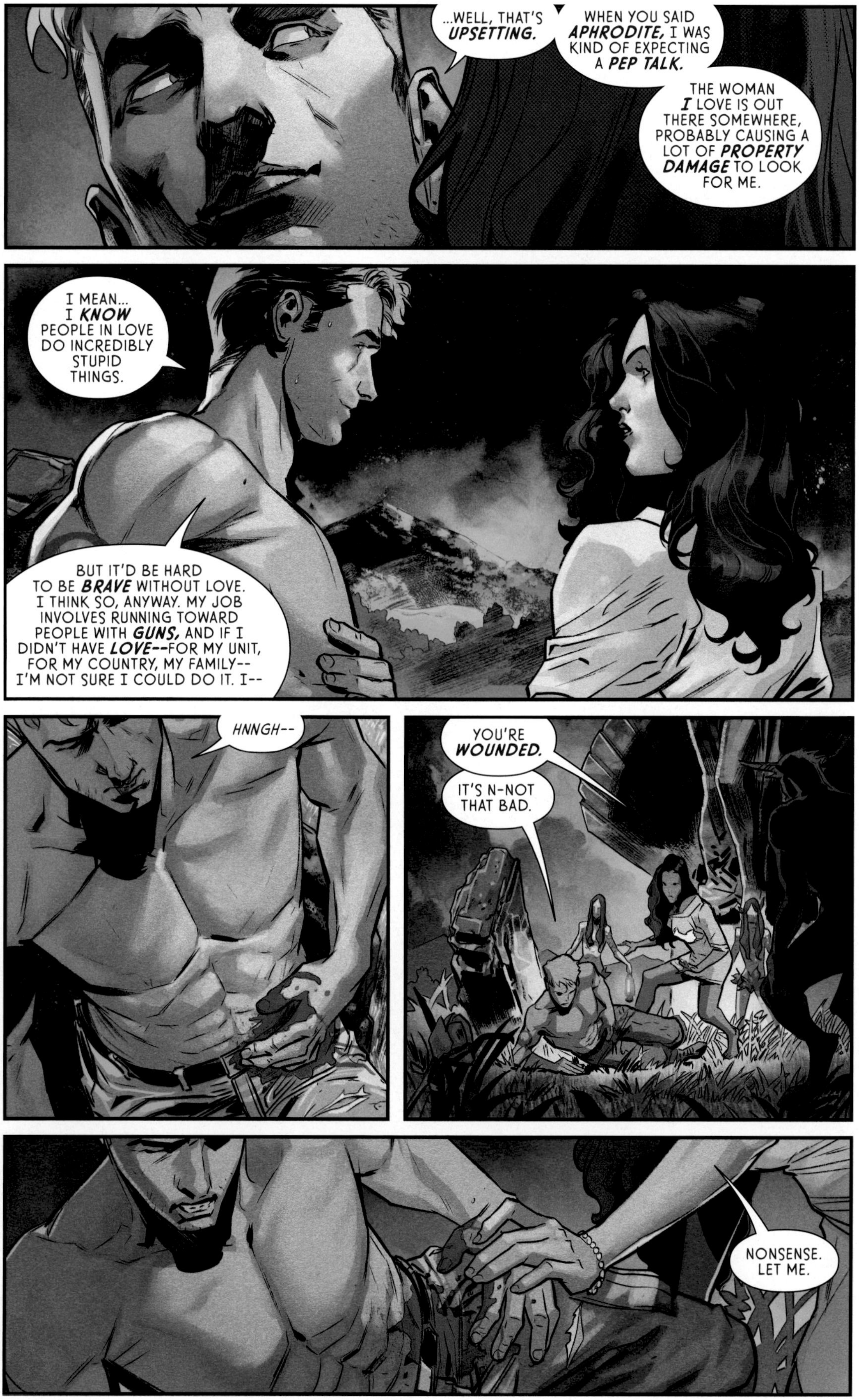
...WELL, THAT'S UPSETTING.
WHEN YOU SAID APHRODITE, I WAS KIND OF EXPECTING A PEP TALK.
THE WOMAN I LOVE IS OUT THERE SOMEWHERE, PROBABLY CAUSING A LOT OF PROPERTY DAMAGE TO LOOK FOR ME.
I MEAN... I KNOW PEOPLE IN LOVE DO INCREDIBLY STUPID THINGS.
BUT IT'D BE HARD TO BE BRAVE WITHOUT LOVE. I THINK SO, ANYWAY. MY JOB INVOLVES RUNNING TOWARD PEOPLE WITH GUNS, AND IF I DIDN'T HAVE LOVE--FOR MY UNIT, FOR MY COUNTRY, MY FAMILY-- I'M NOT SURE I COULD DO IT. I--
HNNGH--
YOU'RE WOUNDED.
IT'S N-NOT THAT BAD.
NONSENSE. LET ME.

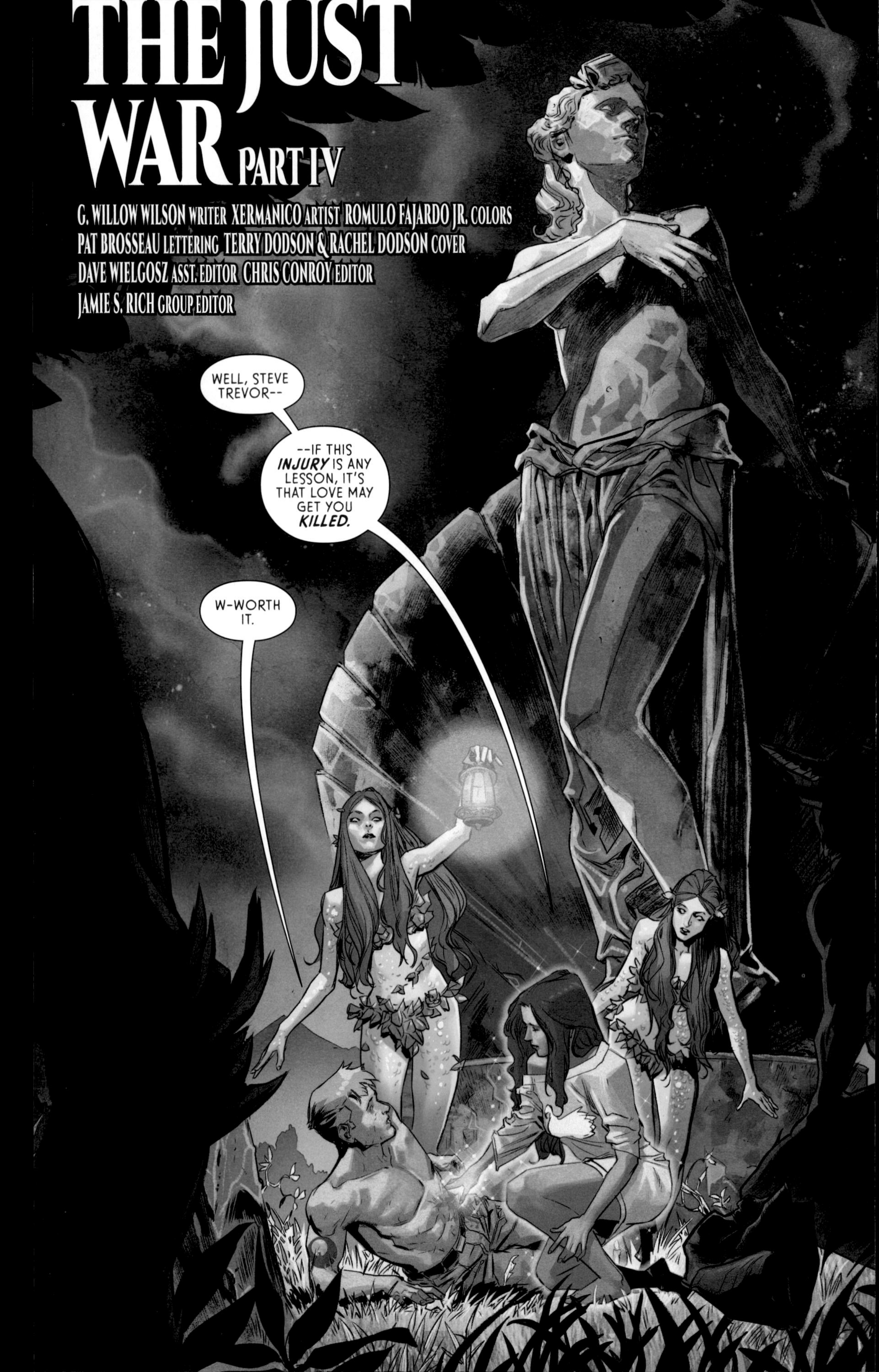
THE JUST WAR PART IV
G. WILLOW WILSON WRITER XERMANICO ARTIST ROMULO FAJARDO JR. COLORS
PAT BROSSEAU LETTERING TERRY DODSON & RACHEL DODSON COVER
DAVE WIELGOSZ ASST. EDITOR CHRIS CONROY EDITOR
JAMIE S. RICH GROUP EDITOR
WELL, STEVE TREVOR--
--IF THIS INJURY IS ANY LESSON, IT'S THAT LOVE MAY GET YOU KILLED.
W-WORTH IT.

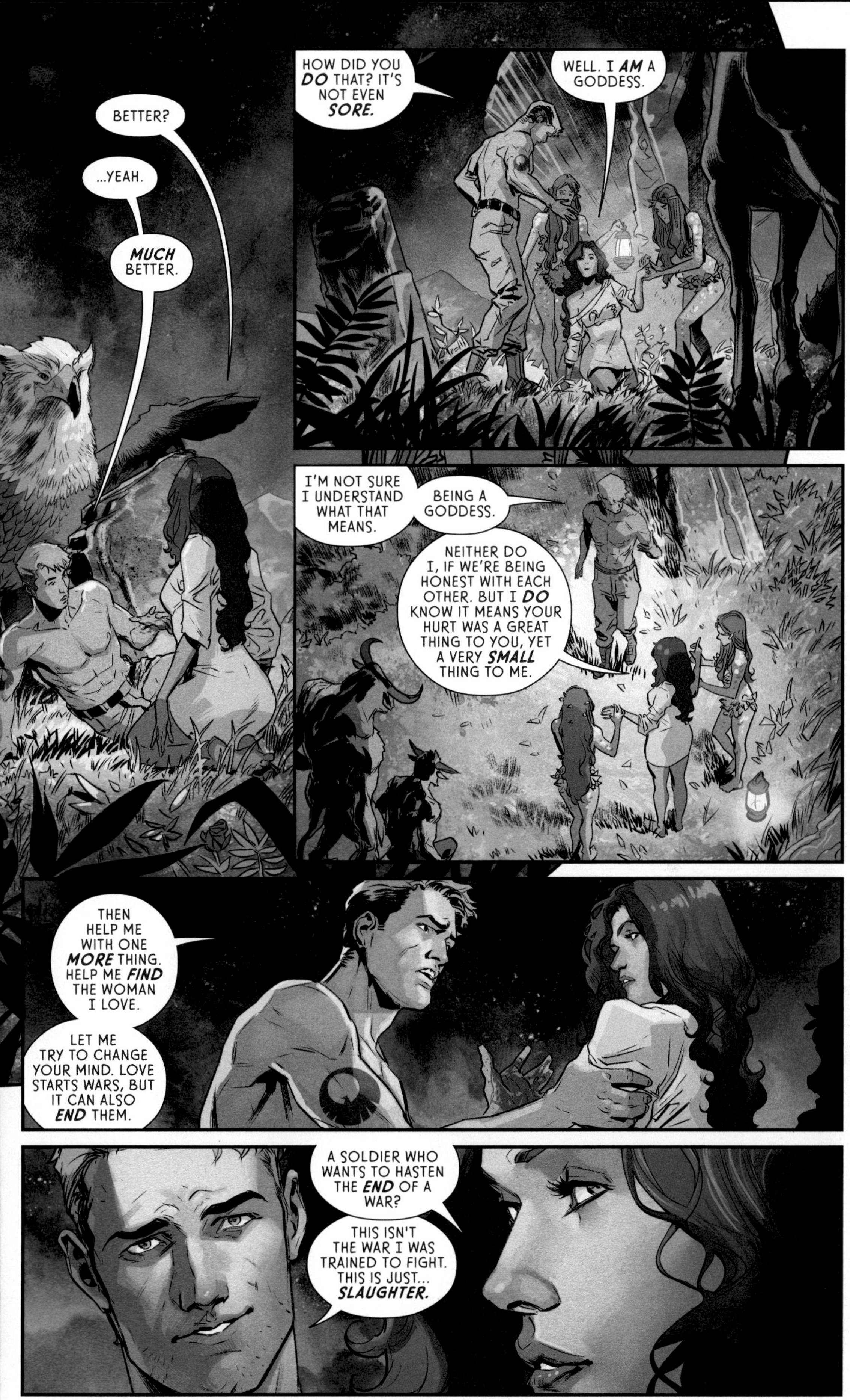
BETTER?
...YEAH.
MUCH BETTER.
HOW DID YOU DO THAT? IT'S NOT EVEN SORE.
WELL. I AM A GODDESS.
I'M NOT SURE I UNDERSTAND WHAT THAT MEANS.
BEING A GODDESS.
NEITHER DO I, IF WE'RE BEING HONEST WITH EACH OTHER. BUT I DO KNOW IT MEANS YOUR HURT WAS A GREAT THING TO YOU, YET A VERY SMALL THING TO ME.
THEN HELP ME WITH ONE MORE THING. HELP ME FIND THE WOMAN I LOVE.
LET ME TRY TO CHANGE YOUR MIND. LOVE STARTS WARS, BUT IT CAN ALSO END THEM.
A SOLDIER WHO WANTS TO HASTEN THE END OF A WAR?
THIS ISN'T THE WAR I WAS TRAINED TO FIGHT. THIS IS JUST... SLAUGHTER.

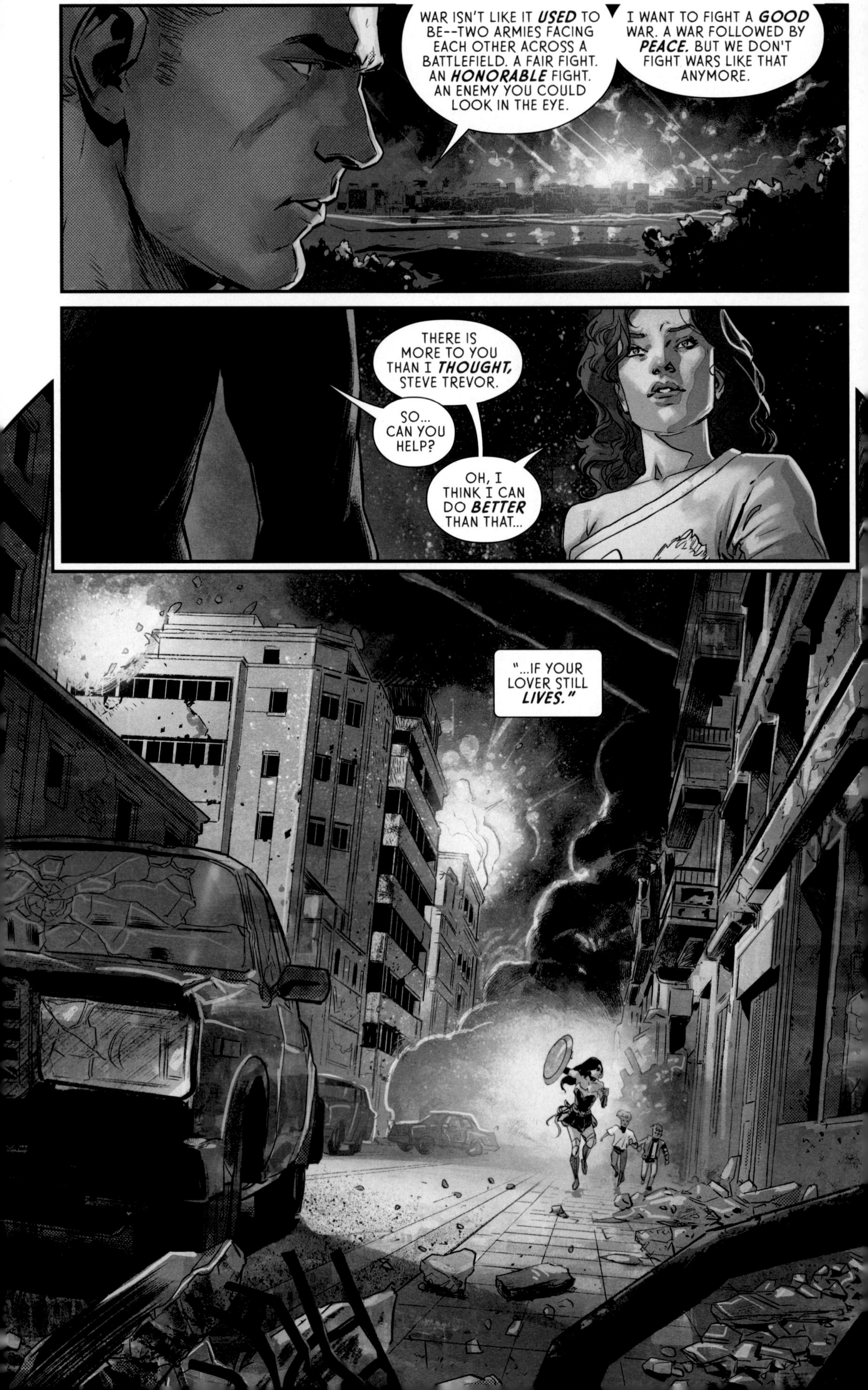
WAR ISN'T LIKE IT USED TO BE--TWO ARMIES FACING EACH OTHER ACROSS A BATTLEFIELD. A FAIR FIGHT. AN HONORABLE FIGHT. AN ENEMY YOU COULD LOOK IN THE EYE.
I WANT TO FIGHT A GOOD WAR. A WAR FOLLOWED BY PEACE. BUT WE DON'T FIGHT WARS LIKE THAT ANYMORE.
THERE IS MORE TO YOU THAN I THOUGHT, STEVE TREVOR.
SO... CAN YOU HELP?
OH, I THINK I CAN DO BETTER THAN THAT...
"...IF YOUR LOVER STILL LIVES."

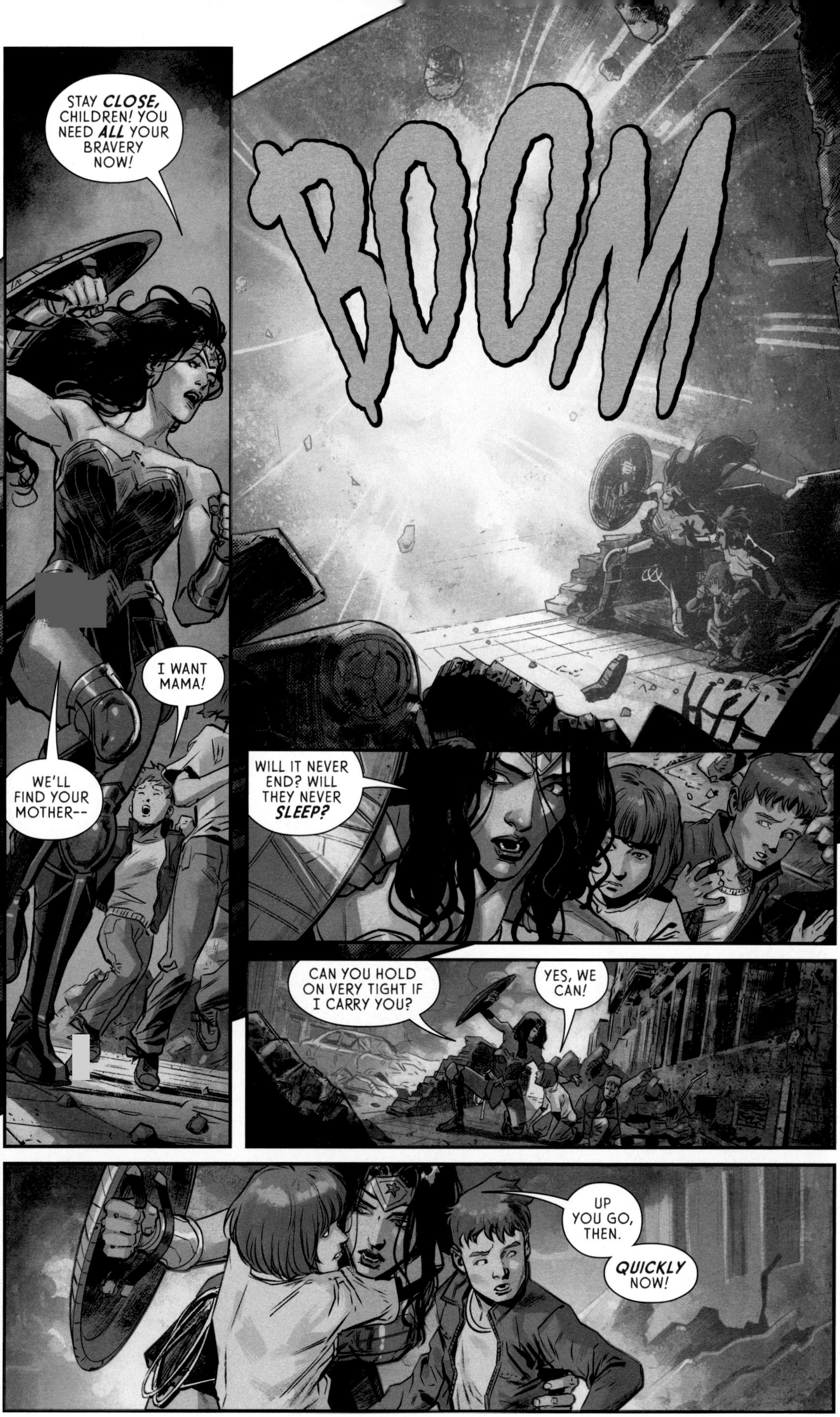
STAY CLOSE, CHILDREN! YOU NEED ALL YOUR BRAVERY NOW!
I WANT MAMA!
WE'LL FIND YOUR MOTHER--
BOOM
WILL IT NEVER END? WILL THEY NEVER SLEEP?
CAN YOU HOLD ON VERY TIGHT IF I CARRY YOU?
YES, WE CAN!
UP YOU GO, THEN.
QUICKLY NOW!

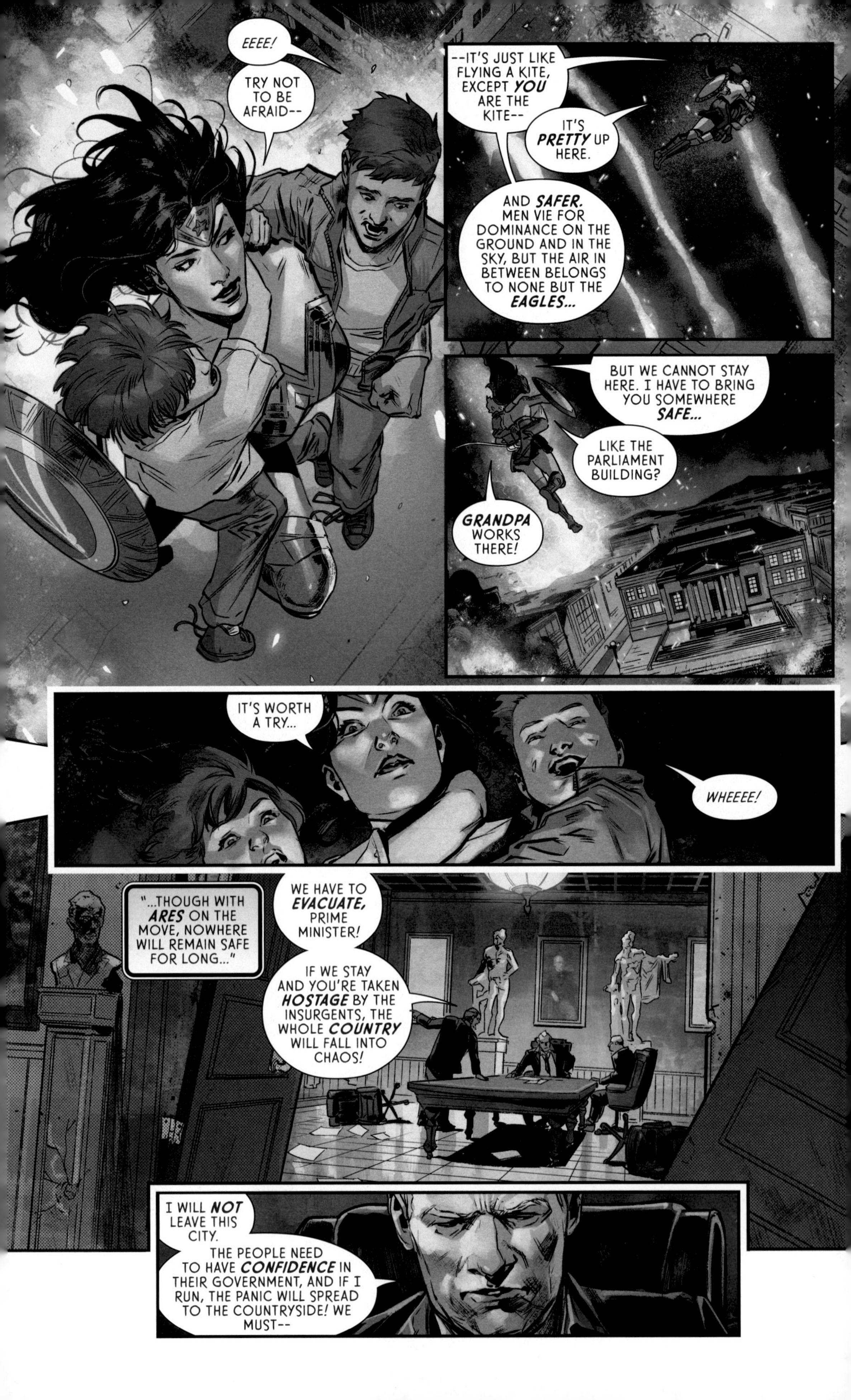

EEEE!
TRY NOT TO BE AFRAID--
--IT'S JUST LIKE FLYING A KITE, EXCEPT YOU ARE THE KITE--
IT'S PRETTY UP HERE.
AND SAFER. MEN VIE FOR DOMINANCE ON THE GROUND AND IN THE SKY, BUT THE AIR IN BETWEEN BELONGS TO NONE BUT THE EAGLES...
BUT WE CANNOT STAY HERE. I HAVE TO BRING YOU SOMEWHERE SAFE...
LIKE THE PARLIAMENT BUILDING?
GRANDPA WORKS THERE!
IT'S WORTH A TRY...
WHEEEE!
"...THOUGH WITH ARES ON THE MOVE, NOWHERE WILL REMAIN SAFE FOR LONG..."
WE HAVE TO EVACUATE, PRIME MINISTER!
IF WE STAY AND YOU'RE TAKEN HOSTAGE BY THE INSURGENTS, THE WHOLE COUNTRY WILL FALL INTO CHAOS!
I WILL NOT LEAVE THIS CITY.
THE PEOPLE NEED TO HAVE CONFIDENCE IN THEIR GOVERNMENT, AND IF I RUN, THE PANIC WILL SPREAD TO THE COUNTRYSIDE! WE MUST--

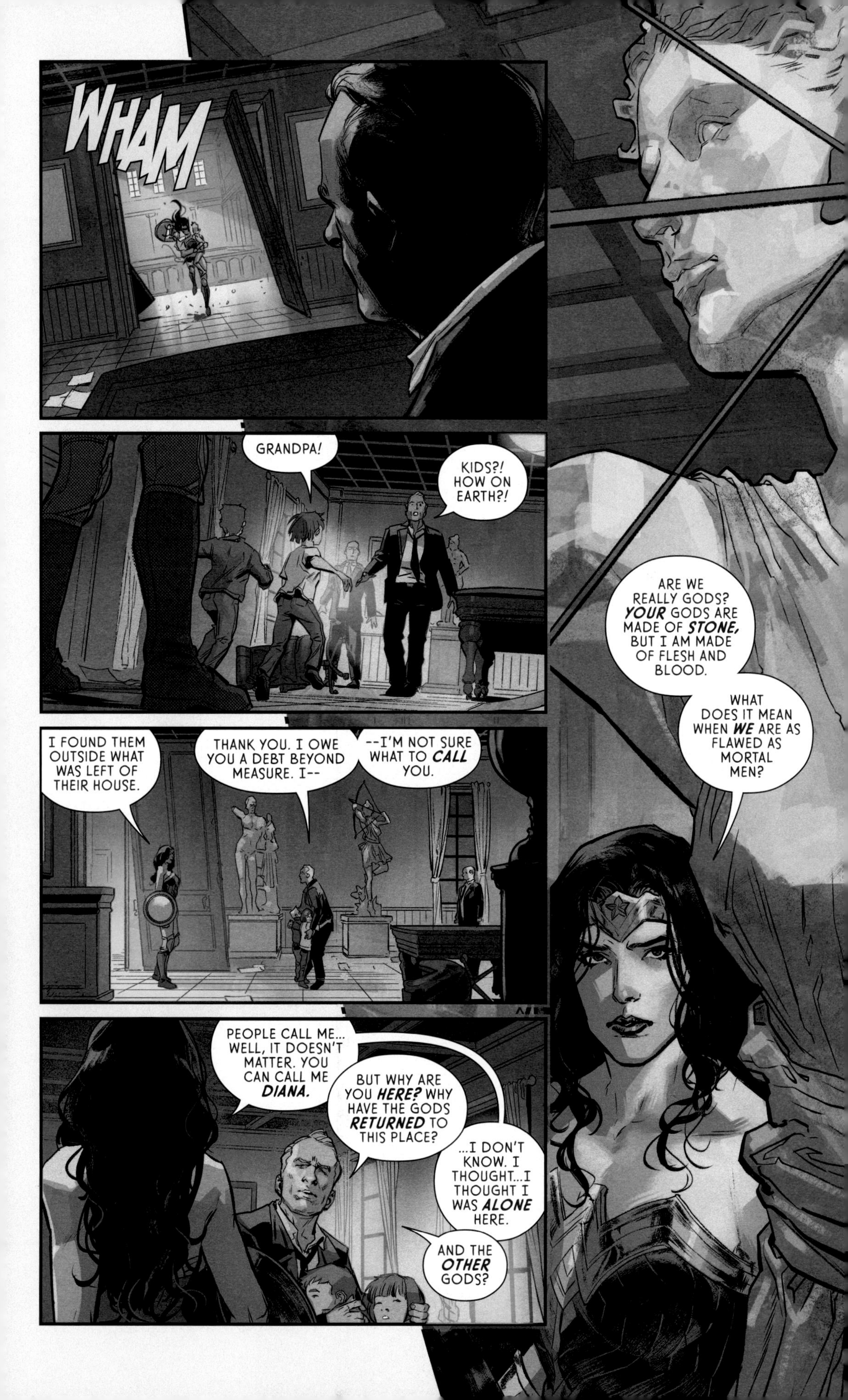
WHAM
GRANDPA!
KIDS?! HOW ON EARTH?!
I FOUND THEM OUTSIDE WHAT WAS LEFT OF THEIR HOUSE.
THANK YOU. I OWE YOU A DEBT BEYOND MEASURE. I--
--I'M NOT SURE WHAT TO CALL YOU.
PEOPLE CALL ME... WELL, IT DOESN'T MATTER. YOU CAN CALL ME DIANA.
BUT WHY ARE YOU HERE? WHY HAVE THE GODS RETURNED TO THIS PLACE?
...I DON'T KNOW. I THOUGHT...I THOUGHT I WAS ALONE HERE.
AND THE OTHER GODS?
ARE WE REALLY GODS? YOUR GODS ARE MADE OF STONE, BUT I AM MADE OF FLESH AND BLOOD.
WHAT DOES IT MEAN WHEN WE ARE AS FLAWED AS MORTAL MEN?

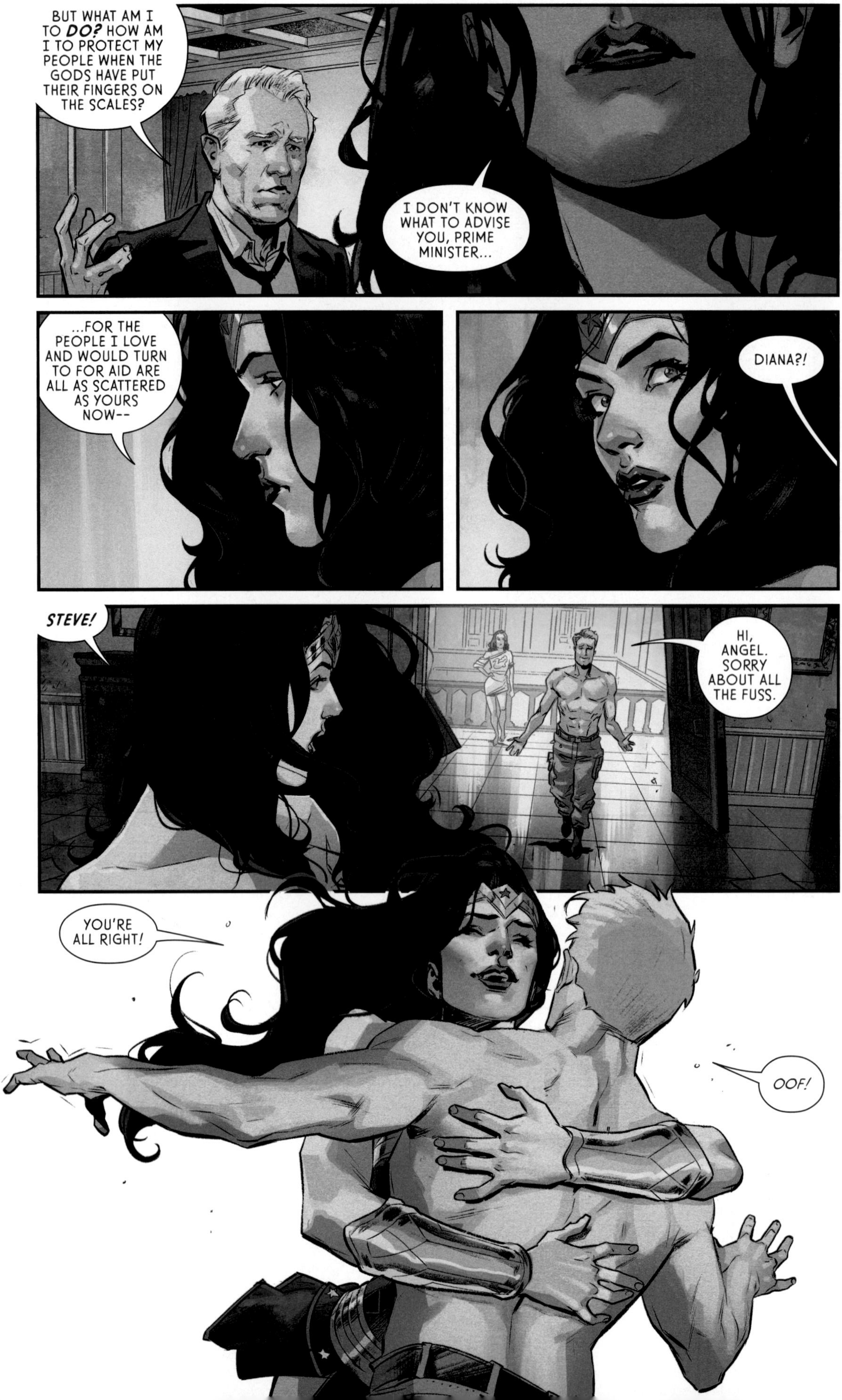
BUT WHAT AM I TO DO? HOW AM I TO PROTECT MY PEOPLE WHEN THE GODS HAVE PUT THEIR FINGERS ON THE SCALES?
I DON'T KNOW WHAT TO ADVISE YOU, PRIME MINISTER...
...FOR THE PEOPLE I LOVE AND WOULD TURN TO FOR AID ARE ALL AS SCATTERED AS YOURS NOW--
DIANA?!
STEVE!
HI, ANGEL. SORRY ABOUT ALL THE FUSS.
YOU'RE ALL RIGHT!
OOF!

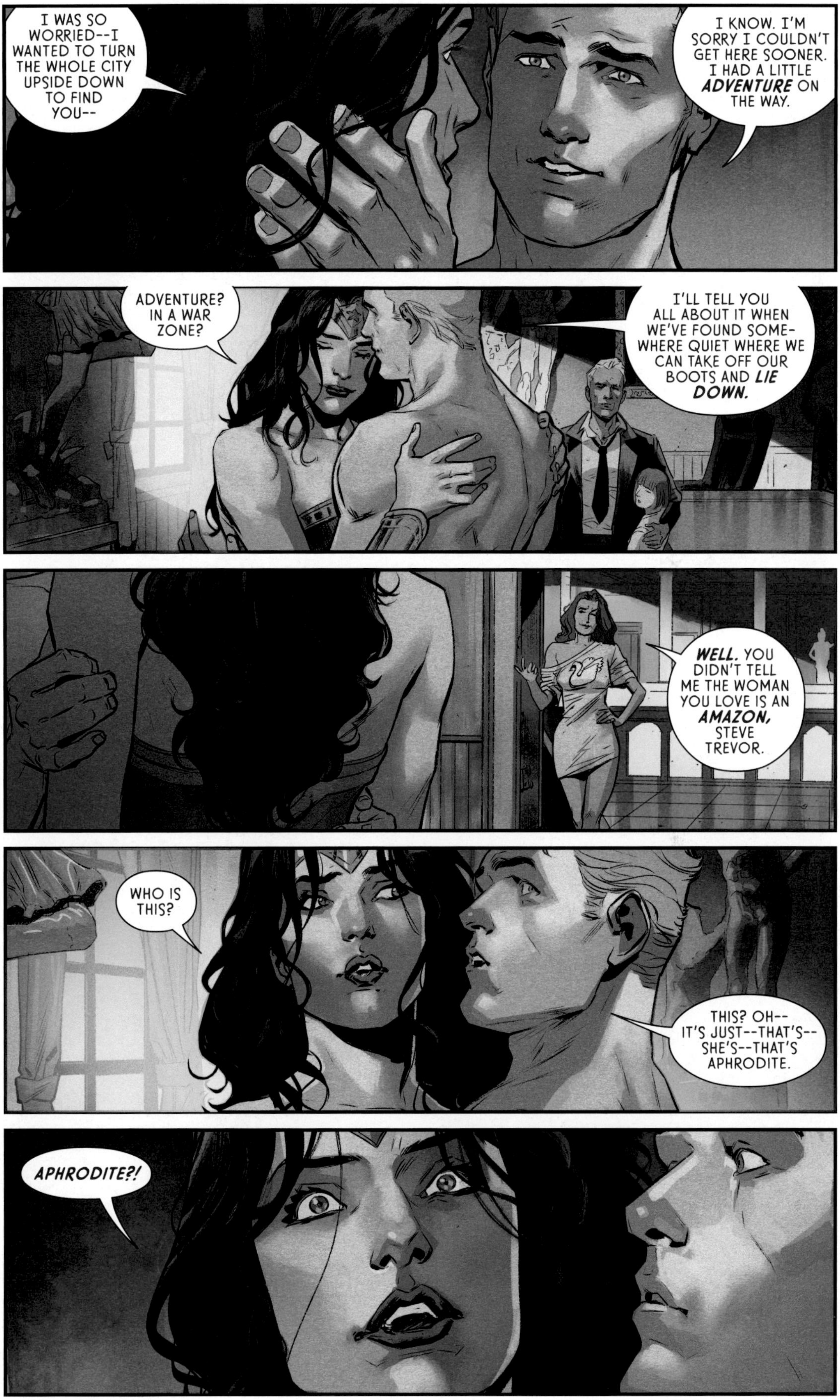
I WAS SO WORRIED--I WANTED TO TURN THE WHOLE CITY UPSIDE DOWN TO FIND YOU--
I KNOW. I'M SORRY I COULDN'T GET HERE SOONER. I HAD A LITTLE *ADVENTURE* ON THE WAY.
ADVENTURE? IN A WAR ZONE?
I'LL TELL YOU ALL ABOUT IT WHEN WE'VE FOUND SOMEWHERE QUIET WHERE WE CAN TAKE OFF OUR BOOTS AND *LIE DOWN.*
WELL. YOU DIDN'T TELL ME THE WOMAN YOU LOVE IS AN *AMAZON,* STEVE TREVOR.
WHO IS THIS?
THIS? OH-- IT'S JUST--THAT'S-- SHE'S--THAT'S APHRODITE.
APHRODITE?!

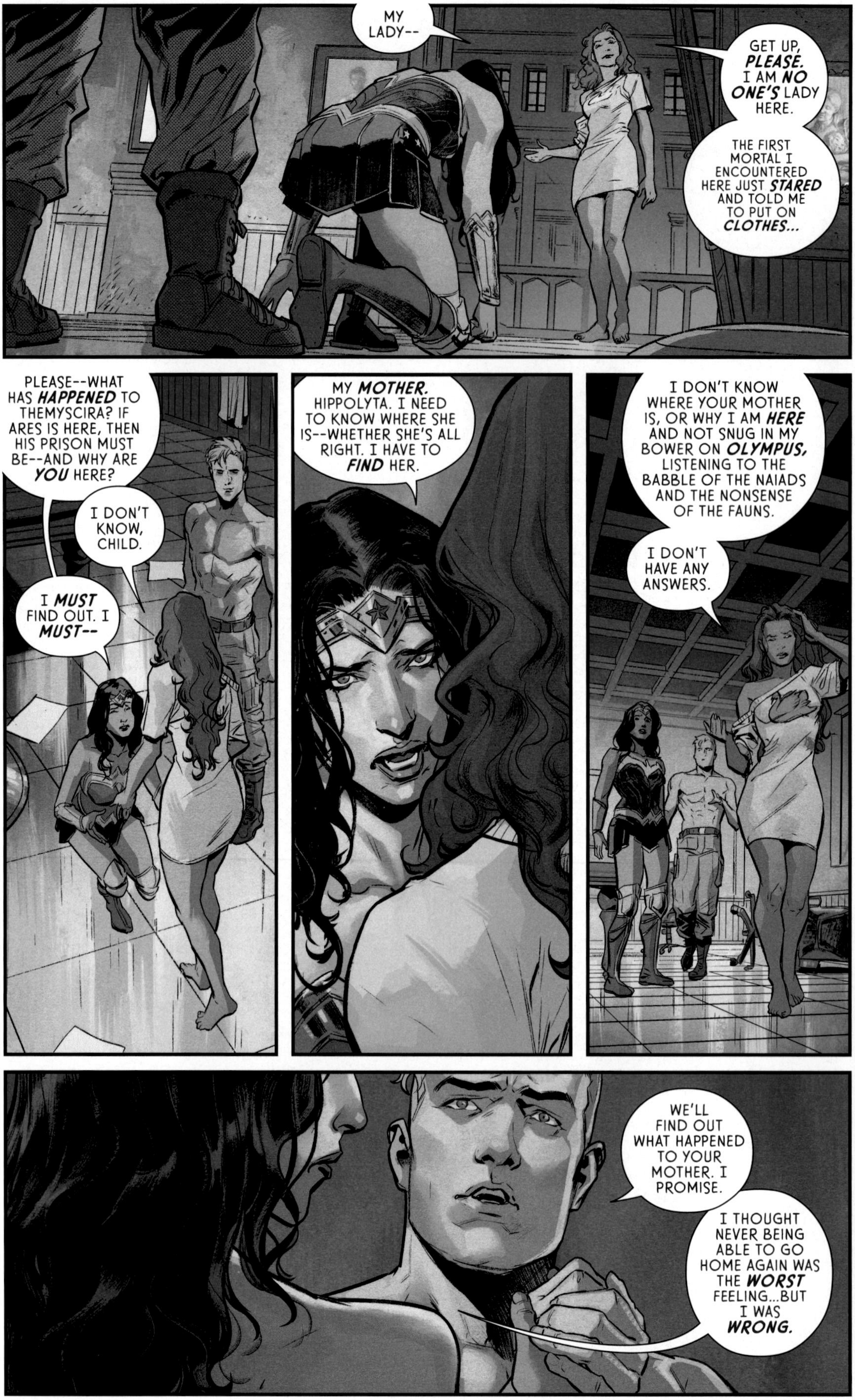
MY LADY--
GET UP, PLEASE. I AM NO ONE'S LADY HERE.
THE FIRST MORTAL I ENCOUNTERED HERE JUST STARED AND TOLD ME TO PUT ON CLOTHES...
PLEASE--WHAT HAS HAPPENED TO THEMYSCIRA? IF ARES IS HERE, THEN HIS PRISON MUST BE--AND WHY ARE YOU HERE?
I DON'T KNOW, CHILD.
I MUST FIND OUT. I MUST--
MY MOTHER. HIPPOLYTA. I NEED TO KNOW WHERE SHE IS--WHETHER SHE'S ALL RIGHT. I HAVE TO FIND HER.
I DON'T KNOW WHERE YOUR MOTHER IS, OR WHY I AM HERE AND NOT SNUG IN MY BOWER ON OLYMPUS, LISTENING TO THE BABBLE OF THE NAIADS AND THE NONSENSE OF THE FAUNS.
I DON'T HAVE ANY ANSWERS.
WE'LL FIND OUT WHAT HAPPENED TO YOUR MOTHER. I PROMISE.
I THOUGHT NEVER BEING ABLE TO GO HOME AGAIN WAS THE WORST FEELING...BUT I WAS WRONG.

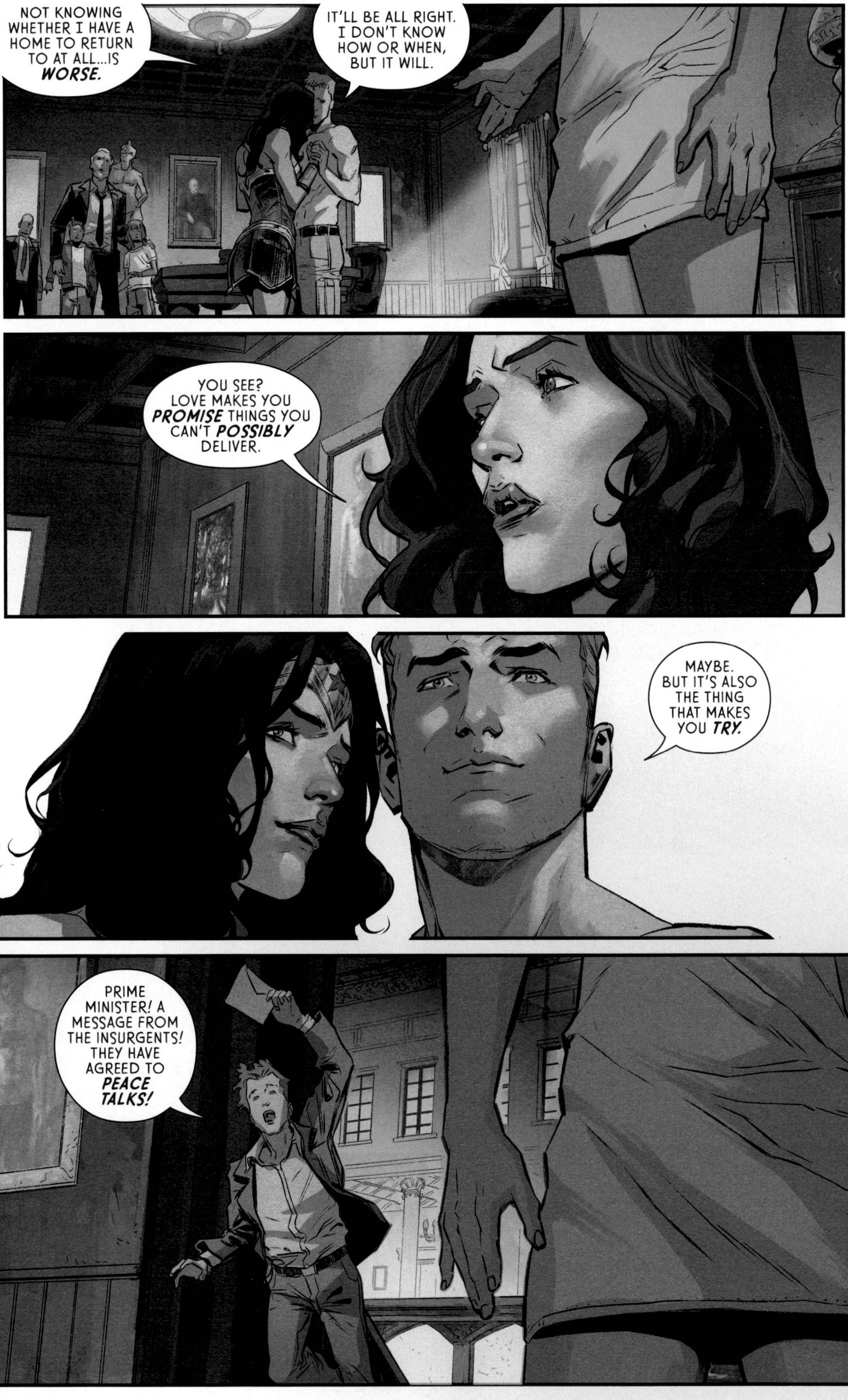
NOT KNOWING WHETHER I HAVE A HOME TO RETURN TO AT ALL...IS WORSE.
IT'LL BE ALL RIGHT. I DON'T KNOW HOW OR WHEN, BUT IT WILL.
YOU SEE? LOVE MAKES YOU PROMISE THINGS YOU CAN'T POSSIBLY DELIVER.
MAYBE. BUT IT'S ALSO THE THING THAT MAKES YOU TRY.
PRIME MINISTER! A MESSAGE FROM THE INSURGENTS! THEY HAVE AGREED TO PEACE TALKS!

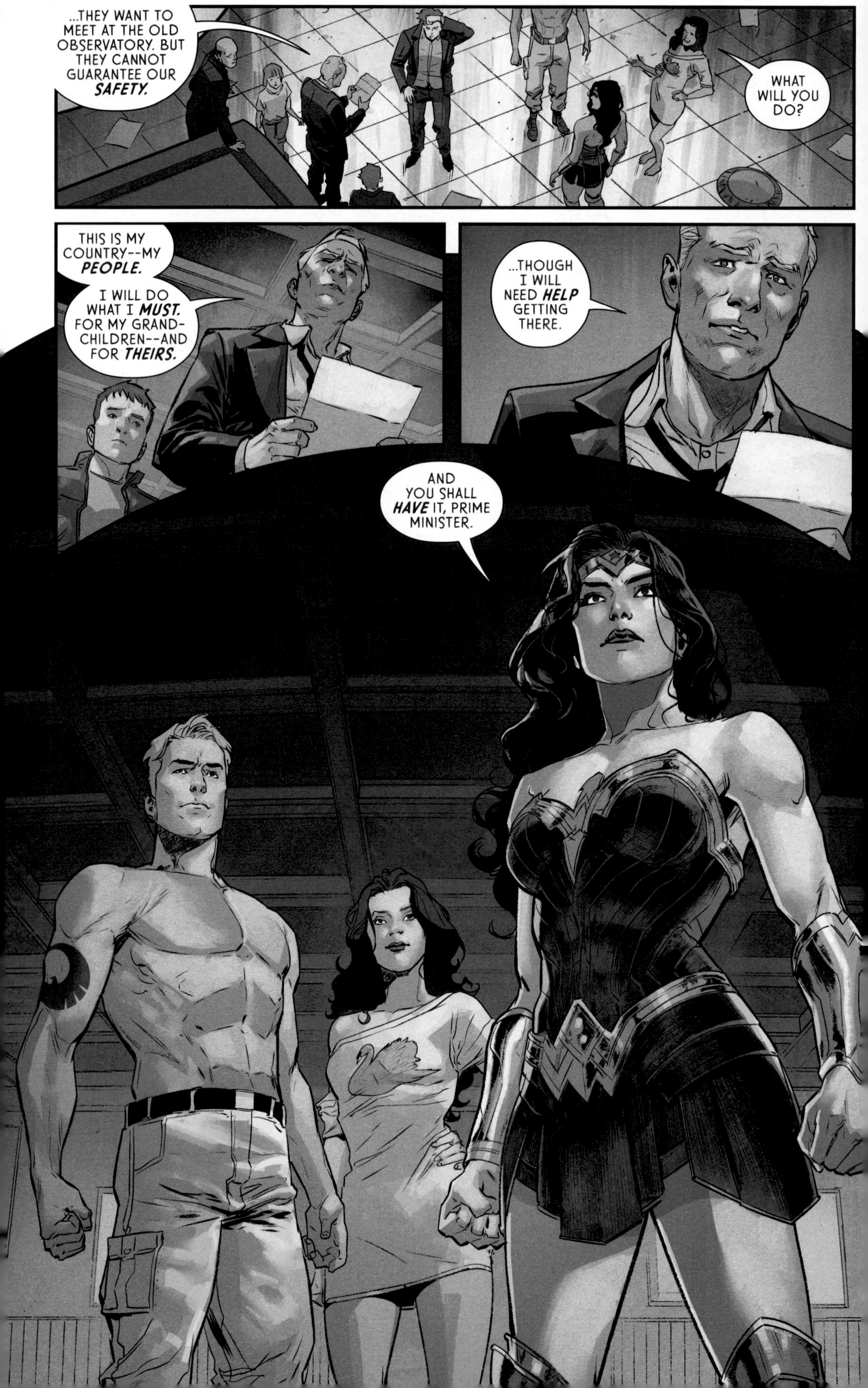

...THEY WANT TO MEET AT THE OLD OBSERVATORY. BUT THEY CANNOT GUARANTEE OUR **SAFETY.**
WHAT WILL YOU DO?
THIS IS MY COUNTRY--MY **PEOPLE.**
I WILL DO WHAT I **MUST.** FOR MY GRAND-CHILDREN--AND FOR **THEIRS.**
...THOUGH I WILL NEED **HELP** GETTING THERE.
AND YOU SHALL **HAVE** IT, PRIME MINISTER.

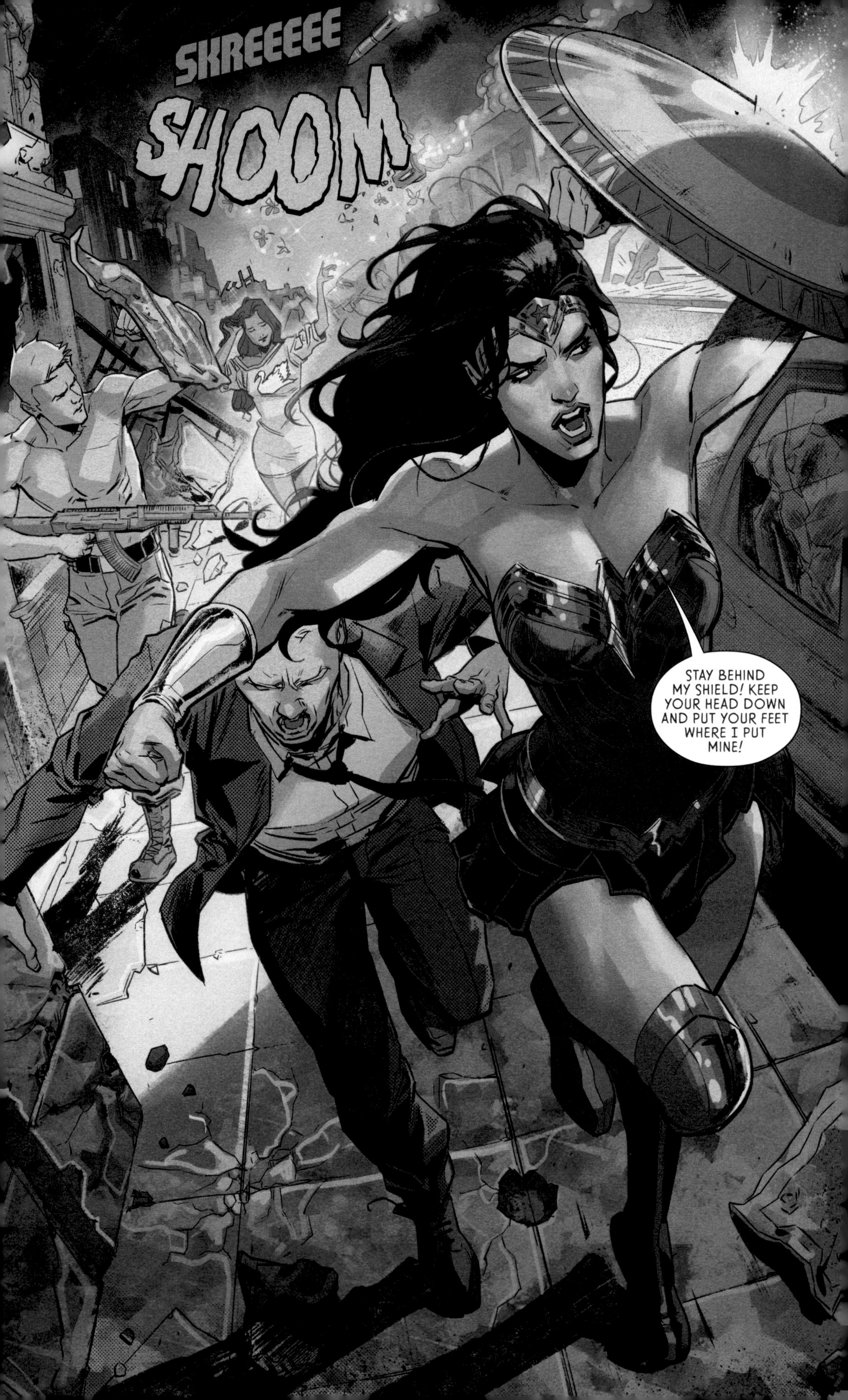
SKREEEEE
SHOOM
STAY BEHIND MY SHIELD! KEEP YOUR HEAD DOWN AND PUT YOUR FEET WHERE I PUT MINE!

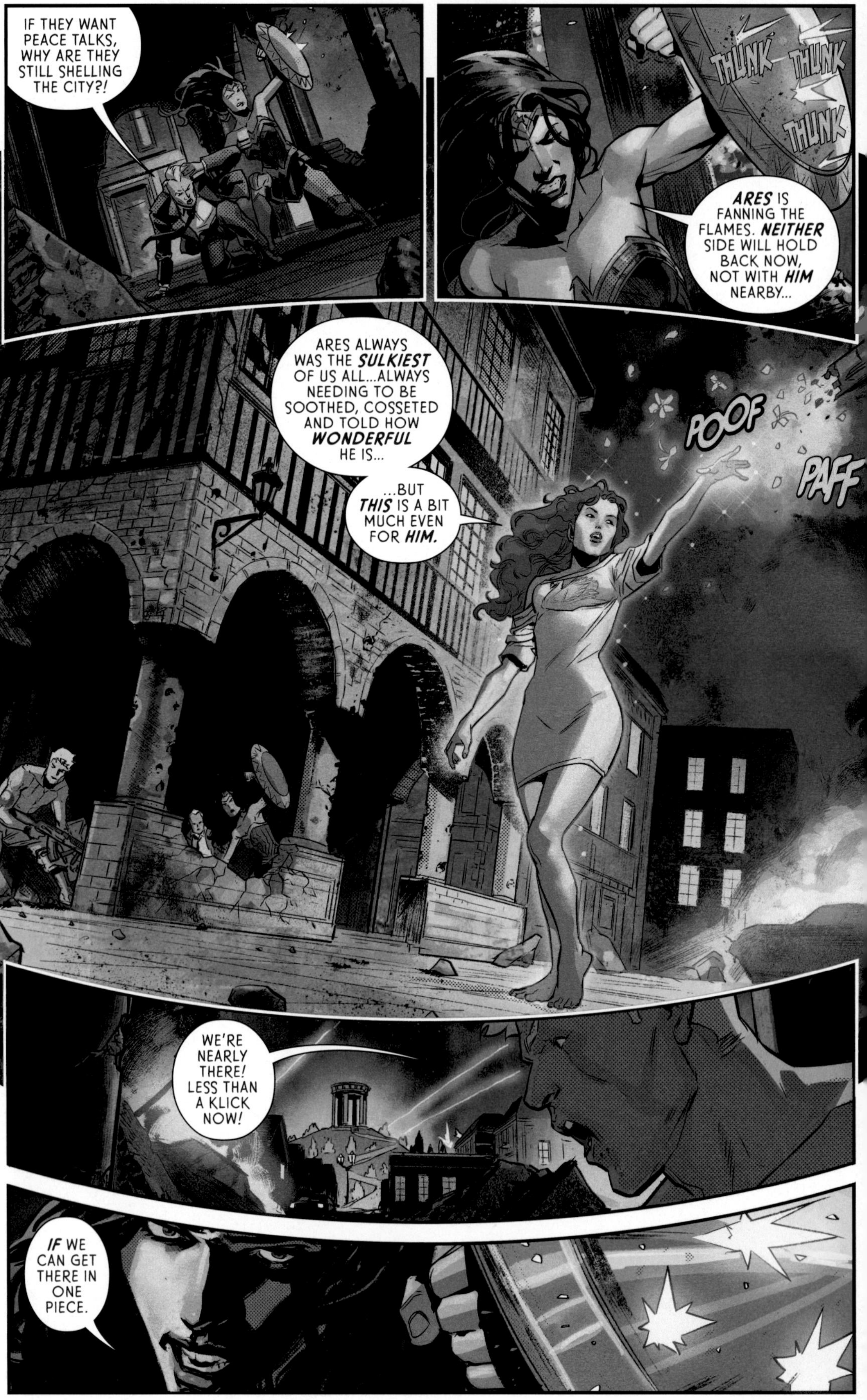
IF THEY WANT PEACE TALKS, WHY ARE THEY STILL SHELLING THE CITY?!
THUNK THUNK
THUNK
ARES IS FANNING THE FLAMES. NEITHER SIDE WILL HOLD BACK NOW, NOT WITH HIM NEARBY...
ARES ALWAYS WAS THE SULKIEST OF US ALL...ALWAYS NEEDING TO BE SOOTHED, COSSETED AND TOLD HOW WONDERFUL HE IS...
...BUT THIS IS A BIT MUCH EVEN FOR HIM.
POOF
PAFF
WE'RE NEARLY THERE! LESS THAN A KLICK NOW!
IF WE CAN GET THERE IN ONE PIECE.

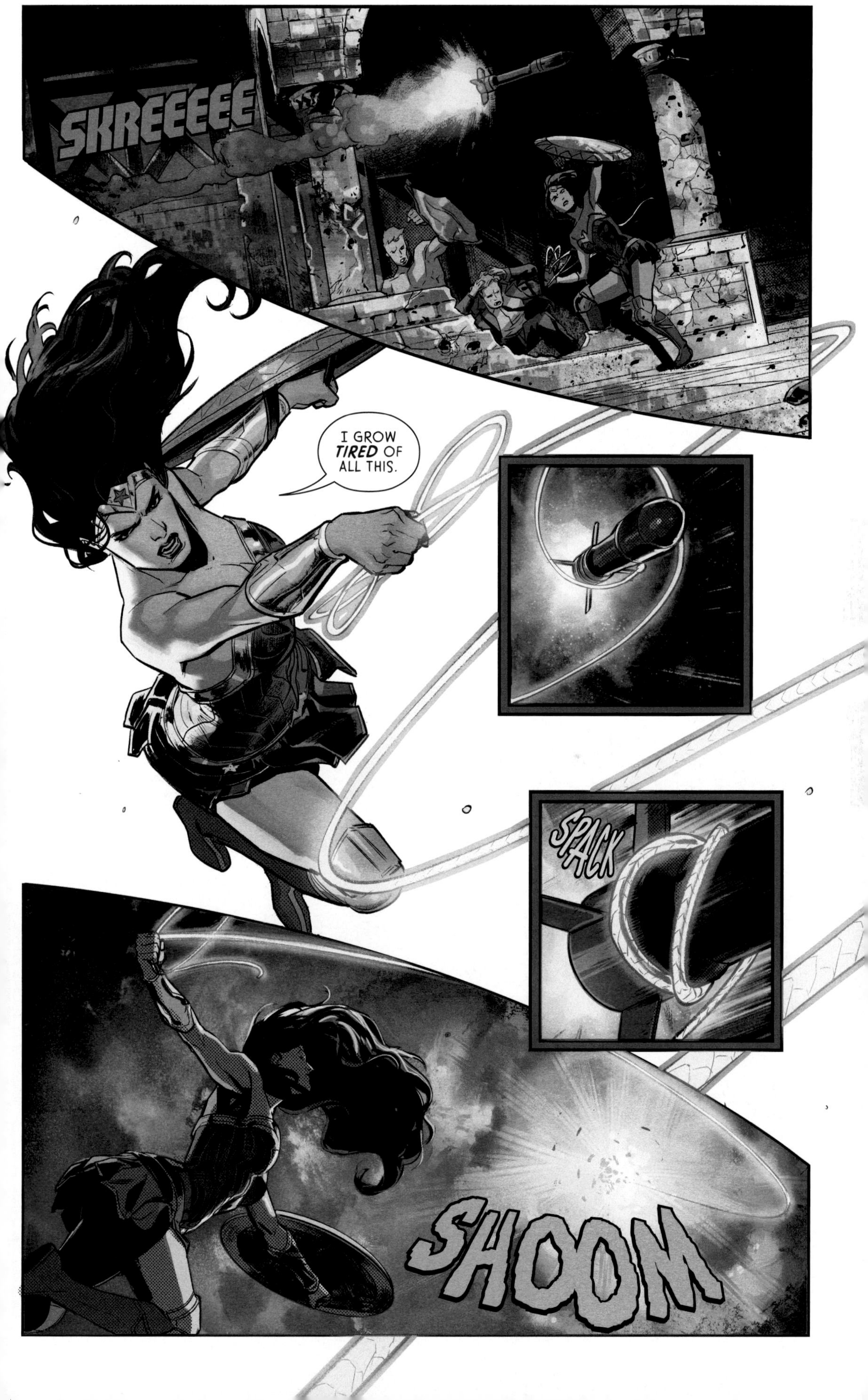
SKREEEEEE
I GROW *TIRED* OF ALL THIS.
SPACK
SHOOM

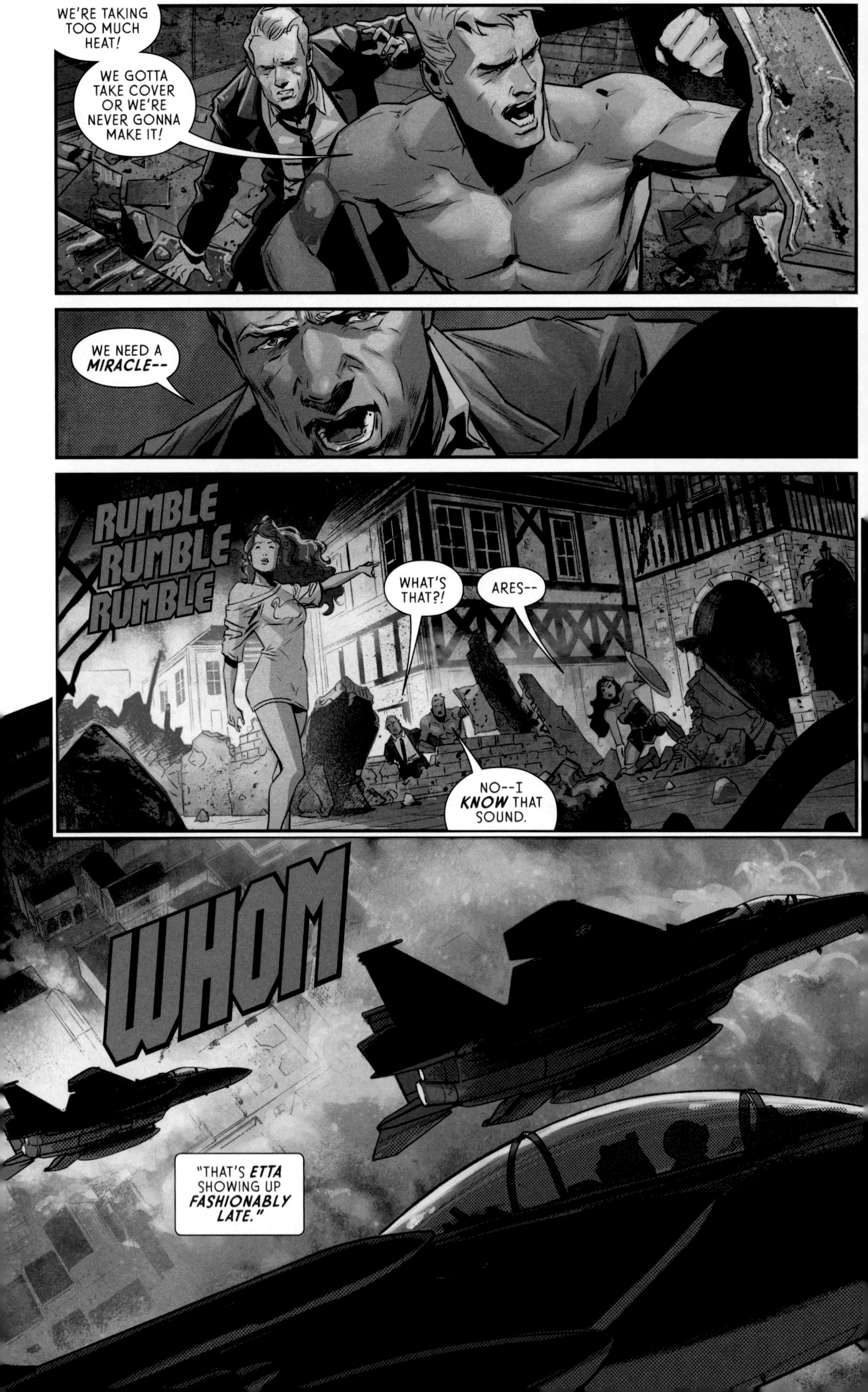
WE'RE TAKING TOO MUCH HEAT!
WE GOTTA TAKE COVER OR WE'RE NEVER GONNA MAKE IT!
WE NEED A MIRACLE--
RUMBLE RUMBLE RUMBLE
WHAT'S THAT?!
ARES--
NO--I KNOW THAT SOUND.
WHOM
"THAT'S ETTA SHOWING UP FASHIONABLY LATE."

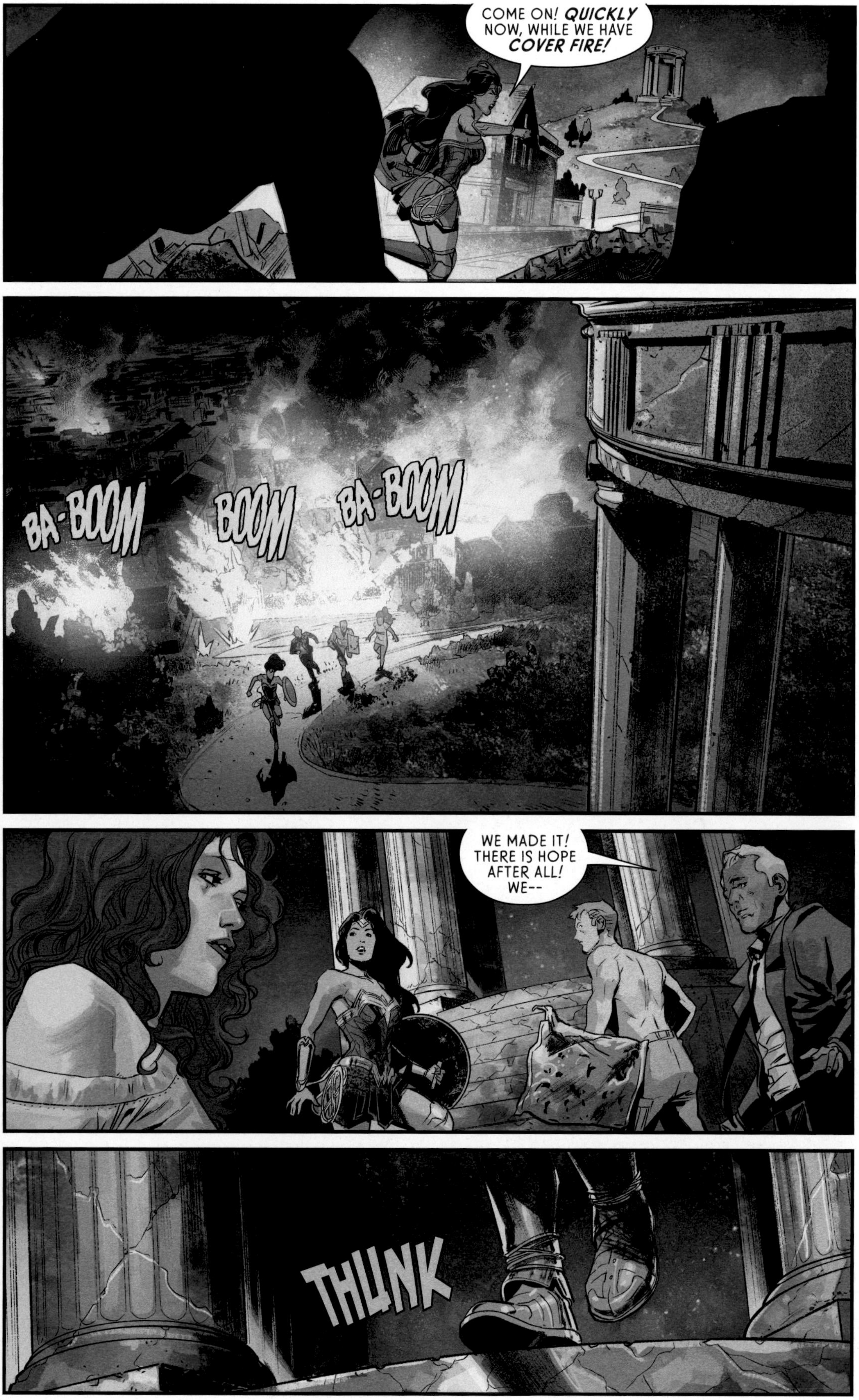
COME ON! QUICKLY NOW, WHILE WE HAVE COVER FIRE!
BA-BOOM
BOOM
BA-BOOM
WE MADE IT! THERE IS HOPE AFTER ALL! WE--
THUNK

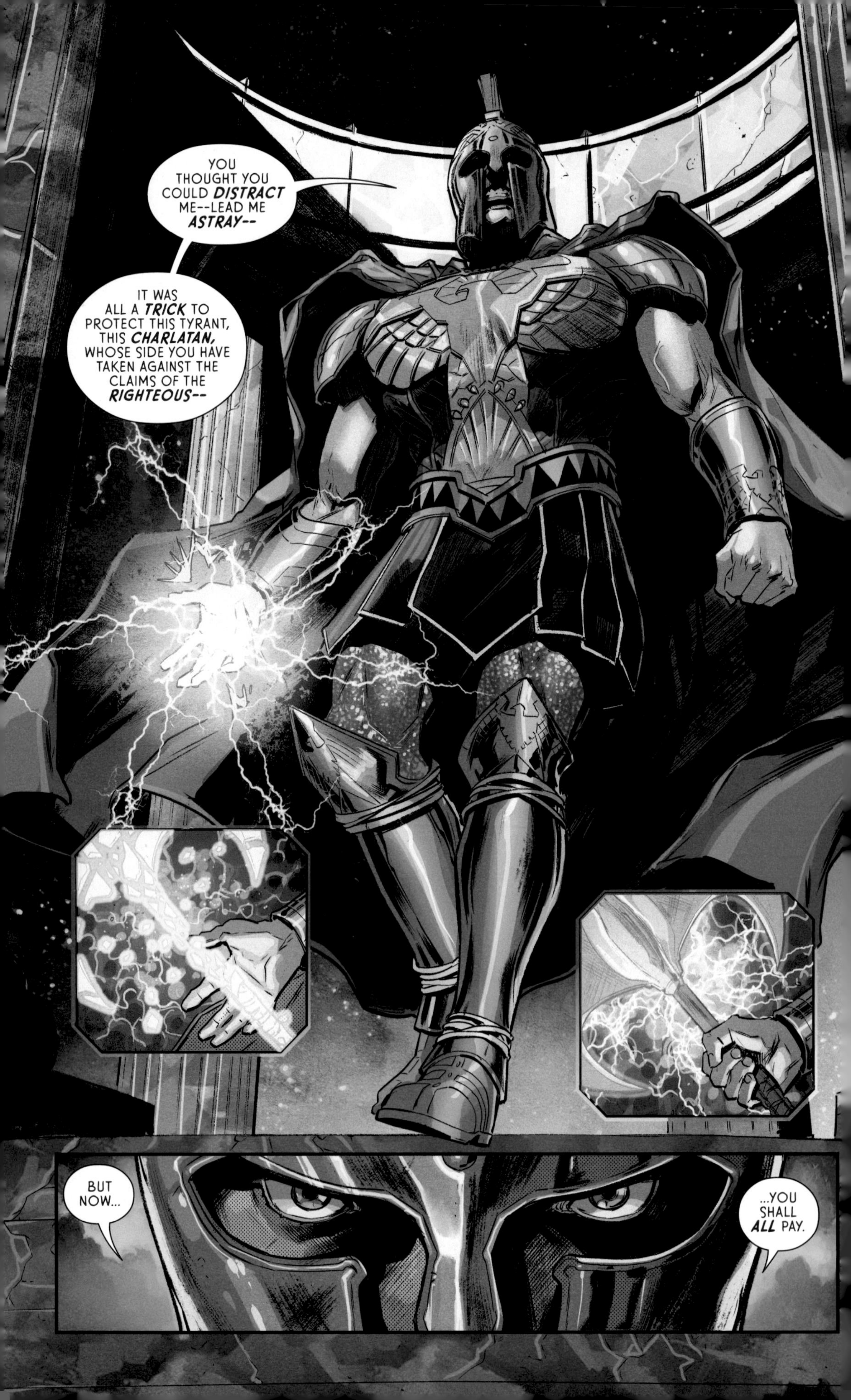
YOU THOUGHT YOU COULD DISTRACT ME--LEAD ME ASTRAY--
IT WAS ALL A TRICK TO PROTECT THIS TYRANT, THIS CHARLATAN, WHOSE SIDE YOU HAVE TAKEN AGAINST THE CLAIMS OF THE RIGHTEOUS--
BUT NOW...
...YOU SHALL ALL PAY.

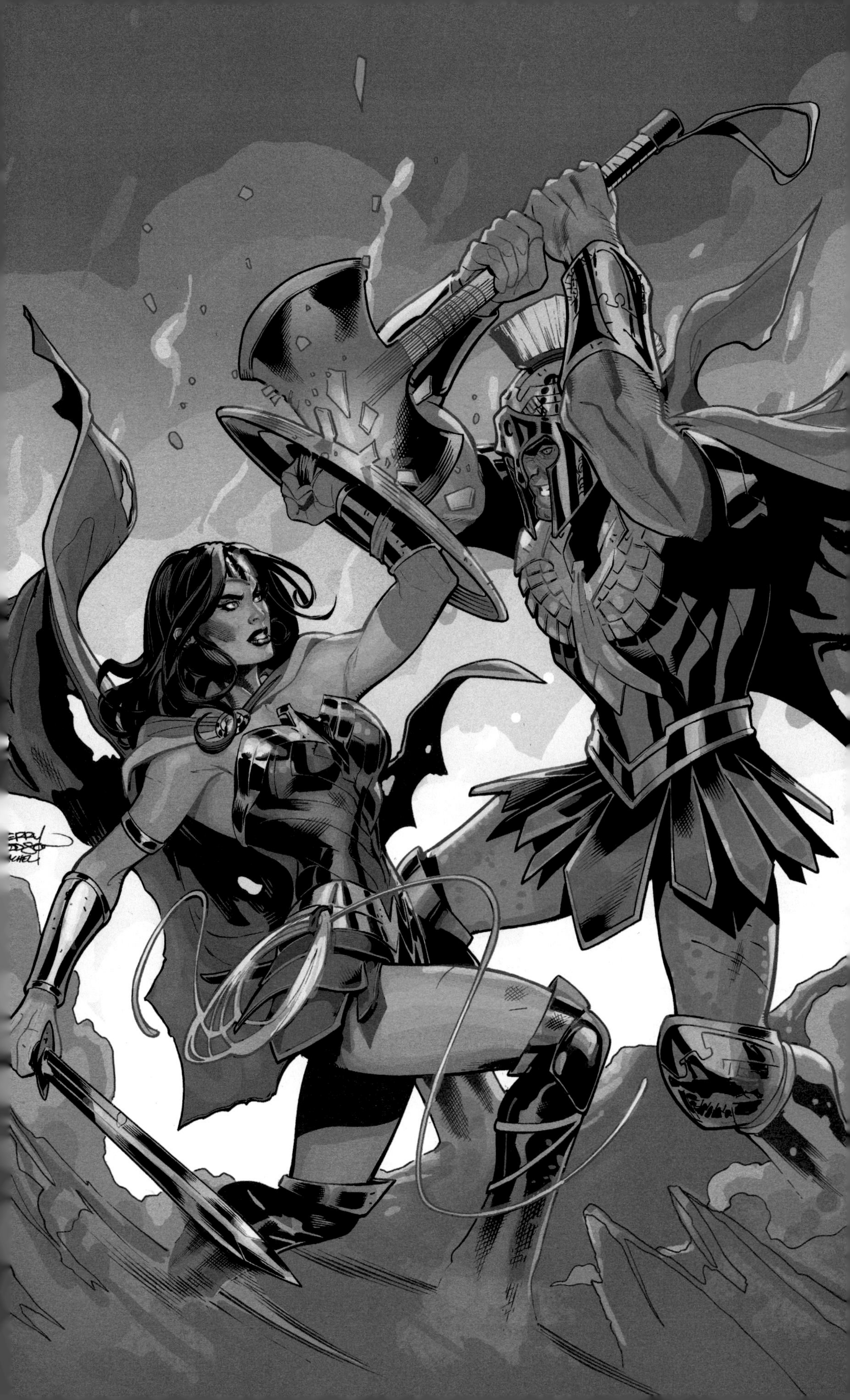

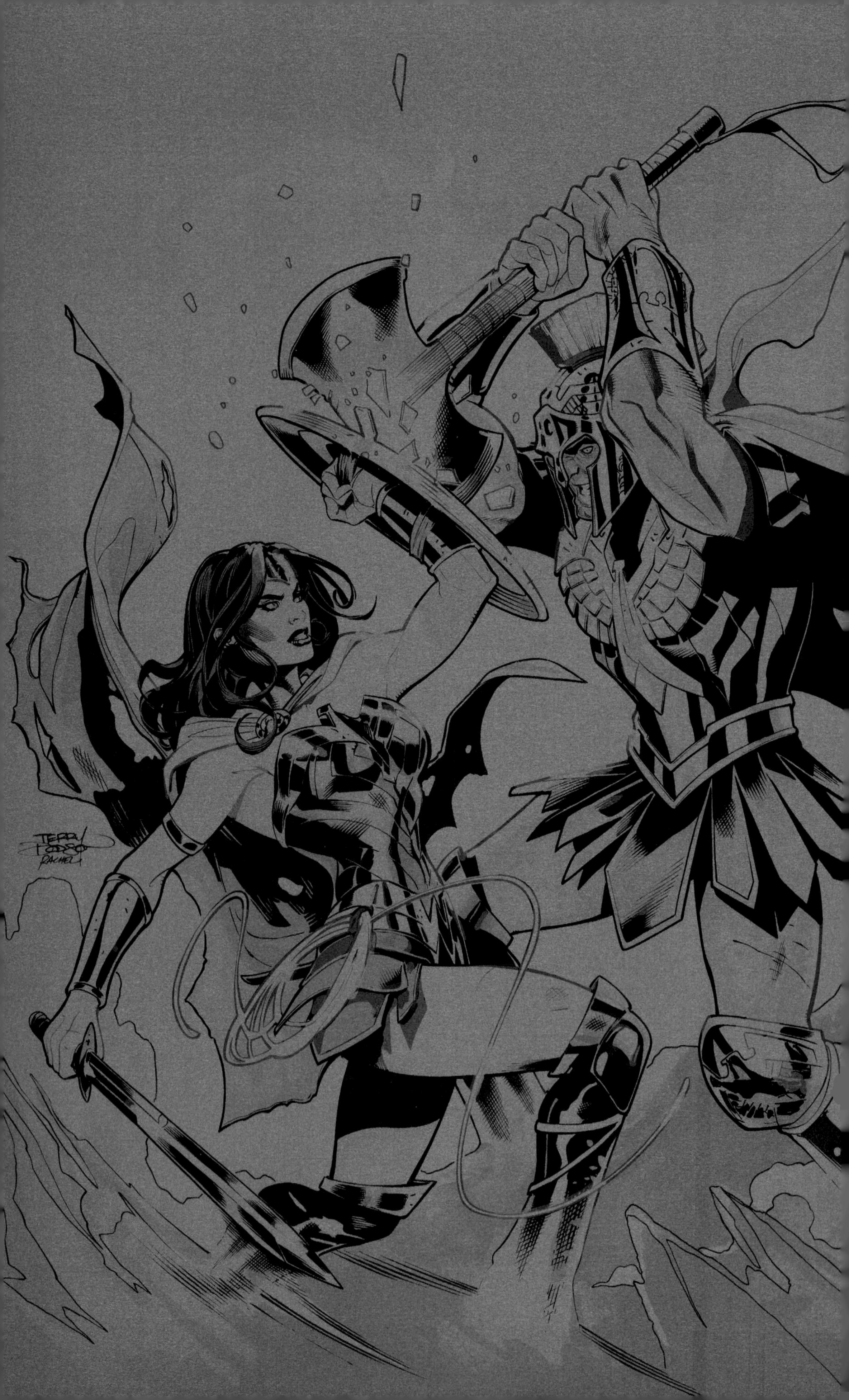

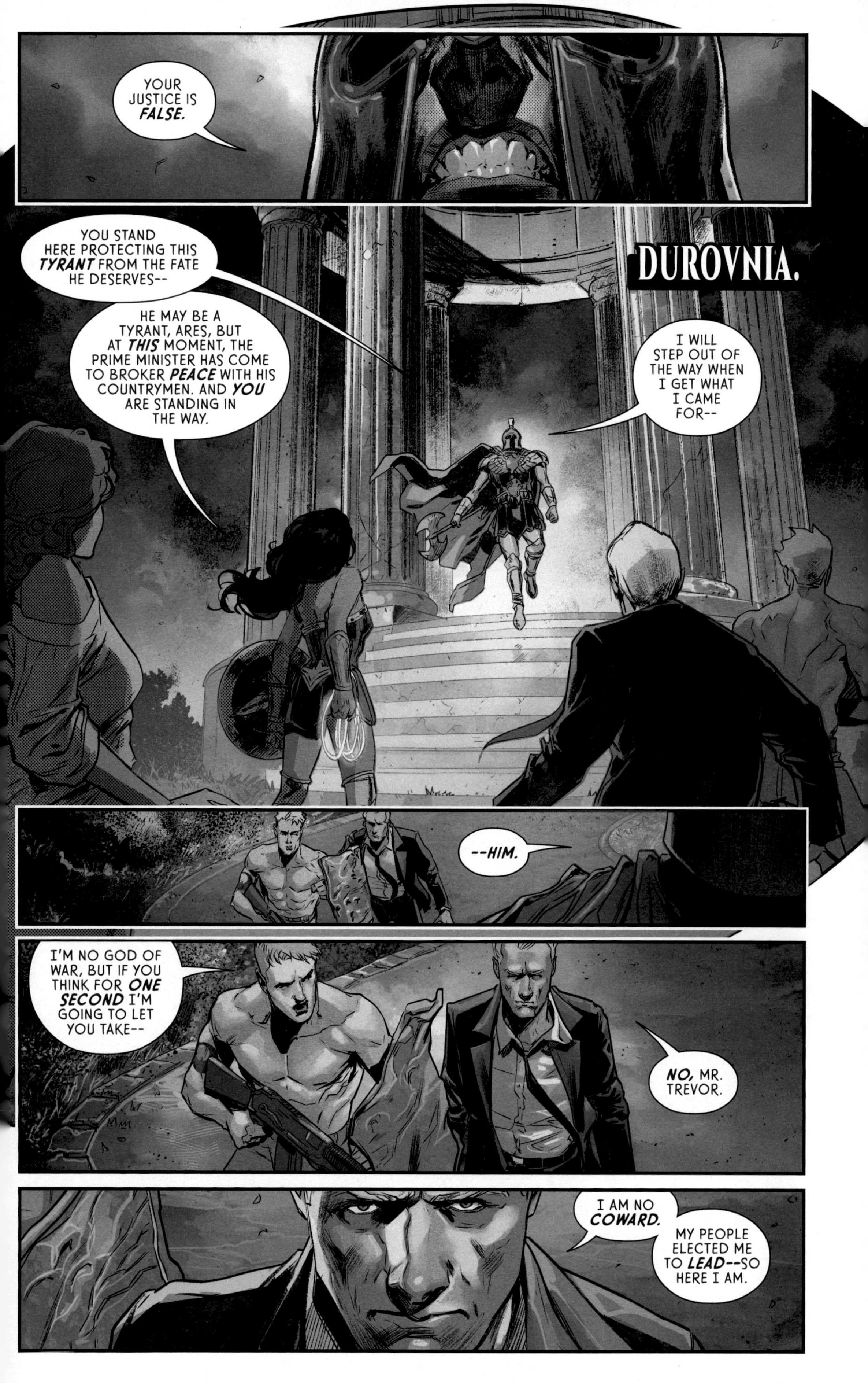
YOUR JUSTICE IS FALSE.
YOU STAND HERE PROTECTING THIS TYRANT FROM THE FATE HE DESERVES--
DUROVNIA.
HE MAY BE A TYRANT, ARES, BUT AT THIS MOMENT, THE PRIME MINISTER HAS COME TO BROKER PEACE WITH HIS COUNTRYMEN. AND YOU ARE STANDING IN THE WAY.
I WILL STEP OUT OF THE WAY WHEN I GET WHAT I CAME FOR--
--HIM.
I'M NO GOD OF WAR, BUT IF YOU THINK FOR ONE SECOND I'M GOING TO LET YOU TAKE--
NO, MR. TREVOR.
I AM NO COWARD.
MY PEOPLE ELECTED ME TO LEAD--SO HERE I AM.

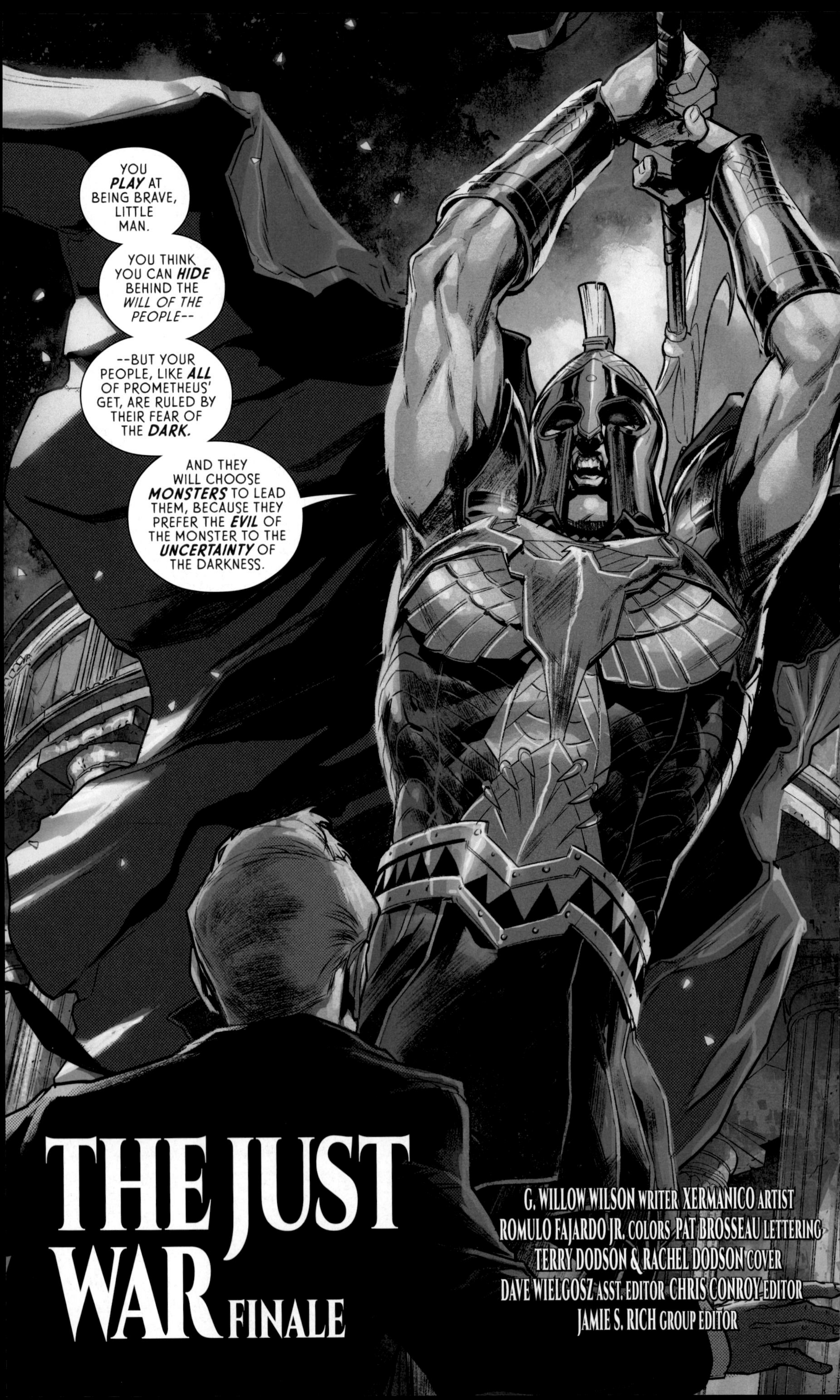
YOU PLAY AT BEING BRAVE, LITTLE MAN.
YOU THINK YOU CAN HIDE BEHIND THE WILL OF THE PEOPLE--
--BUT YOUR PEOPLE, LIKE ALL OF PROMETHEUS' GET, ARE RULED BY THEIR FEAR OF THE DARK.
AND THEY WILL CHOOSE MONSTERS TO LEAD THEM, BECAUSE THEY PREFER THE EVIL OF THE MONSTER TO THE UNCERTAINTY OF THE DARKNESS.
THE JUST WAR FINALE
G. WILLOW WILSON WRITER XERMANICO ARTIST
ROMULO FAJARDO JR. COLORS PAT BROSSEAU LETTERING
TERRY DODSON & RACHEL DODSON COVER
DAVE WIELGOSZ ASST. EDITOR CHRIS CONROY EDITOR
JAMIE S. RICH GROUP EDITOR

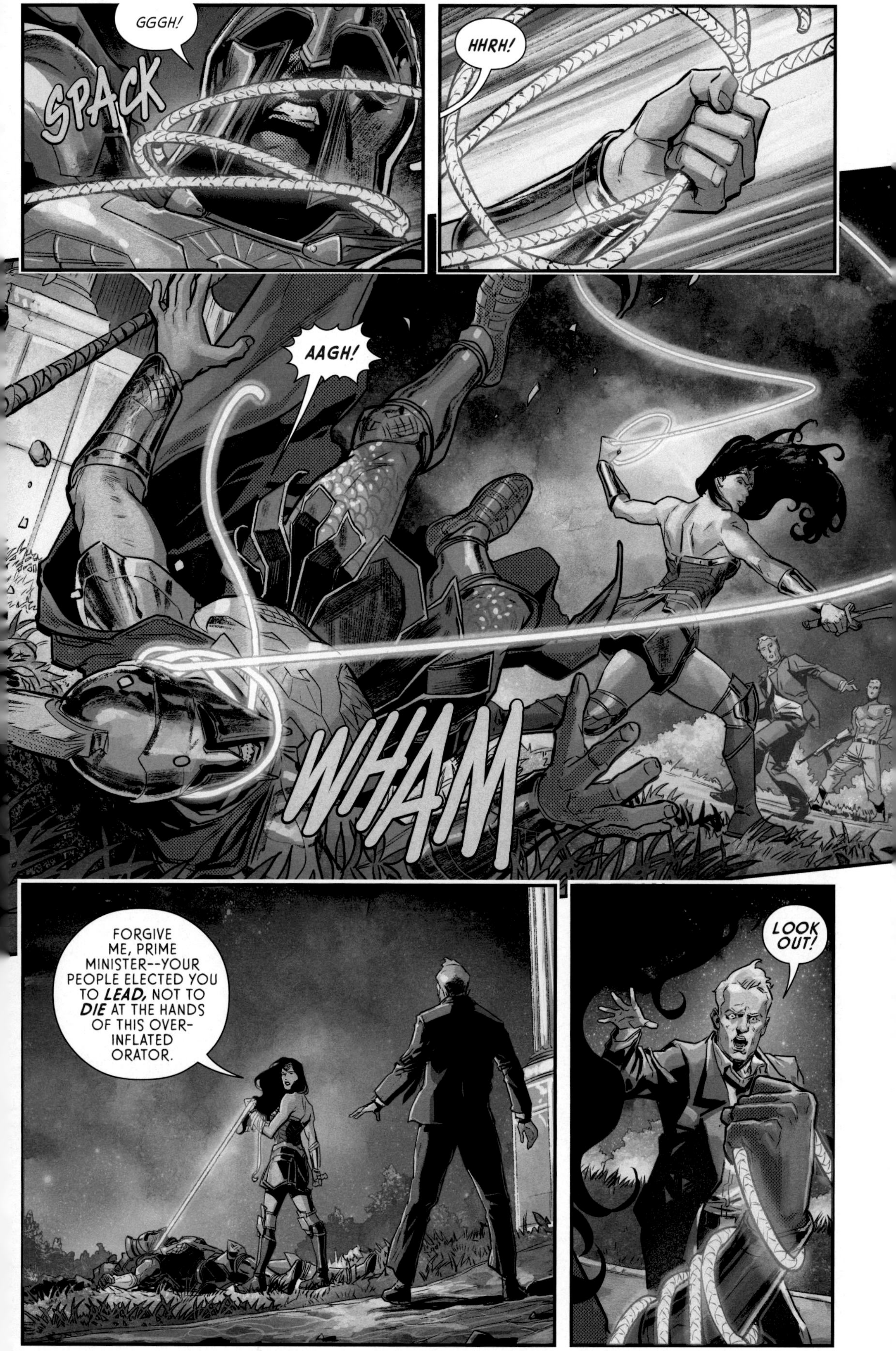
GGGH!
SPACK
HHRH!
AAGH!
WHAM
FORGIVE ME, PRIME MINISTER--YOUR PEOPLE ELECTED YOU TO LEAD, NOT TO DIE AT THE HANDS OF THIS OVER-INFLATED ORATOR.
LOOK OUT!

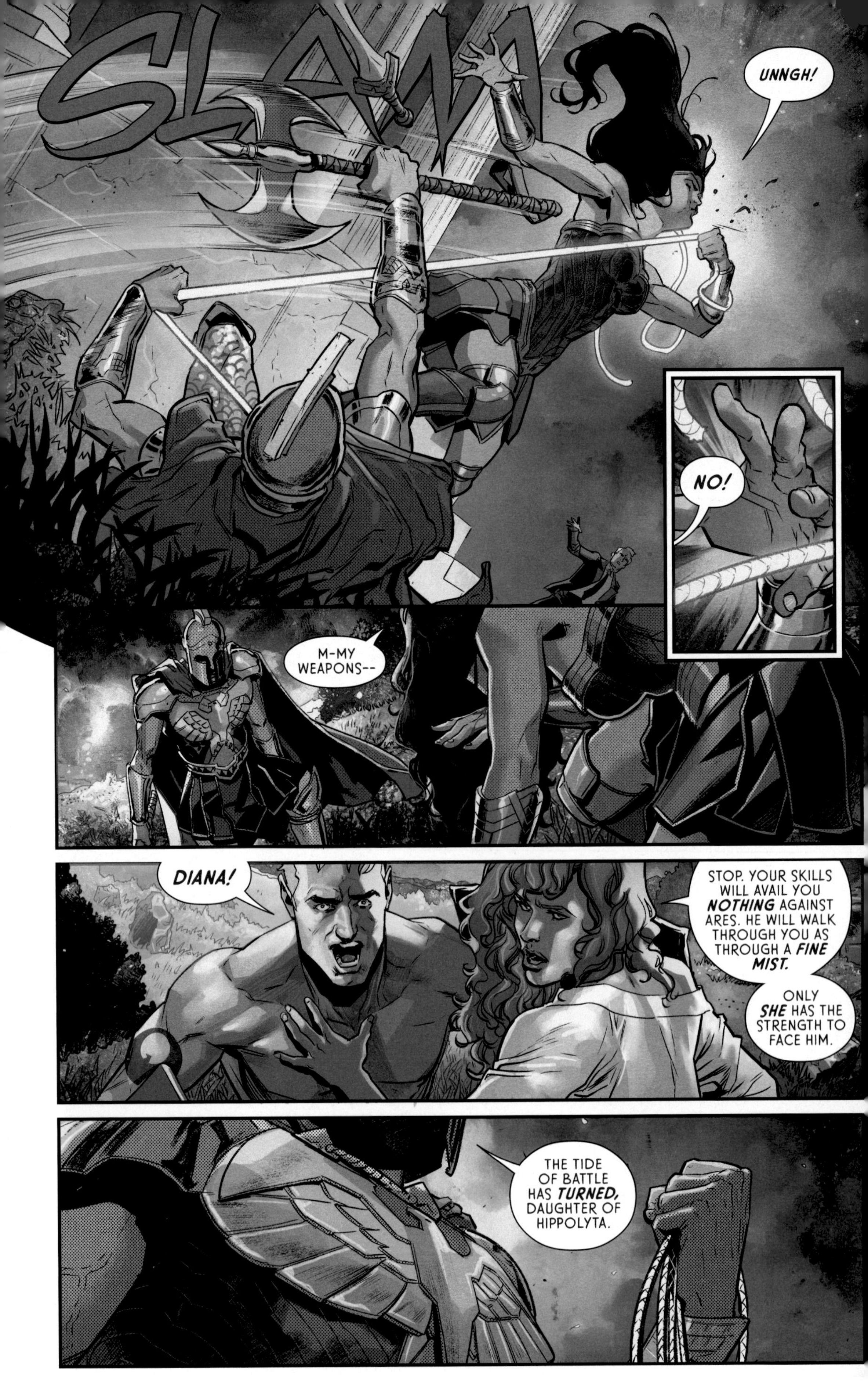
SLAM
UNNGH!
NO!
M-MY WEAPONS--
DIANA!
STOP. YOUR SKILLS WILL AVAIL YOU NOTHING AGAINST ARES. HE WILL WALK THROUGH YOU AS THROUGH A FINE MIST.
ONLY SHE HAS THE STRENGTH TO FACE HIM.
THE TIDE OF BATTLE HAS TURNED, DAUGHTER OF HIPPOLYTA.

Man: APHRODITE... HE'S GOT THE *LASSO OF TRUTH.*

Woman: STEADY. HE *HOLDS* IT, BUT HE HAS NOT YET *USED* IT...

DO YOU THINK JUSTICE IS THIS *EASY,* GOD OF WAR?

YOU THINK BY KILLING THE PRIME MINISTER--BY KILLING ME--YOU CAN WIN THIS WAR FOR THE SIDE YOU HAVE CHOSEN?

FOLLY. YOU WILL ONLY CONDEMN THESE PEOPLE TO ANOTHER DECADE OF *WAR.*

JUSTICE IS NOT WHAT MAKES YOU FEEL GOOD. SOMETIMES JUSTICE DOESN'T BENEFIT *YOU* AT ALL--SOMETIMES YOU MUST *GIVE UP* THAT WHICH YOU TREASURE MOST, SO THAT SOMEONE *ELSE* MAY BENEFIT FROM IT.

YOU HAVEN'T CHANGED, ARES. YOU HAVEN'T *LEARNED.* YOU DO NOT KNOW JUSTICE--YOU KNOW ONLY *WAR.*

OH, DAUGHTER OF WOMEN...

...I KNOW A *GREAT DEAL* MORE THAN THAT.

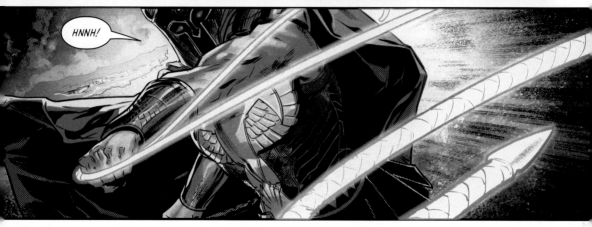

HNNH!

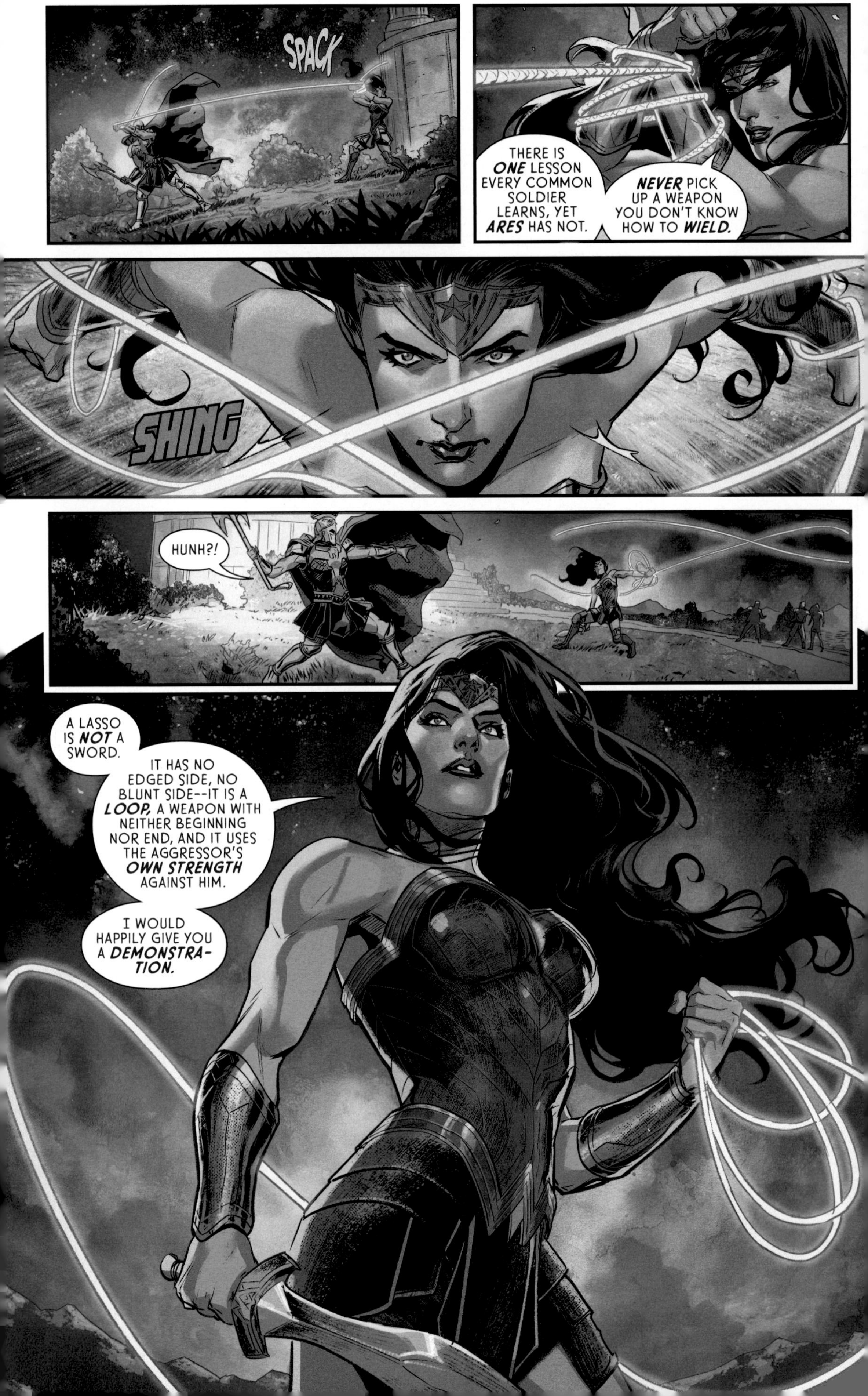
SPACK
THERE IS ONE LESSON EVERY COMMON SOLDIER LEARNS, YET ARES HAS NOT.
NEVER PICK UP A WEAPON YOU DON'T KNOW HOW TO WIELD.
SHING
HUNH?!
A LASSO IS NOT A SWORD.
IT HAS NO EDGED SIDE, NO BLUNT SIDE--IT IS A LOOP, A WEAPON WITH NEITHER BEGINNING NOR END, AND IT USES THE AGGRESSOR'S OWN STRENGTH AGAINST HIM.
I WOULD HAPPILY GIVE YOU A DEMONSTRATION.

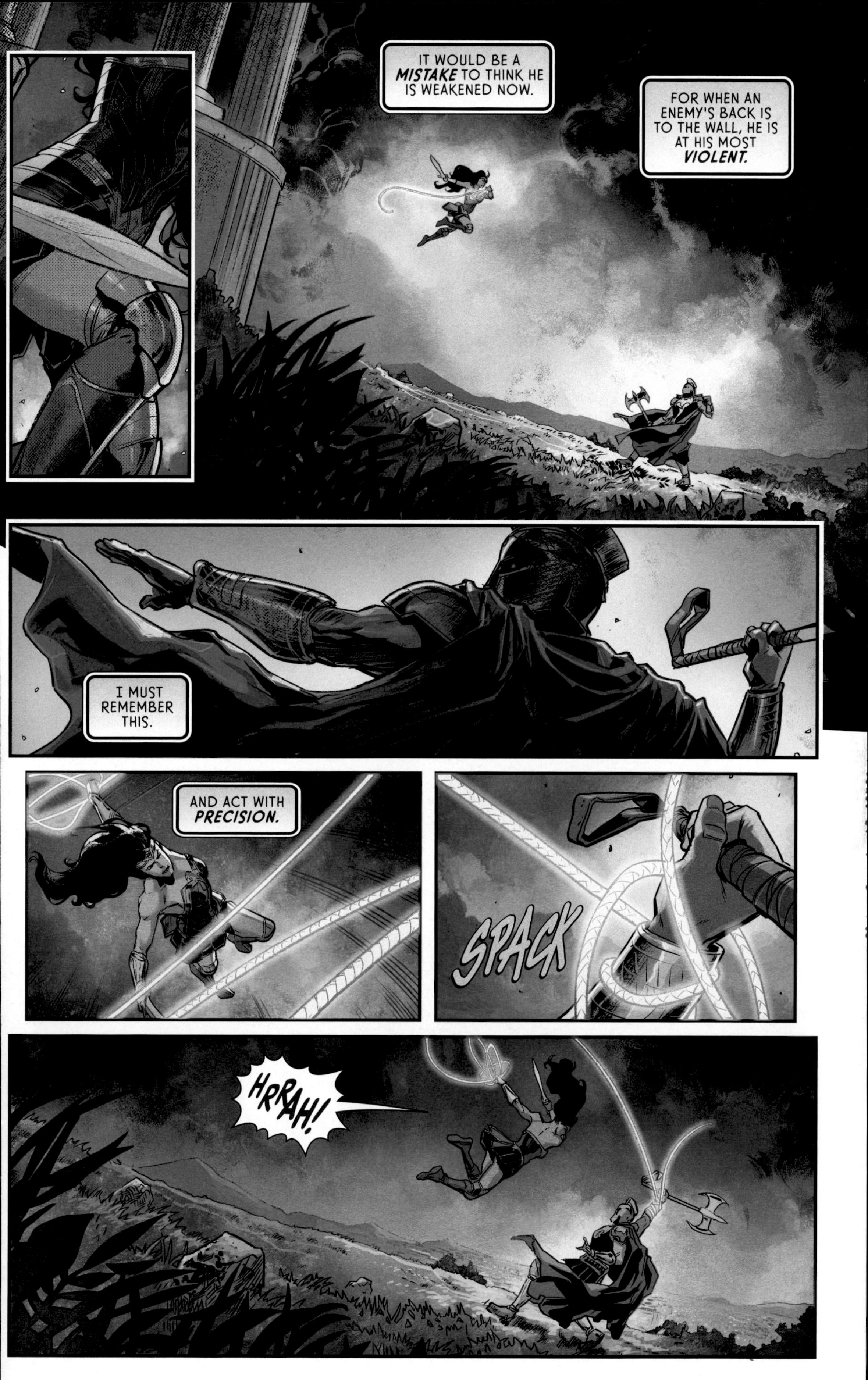
IT WOULD BE A MISTAKE TO THINK HE IS WEAKENED NOW.
FOR WHEN AN ENEMY'S BACK IS TO THE WALL, HE IS AT HIS MOST VIOLENT.
I MUST REMEMBER THIS.
AND ACT WITH PRECISION.
SPACK
HRRAH!

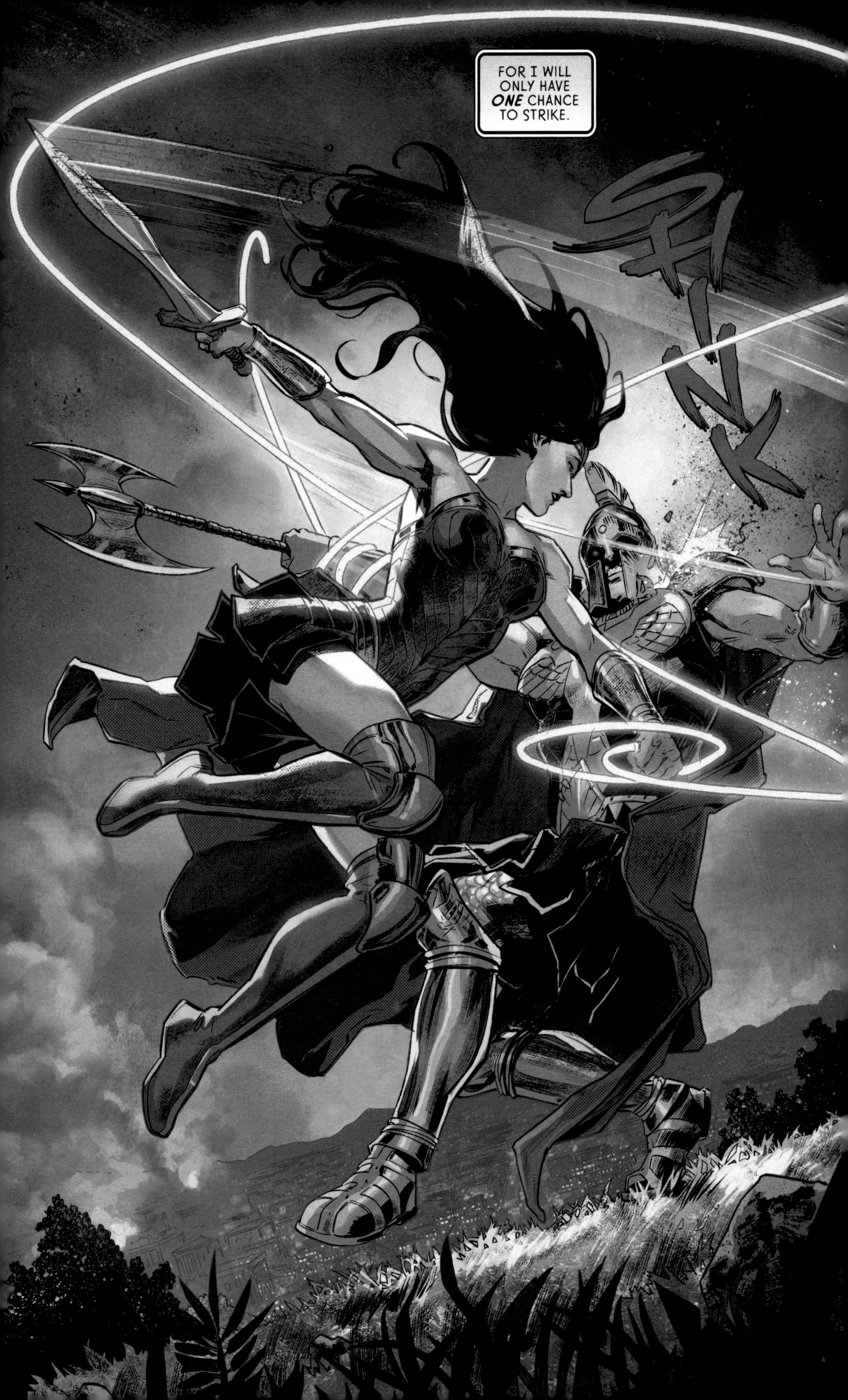
FOR I WILL ONLY HAVE *ONE* CHANCE TO STRIKE.
SHINK

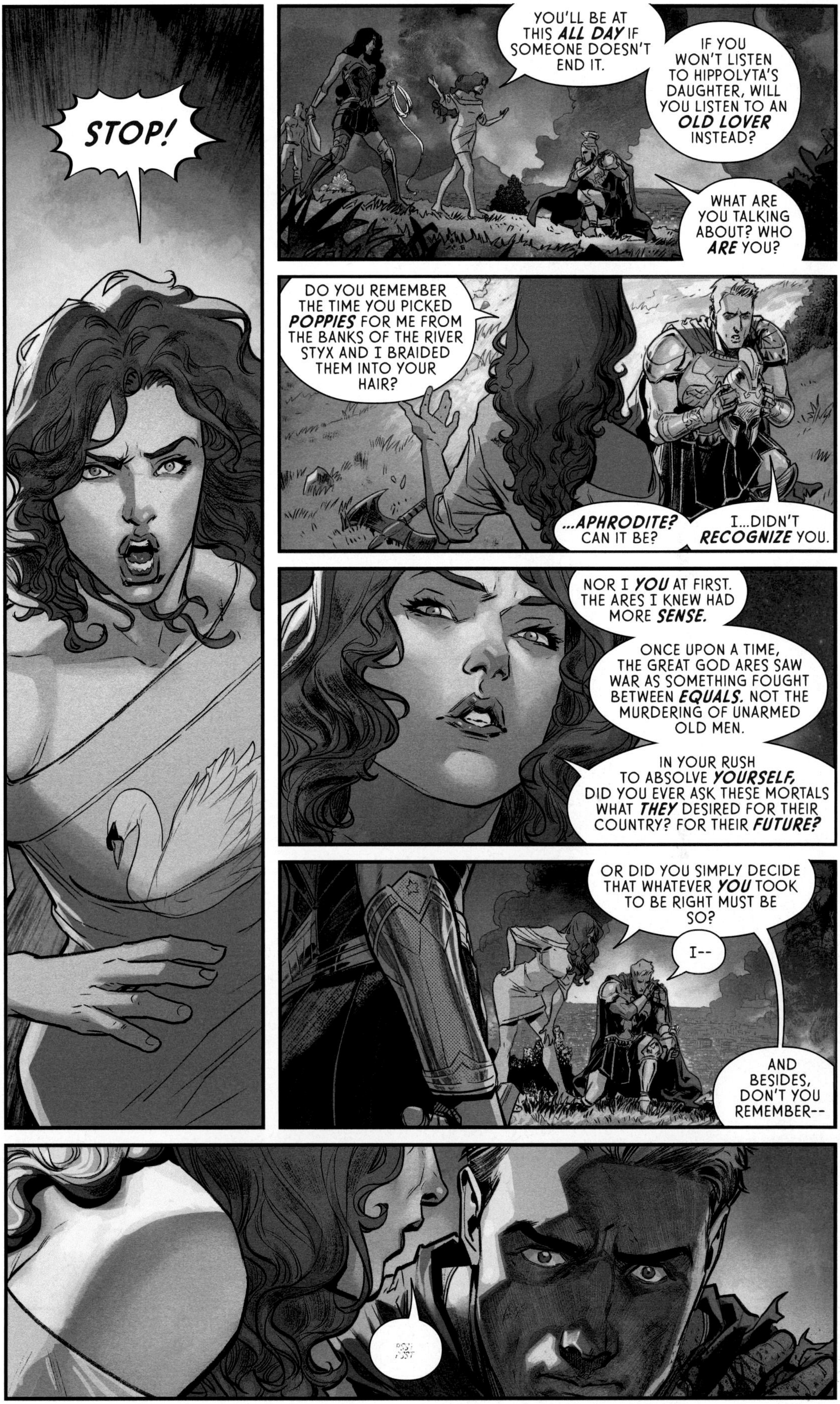
STOP!
YOU'LL BE AT THIS ALL DAY IF SOMEONE DOESN'T END IT.
IF YOU WON'T LISTEN TO HIPPOLYTA'S DAUGHTER, WILL YOU LISTEN TO AN OLD LOVER INSTEAD?
WHAT ARE YOU TALKING ABOUT? WHO ARE YOU?
DO YOU REMEMBER THE TIME YOU PICKED POPPIES FOR ME FROM THE BANKS OF THE RIVER STYX AND I BRAIDED THEM INTO YOUR HAIR?
...APHRODITE? CAN IT BE?
I...DIDN'T RECOGNIZE YOU.
NOR I YOU AT FIRST. THE ARES I KNEW HAD MORE SENSE.
ONCE UPON A TIME, THE GREAT GOD ARES SAW WAR AS SOMETHING FOUGHT BETWEEN EQUALS. NOT THE MURDERING OF UNARMED OLD MEN.
IN YOUR RUSH TO ABSOLVE YOURSELF, DID YOU EVER ASK THESE MORTALS WHAT THEY DESIRED FOR THEIR COUNTRY? FOR THEIR FUTURE?
OR DID YOU SIMPLY DECIDE THAT WHATEVER YOU TOOK TO BE RIGHT MUST BE SO?
I--
AND BESIDES, DON'T YOU REMEMBER--

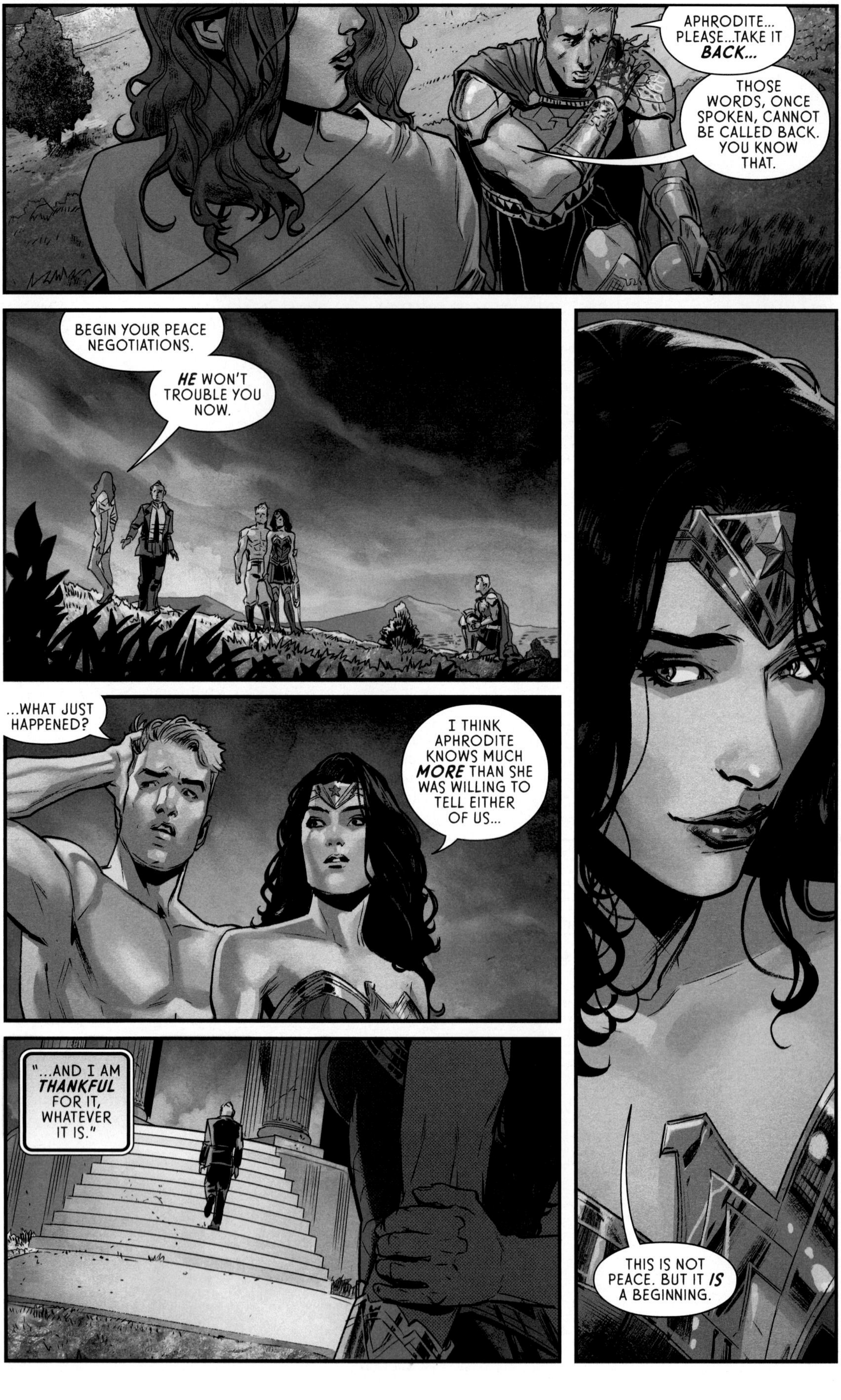
APHRODITE... PLEASE...TAKE IT BACK...
THOSE WORDS, ONCE SPOKEN, CANNOT BE CALLED BACK. YOU KNOW THAT.
BEGIN YOUR PEACE NEGOTIATIONS.
HE WON'T TROUBLE YOU NOW.
...WHAT JUST HAPPENED?
I THINK APHRODITE KNOWS MUCH MORE THAN SHE WAS WILLING TO TELL EITHER OF US...
"...AND I AM THANKFUL FOR IT, WHATEVER IT IS."
THIS IS NOT PEACE. BUT IT IS A BEGINNING.

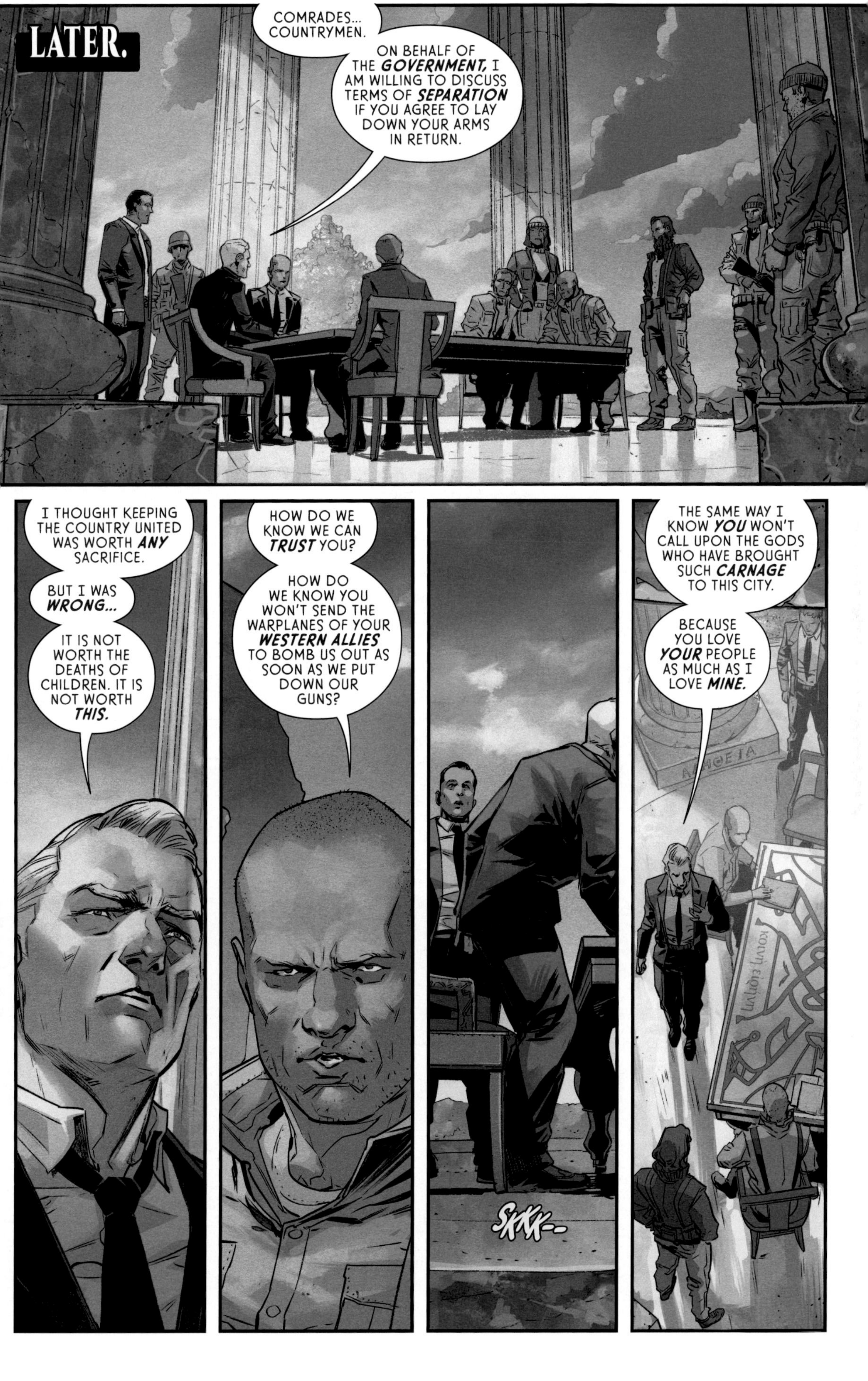

LATER.
COMRADES... COUNTRYMEN.
ON BEHALF OF THE GOVERNMENT, I AM WILLING TO DISCUSS TERMS OF SEPARATION IF YOU AGREE TO LAY DOWN YOUR ARMS IN RETURN.
I THOUGHT KEEPING THE COUNTRY UNITED WAS WORTH ANY SACRIFICE.
BUT I WAS WRONG...
IT IS NOT WORTH THE DEATHS OF CHILDREN. IT IS NOT WORTH THIS.
HOW DO WE KNOW WE CAN TRUST YOU?
HOW DO WE KNOW YOU WON'T SEND THE WARPLANES OF YOUR WESTERN ALLIES TO BOMB US OUT AS SOON AS WE PUT DOWN OUR GUNS?
SKKK--
THE SAME WAY I KNOW YOU WON'T CALL UPON THE GODS WHO HAVE BROUGHT SUCH CARNAGE TO THIS CITY.
BECAUSE YOU LOVE YOUR PEOPLE AS MUCH AS I LOVE MINE.

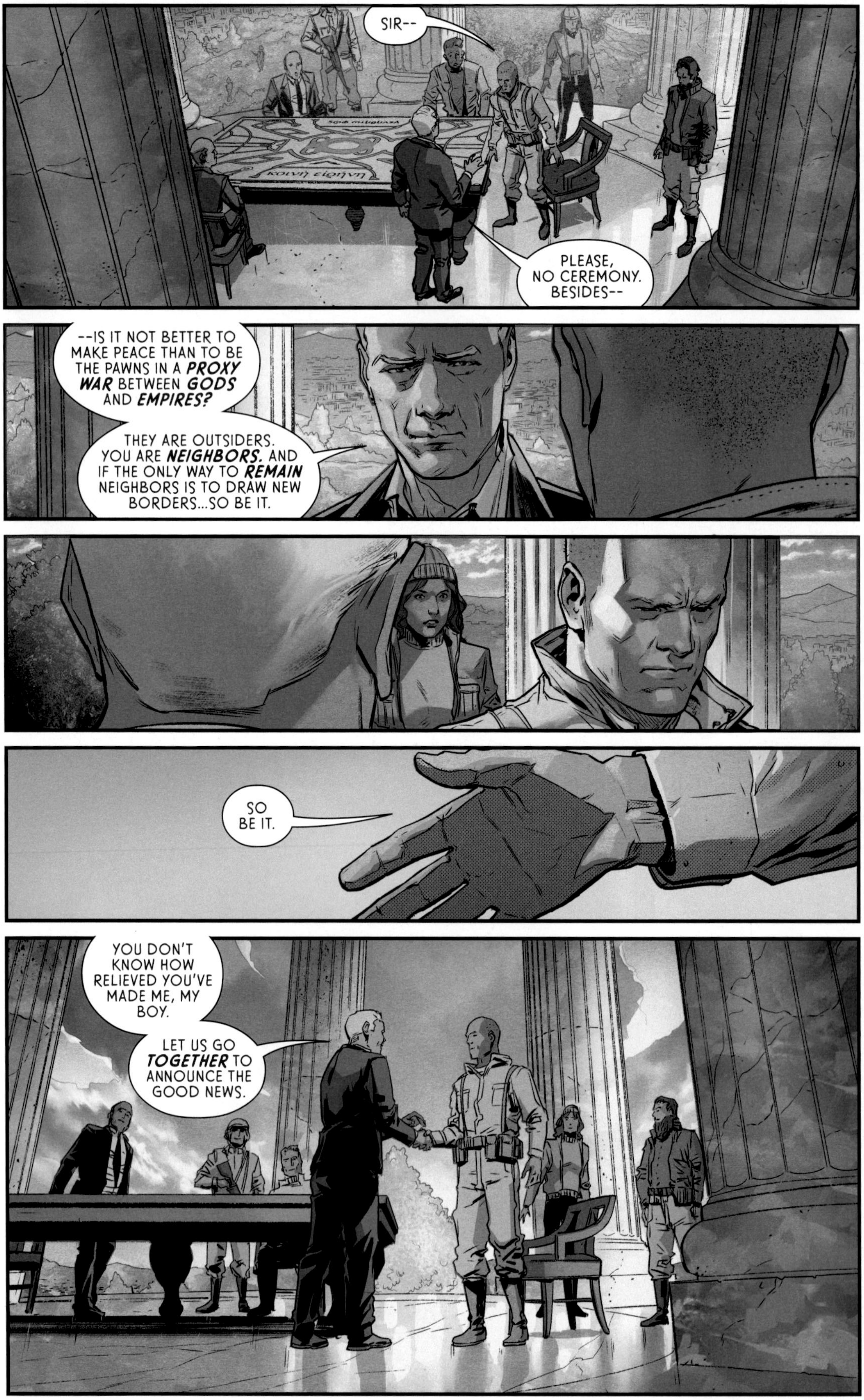
SIR--
PLEASE, NO CEREMONY. BESIDES--
--IS IT NOT BETTER TO MAKE PEACE THAN TO BE THE PAWNS IN A PROXY WAR BETWEEN GODS AND EMPIRES?
THEY ARE OUTSIDERS. YOU ARE NEIGHBORS. AND IF THE ONLY WAY TO REMAIN NEIGHBORS IS TO DRAW NEW BORDERS...SO BE IT.
SO BE IT.
YOU DON'T KNOW HOW RELIEVED YOU'VE MADE ME, MY BOY.
LET US GO TOGETHER TO ANNOUNCE THE GOOD NEWS.

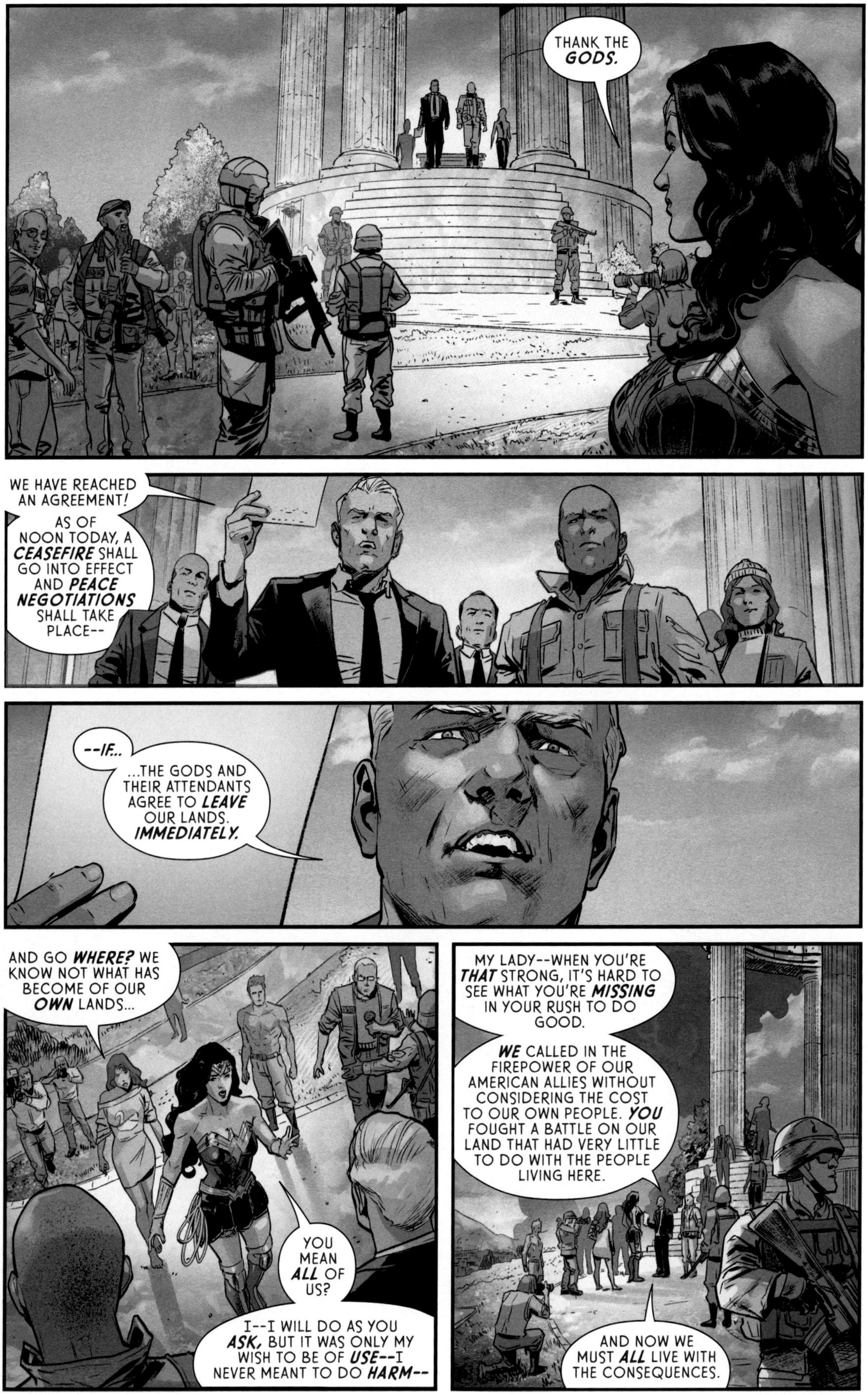
THANK THE GODS.
WE HAVE REACHED AN AGREEMENT!
AS OF NOON TODAY, A CEASEFIRE SHALL GO INTO EFFECT AND PEACE NEGOTIATIONS SHALL TAKE PLACE--
--IF...
...THE GODS AND THEIR ATTENDANTS AGREE TO LEAVE OUR LANDS. IMMEDIATELY.
AND GO WHERE? WE KNOW NOT WHAT HAS BECOME OF OUR OWN LANDS...
YOU MEAN ALL OF US?
I--I WILL DO AS YOU ASK, BUT IT WAS ONLY MY WISH TO BE OF USE--I NEVER MEANT TO DO HARM--
MY LADY--WHEN YOU'RE THAT STRONG, IT'S HARD TO SEE WHAT YOU'RE MISSING IN YOUR RUSH TO DO GOOD.
WE CALLED IN THE FIREPOWER OF OUR AMERICAN ALLIES WITHOUT CONSIDERING THE COST TO OUR OWN PEOPLE. YOU FOUGHT A BATTLE ON OUR LAND THAT HAD VERY LITTLE TO DO WITH THE PEOPLE LIVING HERE.
AND NOW WE MUST ALL LIVE WITH THE CONSEQUENCES.

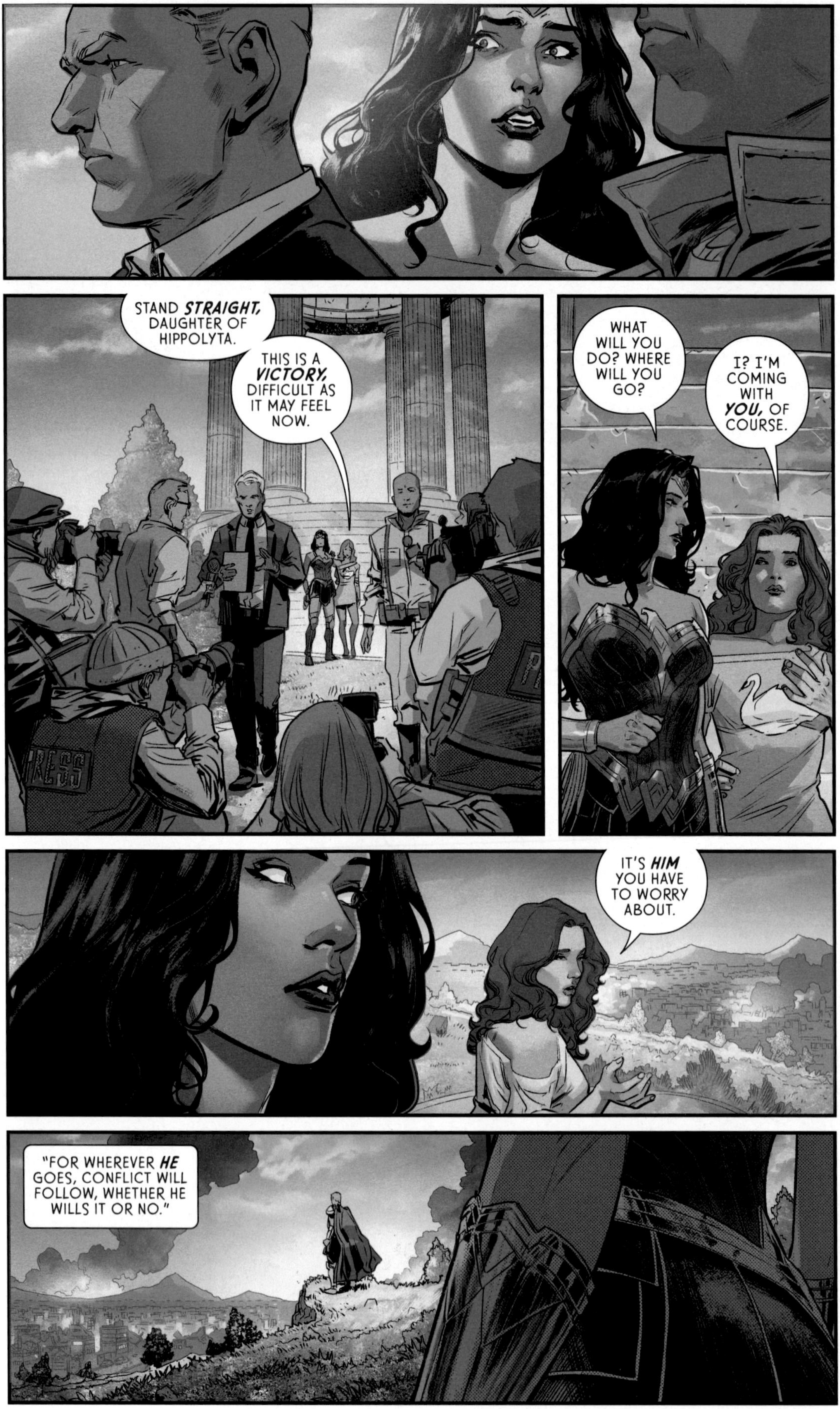
STAND STRAIGHT, DAUGHTER OF HIPPOLYTA.
THIS IS A VICTORY, DIFFICULT AS IT MAY FEEL NOW.
WHAT WILL YOU DO? WHERE WILL YOU GO?
I? I'M COMING WITH YOU, OF COURSE.
IT'S HIM YOU HAVE TO WORRY ABOUT.
"FOR WHEREVER HE GOES, CONFLICT WILL FOLLOW, WHETHER HE WILLS IT OR NO."
PRESS

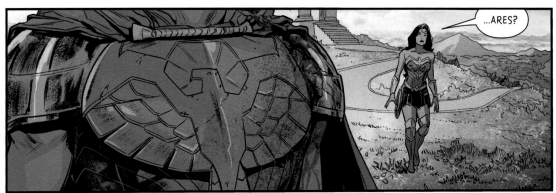

...ARES?

IS THIS WHAT *PEACE* LOOKS LIKE?

PEACE WILL BE WHEN THIS CITY IS *REBUILT* AND ITS PEOPLE *RECONCILED.*

THIS IS MERELY THE END OF CONFLICT.

WHAT AM I MEANT TO DO? IN A TIME OF ENDLESS WAR, WHO IS TO SAY I AM GOD OF *ANYTHING?*

ARE EVEN MY *BEST INTENTIONS* SO POISONOUS TO MORTAL MEN?

I WOULDN'T DARE ADVISE YOU. THESE ARE QUESTIONS WITHOUT CLEAR ANSWERS. YOU WOULD NEED THE WISDOM OF *ATHENA* TO ARRIVE AT THE END OF THEM.

ATHENA-- YES, IT IS *SHE* I MUST SEEK.

IF *ANYONE* UNDERSTANDS WHAT HAS HAPPENED TO ME--TO *ALL* OF US--IT WILL BE *HER...*

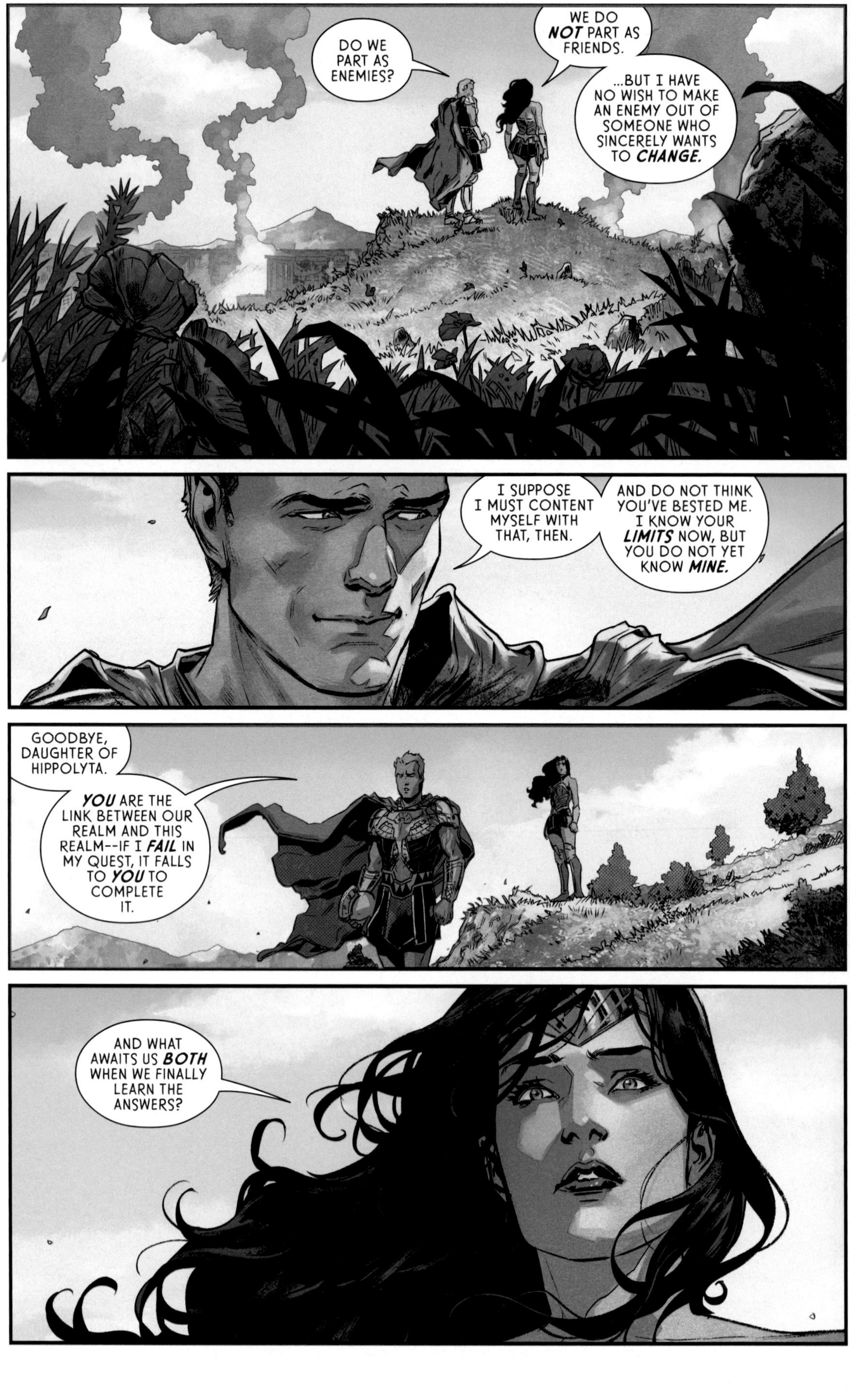
DO WE PART AS ENEMIES?
WE DO *NOT* PART AS FRIENDS.
...BUT I HAVE NO WISH TO MAKE AN ENEMY OUT OF SOMEONE WHO SINCERELY WANTS TO *CHANGE.*
I SUPPOSE I MUST CONTENT MYSELF WITH THAT, THEN.
AND DO NOT THINK YOU'VE BESTED ME. I KNOW YOUR *LIMITS* NOW, BUT YOU DO NOT YET KNOW *MINE.*
GOODBYE, DAUGHTER OF HIPPOLYTA.
YOU ARE THE LINK BETWEEN OUR REALM AND THIS REALM--IF I *FAIL* IN MY QUEST, IT FALLS TO *YOU* TO COMPLETE IT.
AND WHAT AWAITS US *BOTH* WHEN WE FINALLY LEARN THE ANSWERS?

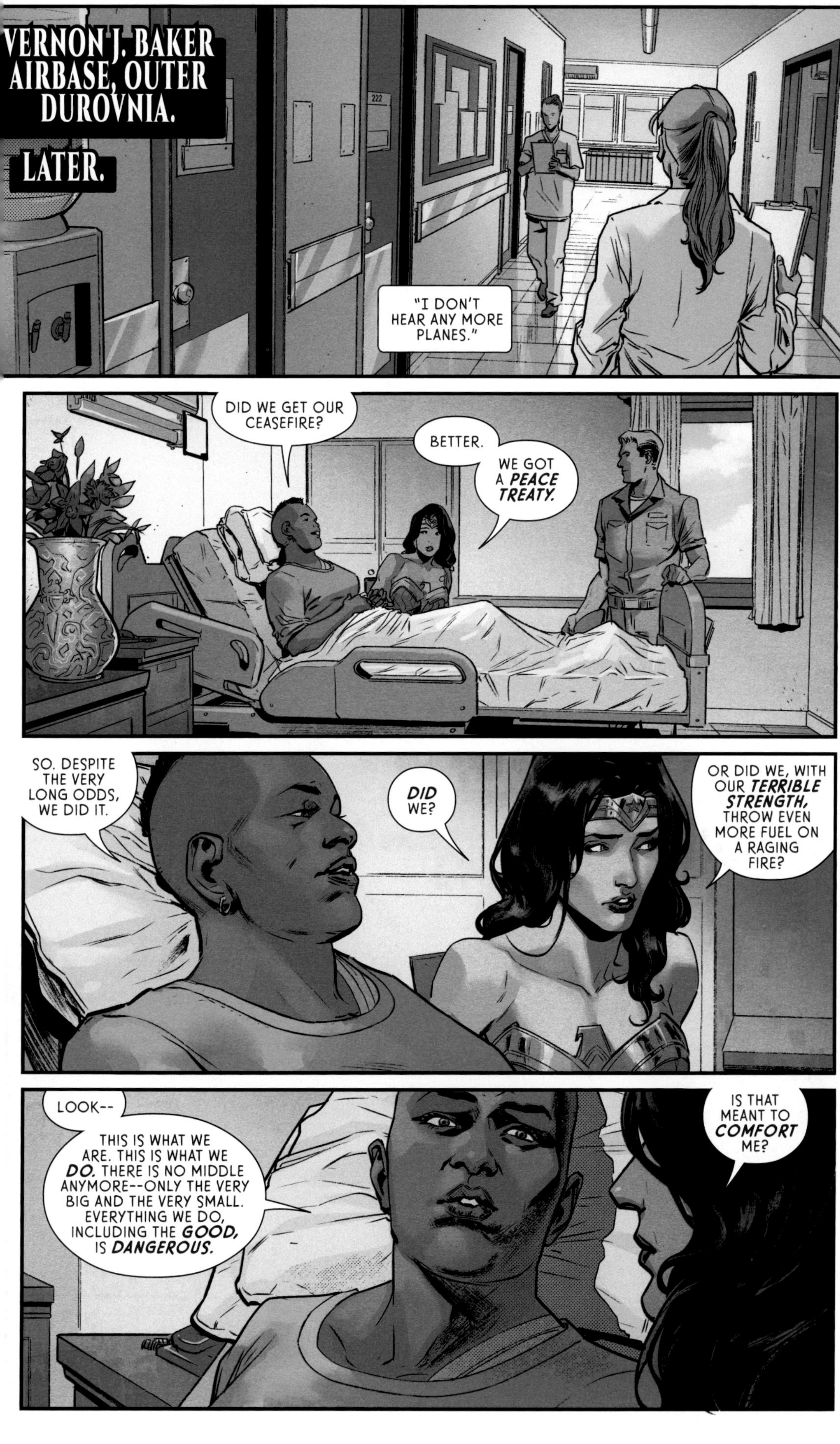
VERNON J. BAKER AIRBASE, OUTER DUROVNIA.
LATER.
"I DON'T HEAR ANY MORE PLANES."
DID WE GET OUR CEASEFIRE?
BETTER.
WE GOT A PEACE TREATY.
SO. DESPITE THE VERY LONG ODDS, WE DID IT.
DID WE?
OR DID WE, WITH OUR TERRIBLE STRENGTH, THROW EVEN MORE FUEL ON A RAGING FIRE?
LOOK--
THIS IS WHAT WE ARE. THIS IS WHAT WE DO. THERE IS NO MIDDLE ANYMORE--ONLY THE VERY BIG AND THE VERY SMALL. EVERYTHING WE DO, INCLUDING THE GOOD, IS DANGEROUS.
IS THAT MEANT TO COMFORT ME?

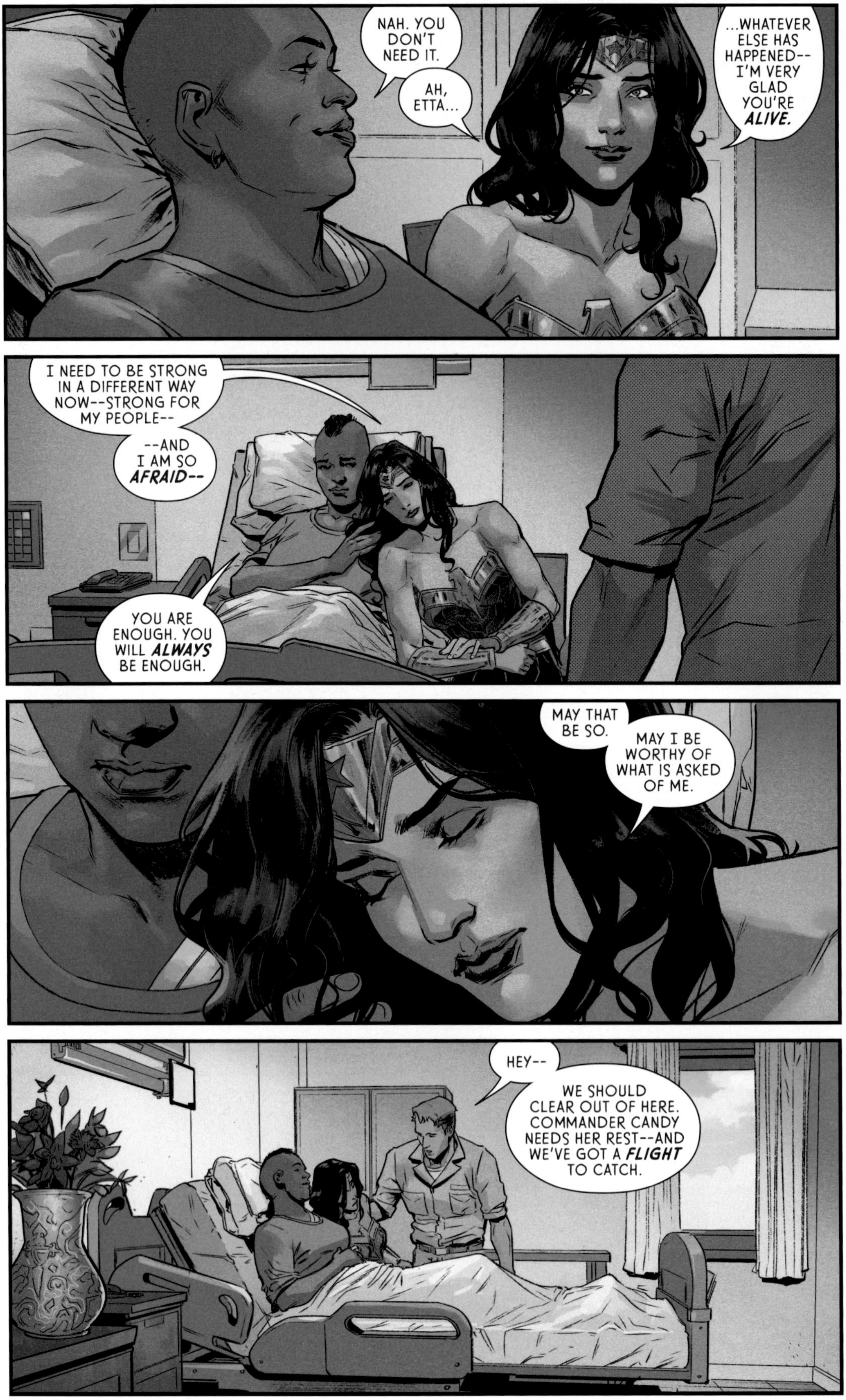
NAH. YOU DON'T NEED IT.
AH, ETTA...
...WHATEVER ELSE HAS HAPPENED-- I'M VERY GLAD YOU'RE ALIVE.
I NEED TO BE STRONG IN A DIFFERENT WAY NOW--STRONG FOR MY PEOPLE--
--AND I AM SO AFRAID--
YOU ARE ENOUGH. YOU WILL ALWAYS BE ENOUGH.
MAY THAT BE SO.
MAY I BE WORTHY OF WHAT IS ASKED OF ME.
HEY--
WE SHOULD CLEAR OUT OF HERE. COMMANDER CANDY NEEDS HER REST--AND WE'VE GOT A FLIGHT TO CATCH.

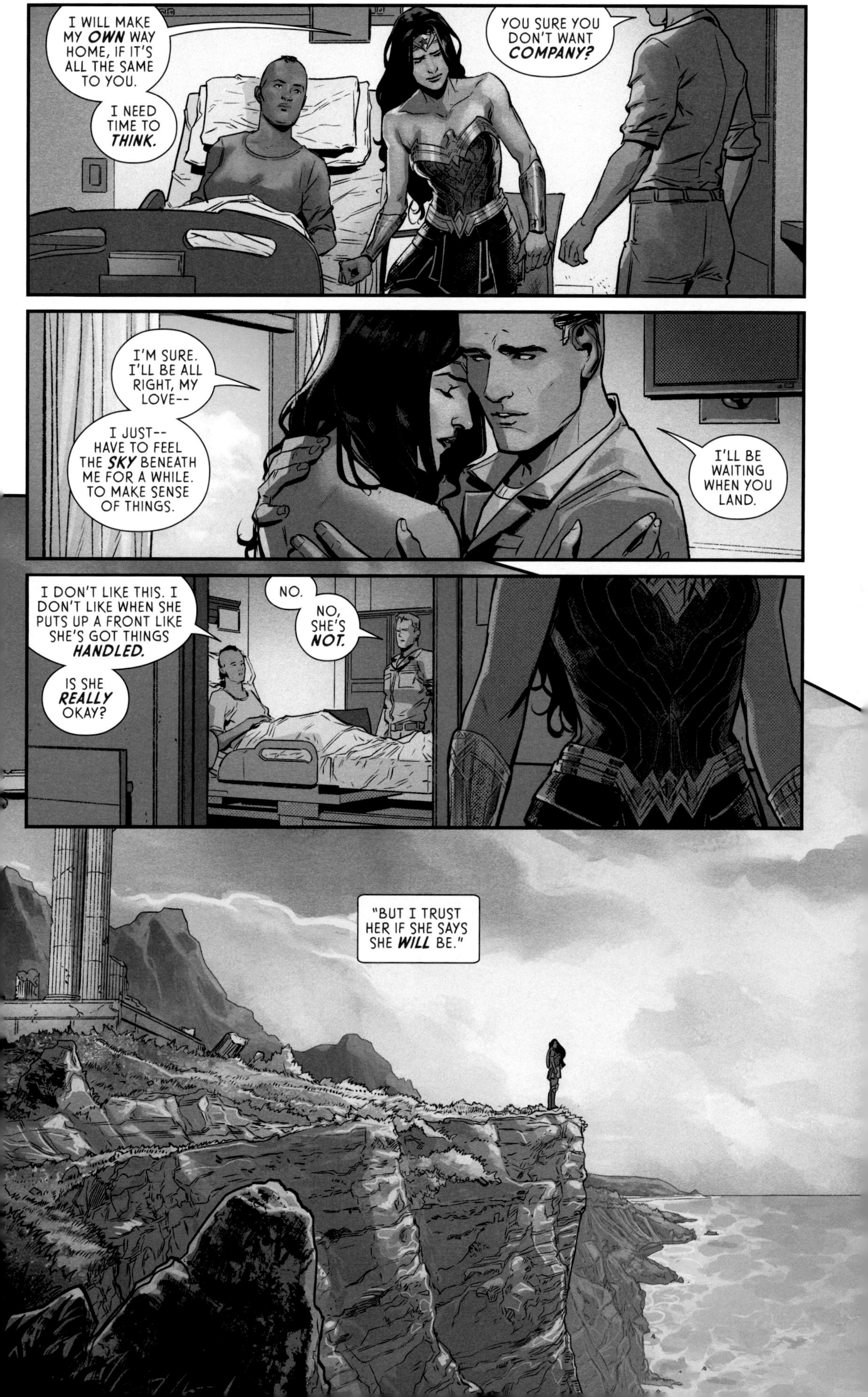

I WILL MAKE MY OWN WAY HOME, IF IT'S ALL THE SAME TO YOU.
I NEED TIME TO THINK.
YOU SURE YOU DON'T WANT COMPANY?
I'M SURE. I'LL BE ALL RIGHT, MY LOVE--
I JUST-- HAVE TO FEEL THE SKY BENEATH ME FOR A WHILE. TO MAKE SENSE OF THINGS.
I'LL BE WAITING WHEN YOU LAND.
I DON'T LIKE THIS. I DON'T LIKE WHEN SHE PUTS UP A FRONT LIKE SHE'S GOT THINGS HANDLED.
IS SHE REALLY OKAY?
NO.
NO, SHE'S NOT.
"BUT I TRUST HER IF SHE SAYS SHE WILL BE."

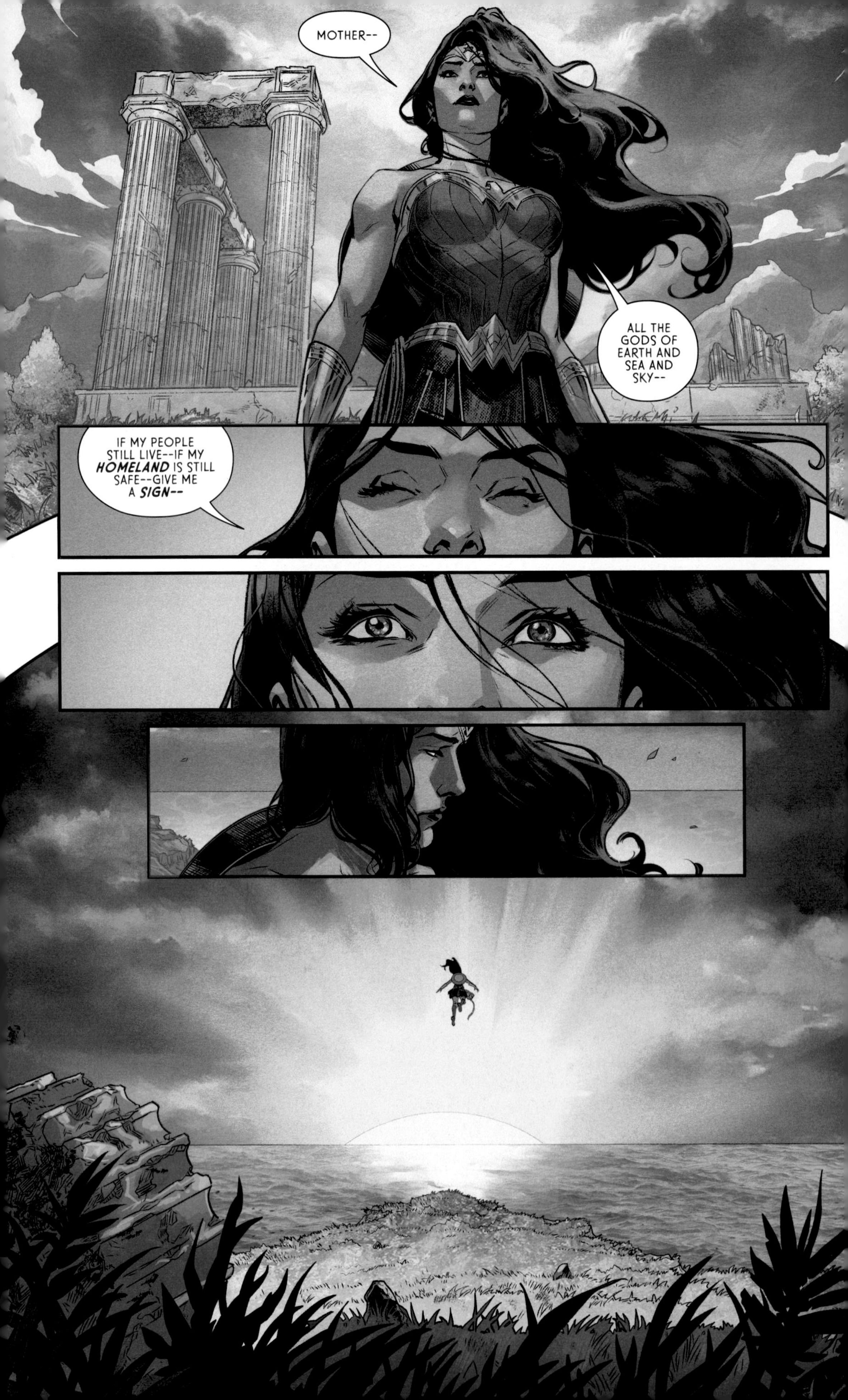

MOTHER--
ALL THE GODS OF EARTH AND SEA AND SKY--
IF MY PEOPLE STILL LIVE--IF MY **HOMELAND** IS STILL SAFE--GIVE ME A **SIGN--**

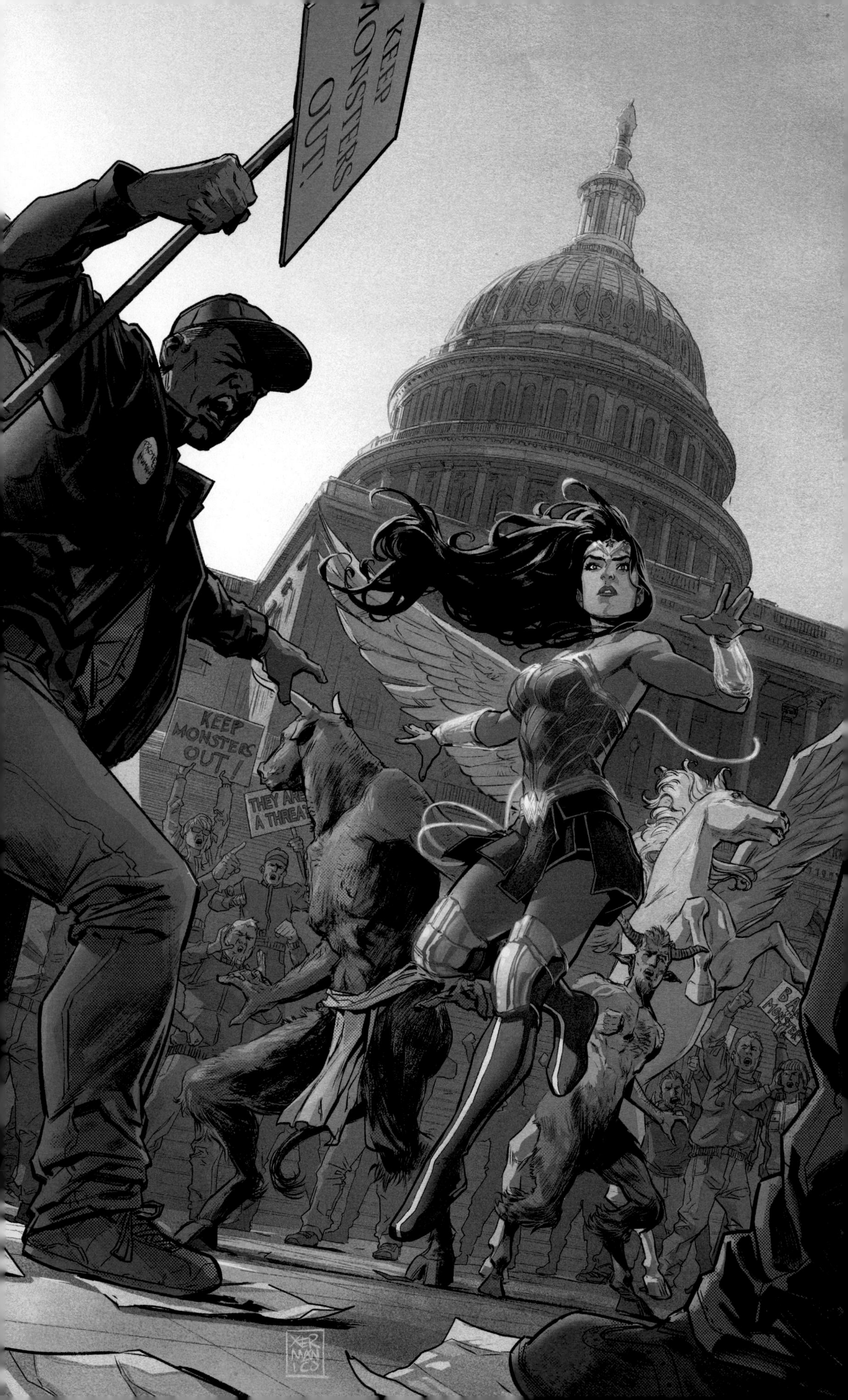
KEEP MONSTERS OUT!
KEEP MONSTERS OUT!
THEY ARE A THREAT
XERMAN '23

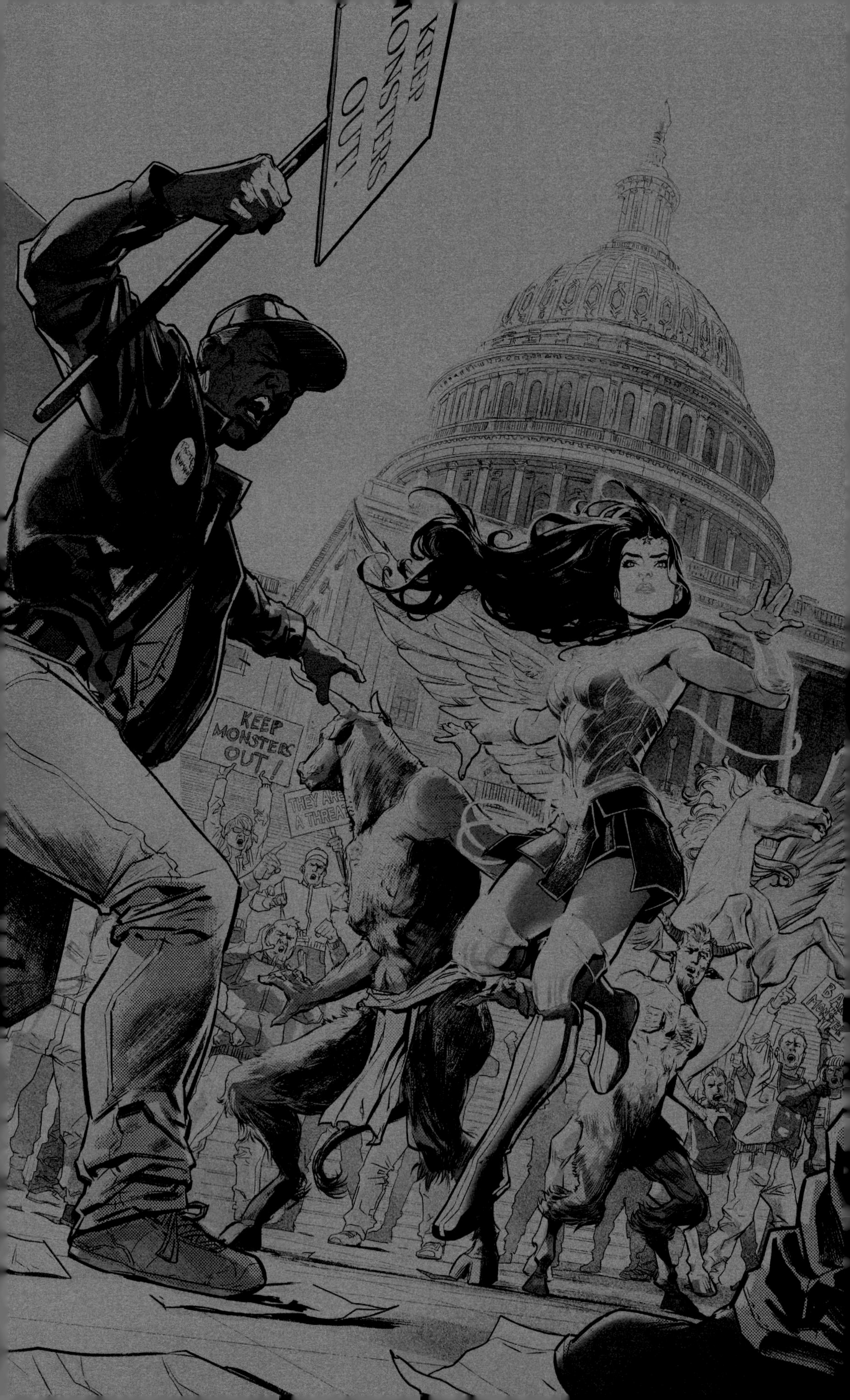
KEEP MONSTERS OUT!
KEEP MONSTERS OUT!
THEY ARE A THREAT

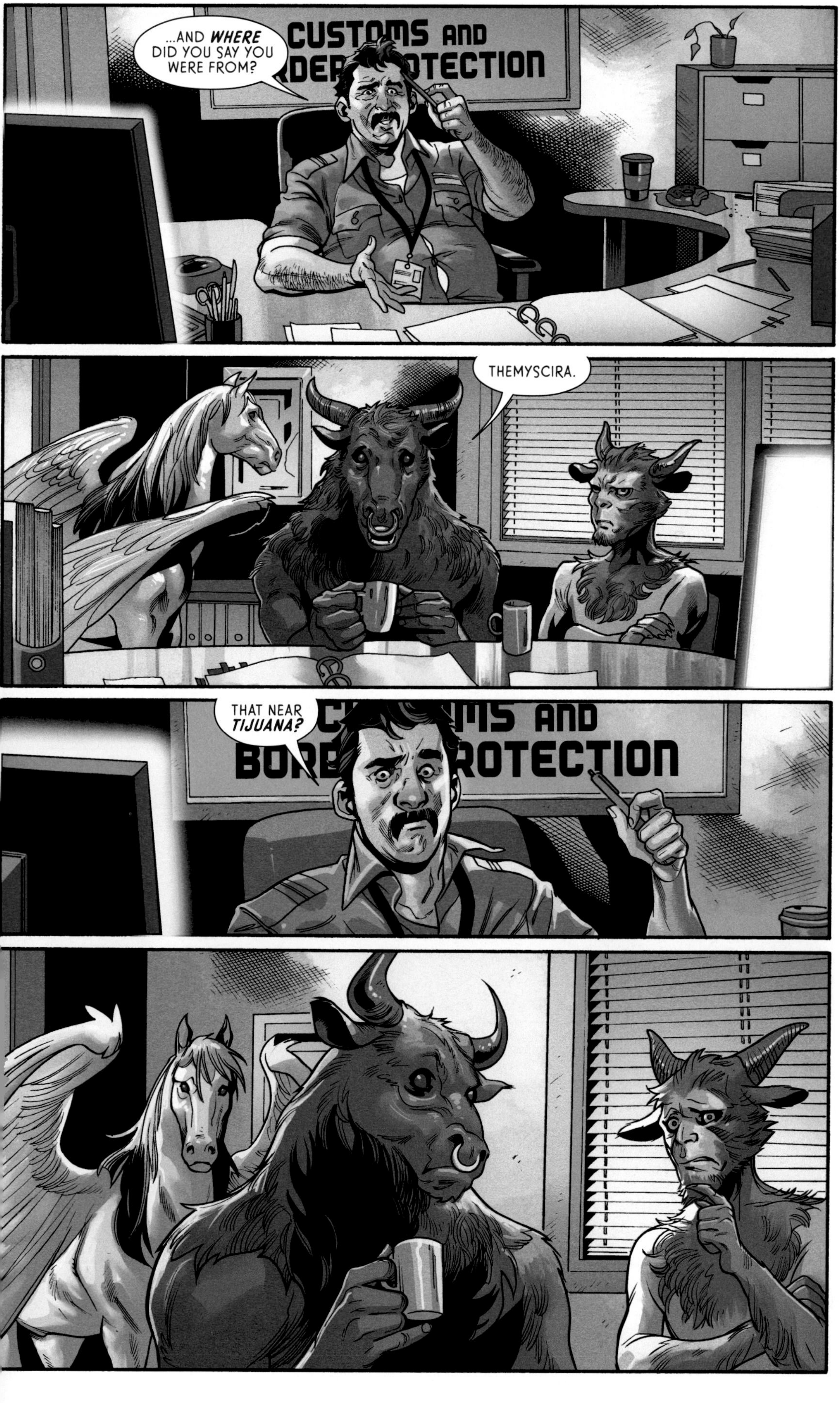
...AND *WHERE* DID YOU SAY YOU WERE FROM?
CUSTOMS AND
THEMYSCIRA.
THAT NEAR *TIJUANA?*

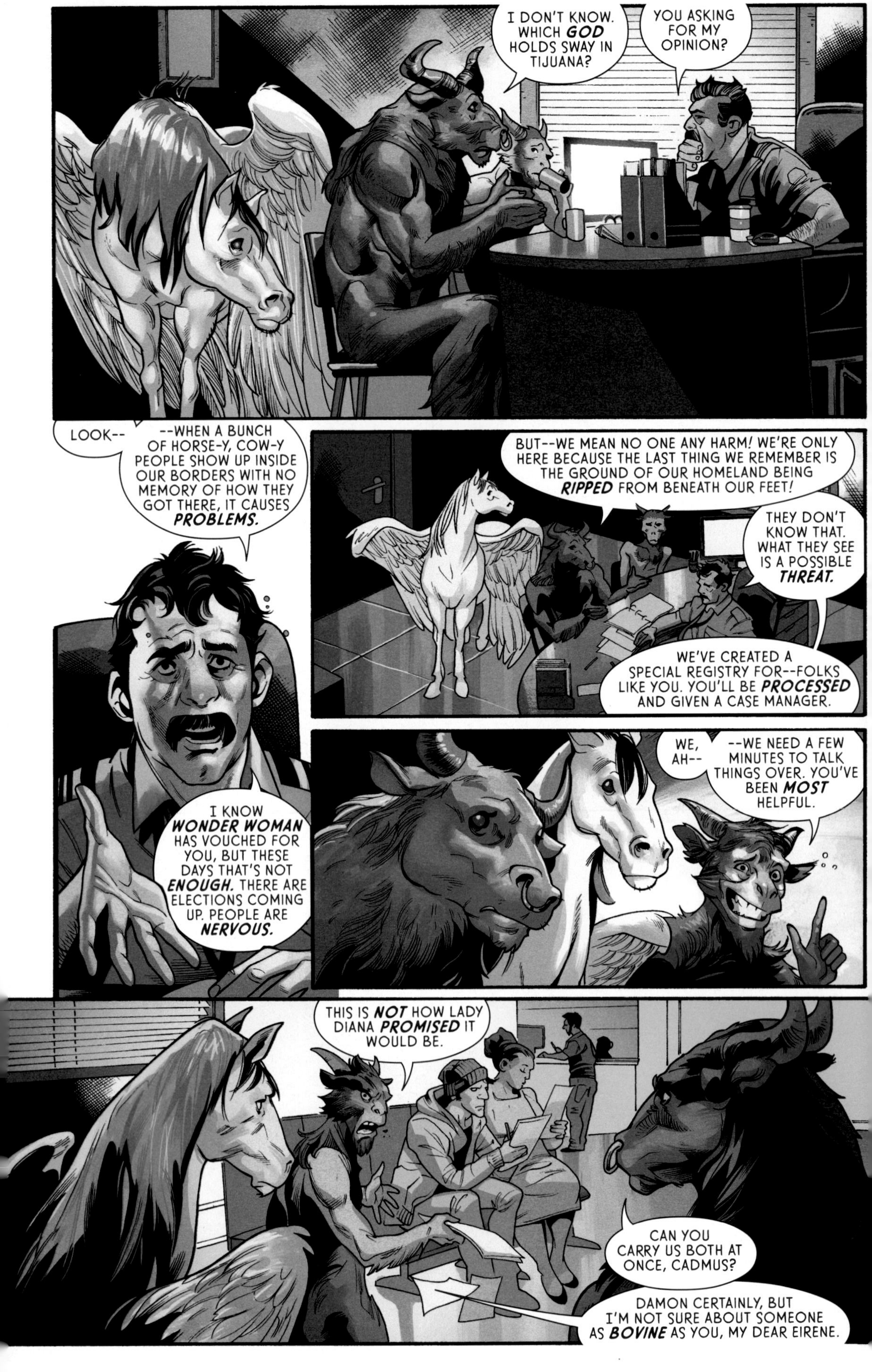

I DON'T KNOW. WHICH GOD HOLDS SWAY IN TIJUANA?
YOU ASKING FOR MY OPINION?
LOOK--
--WHEN A BUNCH OF HORSE-Y, COW-Y PEOPLE SHOW UP INSIDE OUR BORDERS WITH NO MEMORY OF HOW THEY GOT THERE, IT CAUSES PROBLEMS.
BUT--WE MEAN NO ONE ANY HARM! WE'RE ONLY HERE BECAUSE THE LAST THING WE REMEMBER IS THE GROUND OF OUR HOMELAND BEING RIPPED FROM BENEATH OUR FEET!
THEY DON'T KNOW THAT. WHAT THEY SEE IS A POSSIBLE THREAT.
WE'VE CREATED A SPECIAL REGISTRY FOR--FOLKS LIKE YOU. YOU'LL BE PROCESSED AND GIVEN A CASE MANAGER.
I KNOW WONDER WOMAN HAS VOUCHED FOR YOU, BUT THESE DAYS THAT'S NOT ENOUGH. THERE ARE ELECTIONS COMING UP. PEOPLE ARE NERVOUS.
WE, AH--
--WE NEED A FEW MINUTES TO TALK THINGS OVER. YOU'VE BEEN MOST HELPFUL.
THIS IS NOT HOW LADY DIANA PROMISED IT WOULD BE.
CAN YOU CARRY US BOTH AT ONCE, CADMUS?
DAMON CERTAINLY, BUT I'M NOT SURE ABOUT SOMEONE AS BOVINE AS YOU, MY DEAR EIRENE.

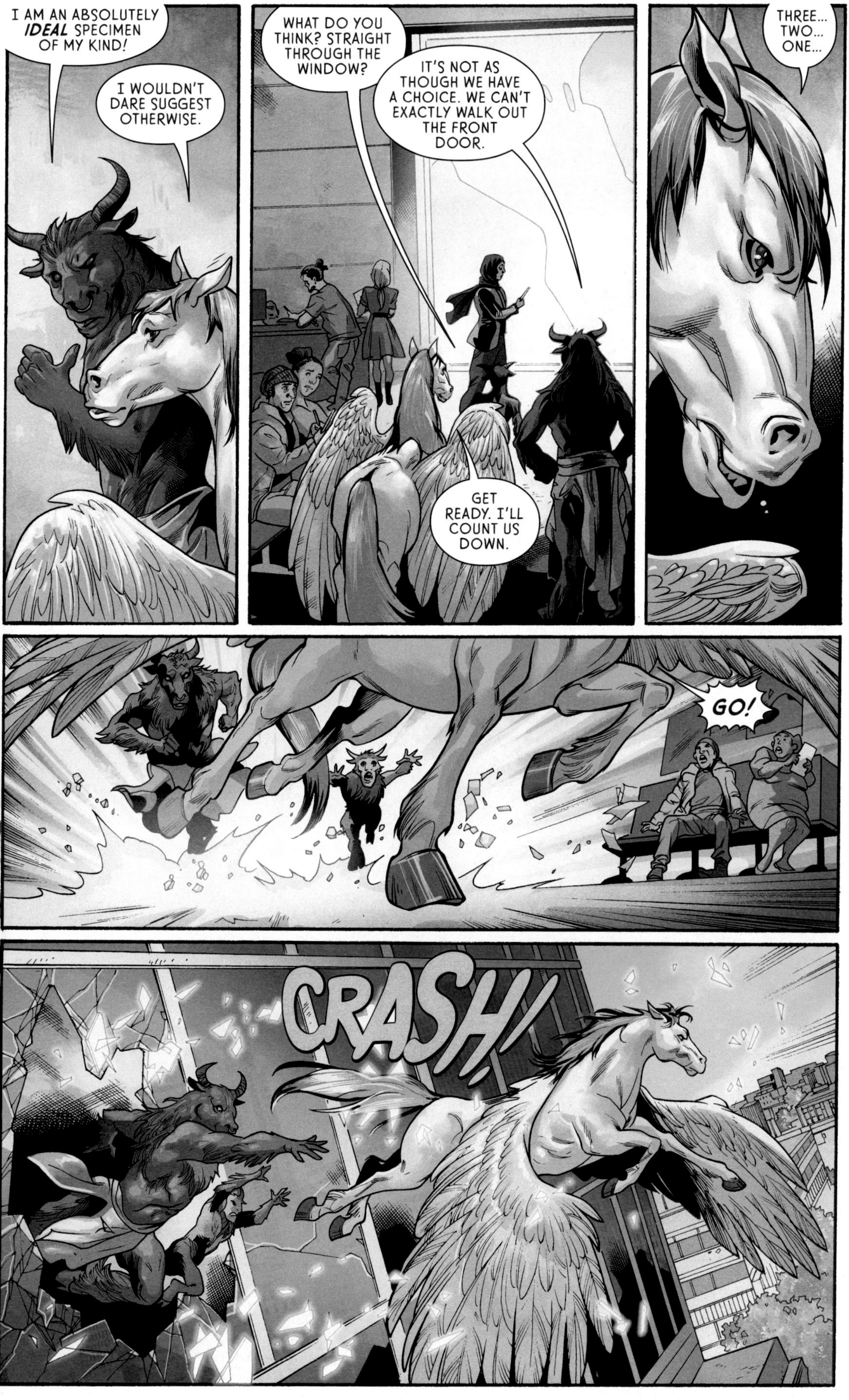

I AM AN ABSOLUTELY *IDEAL* SPECIMEN OF MY KIND!
I WOULDN'T DARE SUGGEST OTHERWISE.
WHAT DO YOU THINK? STRAIGHT THROUGH THE WINDOW?
IT'S NOT AS THOUGH WE HAVE A CHOICE. WE CAN'T EXACTLY WALK OUT THE FRONT DOOR.
GET READY. I'LL COUNT US DOWN.
THREE... TWO... ONE...
GO!
CRASH!

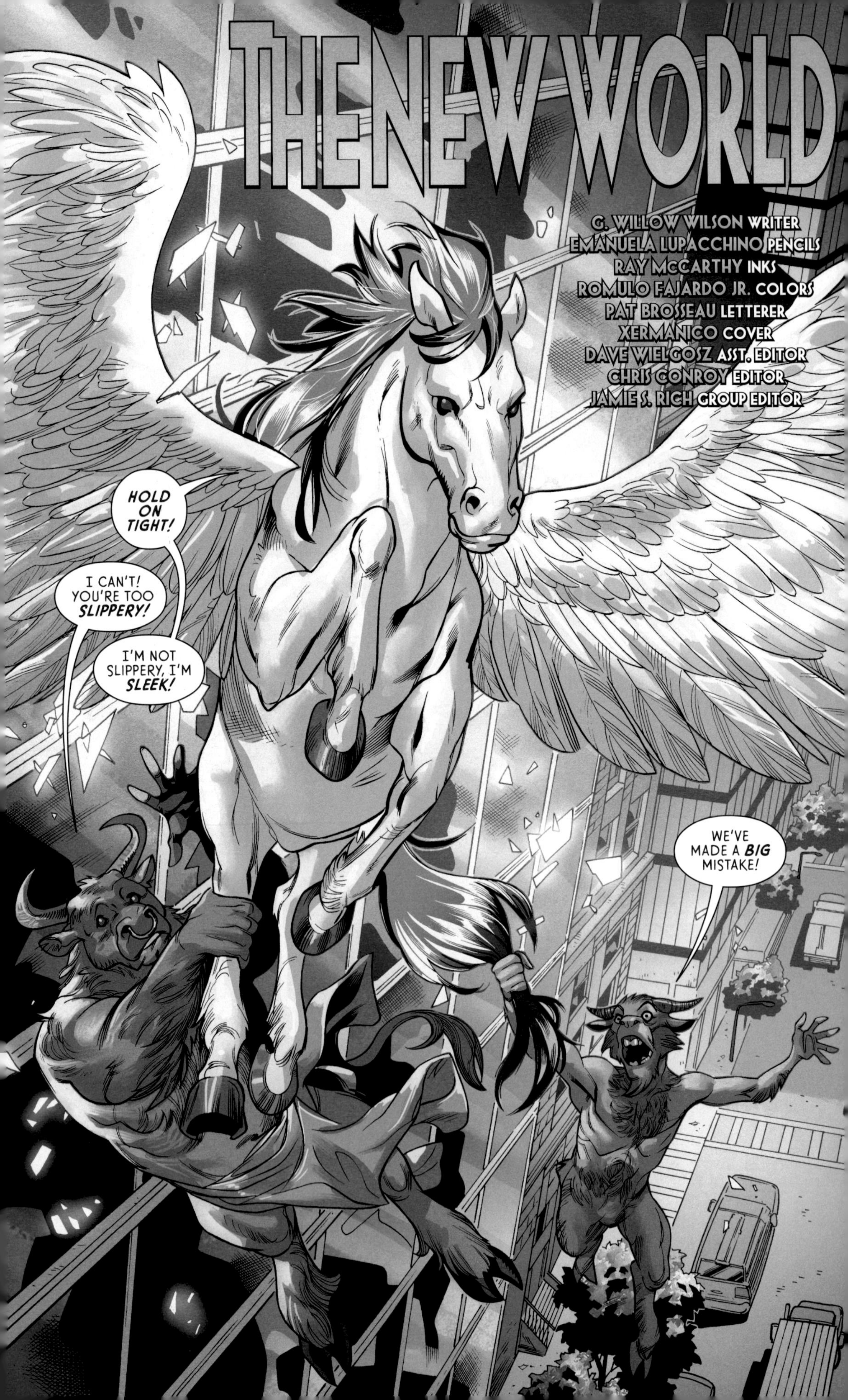
THE NEW WORLD
G. WILLOW WILSON WRITER
EMANUELA LUPACCHINO PENCILS
RAY McCARTHY INKS
ROMULO FAJARDO JR. COLORS
PAT BROSSEAU LETTERER
XERMANICO COVER
DAVE WIELGOSZ ASST. EDITOR
CHRIS CONROY EDITOR
JAMIE S. RICH GROUP EDITOR
HOLD ON TIGHT!
I CAN'T! YOU'RE TOO SLIPPERY!
I'M NOT SLIPPERY, I'M SLEEK!
WE'VE MADE A BIG MISTAKE!

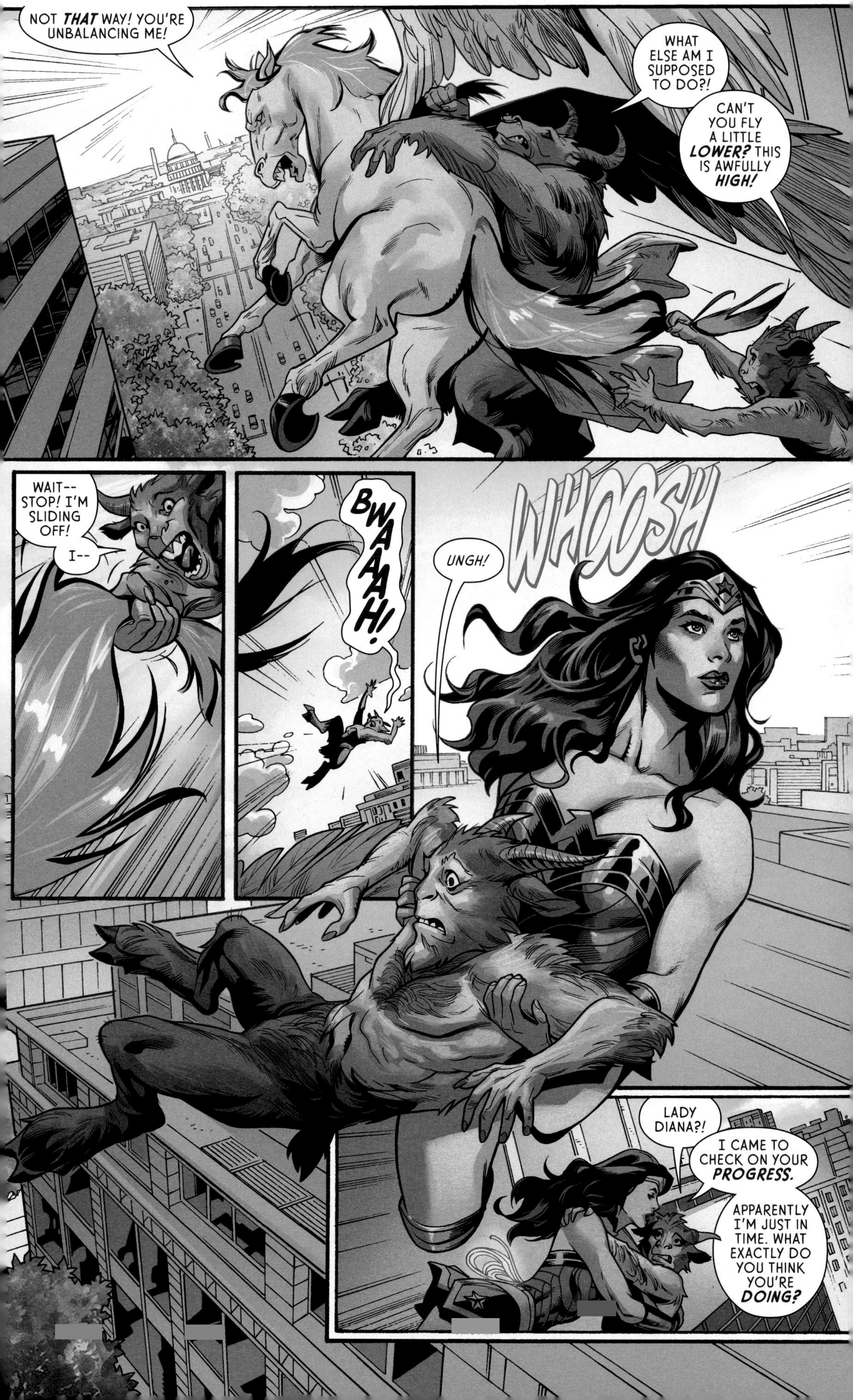

NOT THAT WAY! YOU'RE UNBALANCING ME!
WHAT ELSE AM I SUPPOSED TO DO?!
CAN'T YOU FLY A LITTLE LOWER? THIS IS AWFULLY HIGH!
WAIT-- STOP! I'M SLIDING OFF!
I--
BWAAAAH!
WHOOSH
UNGH!
LADY DIANA?!
I CAME TO CHECK ON YOUR PROGRESS.
APPARENTLY I'M JUST IN TIME. WHAT EXACTLY DO YOU THINK YOU'RE DOING?

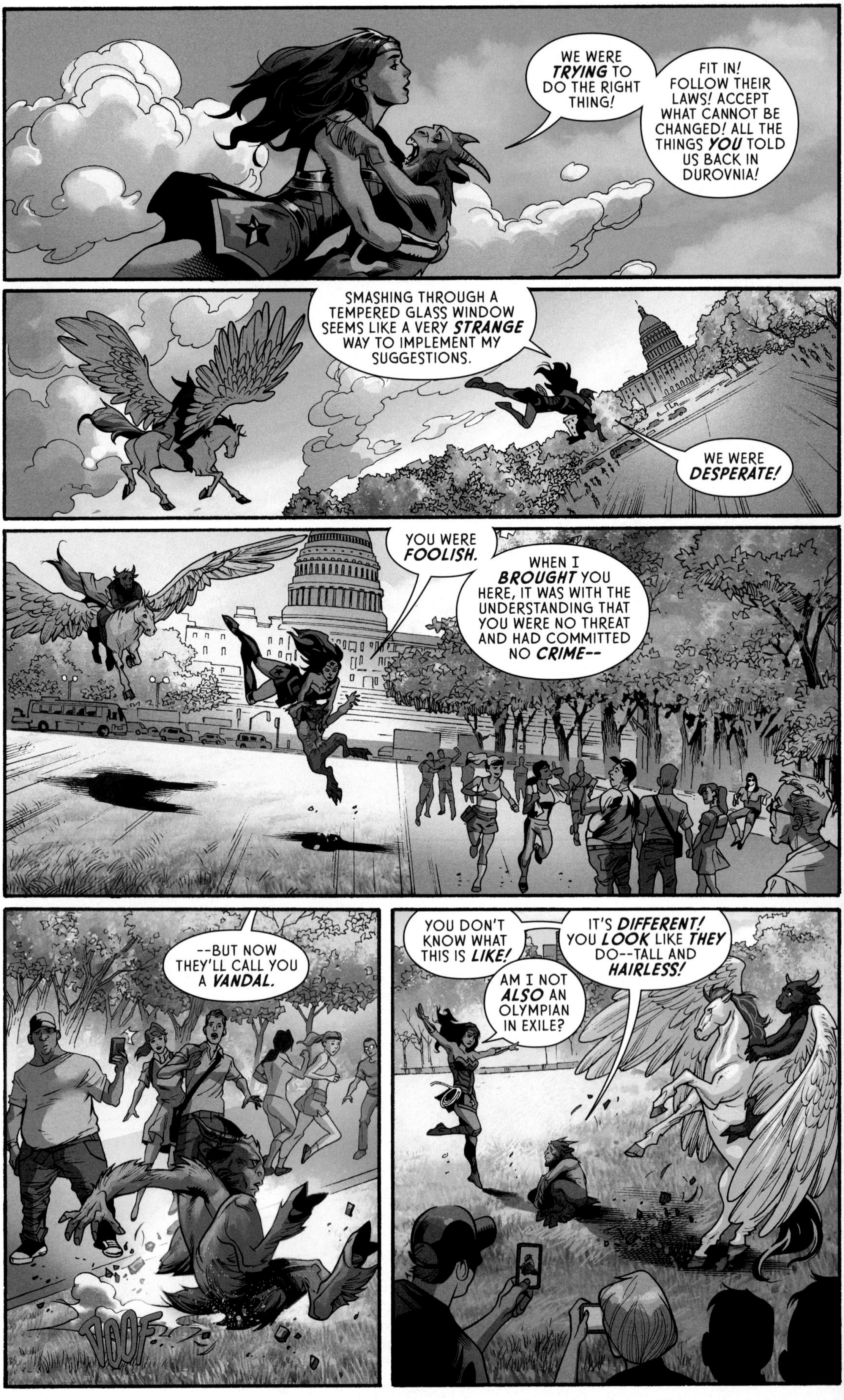

WE WERE TRYING TO DO THE RIGHT THING!
FIT IN! FOLLOW THEIR LAWS! ACCEPT WHAT CANNOT BE CHANGED! ALL THE THINGS YOU TOLD US BACK IN DUROVNIA!
SMASHING THROUGH A TEMPERED GLASS WINDOW SEEMS LIKE A VERY STRANGE WAY TO IMPLEMENT MY SUGGESTIONS.
WE WERE DESPERATE!
YOU WERE FOOLISH.
WHEN I BROUGHT YOU HERE, IT WAS WITH THE UNDERSTANDING THAT YOU WERE NO THREAT AND HAD COMMITTED NO CRIME--
--BUT NOW THEY'LL CALL YOU A VANDAL.
DOOF
YOU DON'T KNOW WHAT THIS IS LIKE!
IT'S DIFFERENT! YOU LOOK LIKE THEY DO--TALL AND HAIRLESS!
AM I NOT ALSO AN OLYMPIAN IN EXILE?

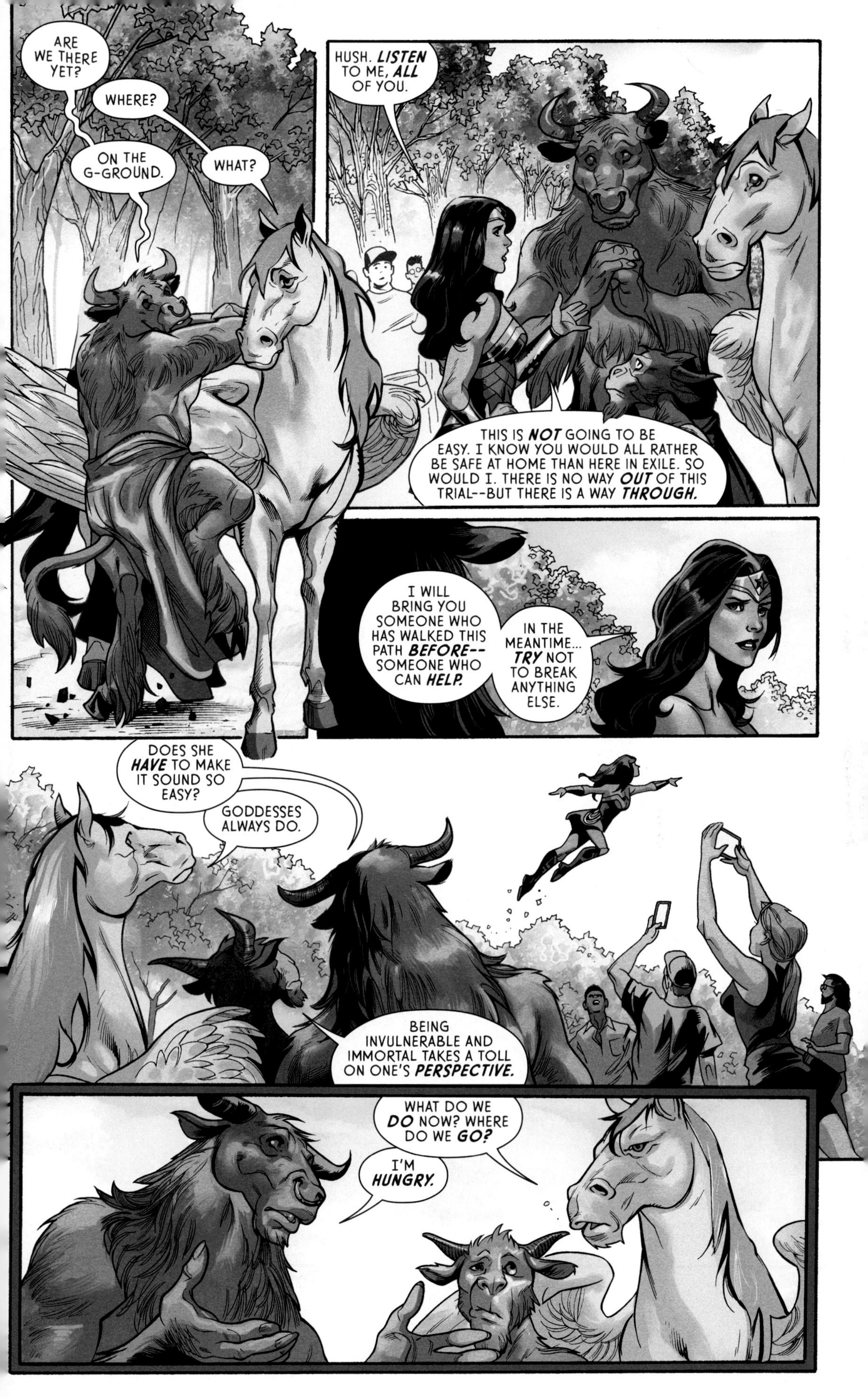
ARE WE THERE YET?
WHERE?
ON THE G-GROUND.
WHAT?
HUSH. LISTEN TO ME, ALL OF YOU.
THIS IS NOT GOING TO BE EASY. I KNOW YOU WOULD ALL RATHER BE SAFE AT HOME THAN HERE IN EXILE. SO WOULD I. THERE IS NO WAY OUT OF THIS TRIAL--BUT THERE IS A WAY THROUGH.
I WILL BRING YOU SOMEONE WHO HAS WALKED THIS PATH BEFORE-- SOMEONE WHO CAN HELP.
IN THE MEANTIME... TRY NOT TO BREAK ANYTHING ELSE.
DOES SHE HAVE TO MAKE IT SOUND SO EASY?
GODDESSES ALWAYS DO.
BEING INVULNERABLE AND IMMORTAL TAKES A TOLL ON ONE'S PERSPECTIVE.
WHAT DO WE DO NOW? WHERE DO WE GO?
I'M HUNGRY.

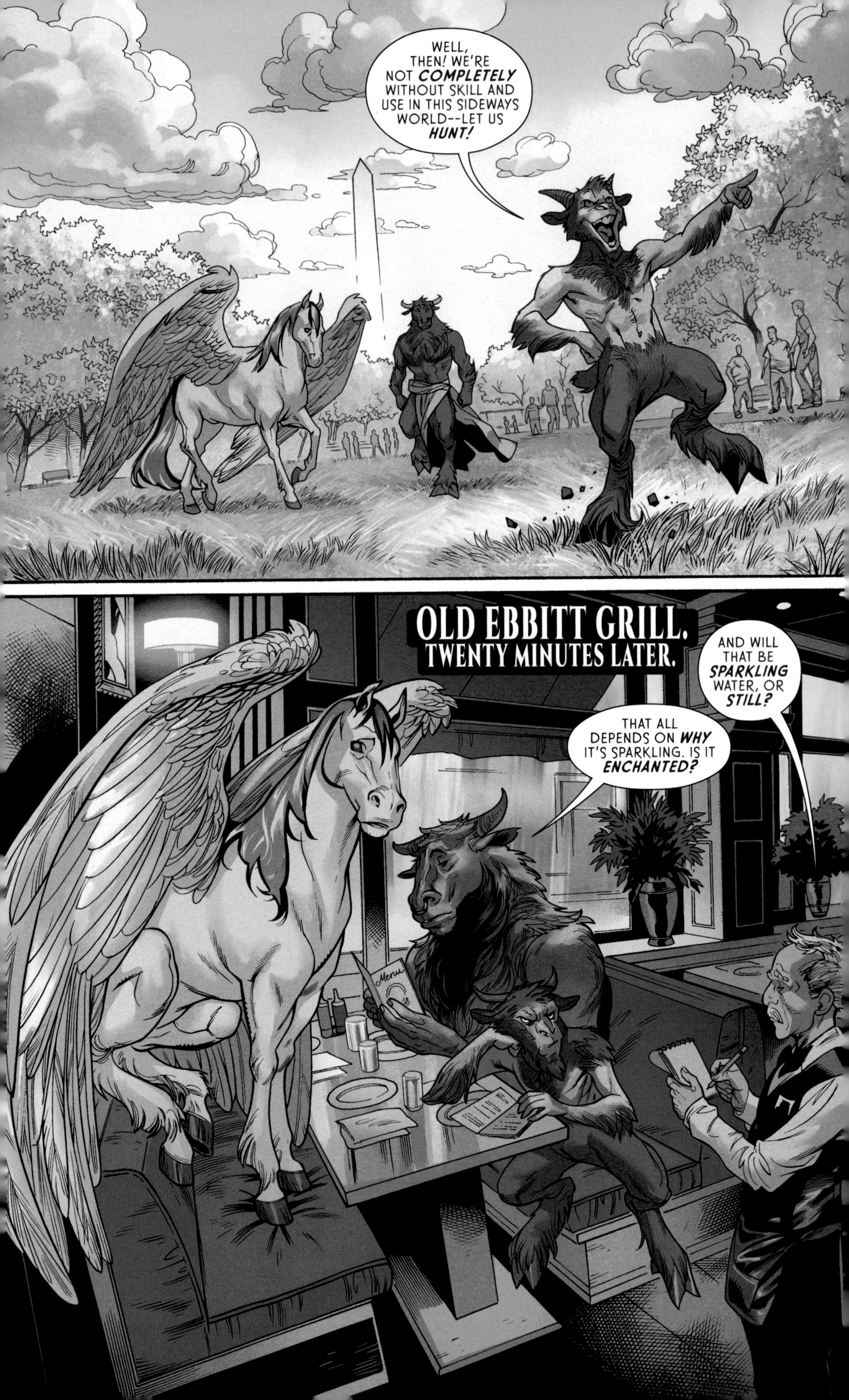
WELL, THEN! WE'RE NOT COMPLETELY WITHOUT SKILL AND USE IN THIS SIDEWAYS WORLD--LET US HUNT!
OLD EBBITT GRILL. TWENTY MINUTES LATER.
AND WILL THAT BE SPARKLING WATER, OR STILL?
THAT ALL DEPENDS ON WHY IT'S SPARKLING. IS IT ENCHANTED?
Menu

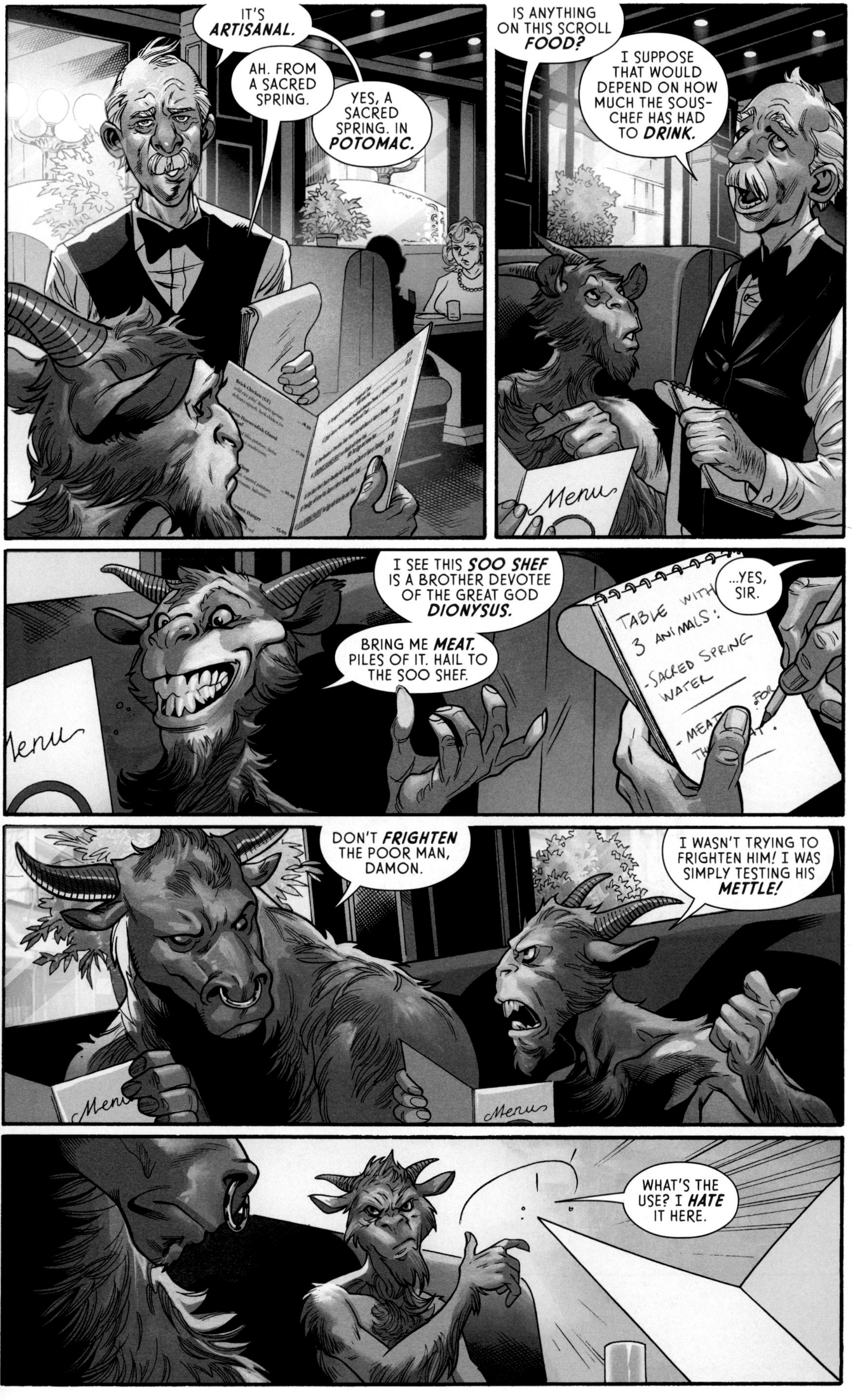

IT'S *ARTISANAL.*
AH. FROM A SACRED SPRING.
YES, A SACRED SPRING. IN *POTOMAC.*
IS ANYTHING ON THIS SCROLL *FOOD?*
I SUPPOSE THAT WOULD DEPEND ON HOW MUCH THE SOUS-CHEF HAS HAD TO *DRINK.*
Menu
I SEE THIS *SOO SHEF* IS A BROTHER DEVOTEE OF THE GREAT GOD *DIONYSUS.*
BRING ME *MEAT.* PILES OF IT. HAIL TO THE SOO SHEF.
TABLE WITH 3 ANIMALS:
-SACRED SPRING WATER
...YES, SIR.
DON'T *FRIGHTEN* THE POOR MAN, DAMON.
I WASN'T TRYING TO FRIGHTEN HIM! I WAS SIMPLY TESTING HIS *METTLE!*
WHAT'S THE USE? I *HATE* IT HERE.

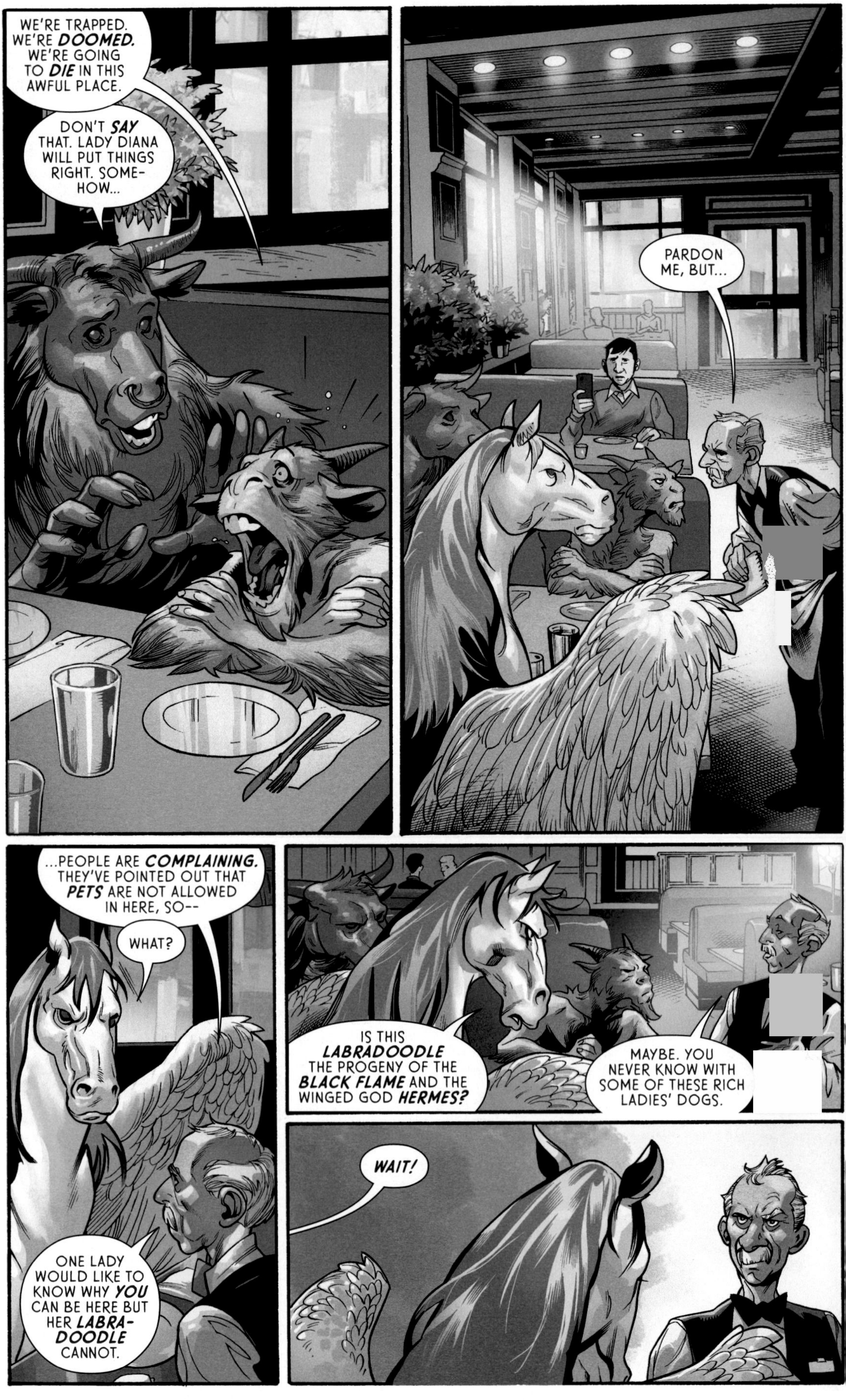
WE'RE TRAPPED. WE'RE DOOMED. WE'RE GOING TO DIE IN THIS AWFUL PLACE.
DON'T SAY THAT. LADY DIANA WILL PUT THINGS RIGHT. SOME-HOW...
PARDON ME, BUT...
...PEOPLE ARE COMPLAINING. THEY'VE POINTED OUT THAT PETS ARE NOT ALLOWED IN HERE, SO--
WHAT?
ONE LADY WOULD LIKE TO KNOW WHY YOU CAN BE HERE BUT HER LABRA-DOODLE CANNOT.
IS THIS LABRADOODLE THE PROGENY OF THE BLACK FLAME AND THE WINGED GOD HERMES?
MAYBE. YOU NEVER KNOW WITH SOME OF THESE RICH LADIES' DOGS.
WAIT!

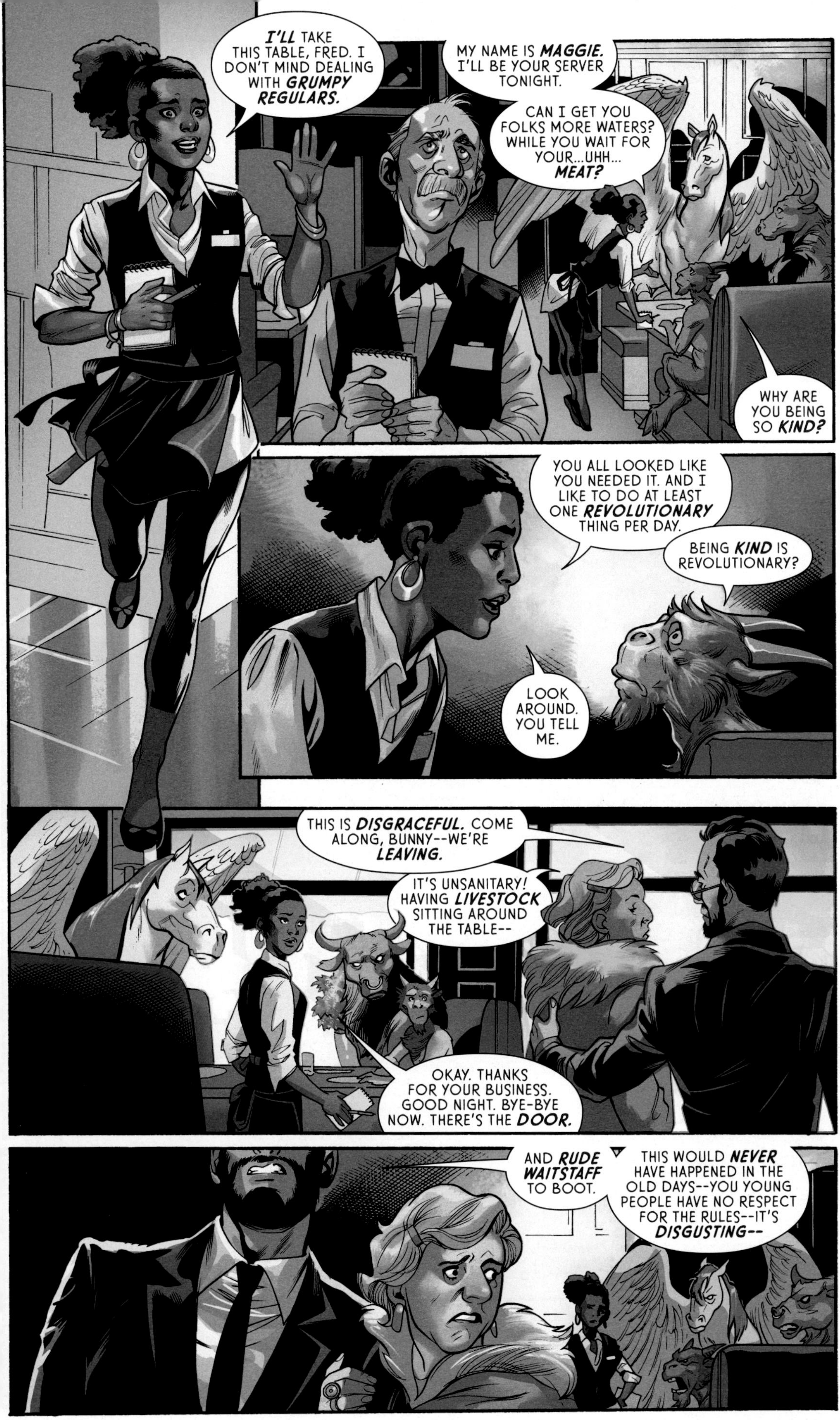

I'LL TAKE THIS TABLE, FRED. I DON'T MIND DEALING WITH GRUMPY REGULARS.
MY NAME IS MAGGIE. I'LL BE YOUR SERVER TONIGHT.
CAN I GET YOU FOLKS MORE WATERS? WHILE YOU WAIT FOR YOUR...UHH... MEAT?
WHY ARE YOU BEING SO KIND?
YOU ALL LOOKED LIKE YOU NEEDED IT. AND I LIKE TO DO AT LEAST ONE REVOLUTIONARY THING PER DAY.
BEING KIND IS REVOLUTIONARY?
LOOK AROUND. YOU TELL ME.
THIS IS DISGRACEFUL. COME ALONG, BUNNY--WE'RE LEAVING.
IT'S UNSANITARY! HAVING LIVESTOCK SITTING AROUND THE TABLE--
OKAY. THANKS FOR YOUR BUSINESS. GOOD NIGHT. BYE-BYE NOW. THERE'S THE DOOR.
AND RUDE WAITSTAFF TO BOOT.
THIS WOULD NEVER HAVE HAPPENED IN THE OLD DAYS--YOU YOUNG PEOPLE HAVE NO RESPECT FOR THE RULES--IT'S DISGUSTING--

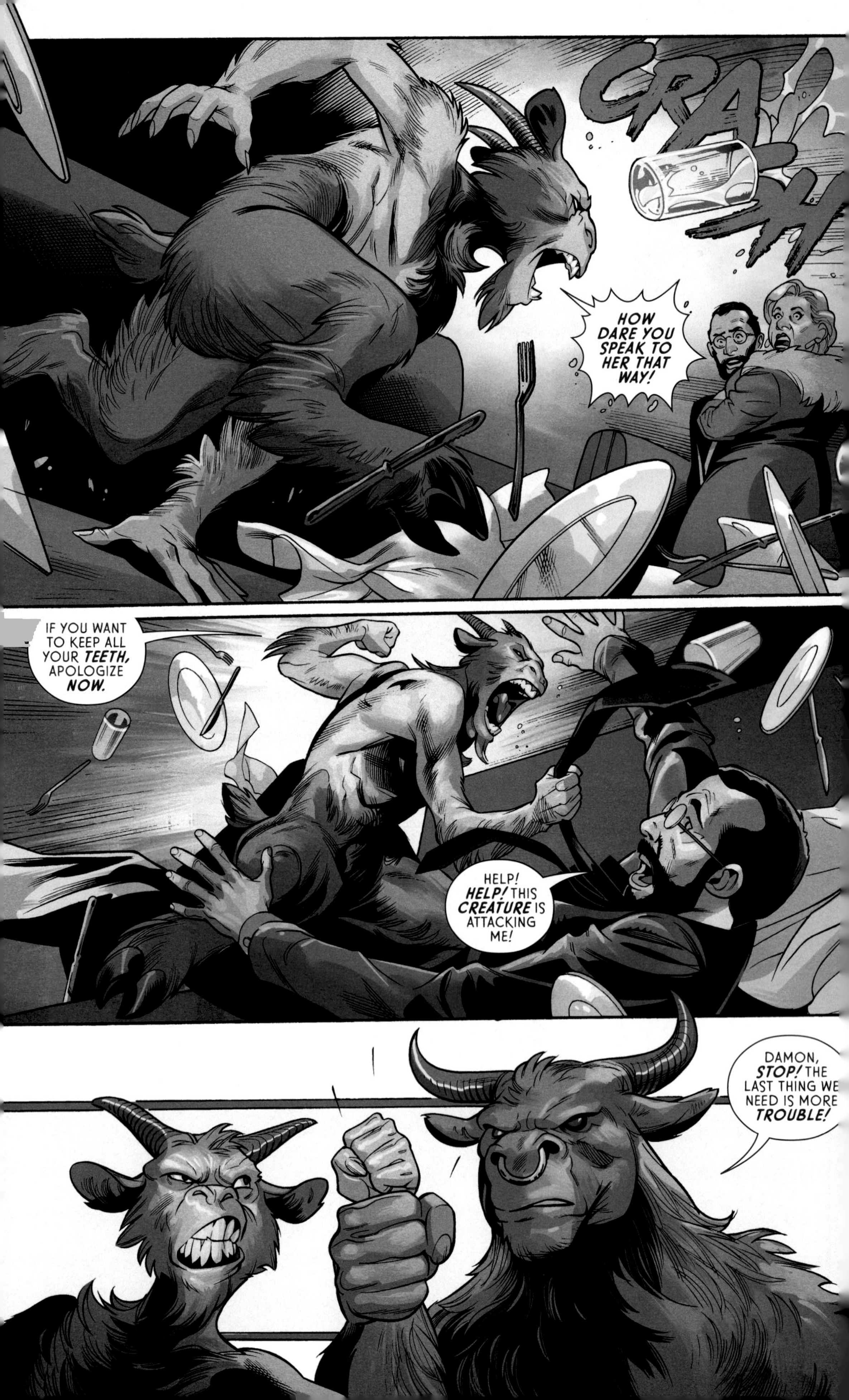
CRASH
HOW DARE YOU SPEAK TO HER THAT WAY!
IF YOU WANT TO KEEP ALL YOUR TEETH, APOLOGIZE NOW.
HELP! HELP! THIS CREATURE IS ATTACKING ME!
DAMON, STOP! THE LAST THING WE NEED IS MORE TROUBLE!

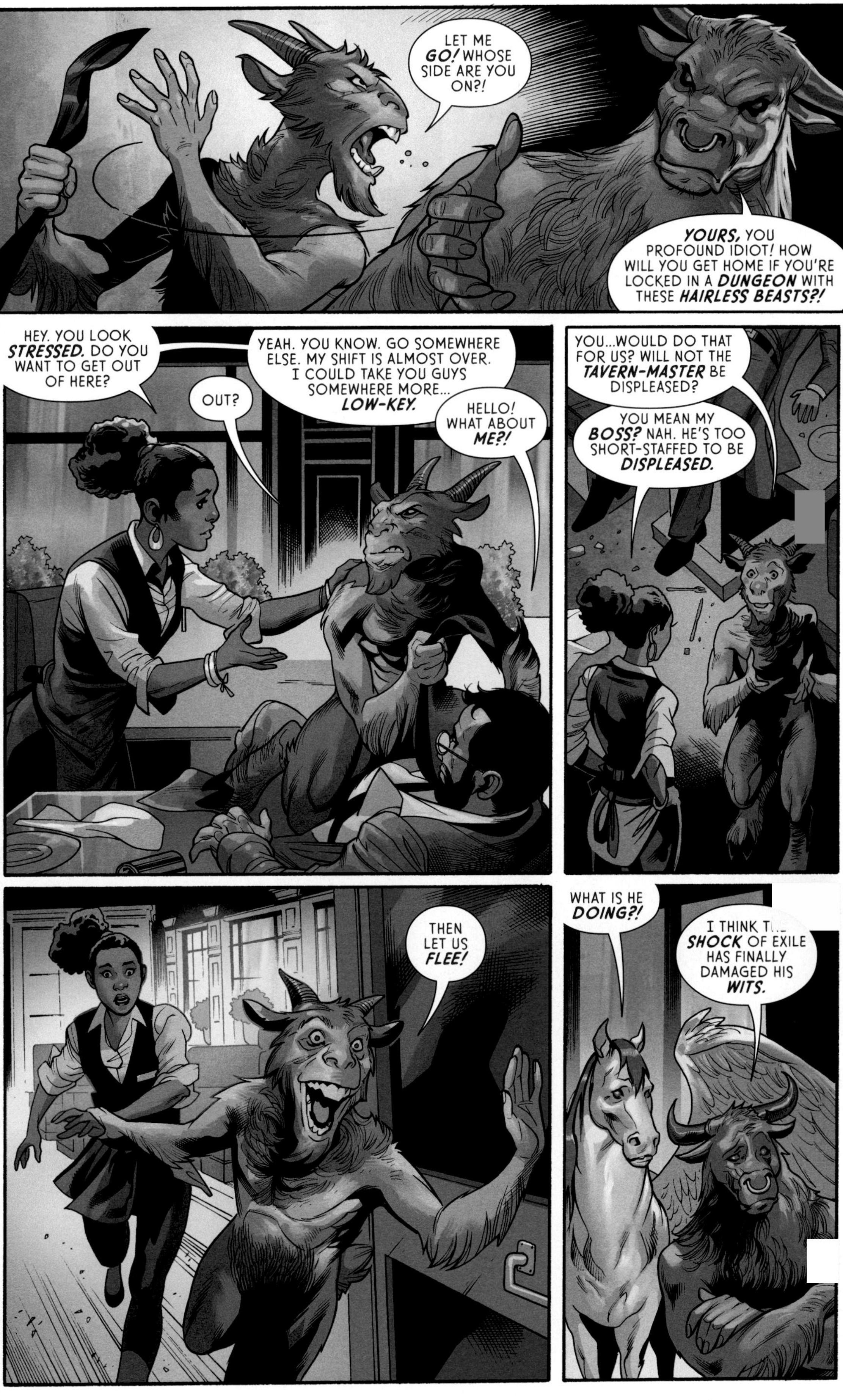

LET ME GO! WHOSE SIDE ARE YOU ON?!
YOURS, YOU PROFOUND IDIOT! HOW WILL YOU GET HOME IF YOU'RE LOCKED IN A DUNGEON WITH THESE HAIRLESS BEASTS?!
HEY. YOU LOOK STRESSED. DO YOU WANT TO GET OUT OF HERE?
OUT?
YEAH. YOU KNOW. GO SOMEWHERE ELSE. MY SHIFT IS ALMOST OVER. I COULD TAKE YOU GUYS SOMEWHERE MORE... LOW-KEY.
HELLO! WHAT ABOUT ME?!
YOU...WOULD DO THAT FOR US? WILL NOT THE TAVERN-MASTER BE DISPLEASED?
YOU MEAN MY BOSS? NAH. HE'S TOO SHORT-STAFFED TO BE DISPLEASED.
THEN LET US FLEE!
WHAT IS HE DOING?!
I THINK TH SHOCK OF EXILE HAS FINALLY DAMAGED HIS WITS.

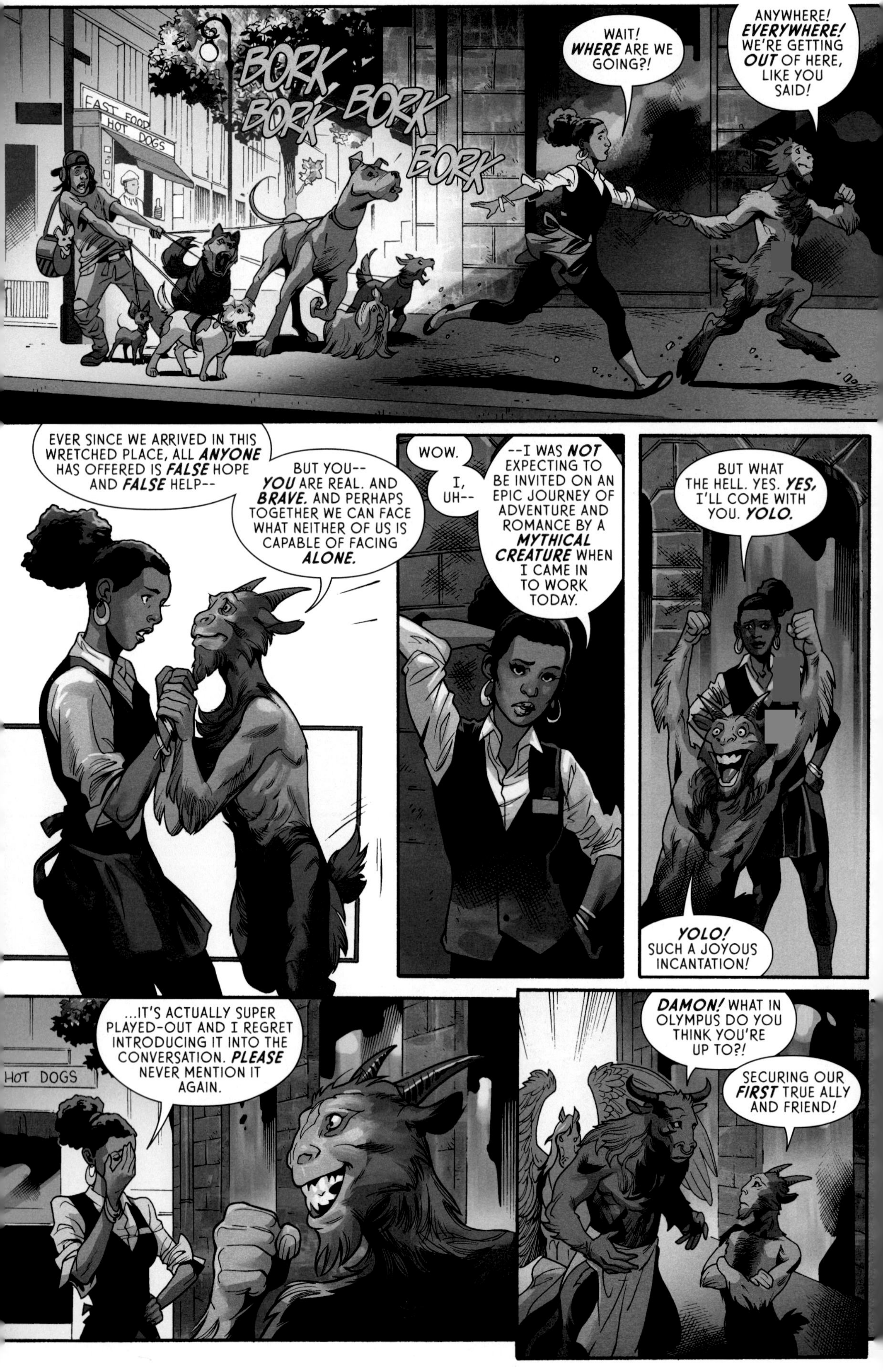
BORK BORK BORK BORK
WAIT! WHERE ARE WE GOING?!
ANYWHERE! EVERYWHERE! WE'RE GETTING OUT OF HERE, LIKE YOU SAID!
FAST FOOD
HOT DOGS
EVER SINCE WE ARRIVED IN THIS WRETCHED PLACE, ALL ANYONE HAS OFFERED IS FALSE HOPE AND FALSE HELP--
BUT YOU-- YOU ARE REAL. AND BRAVE. AND PERHAPS TOGETHER WE CAN FACE WHAT NEITHER OF US IS CAPABLE OF FACING ALONE.
WOW.
I, UH--
--I WAS NOT EXPECTING TO BE INVITED ON AN EPIC JOURNEY OF ADVENTURE AND ROMANCE BY A MYTHICAL CREATURE WHEN I CAME IN TO WORK TODAY.
BUT WHAT THE HELL. YES. YES, I'LL COME WITH YOU. YOLO.
YOLO! SUCH A JOYOUS INCANTATION!
HOT DOGS
...IT'S ACTUALLY SUPER PLAYED-OUT AND I REGRET INTRODUCING IT INTO THE CONVERSATION. PLEASE NEVER MENTION IT AGAIN.
DAMON! WHAT IN OLYMPUS DO YOU THINK YOU'RE UP TO?!
SECURING OUR FIRST TRUE ALLY AND FRIEND!

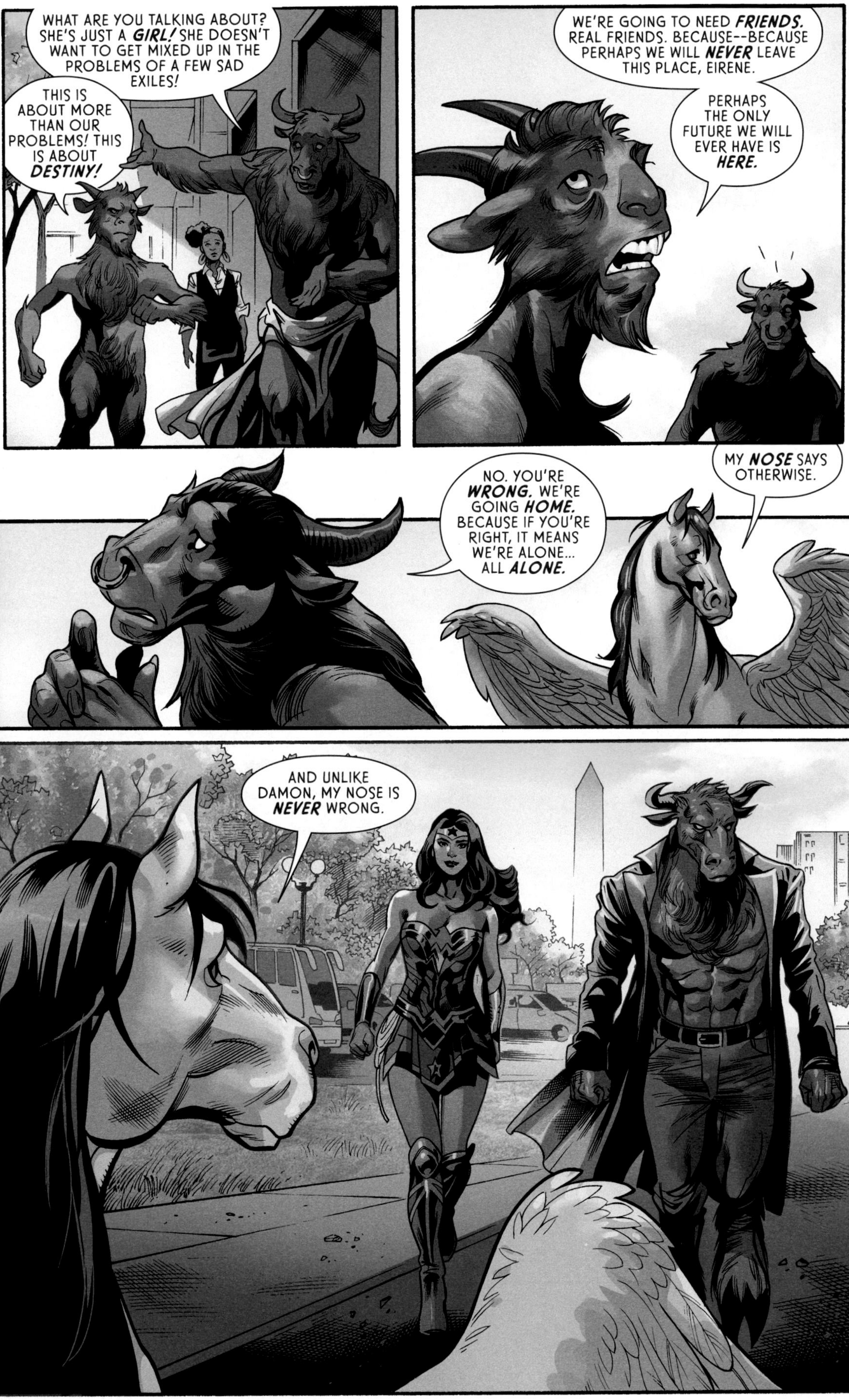
WHAT ARE YOU TALKING ABOUT? SHE'S JUST A *GIRL!* SHE DOESN'T WANT TO GET MIXED UP IN THE PROBLEMS OF A FEW SAD EXILES!
THIS IS ABOUT MORE THAN OUR PROBLEMS! THIS IS ABOUT *DESTINY!*
WE'RE GOING TO NEED *FRIENDS.* REAL FRIENDS. BECAUSE--BECAUSE PERHAPS WE WILL *NEVER* LEAVE THIS PLACE, EIRENE.
PERHAPS THE ONLY FUTURE WE WILL EVER HAVE IS *HERE.*
NO. YOU'RE *WRONG.* WE'RE GOING *HOME.* BECAUSE IF YOU'RE RIGHT, IT MEANS WE'RE ALONE... ALL *ALONE.*
MY *NOSE* SAYS OTHERWISE.
AND UNLIKE DAMON, MY NOSE IS *NEVER* WRONG.

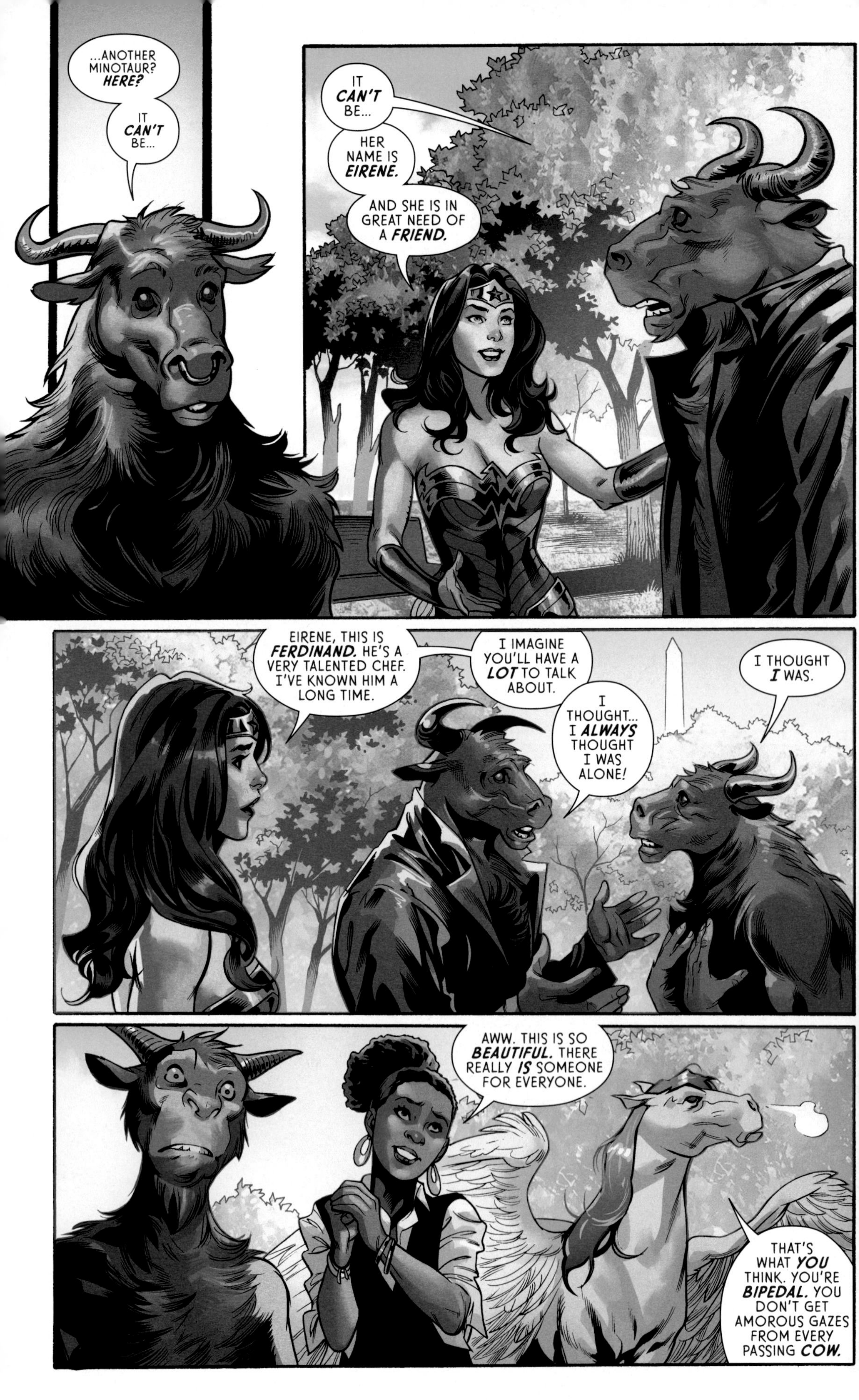
...ANOTHER MINOTAUR? **HERE?**
IT **CAN'T** BE...
IT **CAN'T** BE...
HER NAME IS **EIRENE.**
AND SHE IS IN GREAT NEED OF A **FRIEND.**
EIRENE, THIS IS **FERDINAND.** HE'S A VERY TALENTED CHEF. I'VE KNOWN HIM A LONG TIME.
I IMAGINE YOU'LL HAVE A **LOT** TO TALK ABOUT.
I THOUGHT... I **ALWAYS** THOUGHT I WAS ALONE!
I THOUGHT **I** WAS.
AWW. THIS IS SO **BEAUTIFUL.** THERE REALLY **IS** SOMEONE FOR EVERYONE.
THAT'S WHAT **YOU** THINK. YOU'RE **BIPEDAL.** YOU DON'T GET AMOROUS GAZES FROM EVERY PASSING **COW.**

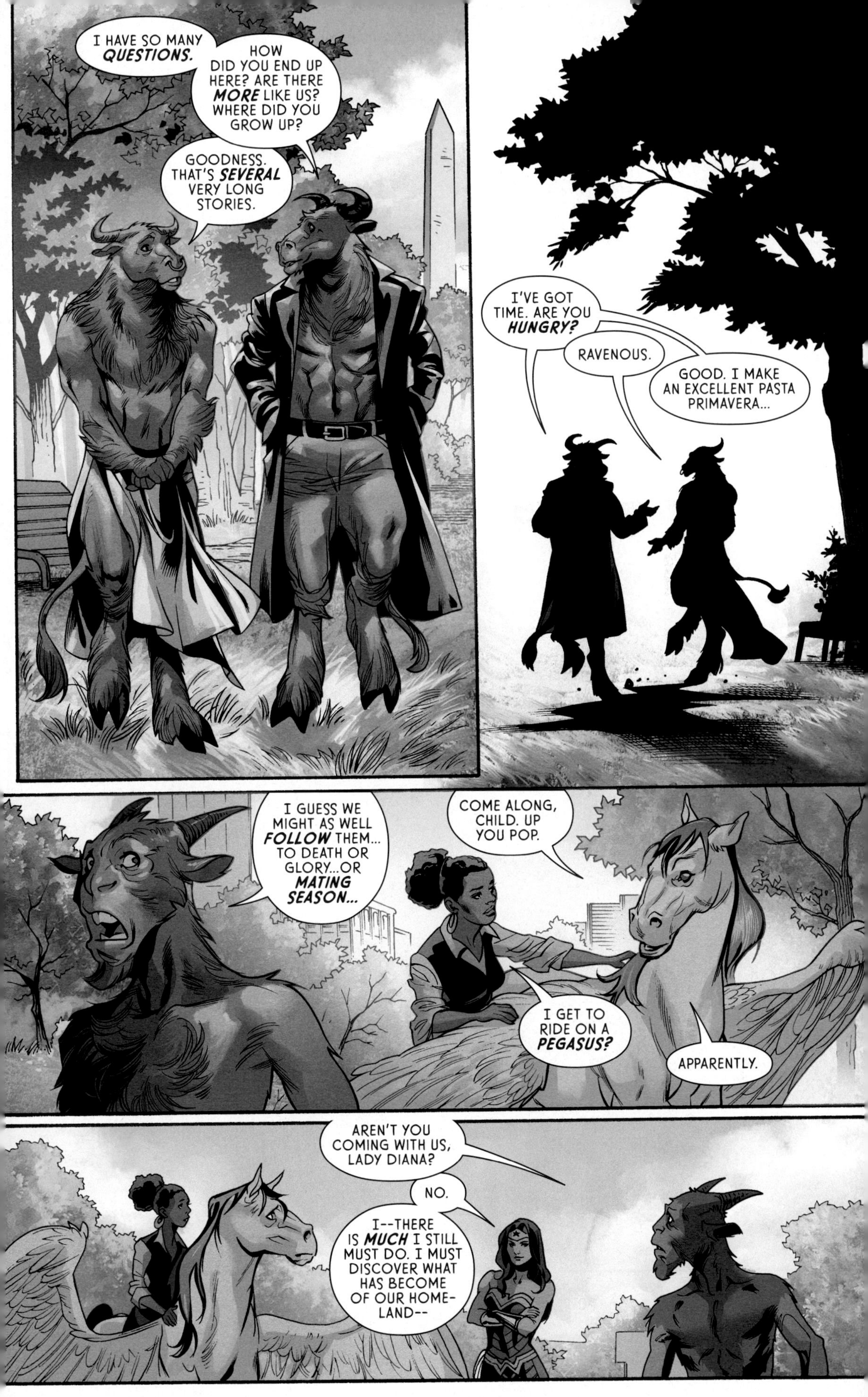
I HAVE SO MANY QUESTIONS.
HOW DID YOU END UP HERE? ARE THERE MORE LIKE US? WHERE DID YOU GROW UP?
GOODNESS. THAT'S SEVERAL VERY LONG STORIES.
I'VE GOT TIME. ARE YOU HUNGRY?
RAVENOUS.
GOOD. I MAKE AN EXCELLENT PASTA PRIMAVERA...
I GUESS WE MIGHT AS WELL FOLLOW THEM... TO DEATH OR GLORY...OR MATING SEASON...
COME ALONG, CHILD. UP YOU POP.
I GET TO RIDE ON A PEGASUS?
APPARENTLY.
AREN'T YOU COMING WITH US, LADY DIANA?
NO.
I--THERE IS MUCH I STILL MUST DO. I MUST DISCOVER WHAT HAS BECOME OF OUR HOME-LAND--

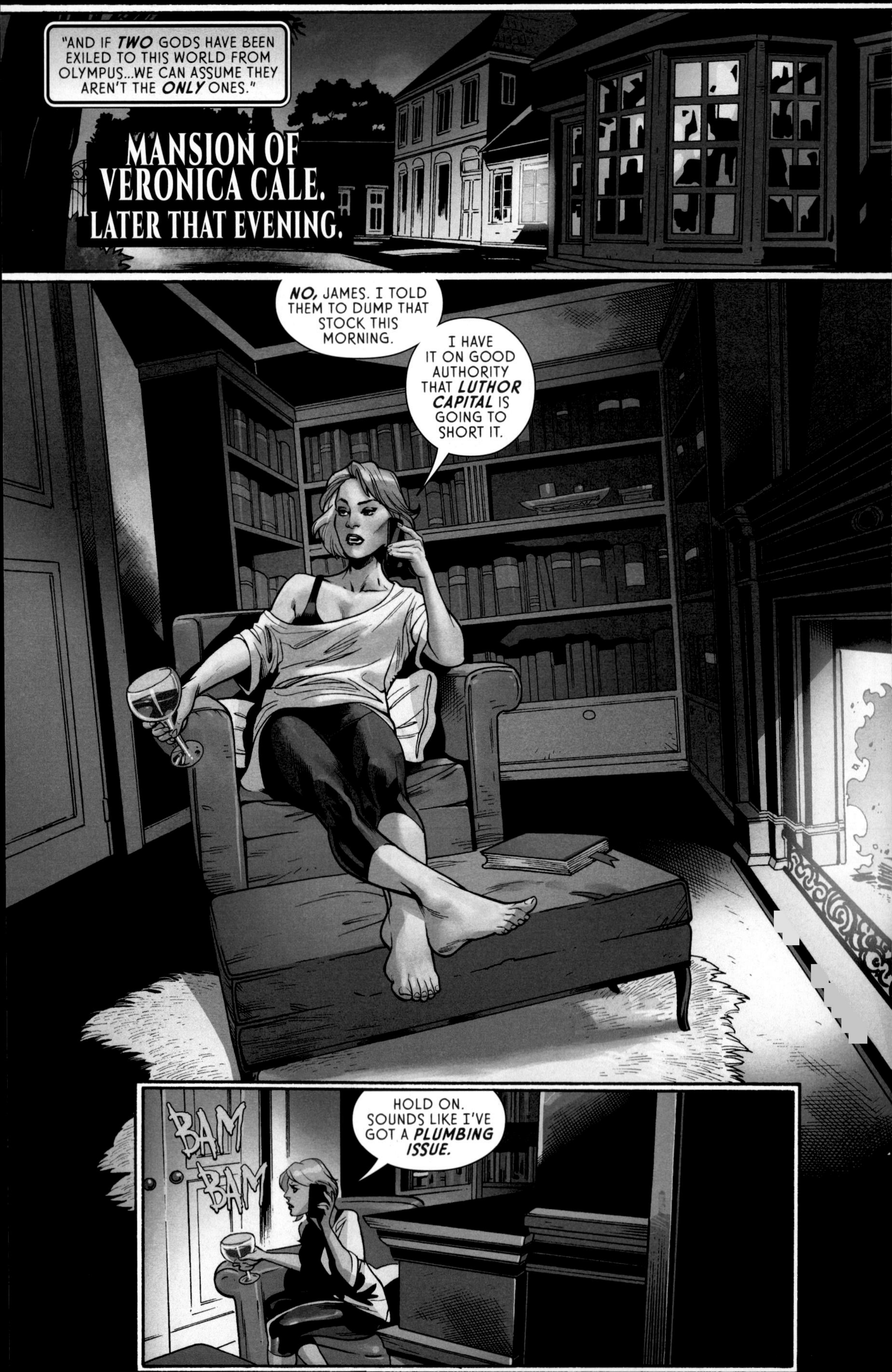
"AND IF TWO GODS HAVE BEEN EXILED TO THIS WORLD FROM OLYMPUS...WE CAN ASSUME THEY AREN'T THE ONLY ONES."
MANSION OF VERONICA CALE. LATER THAT EVENING.
NO, JAMES. I TOLD THEM TO DUMP THAT STOCK THIS MORNING.
I HAVE IT ON GOOD AUTHORITY THAT LUTHOR CAPITAL IS GOING TO SHORT IT.
BAM BAM
HOLD ON. SOUNDS LIKE I'VE GOT A PLUMBING ISSUE.

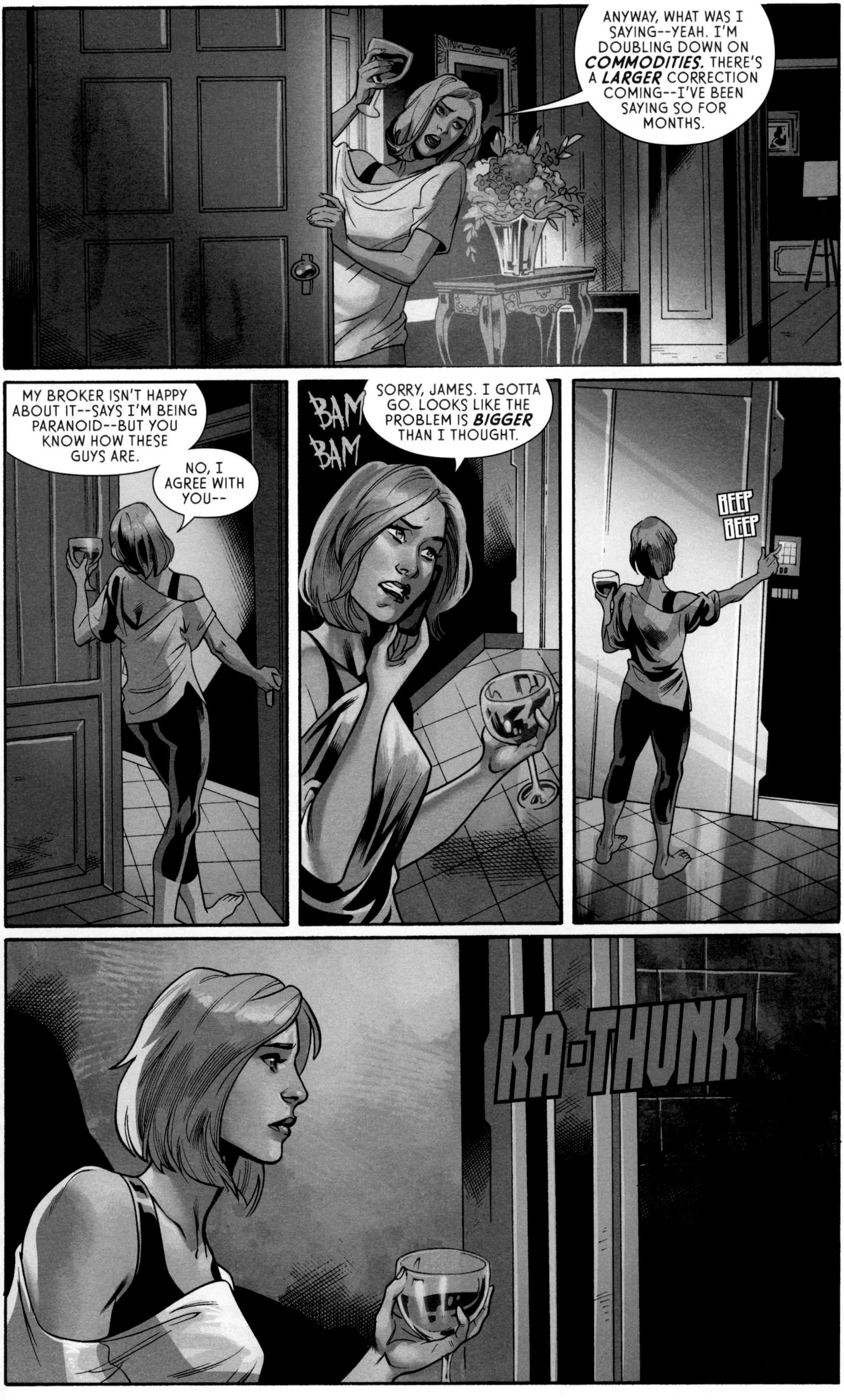
ANYWAY, WHAT WAS I SAYING--YEAH. I'M DOUBLING DOWN ON **COMMODITIES.** THERE'S A **LARGER** CORRECTION COMING--I'VE BEEN SAYING SO FOR MONTHS.
MY BROKER ISN'T HAPPY ABOUT IT--SAYS I'M BEING PARANOID--BUT YOU KNOW HOW THESE GUYS ARE.
NO, I AGREE WITH YOU--
BAM BAM
SORRY, JAMES. I GOTTA GO. LOOKS LIKE THE PROBLEM IS **BIGGER** THAN I THOUGHT.
BEEP BEEP
KA-THUNK

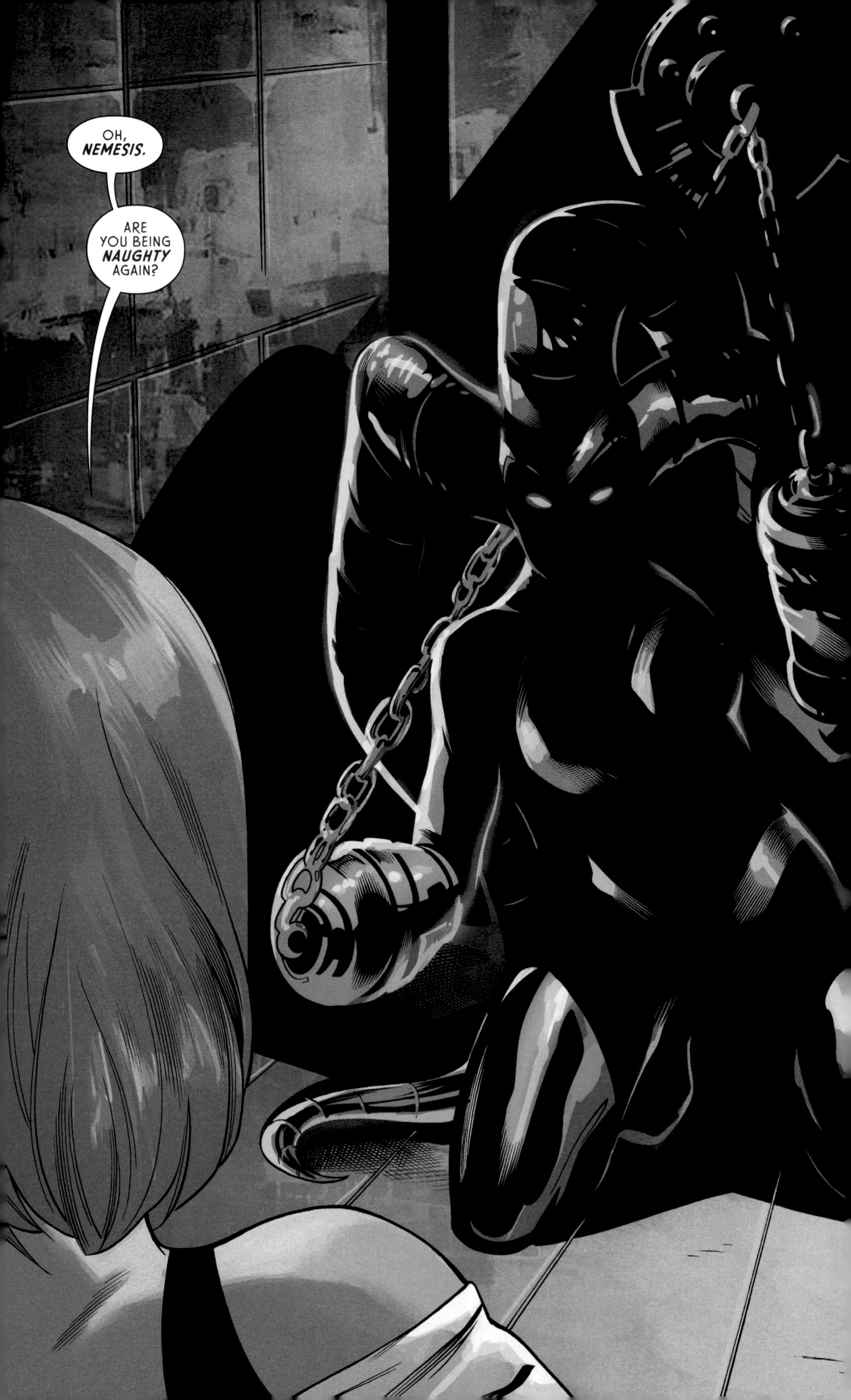
OH, *NEMESIS.*
ARE YOU BEING *NAUGHTY* AGAIN?

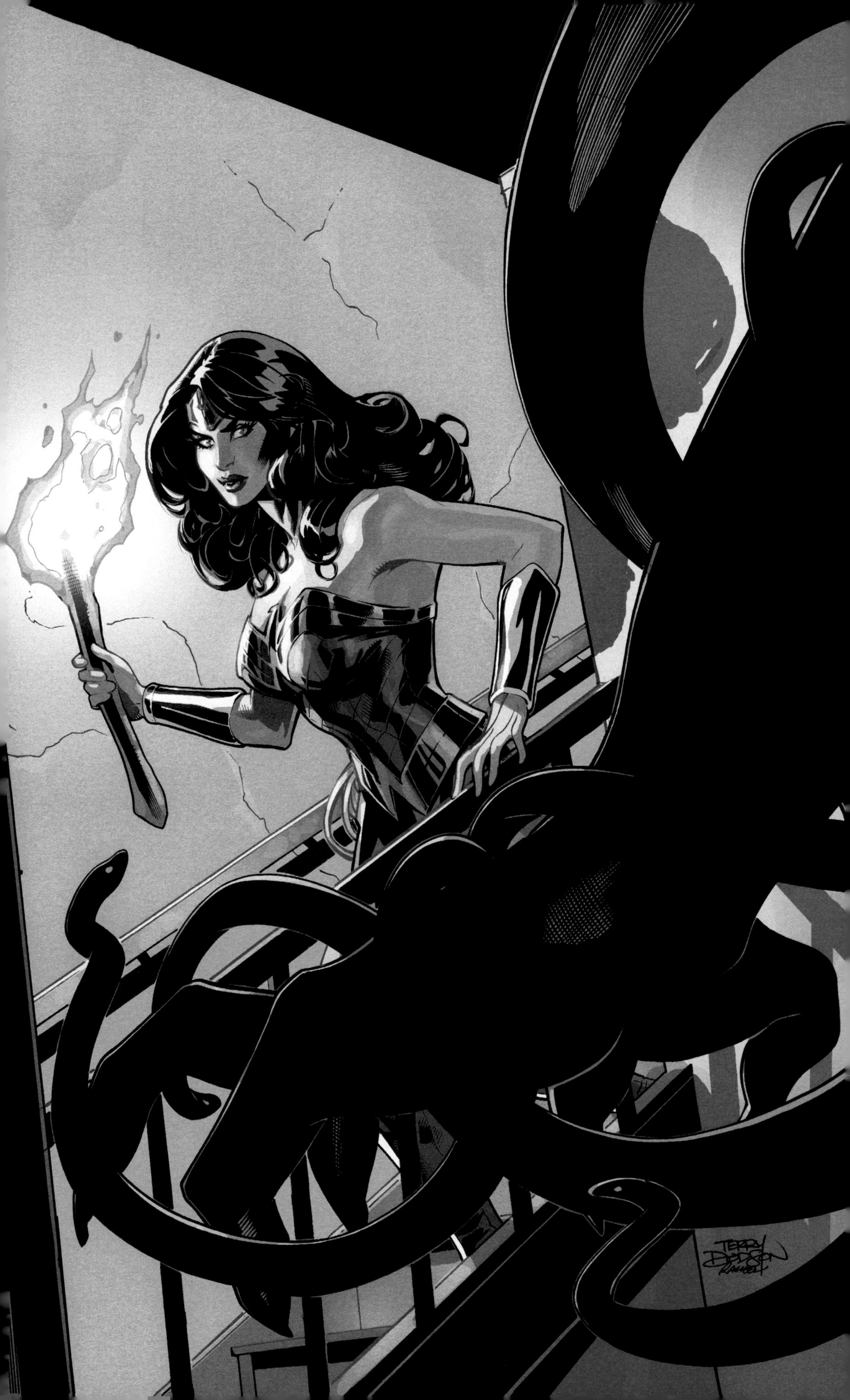
TERRY DODSON

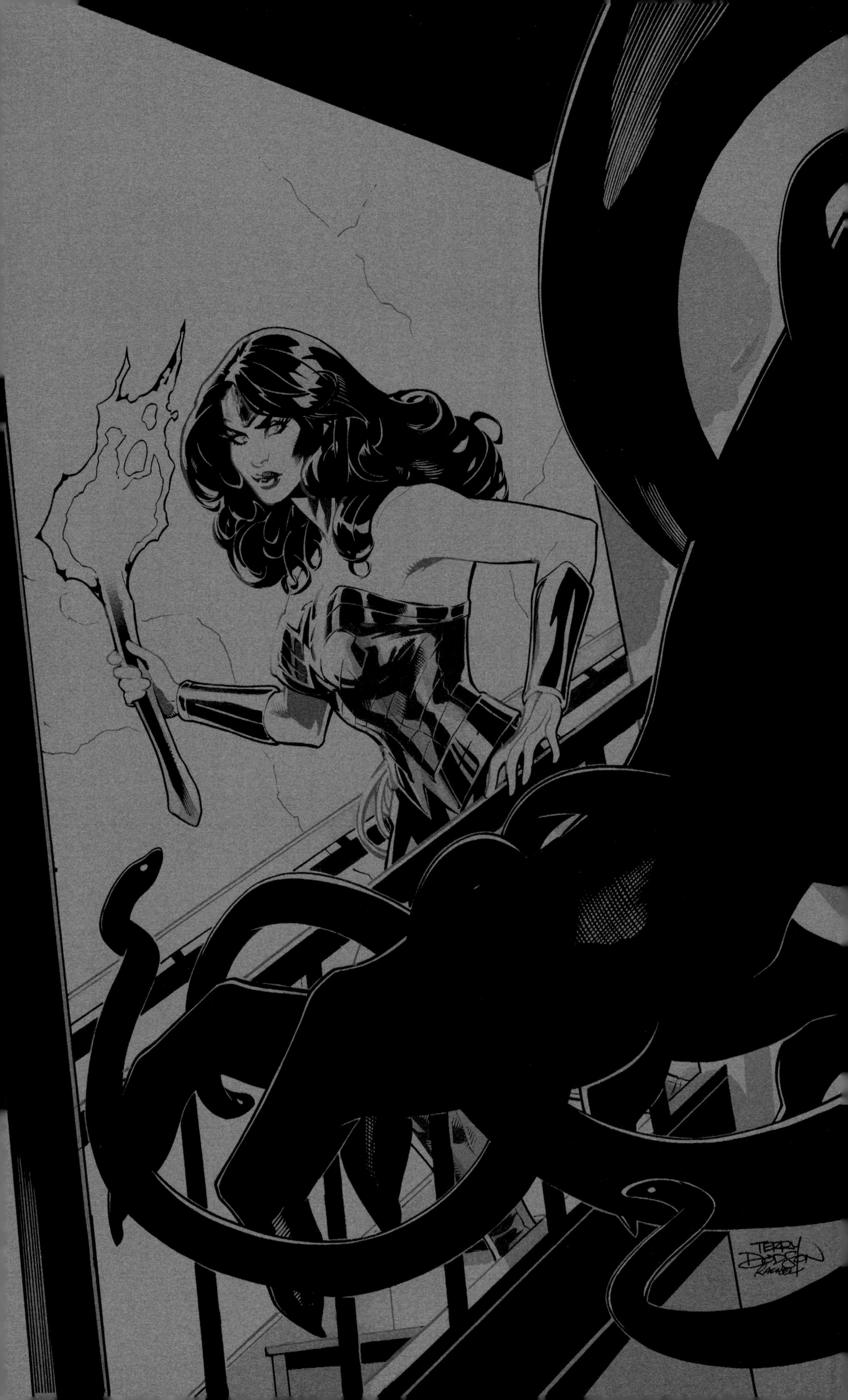
TERRY DODSON

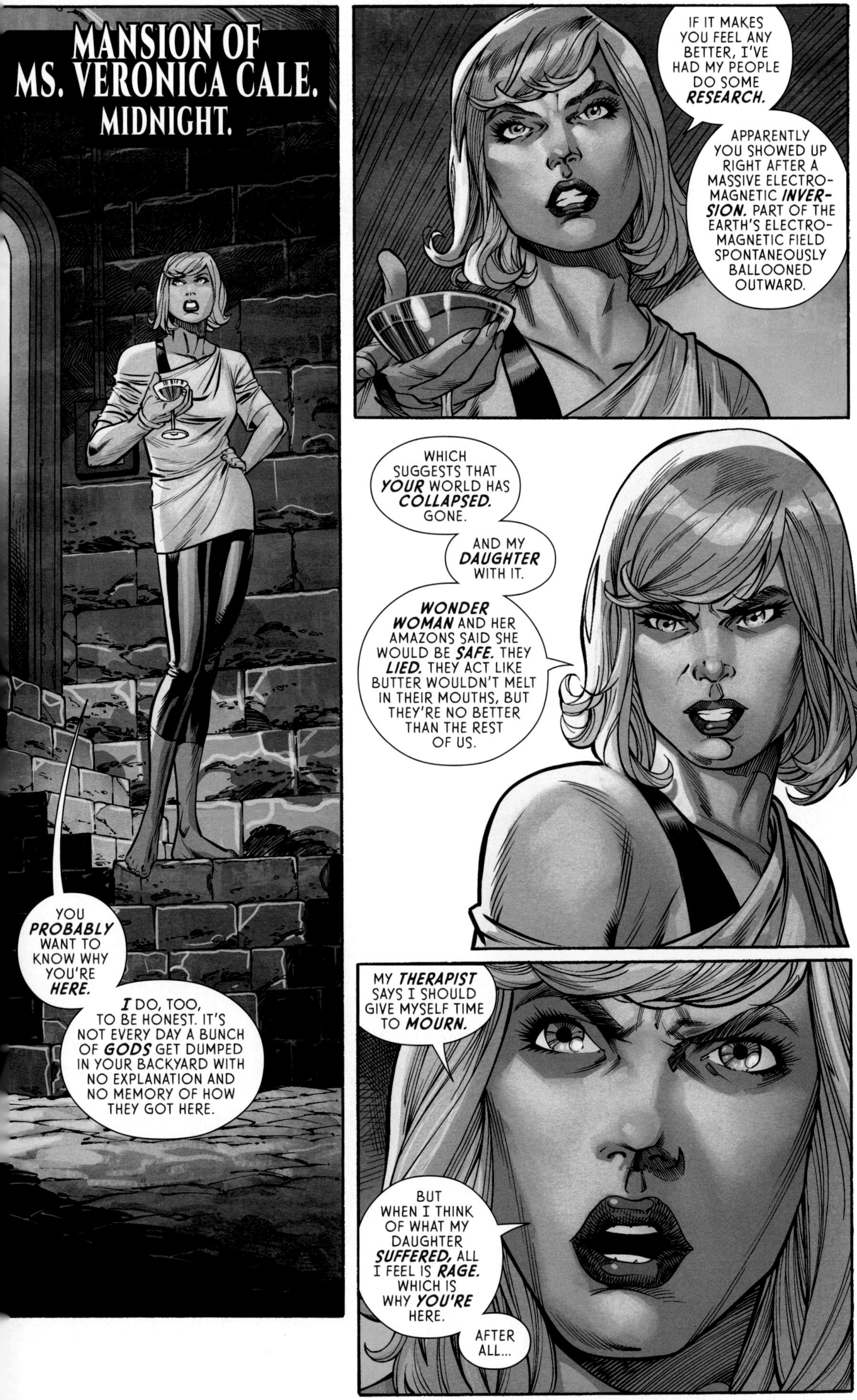
MANSION OF MS. VERONICA CALE. MIDNIGHT.
YOU PROBABLY WANT TO KNOW WHY YOU'RE HERE.
I DO, TOO, TO BE HONEST. IT'S NOT EVERY DAY A BUNCH OF GODS GET DUMPED IN YOUR BACKYARD WITH NO EXPLANATION AND NO MEMORY OF HOW THEY GOT HERE.
IF IT MAKES YOU FEEL ANY BETTER, I'VE HAD MY PEOPLE DO SOME RESEARCH.
APPARENTLY YOU SHOWED UP RIGHT AFTER A MASSIVE ELECTRO-MAGNETIC INVERSION. PART OF THE EARTH'S ELECTRO-MAGNETIC FIELD SPONTANEOUSLY BALLOONED OUTWARD.
WHICH SUGGESTS THAT YOUR WORLD HAS COLLAPSED. GONE.
AND MY DAUGHTER WITH IT.
WONDER WOMAN AND HER AMAZONS SAID SHE WOULD BE SAFE. THEY LIED. THEY ACT LIKE BUTTER WOULDN'T MELT IN THEIR MOUTHS, BUT THEY'RE NO BETTER THAN THE REST OF US.
MY THERAPIST SAYS I SHOULD GIVE MYSELF TIME TO MOURN.
BUT WHEN I THINK OF WHAT MY DAUGHTER SUFFERED, ALL I FEEL IS RAGE. WHICH IS WHY YOU'RE HERE.
AFTER ALL...

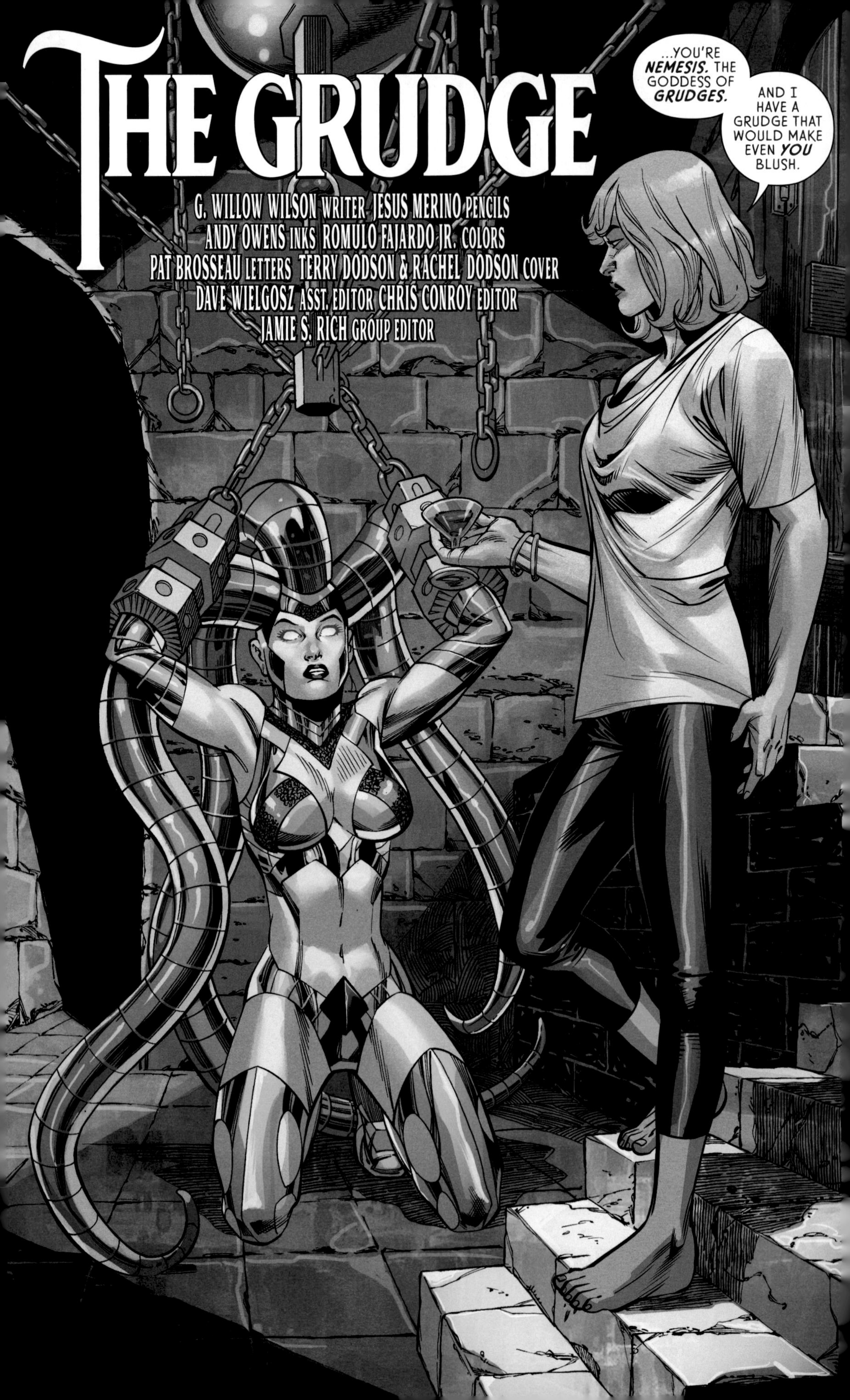
THE GRUDGE
G. WILLOW WILSON WRITER JESUS MERINO PENCILS
ANDY OWENS INKS ROMULO FAJARDO JR. COLORS
PAT BROSSEAU LETTERS TERRY DODSON & RACHEL DODSON COVER
DAVE WIELGOSZ ASST. EDITOR CHRIS CONROY EDITOR
JAMIE S. RICH GROUP EDITOR
...YOU'RE NEMESIS. THE GODDESS OF GRUDGES.
AND I HAVE A GRUDGE THAT WOULD MAKE EVEN YOU BLUSH.

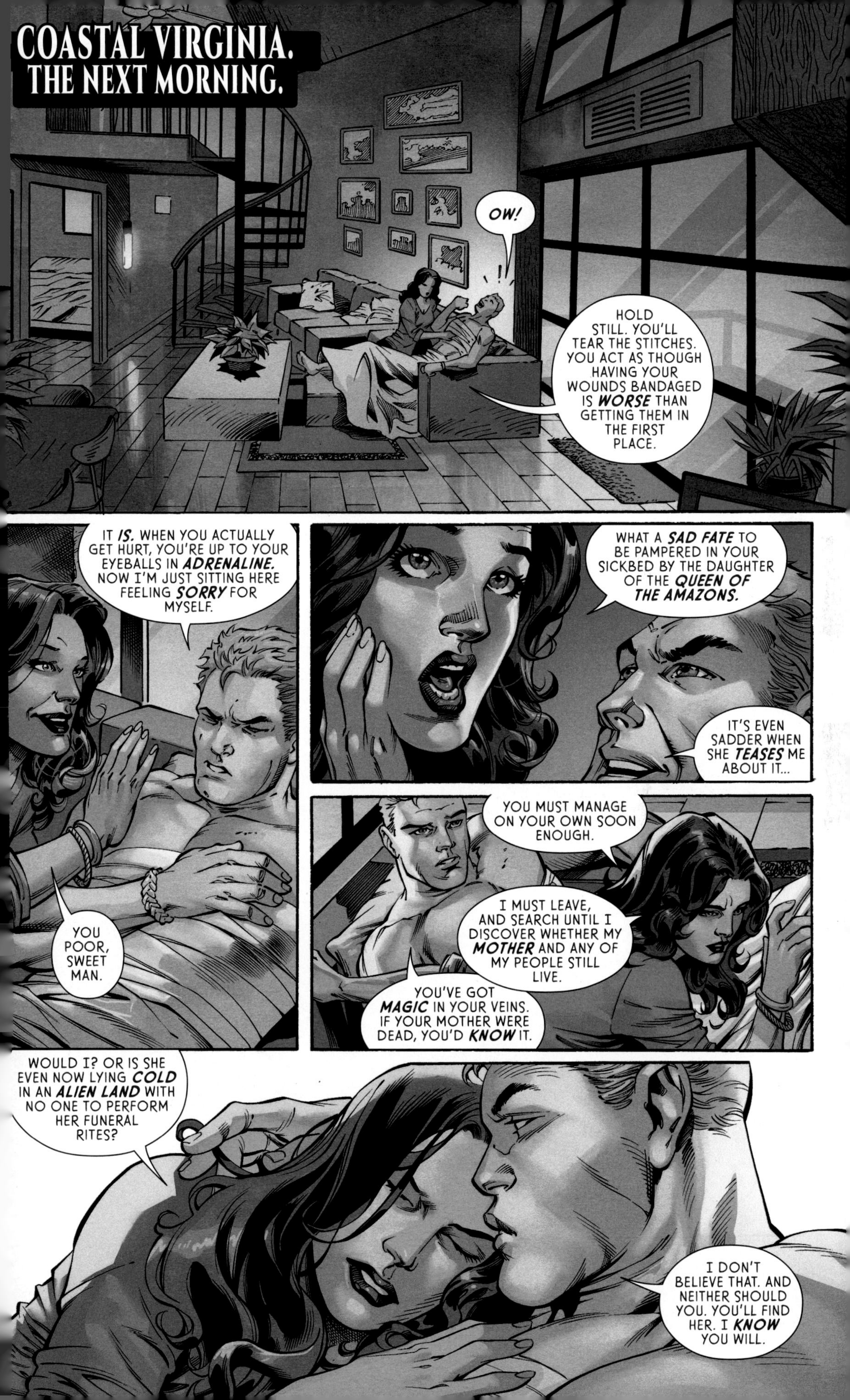
COASTAL VIRGINIA. THE NEXT MORNING.
OW!
HOLD STILL. YOU'LL TEAR THE STITCHES. YOU ACT AS THOUGH HAVING YOUR WOUNDS BANDAGED IS WORSE THAN GETTING THEM IN THE FIRST PLACE.
IT IS. WHEN YOU ACTUALLY GET HURT, YOU'RE UP TO YOUR EYEBALLS IN ADRENALINE. NOW I'M JUST SITTING HERE FEELING SORRY FOR MYSELF.
YOU POOR, SWEET MAN.
WHAT A SAD FATE TO BE PAMPERED IN YOUR SICKBED BY THE DAUGHTER OF THE QUEEN OF THE AMAZONS.
IT'S EVEN SADDER WHEN SHE TEASES ME ABOUT IT...
YOU MUST MANAGE ON YOUR OWN SOON ENOUGH.
I MUST LEAVE, AND SEARCH UNTIL I DISCOVER WHETHER MY MOTHER AND ANY OF MY PEOPLE STILL LIVE.
YOU'VE GOT MAGIC IN YOUR VEINS. IF YOUR MOTHER WERE DEAD, YOU'D KNOW IT.
WOULD I? OR IS SHE EVEN NOW LYING COLD IN AN ALIEN LAND WITH NO ONE TO PERFORM HER FUNERAL RITES?
I DON'T BELIEVE THAT. AND NEITHER SHOULD YOU. YOU'LL FIND HER. I KNOW YOU WILL.

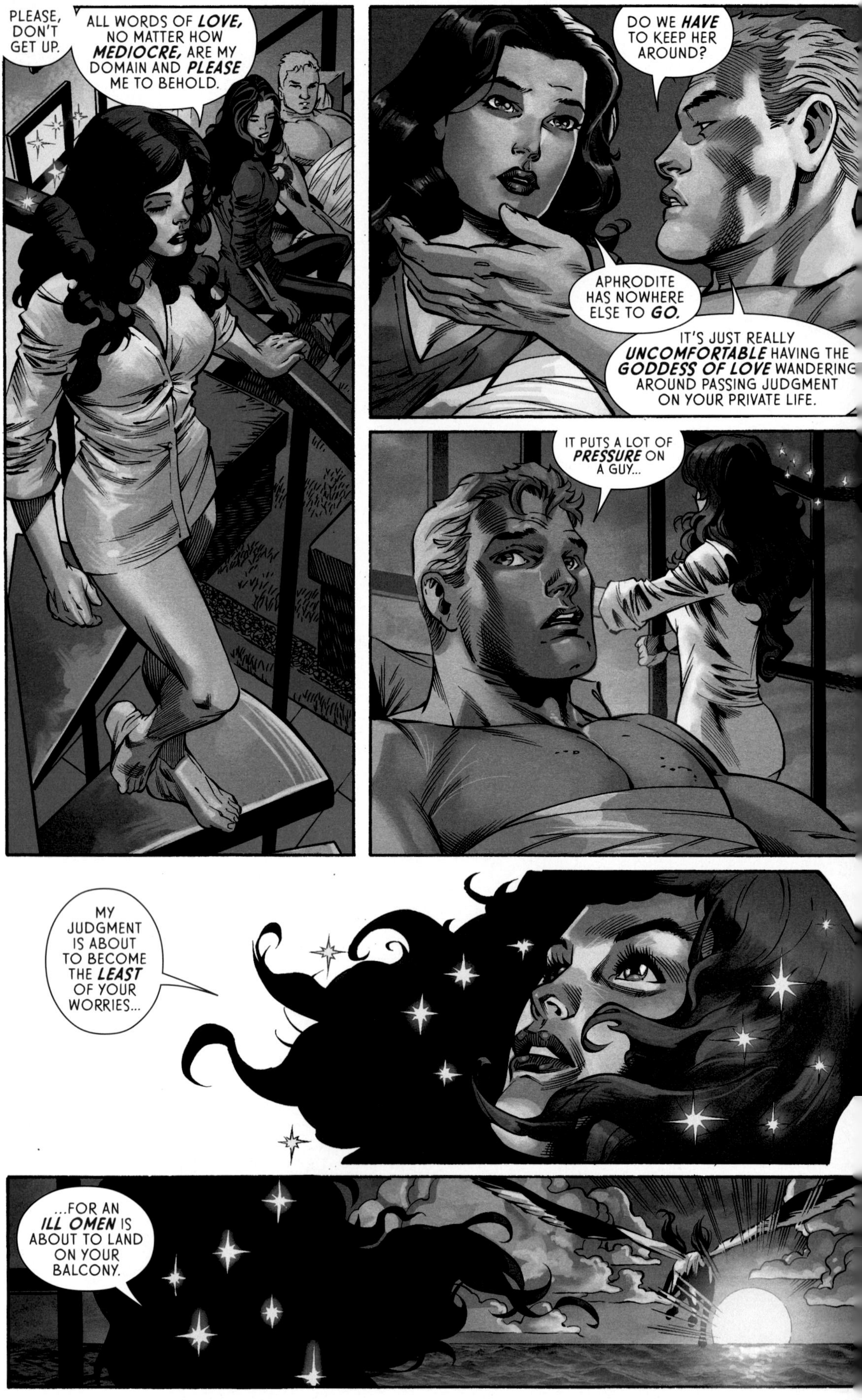
PLEASE, DON'T GET UP.
ALL WORDS OF LOVE, NO MATTER HOW MEDIOCRE, ARE MY DOMAIN AND PLEASE ME TO BEHOLD.
DO WE HAVE TO KEEP HER AROUND?
APHRODITE HAS NOWHERE ELSE TO GO.
IT'S JUST REALLY UNCOMFORTABLE HAVING THE GODDESS OF LOVE WANDERING AROUND PASSING JUDGMENT ON YOUR PRIVATE LIFE.
IT PUTS A LOT OF PRESSURE ON A GUY...
MY JUDGMENT IS ABOUT TO BECOME THE LEAST OF YOUR WORRIES...
...FOR AN ILL OMEN IS ABOUT TO LAND ON YOUR BALCONY.

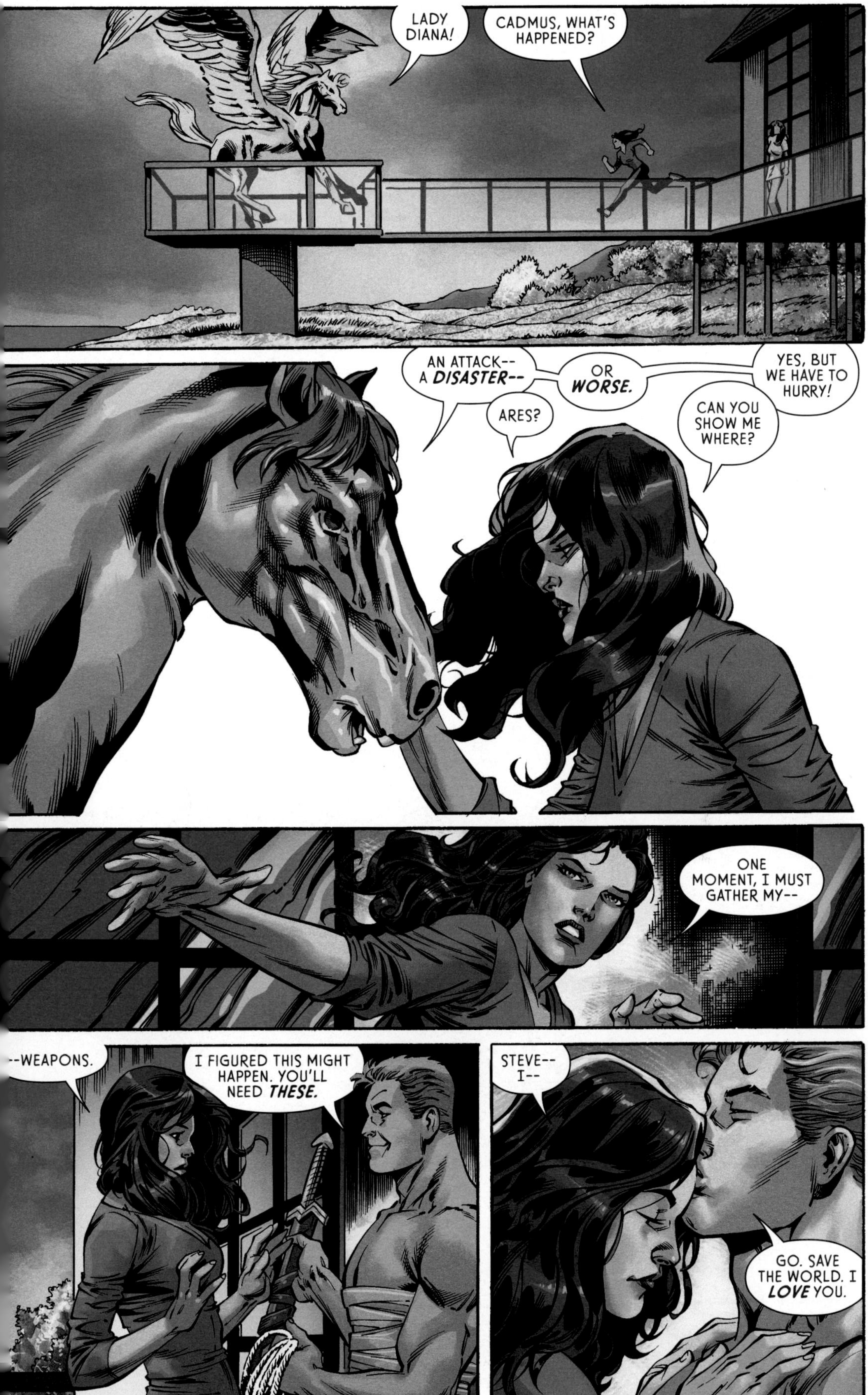
LADY DIANA!
CADMUS, WHAT'S HAPPENED?
AN ATTACK-- A DISASTER--
OR WORSE.
ARES?
YES, BUT WE HAVE TO HURRY!
CAN YOU SHOW ME WHERE?
ONE MOMENT, I MUST GATHER MY--
--WEAPONS.
I FIGURED THIS MIGHT HAPPEN. YOU'LL NEED THESE.
STEVE-- I--
GO. SAVE THE WORLD. I LOVE YOU.

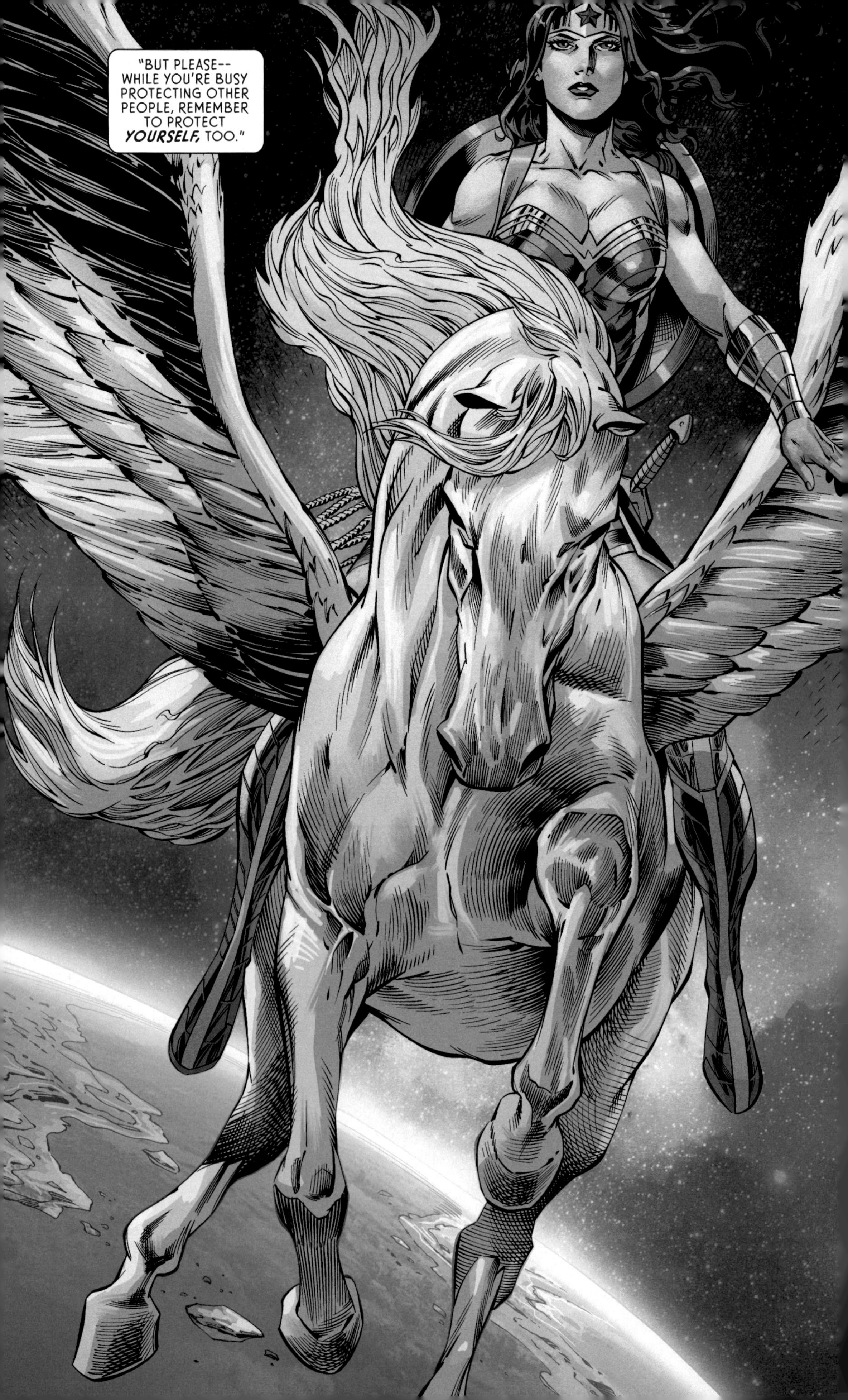
"BUT PLEASE--
WHILE YOU'RE BUSY
PROTECTING OTHER
PEOPLE, REMEMBER
TO PROTECT
YOURSELF, TOO."

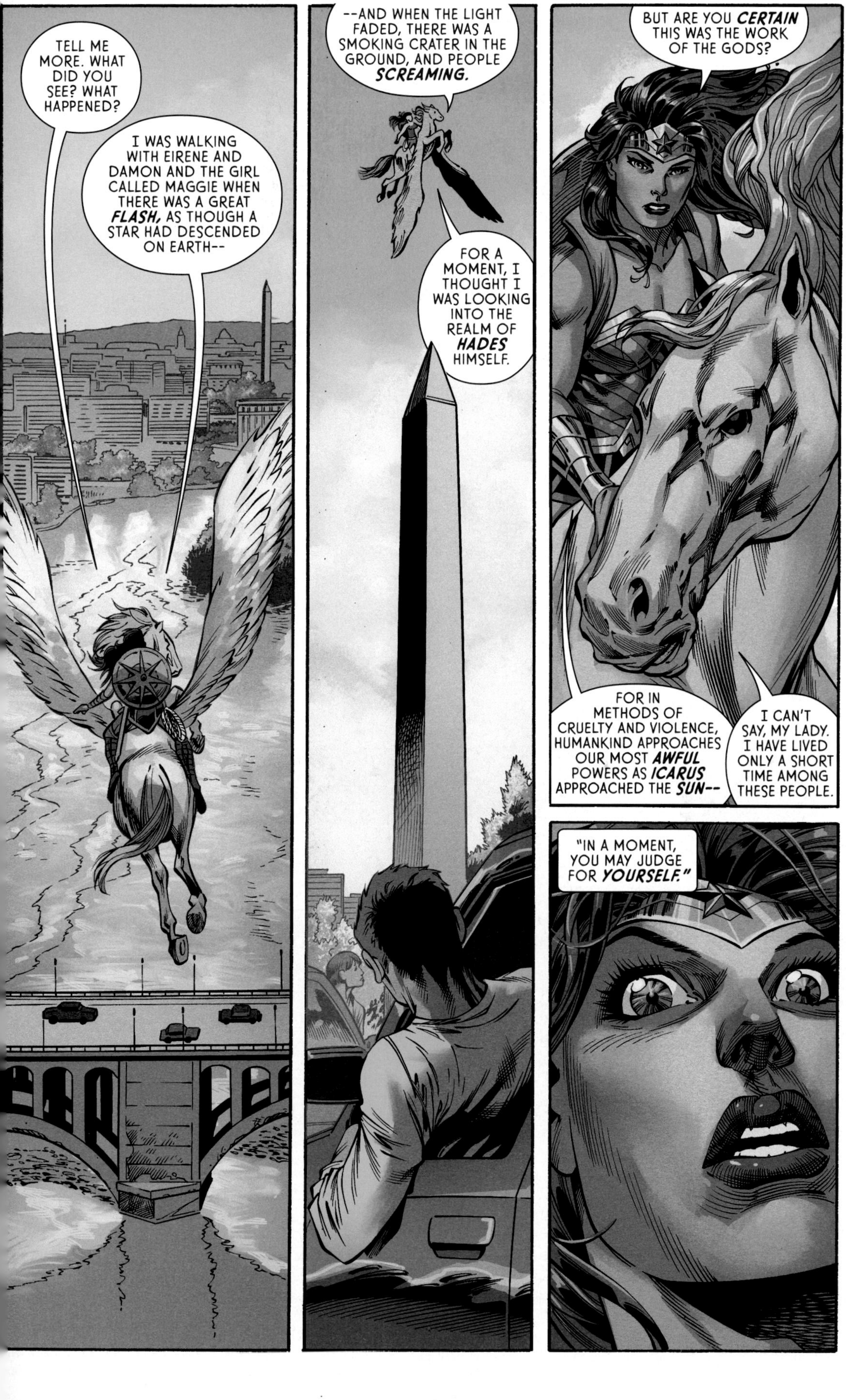
TELL ME MORE. WHAT DID YOU SEE? WHAT HAPPENED?
I WAS WALKING WITH EIRENE AND DAMON AND THE GIRL CALLED MAGGIE WHEN THERE WAS A GREAT FLASH, AS THOUGH A STAR HAD DESCENDED ON EARTH--
--AND WHEN THE LIGHT FADED, THERE WAS A SMOKING CRATER IN THE GROUND, AND PEOPLE SCREAMING.
FOR A MOMENT, I THOUGHT I WAS LOOKING INTO THE REALM OF HADES HIMSELF.
BUT ARE YOU CERTAIN THIS WAS THE WORK OF THE GODS?
FOR IN METHODS OF CRUELTY AND VIOLENCE, HUMANKIND APPROACHES OUR MOST AWFUL POWERS AS ICARUS APPROACHED THE SUN--
I CAN'T SAY, MY LADY. I HAVE LIVED ONLY A SHORT TIME AMONG THESE PEOPLE.
"IN A MOMENT, YOU MAY JUDGE FOR YOURSELF."

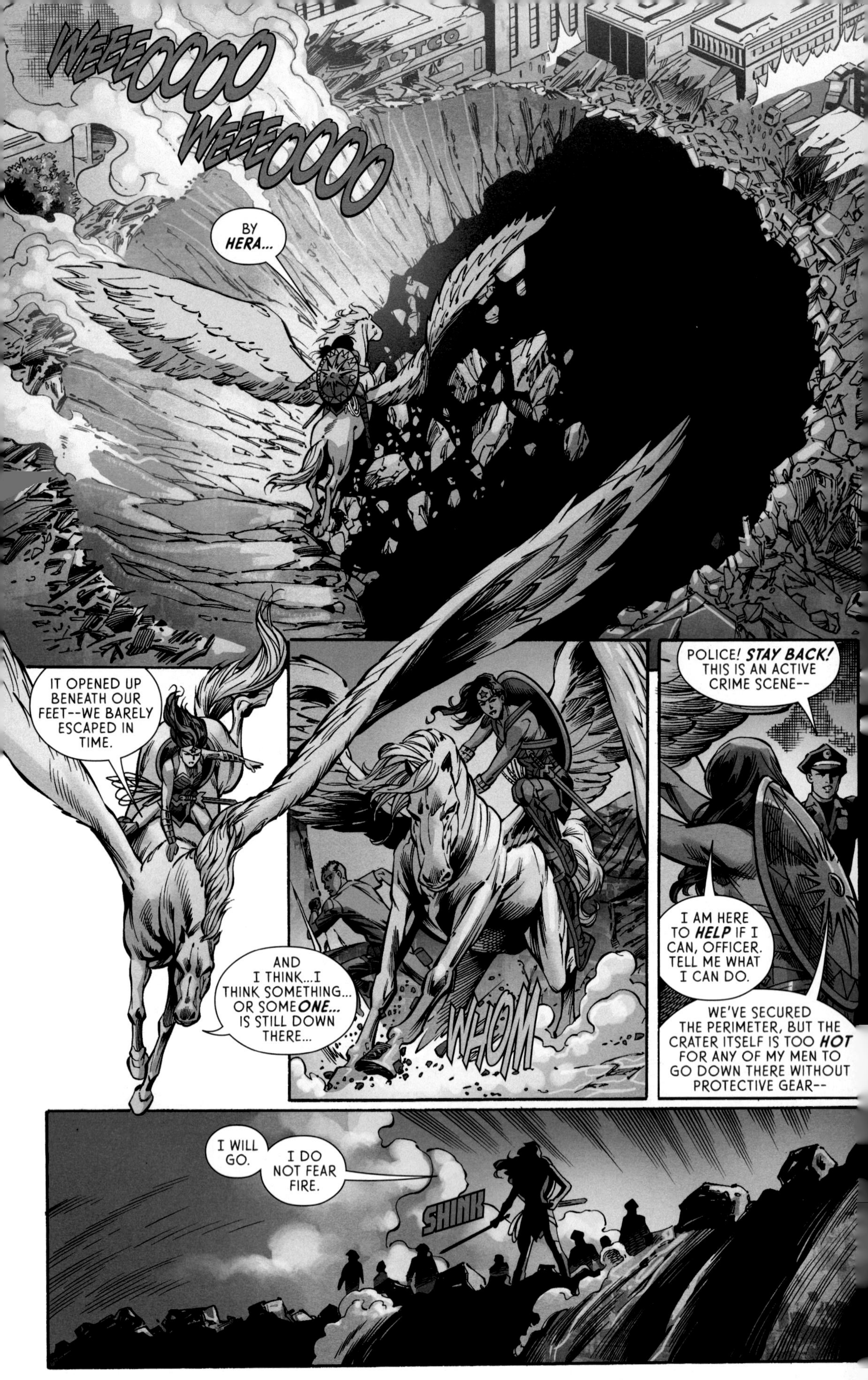
WEEEOOOO
WEEEOOOO
BY HERA...
IT OPENED UP BENEATH OUR FEET--WE BARELY ESCAPED IN TIME.
AND I THINK...I THINK SOMETHING... OR SOMEONE... IS STILL DOWN THERE...
WHOM
POLICE! STAY BACK! THIS IS AN ACTIVE CRIME SCENE--
I AM HERE TO HELP IF I CAN, OFFICER. TELL ME WHAT I CAN DO.
WE'VE SECURED THE PERIMETER, BUT THE CRATER ITSELF IS TOO HOT FOR ANY OF MY MEN TO GO DOWN THERE WITHOUT PROTECTIVE GEAR--
I WILL GO.
I DO NOT FEAR FIRE.
SHINK

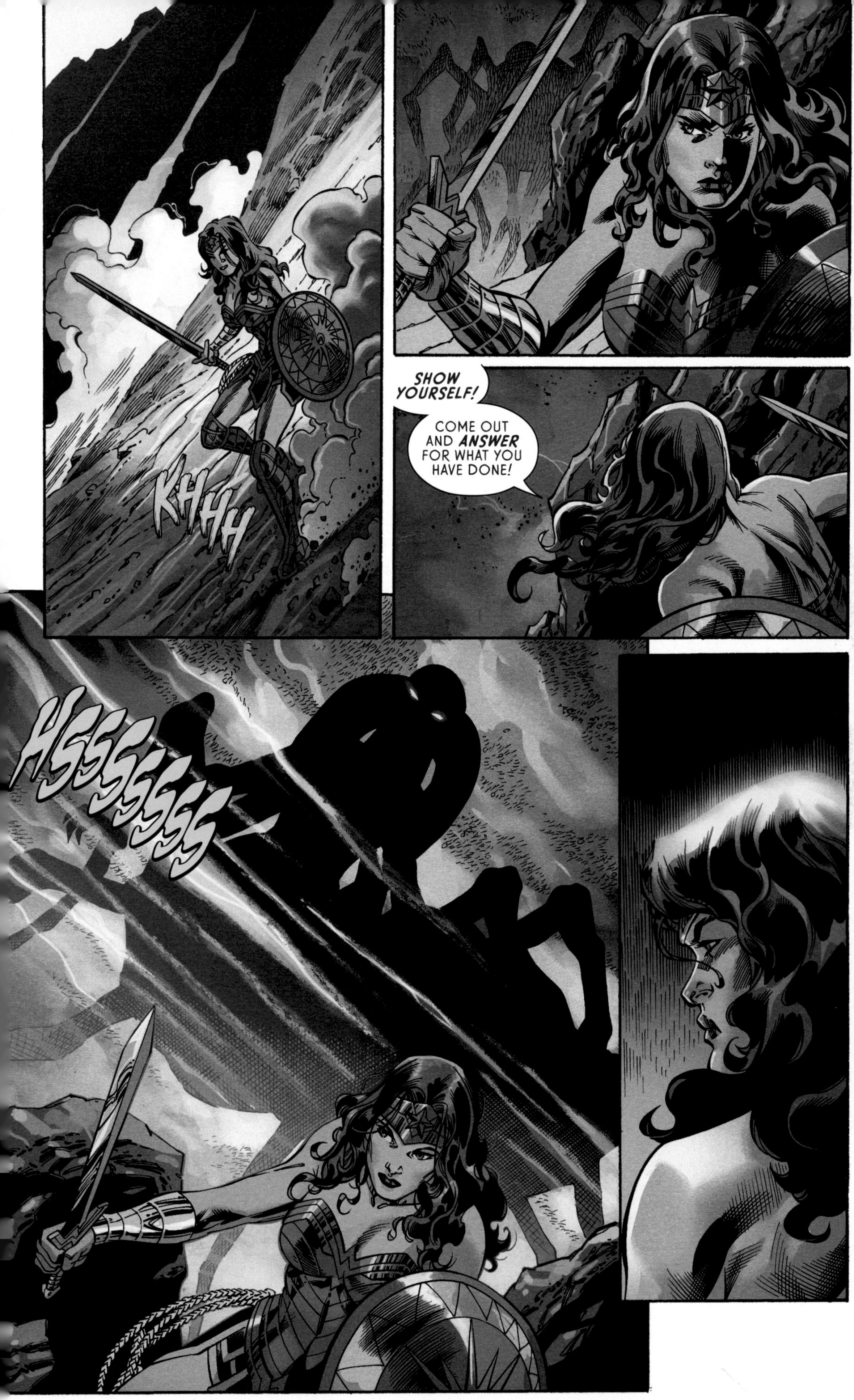
KHHH
SHOW YOURSELF!
COME OUT AND ANSWER FOR WHAT YOU HAVE DONE!
HSSSSSSS

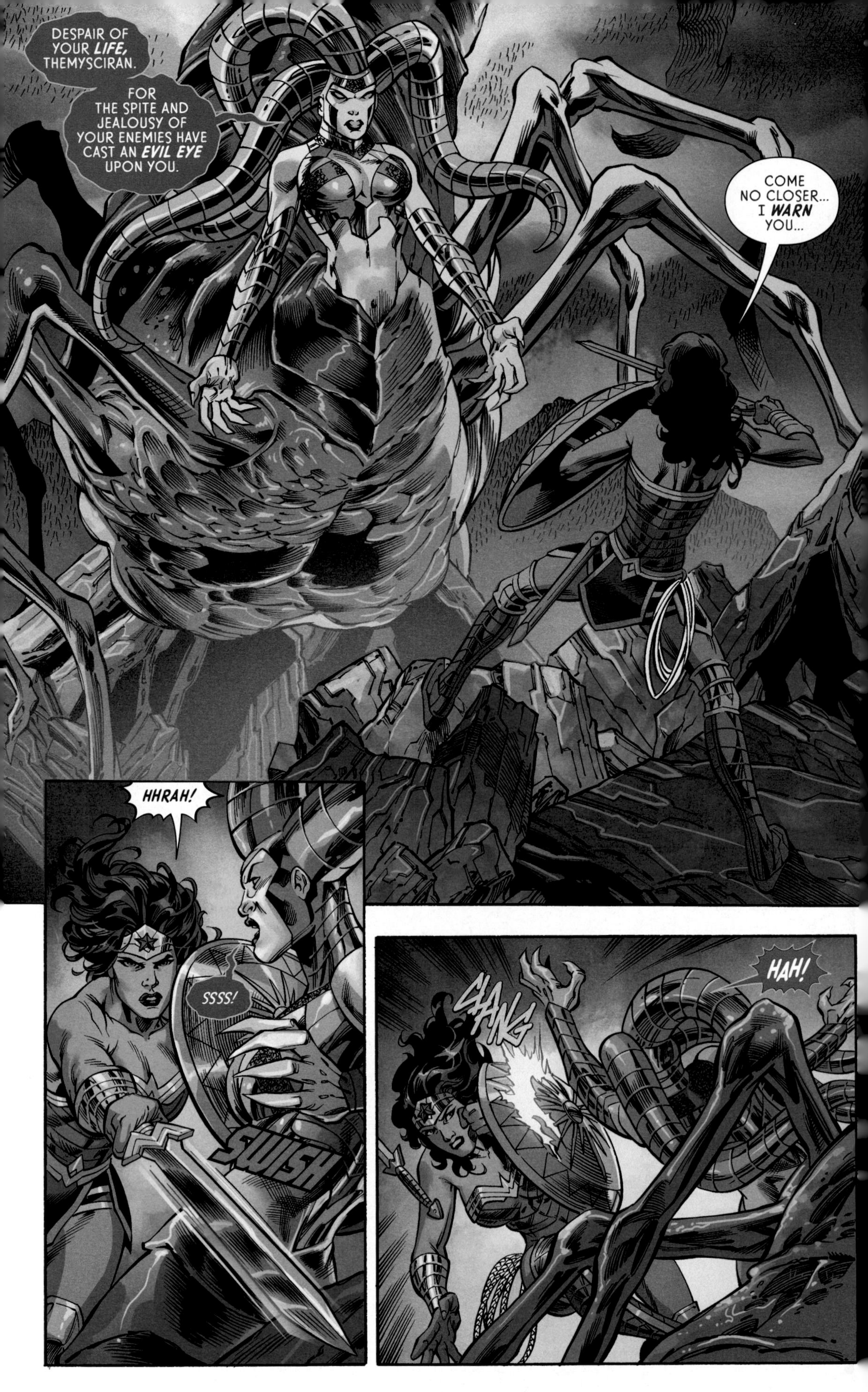
DESPAIR OF YOUR LIFE, THEMYSCIRAN.
FOR THE SPITE AND JEALOUSY OF YOUR ENEMIES HAVE CAST AN EVIL EYE UPON YOU.
COME NO CLOSER... I WARN YOU...
HHRAH!
SSSS!
SWISH
CLANG
HAH!

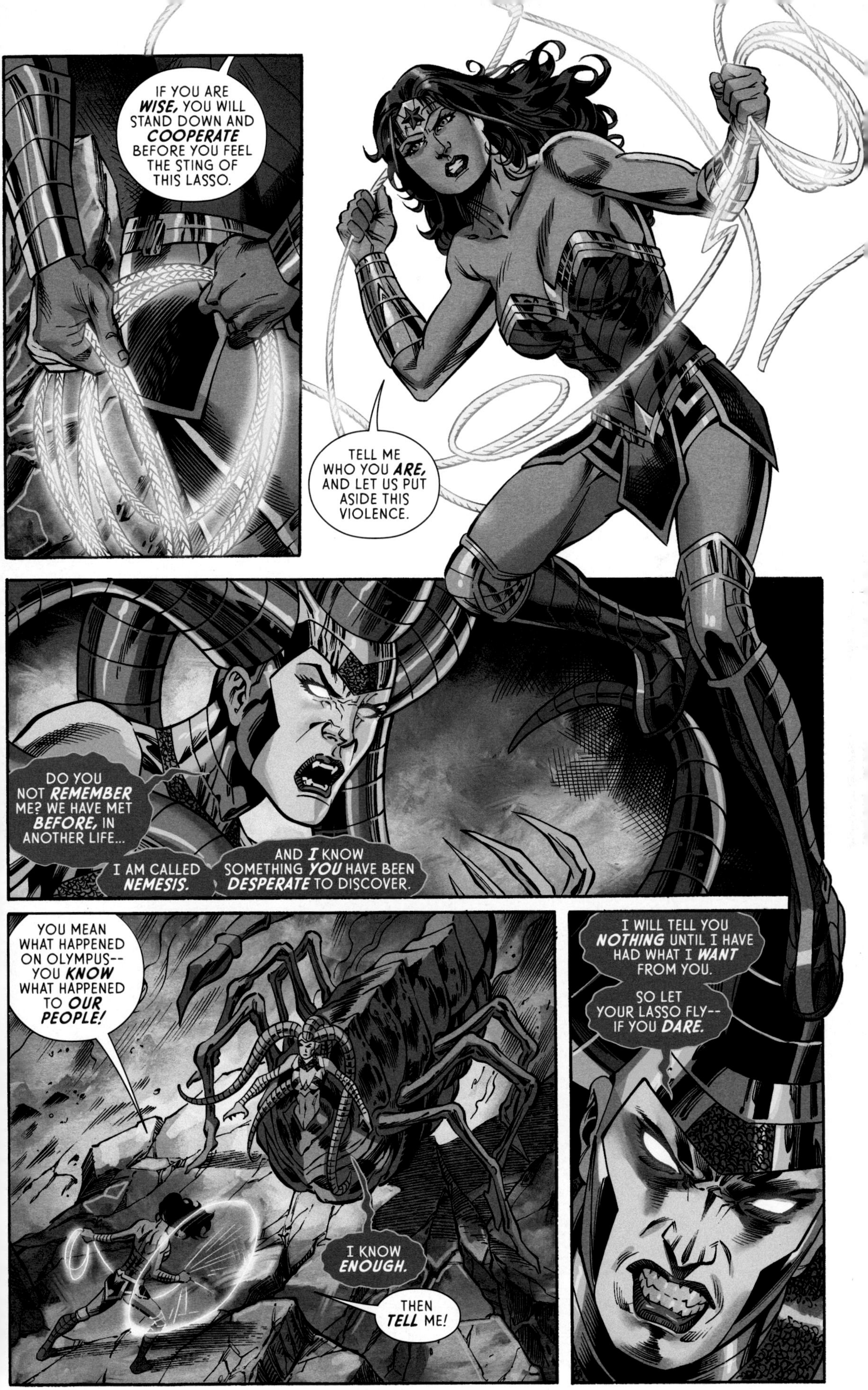
IF YOU ARE WISE, YOU WILL STAND DOWN AND COOPERATE BEFORE YOU FEEL THE STING OF THIS LASSO.
TELL ME WHO YOU ARE, AND LET US PUT ASIDE THIS VIOLENCE.
DO YOU NOT REMEMBER ME? WE HAVE MET BEFORE, IN ANOTHER LIFE...
I AM CALLED NEMESIS.
AND I KNOW SOMETHING YOU HAVE BEEN DESPERATE TO DISCOVER.
YOU MEAN WHAT HAPPENED ON OLYMPUS-- YOU KNOW WHAT HAPPENED TO OUR PEOPLE!
I KNOW ENOUGH.
THEN TELL ME!
I WILL TELL YOU NOTHING UNTIL I HAVE HAD WHAT I WANT FROM YOU.
SO LET YOUR LASSO FLY-- IF YOU DARE.

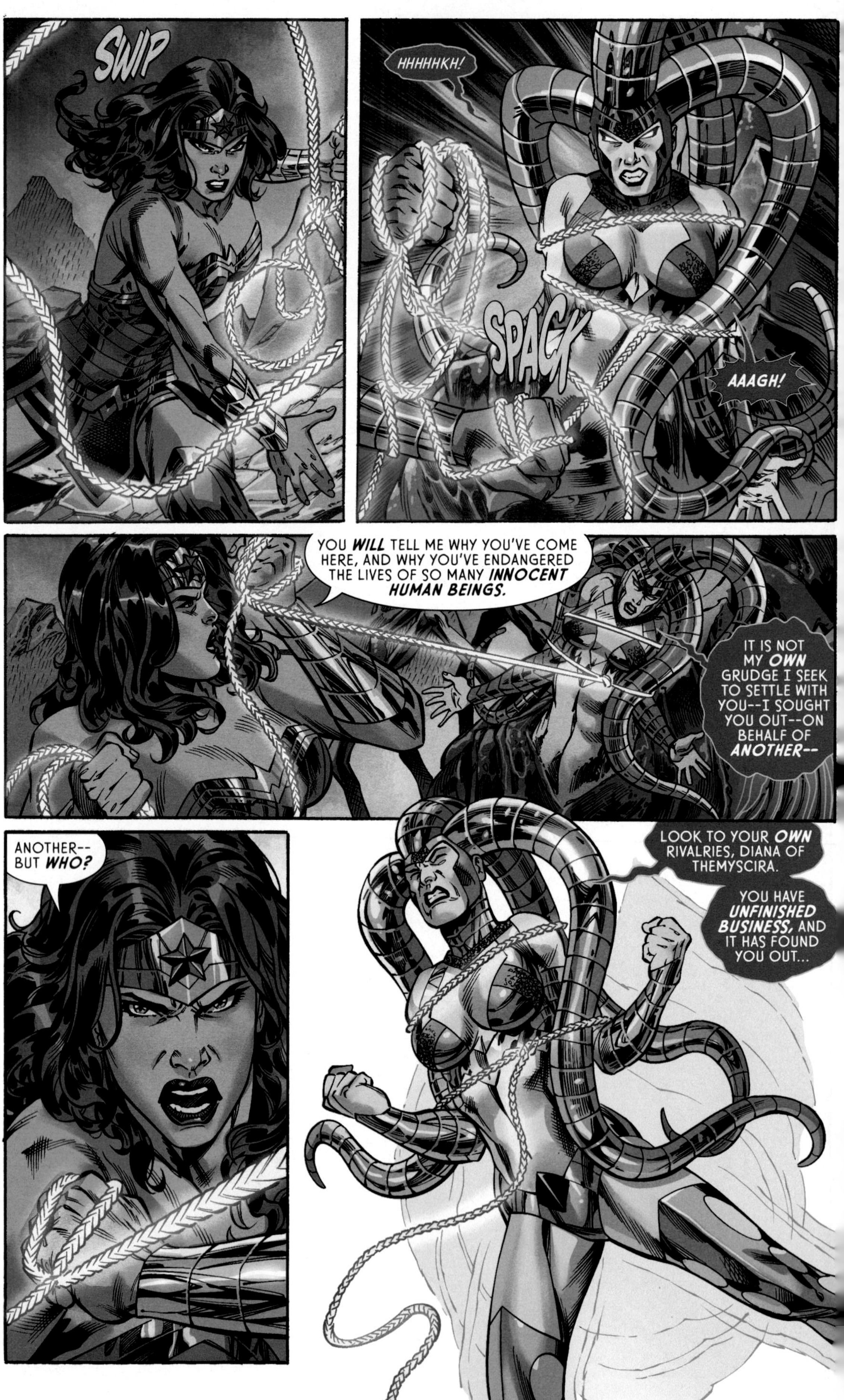
SWIP
HHHHHKH!
SPACK
AAAGH!
YOU WILL TELL ME WHY YOU'VE COME HERE, AND WHY YOU'VE ENDANGERED THE LIVES OF SO MANY INNOCENT HUMAN BEINGS.
IT IS NOT MY OWN GRUDGE I SEEK TO SETTLE WITH YOU--I SOUGHT YOU OUT--ON BEHALF OF ANOTHER--
ANOTHER-- BUT WHO?
LOOK TO YOUR OWN RIVALRIES, DIANA OF THEMYSCIRA.
YOU HAVE UNFINISHED BUSINESS, AND IT HAS FOUND YOU OUT...

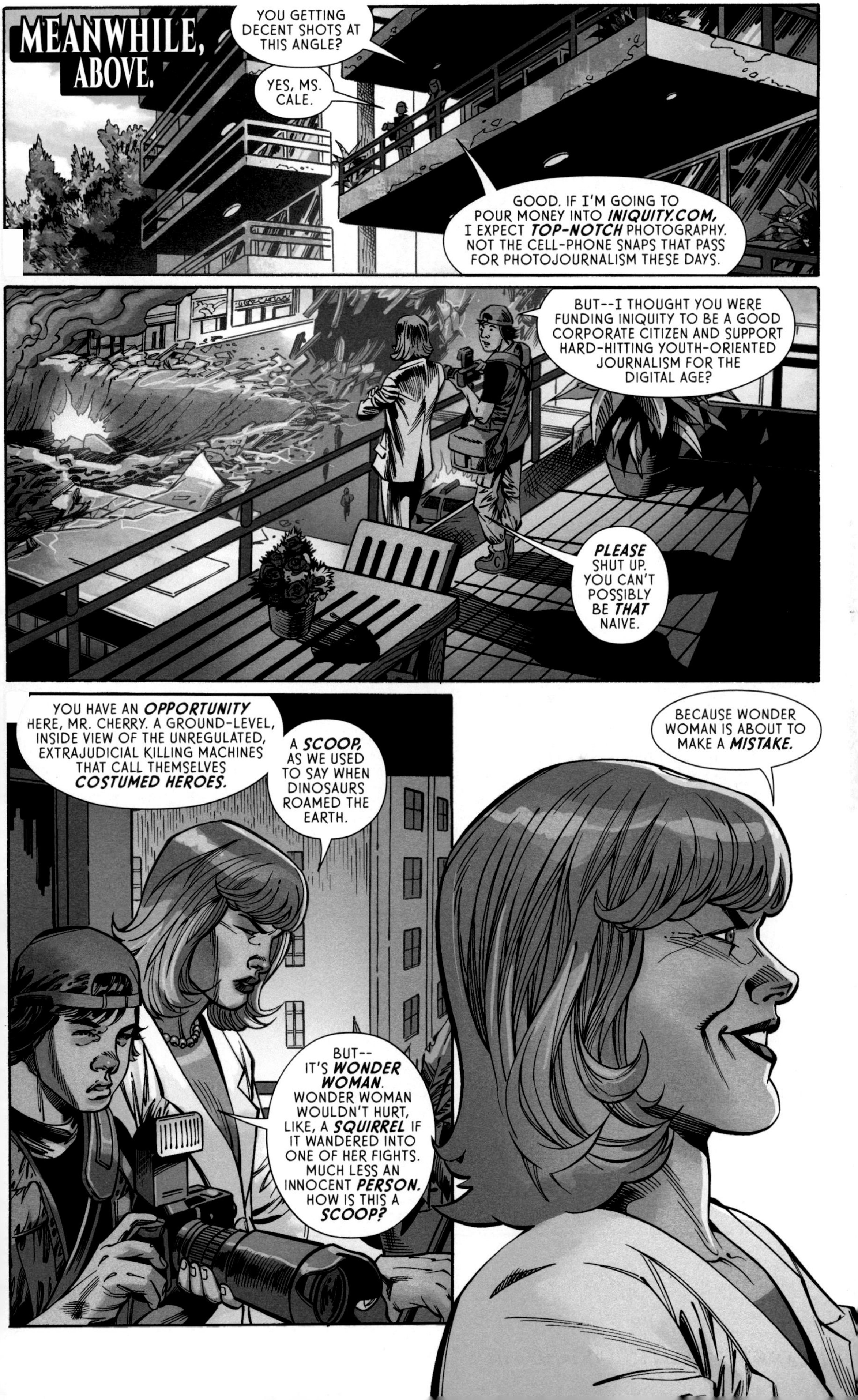
MEANWHILE, ABOVE.
YOU GETTING DECENT SHOTS AT THIS ANGLE?
YES, MS. CALE.
GOOD. IF I'M GOING TO POUR MONEY INTO INIQUITY.COM, I EXPECT TOP-NOTCH PHOTOGRAPHY. NOT THE CELL-PHONE SNAPS THAT PASS FOR PHOTOJOURNALISM THESE DAYS.
BUT--I THOUGHT YOU WERE FUNDING INIQUITY TO BE A GOOD CORPORATE CITIZEN AND SUPPORT HARD-HITTING YOUTH-ORIENTED JOURNALISM FOR THE DIGITAL AGE?
PLEASE SHUT UP. YOU CAN'T POSSIBLY BE THAT NAIVE.
YOU HAVE AN OPPORTUNITY HERE, MR. CHERRY. A GROUND-LEVEL, INSIDE VIEW OF THE UNREGULATED, EXTRAJUDICIAL KILLING MACHINES THAT CALL THEMSELVES COSTUMED HEROES.
A SCOOP, AS WE USED TO SAY WHEN DINOSAURS ROAMED THE EARTH.
BUT-- IT'S WONDER WOMAN. WONDER WOMAN WOULDN'T HURT, LIKE, A SQUIRREL IF IT WANDERED INTO ONE OF HER FIGHTS. MUCH LESS AN INNOCENT PERSON. HOW IS THIS A SCOOP?
BECAUSE WONDER WOMAN IS ABOUT TO MAKE A MISTAKE.

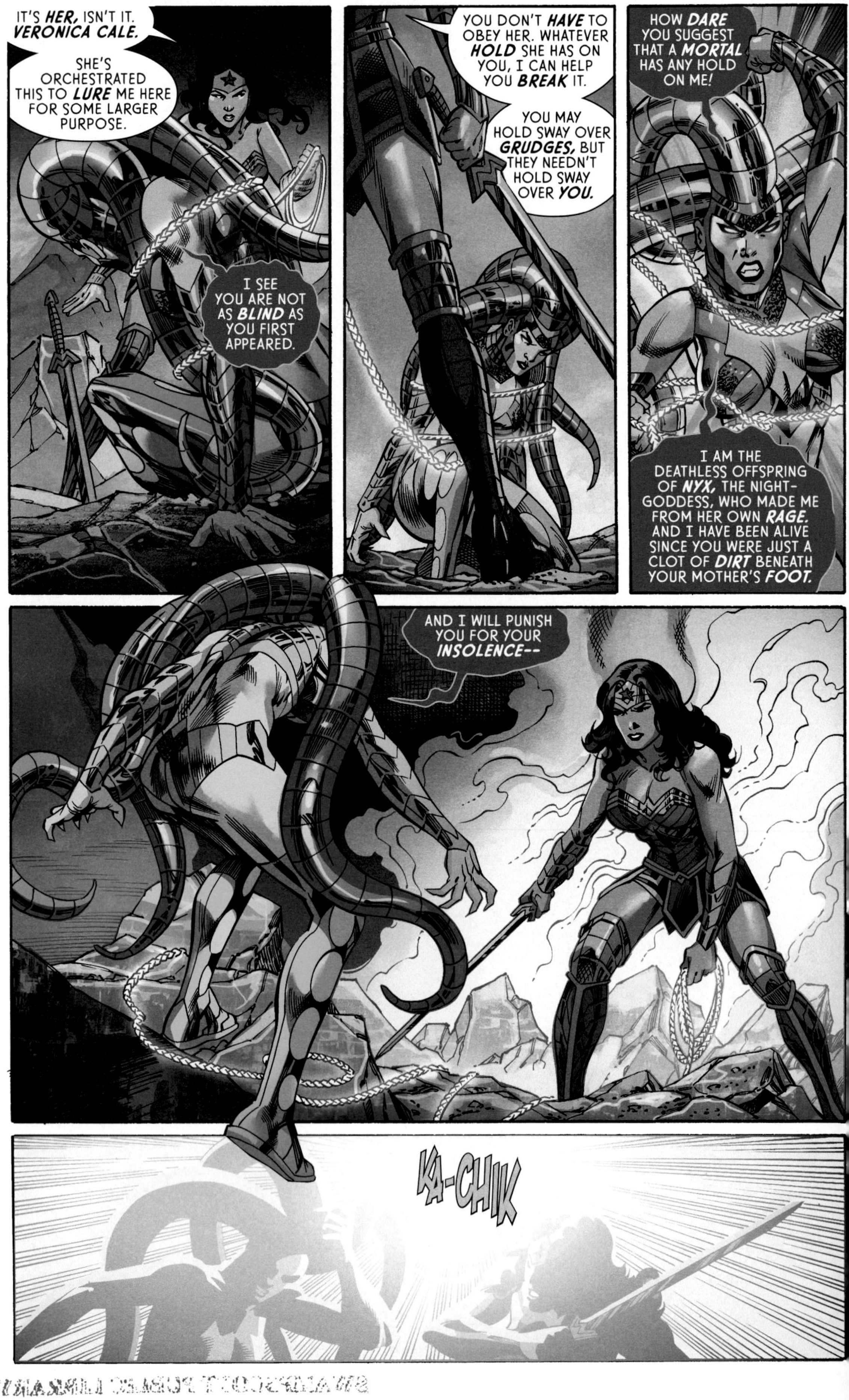
IT'S HER, ISN'T IT. VERONICA CALE.
SHE'S ORCHESTRATED THIS TO LURE ME HERE FOR SOME LARGER PURPOSE.
I SEE YOU ARE NOT AS BLIND AS YOU FIRST APPEARED.
YOU DON'T HAVE TO OBEY HER. WHATEVER HOLD SHE HAS ON YOU, I CAN HELP YOU BREAK IT.
YOU MAY HOLD SWAY OVER GRUDGES, BUT THEY NEEDN'T HOLD SWAY OVER YOU.
HOW DARE YOU SUGGEST THAT A MORTAL HAS ANY HOLD ON ME!
I AM THE DEATHLESS OFFSPRING OF NYX, THE NIGHT-GODDESS, WHO MADE ME FROM HER OWN RAGE. AND I HAVE BEEN ALIVE SINCE YOU WERE JUST A CLOT OF DIRT BENEATH YOUR MOTHER'S FOOT.
AND I WILL PUNISH YOU FOR YOUR INSOLENCE--
KA-CHIK

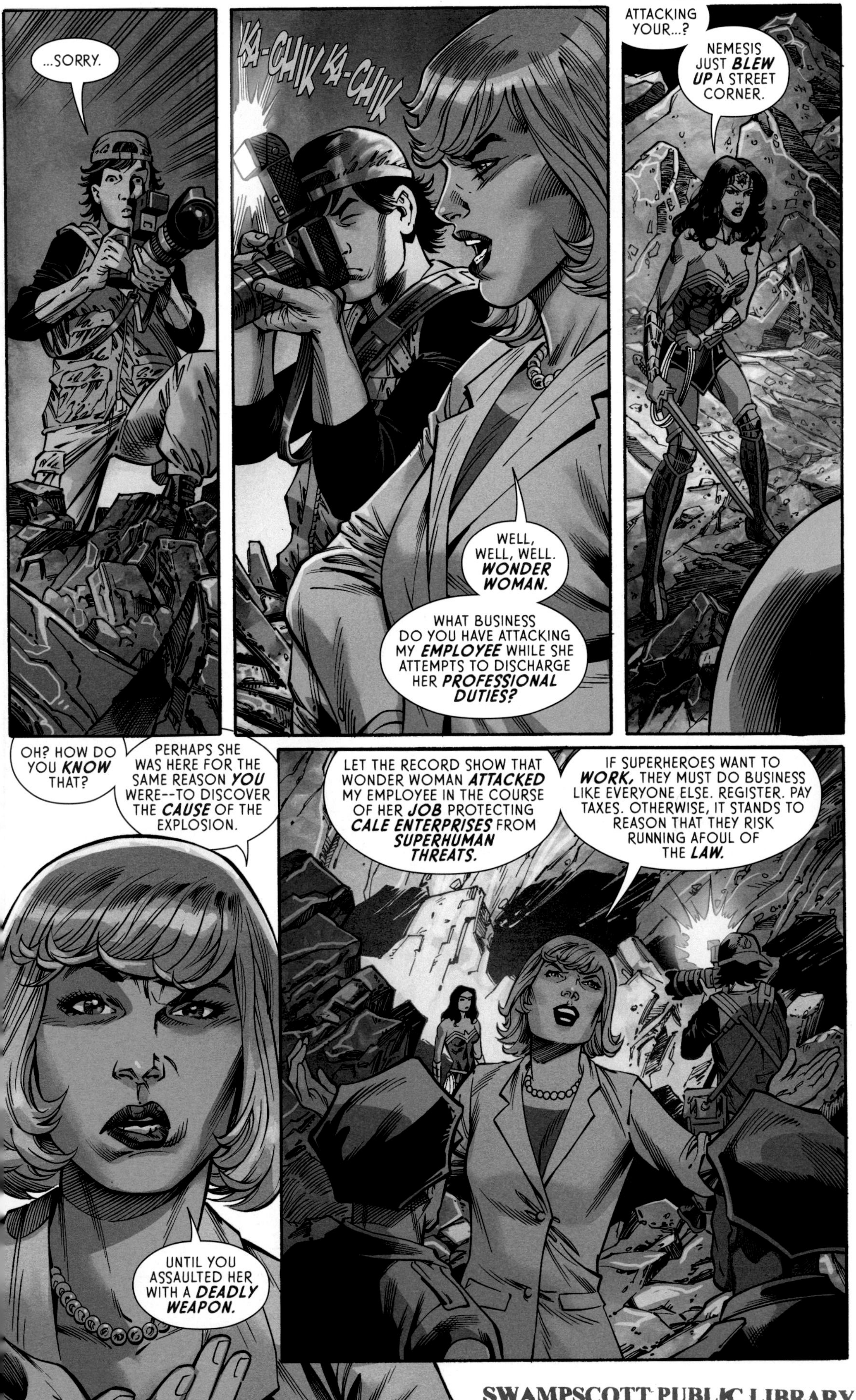
...SORRY.
KA-CHIK KA-CHIK
WELL, WELL, WELL. WONDER WOMAN.
WHAT BUSINESS DO YOU HAVE ATTACKING MY EMPLOYEE WHILE SHE ATTEMPTS TO DISCHARGE HER PROFESSIONAL DUTIES?
ATTACKING YOUR...?
NEMESIS JUST BLEW UP A STREET CORNER.
OH? HOW DO YOU KNOW THAT?
PERHAPS SHE WAS HERE FOR THE SAME REASON YOU WERE--TO DISCOVER THE CAUSE OF THE EXPLOSION.
UNTIL YOU ASSAULTED HER WITH A DEADLY WEAPON.
LET THE RECORD SHOW THAT WONDER WOMAN ATTACKED MY EMPLOYEE IN THE COURSE OF HER JOB PROTECTING CALE ENTERPRISES FROM SUPERHUMAN THREATS.
IF SUPERHEROES WANT TO WORK, THEY MUST DO BUSINESS LIKE EVERYONE ELSE. REGISTER. PAY TAXES. OTHERWISE, IT STANDS TO REASON THAT THEY RISK RUNNING AFOUL OF THE LAW.

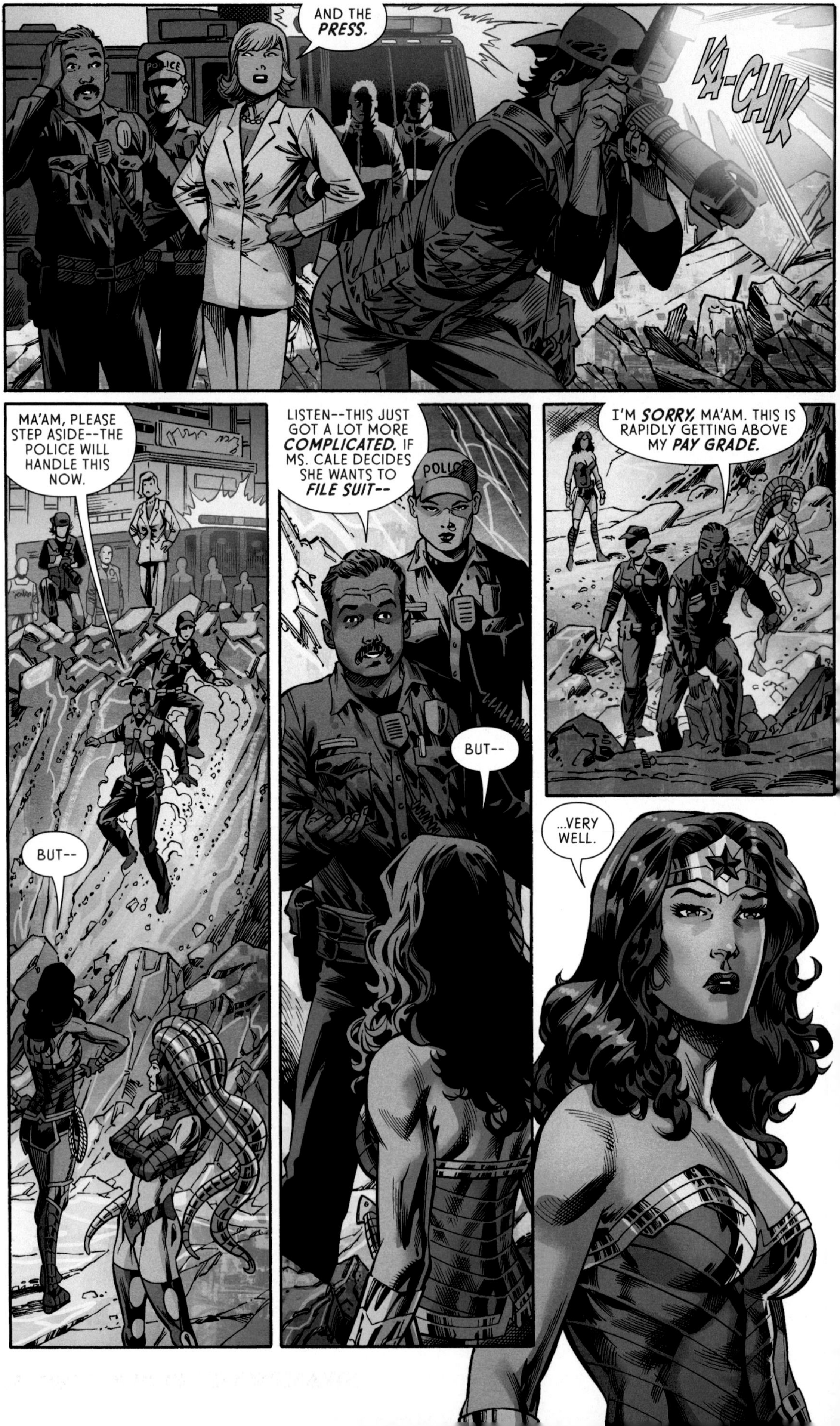
AND THE PRESS.
KA-CHIK
MA'AM, PLEASE STEP ASIDE--THE POLICE WILL HANDLE THIS NOW.
BUT--
LISTEN--THIS JUST GOT A LOT MORE COMPLICATED. IF MS. CALE DECIDES SHE WANTS TO FILE SUIT--
BUT--
I'M SORRY, MA'AM. THIS IS RAPIDLY GETTING ABOVE MY PAY GRADE.
...VERY WELL.

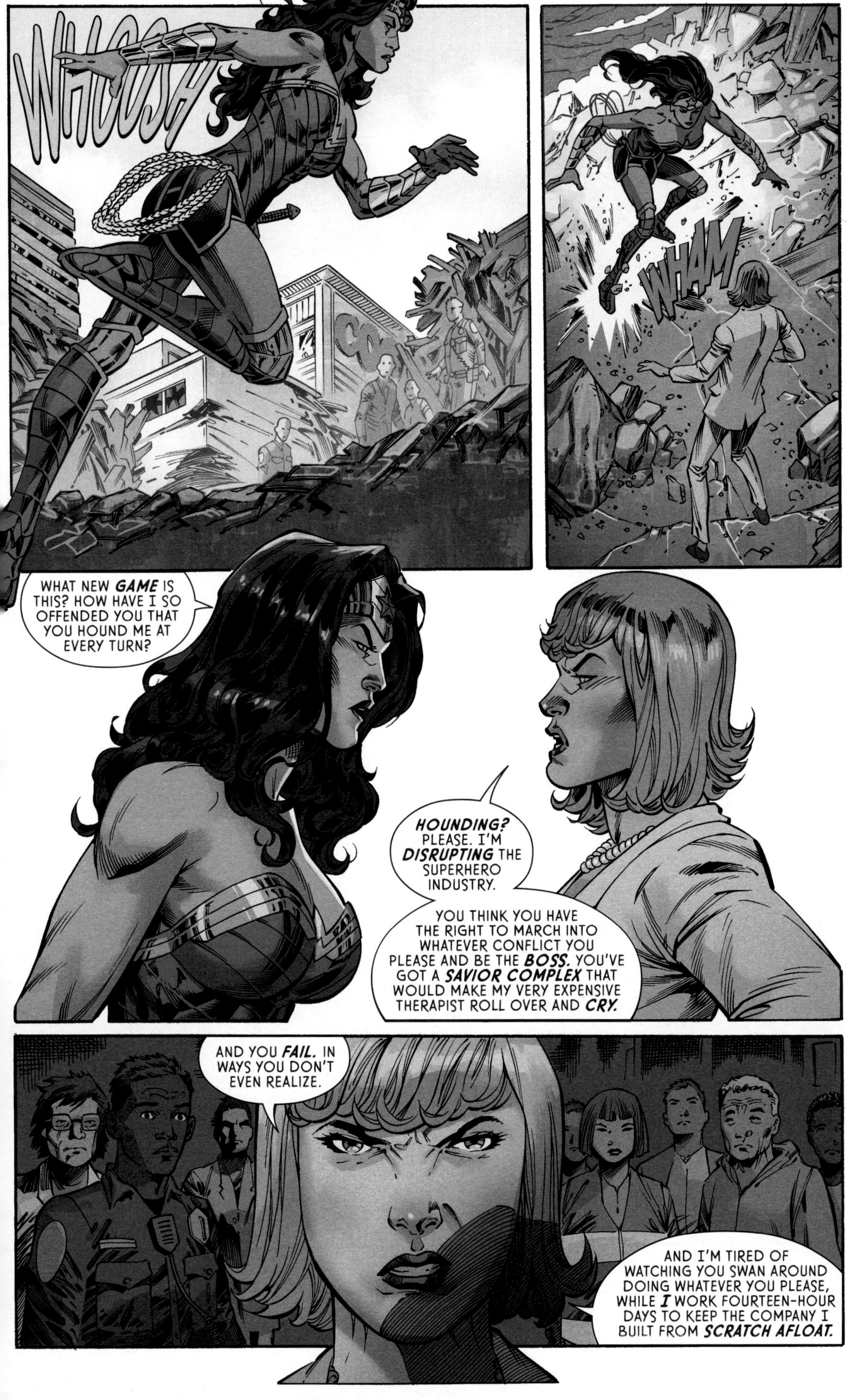
WHOOSH
WHAM
WHAT NEW **GAME** IS THIS? HOW HAVE I SO OFFENDED YOU THAT YOU HOUND ME AT EVERY TURN?
HOUNDING? PLEASE. I'M ***DISRUPTING*** THE SUPERHERO INDUSTRY.
YOU THINK YOU HAVE THE RIGHT TO MARCH INTO WHATEVER CONFLICT YOU PLEASE AND BE THE ***BOSS.*** YOU'VE GOT A ***SAVIOR COMPLEX*** THAT WOULD MAKE MY VERY EXPENSIVE THERAPIST ROLL OVER AND ***CRY.***
AND YOU ***FAIL.*** IN WAYS YOU DON'T EVEN REALIZE.
AND I'M TIRED OF WATCHING YOU SWAN AROUND DOING WHATEVER YOU PLEASE, WHILE ***I*** WORK FOURTEEN-HOUR DAYS TO KEEP THE COMPANY I BUILT FROM ***SCRATCH AFLOAT.***

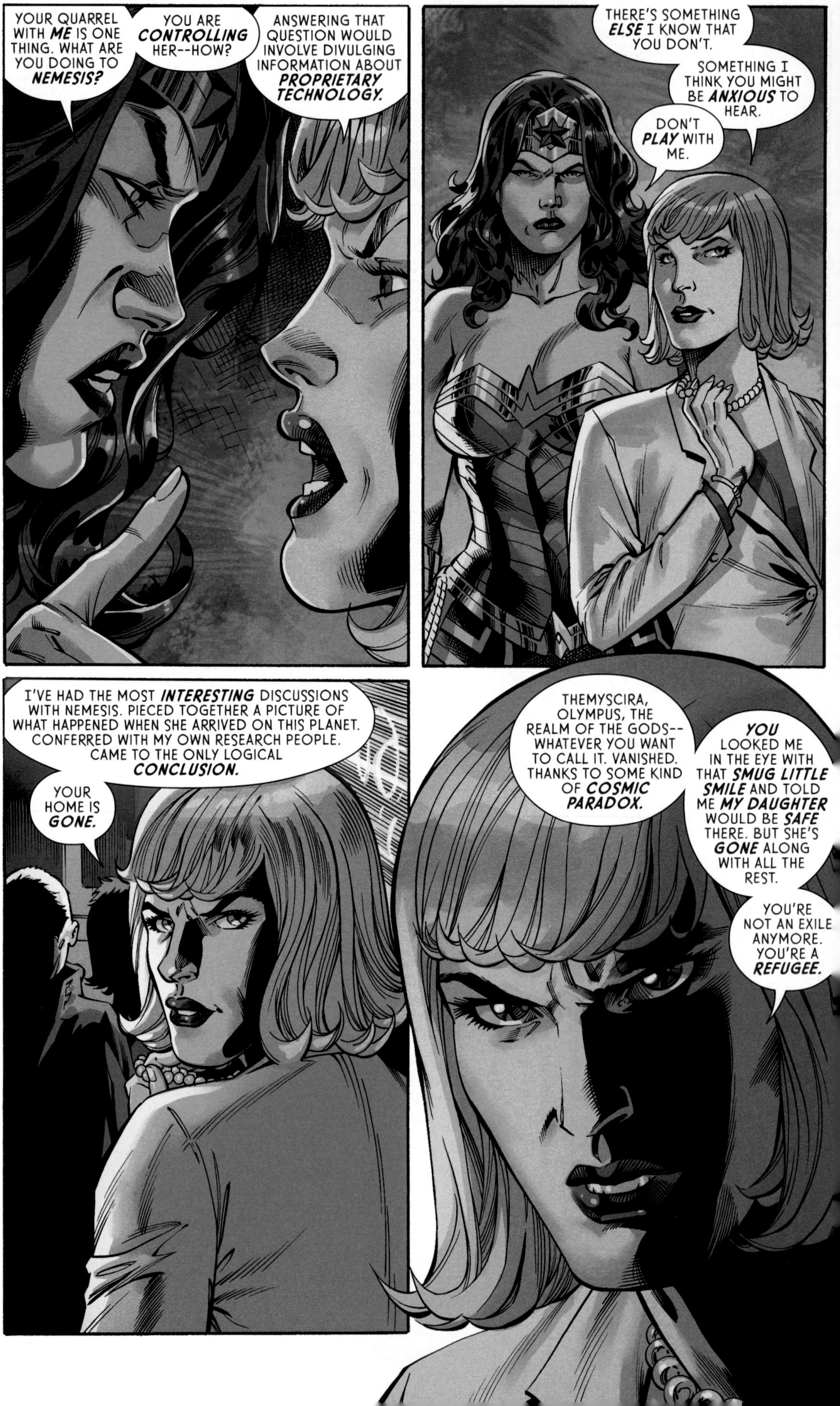
YOUR QUARREL WITH ME IS ONE THING. WHAT ARE YOU DOING TO NEMESIS?
YOU ARE CONTROLLING HER--HOW?
ANSWERING THAT QUESTION WOULD INVOLVE DIVULGING INFORMATION ABOUT PROPRIETARY TECHNOLOGY.
THERE'S SOMETHING ELSE I KNOW THAT YOU DON'T.
SOMETHING I THINK YOU MIGHT BE ANXIOUS TO HEAR.
DON'T PLAY WITH ME.
I'VE HAD THE MOST INTERESTING DISCUSSIONS WITH NEMESIS. PIECED TOGETHER A PICTURE OF WHAT HAPPENED WHEN SHE ARRIVED ON THIS PLANET. CONFERRED WITH MY OWN RESEARCH PEOPLE. CAME TO THE ONLY LOGICAL CONCLUSION.
YOUR HOME IS GONE.
THEMYSCIRA, OLYMPUS, THE REALM OF THE GODS--WHATEVER YOU WANT TO CALL IT. VANISHED. THANKS TO SOME KIND OF COSMIC PARADOX.
YOU LOOKED ME IN THE EYE WITH THAT SMUG LITTLE SMILE AND TOLD ME MY DAUGHTER WOULD BE SAFE THERE. BUT SHE'S GONE ALONG WITH ALL THE REST.
YOU'RE NOT AN EXILE ANYMORE. YOU'RE A REFUGEE.

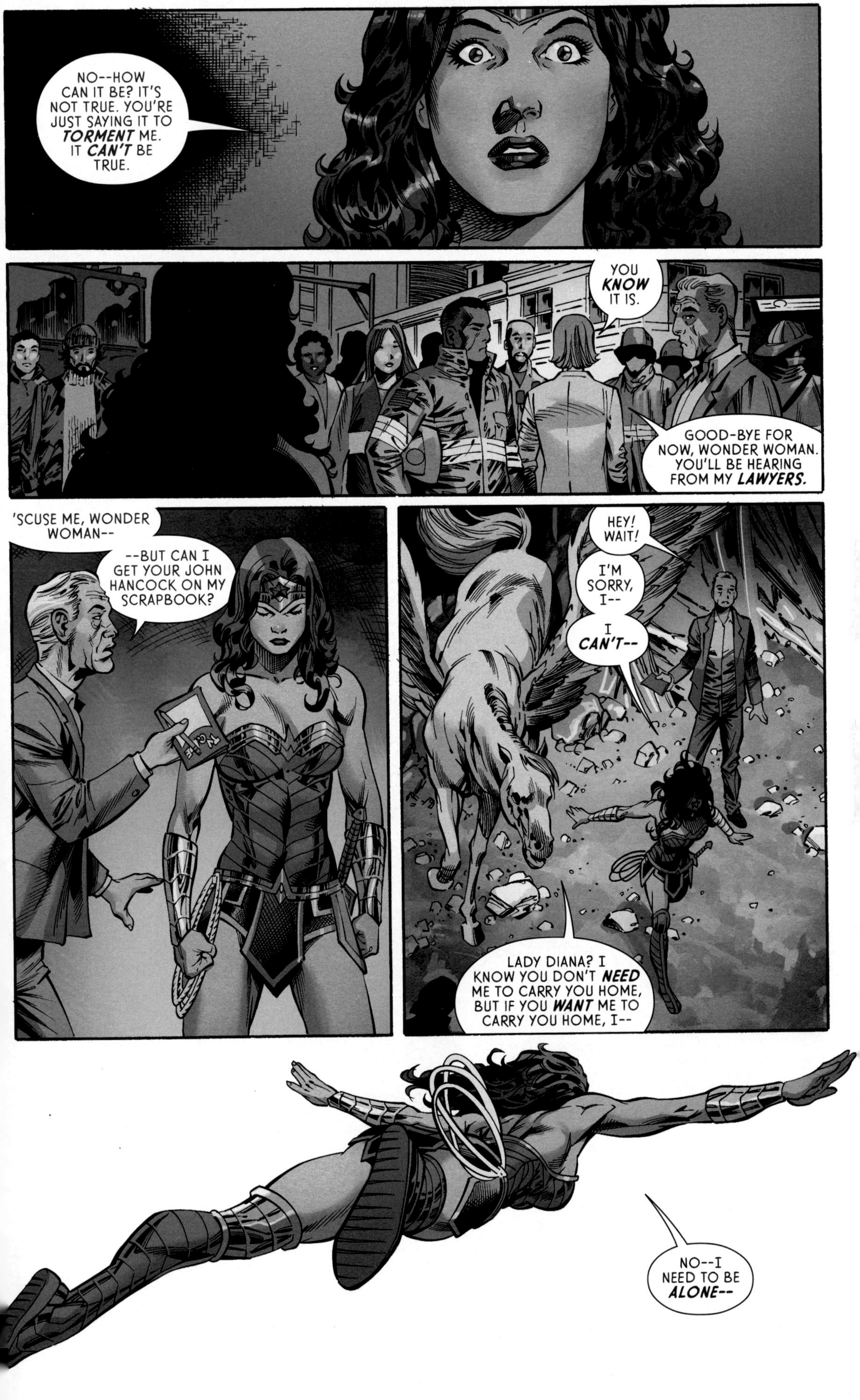
NO--HOW CAN IT BE? IT'S NOT TRUE. YOU'RE JUST SAYING IT TO TORMENT ME. IT CAN'T BE TRUE.
YOU KNOW IT IS.
GOOD-BYE FOR NOW, WONDER WOMAN. YOU'LL BE HEARING FROM MY LAWYERS.
'SCUSE ME, WONDER WOMAN--
--BUT CAN I GET YOUR JOHN HANCOCK ON MY SCRAPBOOK?
HEY! WAIT!
I'M SORRY, I--
I CAN'T--
LADY DIANA? I KNOW YOU DON'T NEED ME TO CARRY YOU HOME, BUT IF YOU WANT ME TO CARRY YOU HOME, I--
NO--I NEED TO BE ALONE--

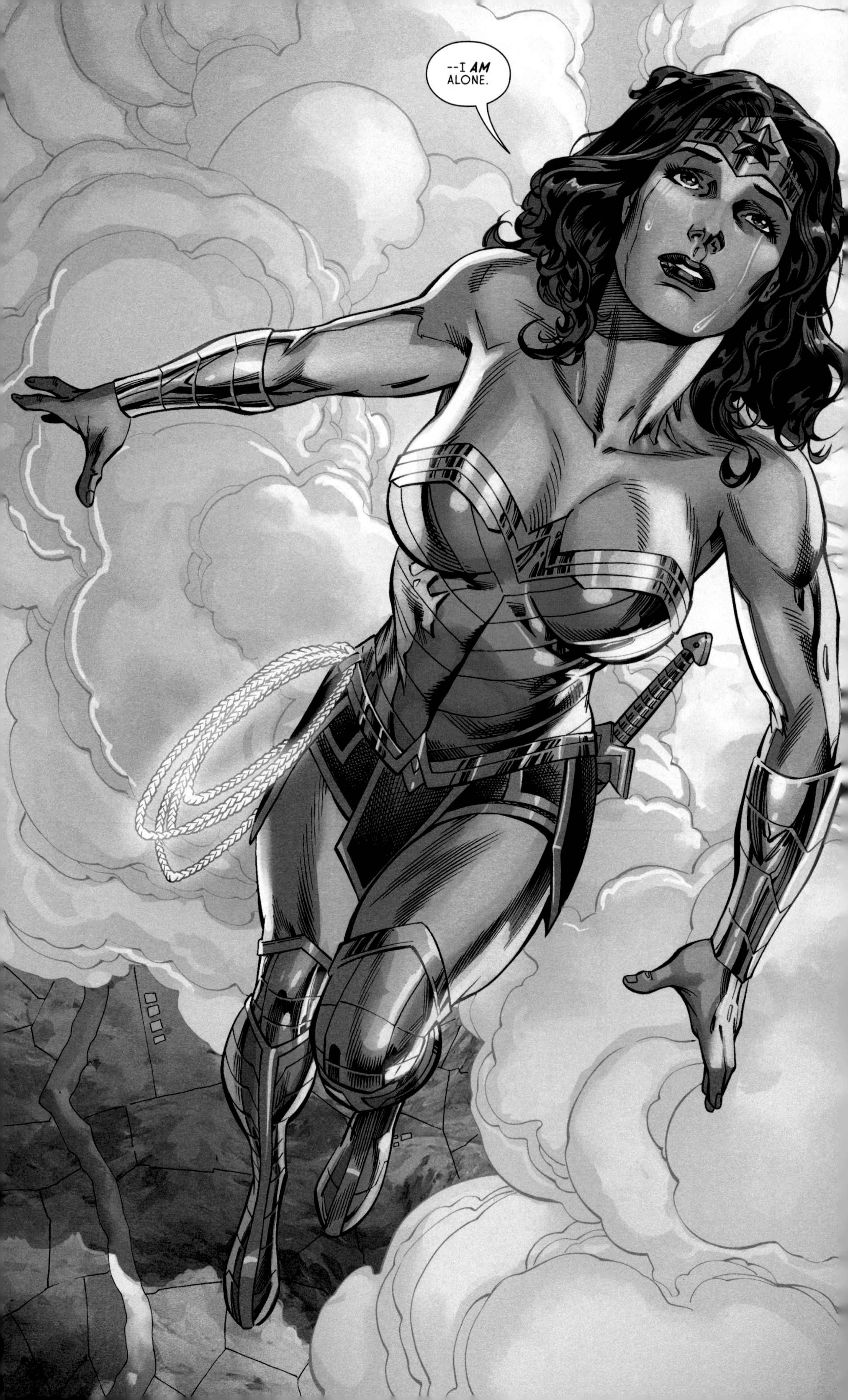
--I AM ALONE.

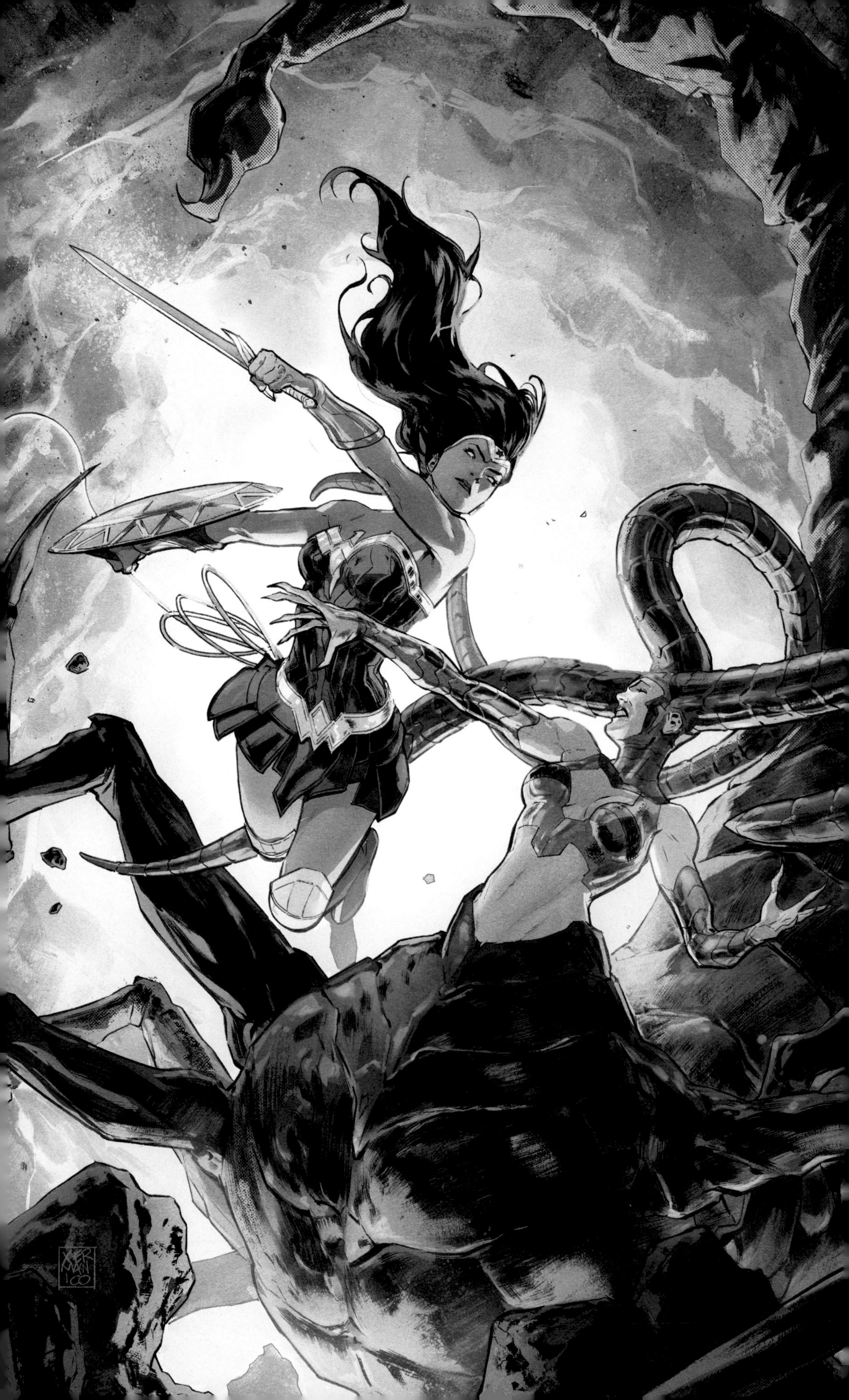

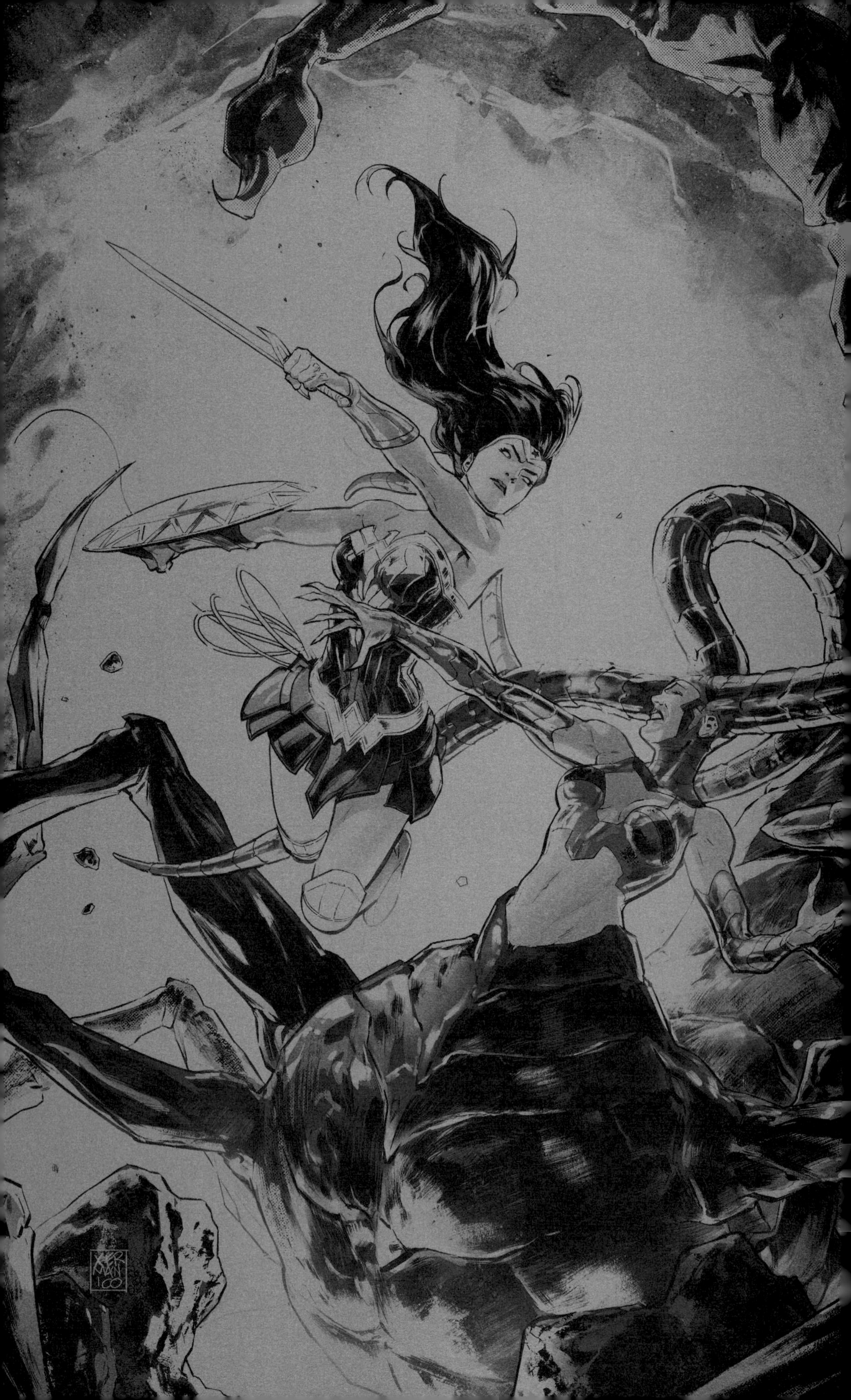

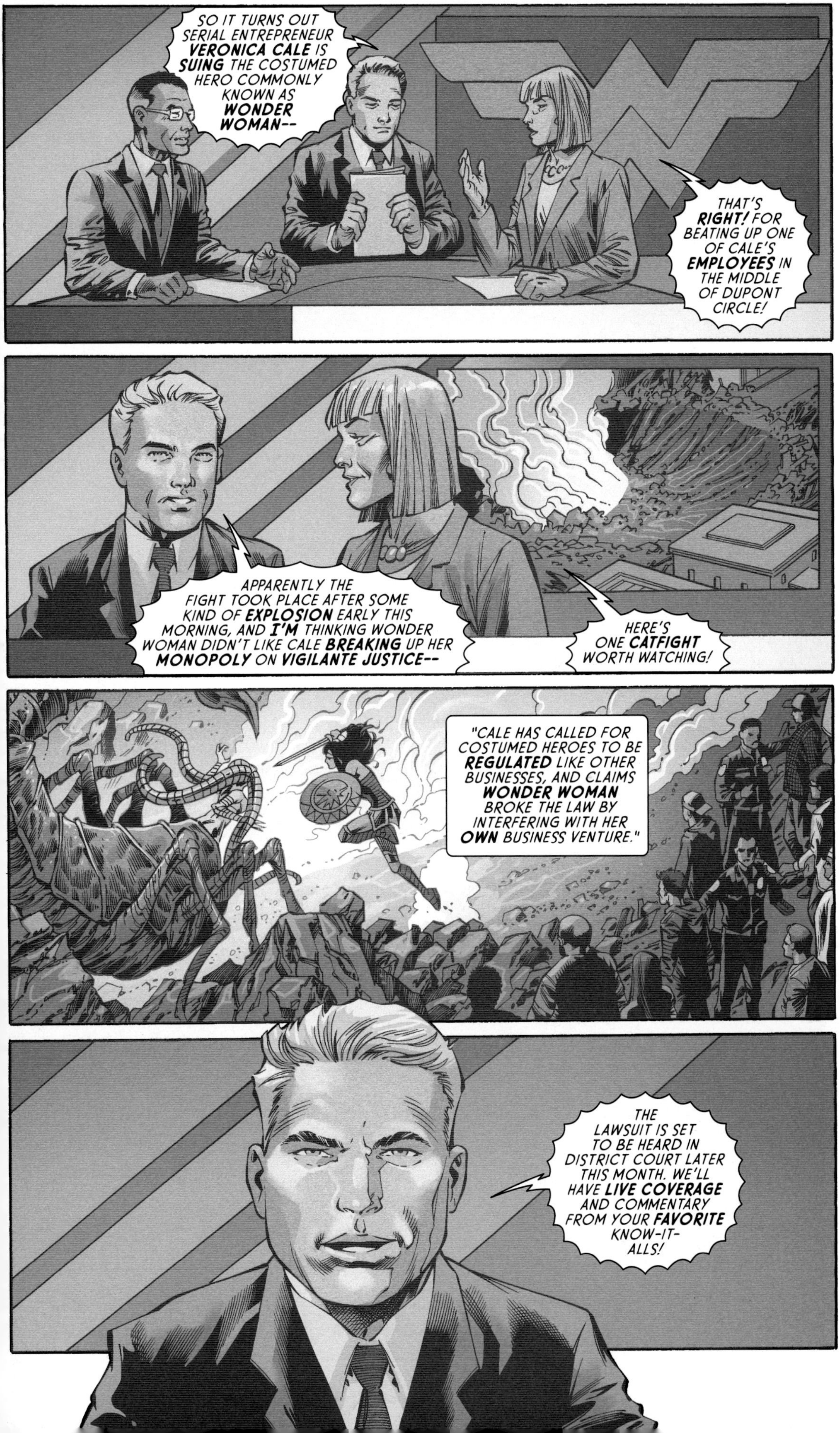
SO IT TURNS OUT SERIAL ENTREPRENEUR VERONICA CALE IS SUING THE COSTUMED HERO COMMONLY KNOWN AS WONDER WOMAN--
THAT'S RIGHT! FOR BEATING UP ONE OF CALE'S EMPLOYEES IN THE MIDDLE OF DUPONT CIRCLE!
APPARENTLY THE FIGHT TOOK PLACE AFTER SOME KIND OF EXPLOSION EARLY THIS MORNING, AND I'M THINKING WONDER WOMAN DIDN'T LIKE CALE BREAKING UP HER MONOPOLY ON VIGILANTE JUSTICE--
HERE'S ONE CATFIGHT WORTH WATCHING!
"CALE HAS CALLED FOR COSTUMED HEROES TO BE REGULATED LIKE OTHER BUSINESSES, AND CLAIMS WONDER WOMAN BROKE THE LAW BY INTERFERING WITH HER OWN BUSINESS VENTURE."
THE LAWSUIT IS SET TO BE HEARD IN DISTRICT COURT LATER THIS MONTH. WE'LL HAVE LIVE COVERAGE AND COMMENTARY FROM YOUR FAVORITE KNOW-IT-ALLS!

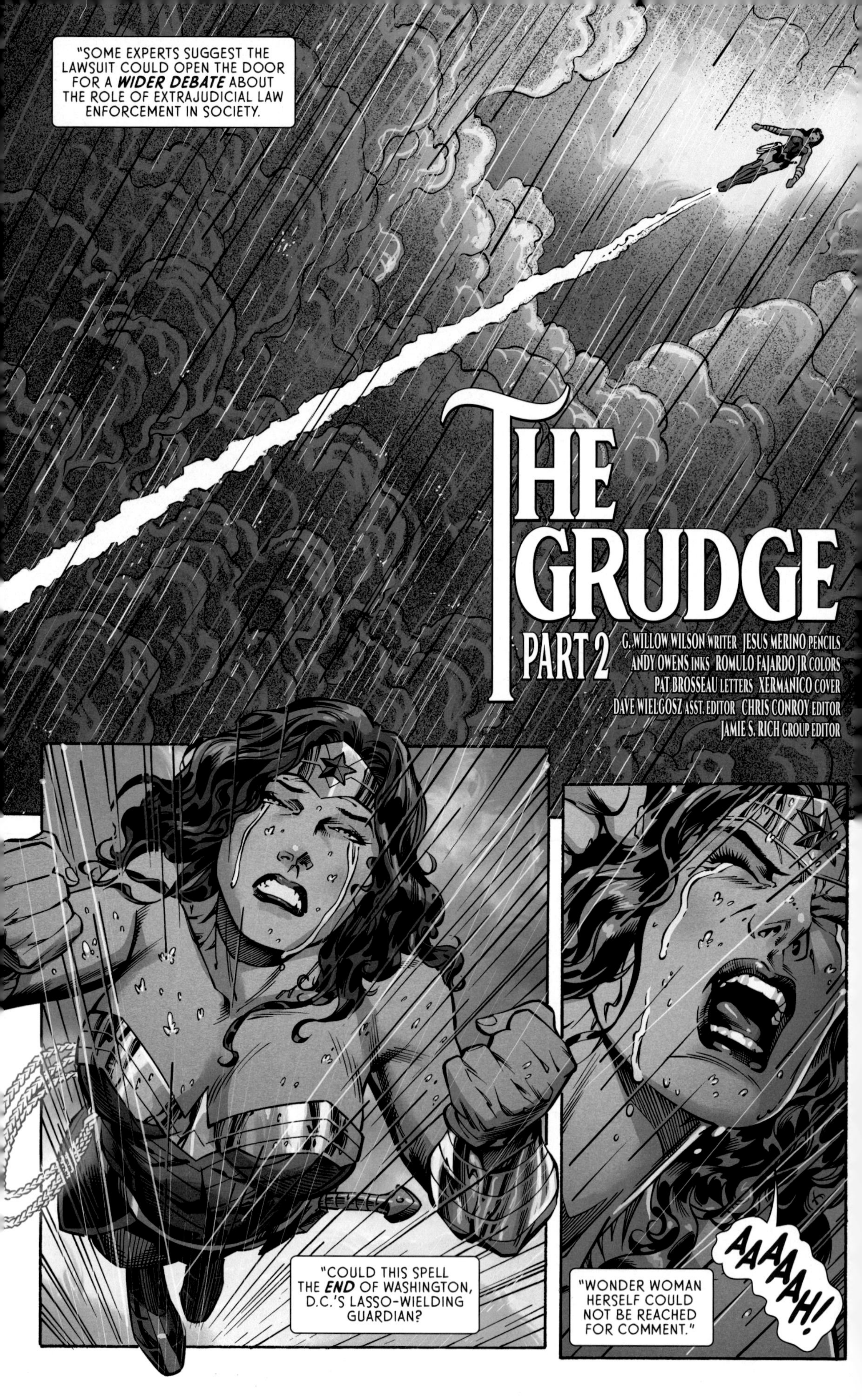
"SOME EXPERTS SUGGEST THE LAWSUIT COULD OPEN THE DOOR FOR A WIDER DEBATE ABOUT THE ROLE OF EXTRAJUDICIAL LAW ENFORCEMENT IN SOCIETY.
THE GRUDGE
PART 2
G. WILLOW WILSON WRITER JESUS MERINO PENCILS
ANDY OWENS INKS ROMULO FAJARDO JR COLORS
PAT BROSSEAU LETTERS XERMANICO COVER
DAVE WIELGOSZ ASST. EDITOR CHRIS CONROY EDITOR
JAMIE S. RICH GROUP EDITOR
"COULD THIS SPELL THE END OF WASHINGTON, D.C.'S LASSO-WIELDING GUARDIAN?
"WONDER WOMAN HERSELF COULD NOT BE REACHED FOR COMMENT."
AAAAAH!

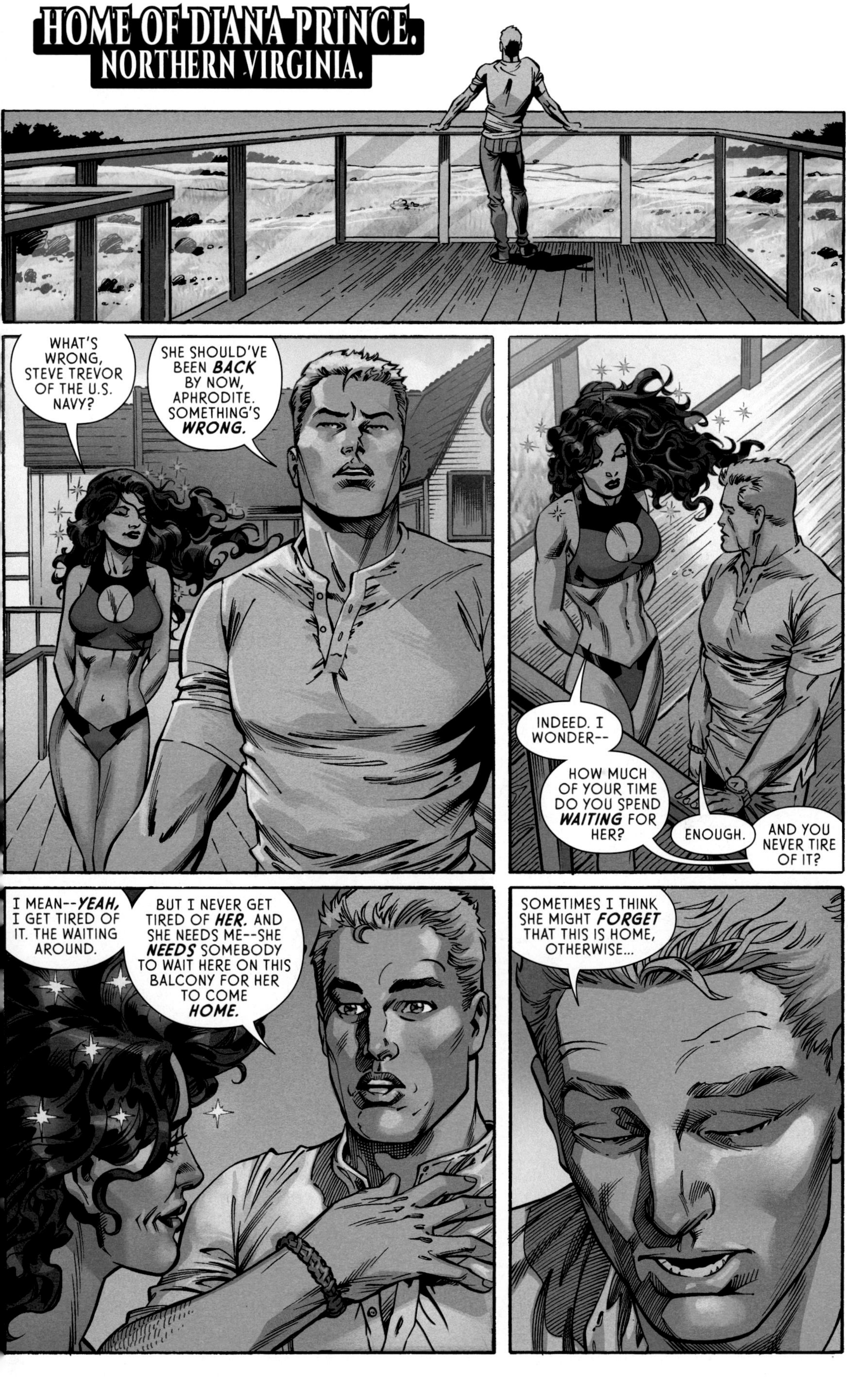
HOME OF DIANA PRINCE.
NORTHERN VIRGINIA.
WHAT'S WRONG, STEVE TREVOR OF THE U.S. NAVY?
SHE SHOULD'VE BEEN BACK BY NOW, APHRODITE. SOMETHING'S WRONG.
INDEED. I WONDER--
HOW MUCH OF YOUR TIME DO YOU SPEND WAITING FOR HER?
ENOUGH.
AND YOU NEVER TIRE OF IT?
I MEAN--YEAH, I GET TIRED OF IT. THE WAITING AROUND.
BUT I NEVER GET TIRED OF HER. AND SHE NEEDS ME--SHE NEEDS SOMEBODY TO WAIT HERE ON THIS BALCONY FOR HER TO COME HOME.
SOMETIMES I THINK SHE MIGHT FORGET THAT THIS IS HOME, OTHERWISE...

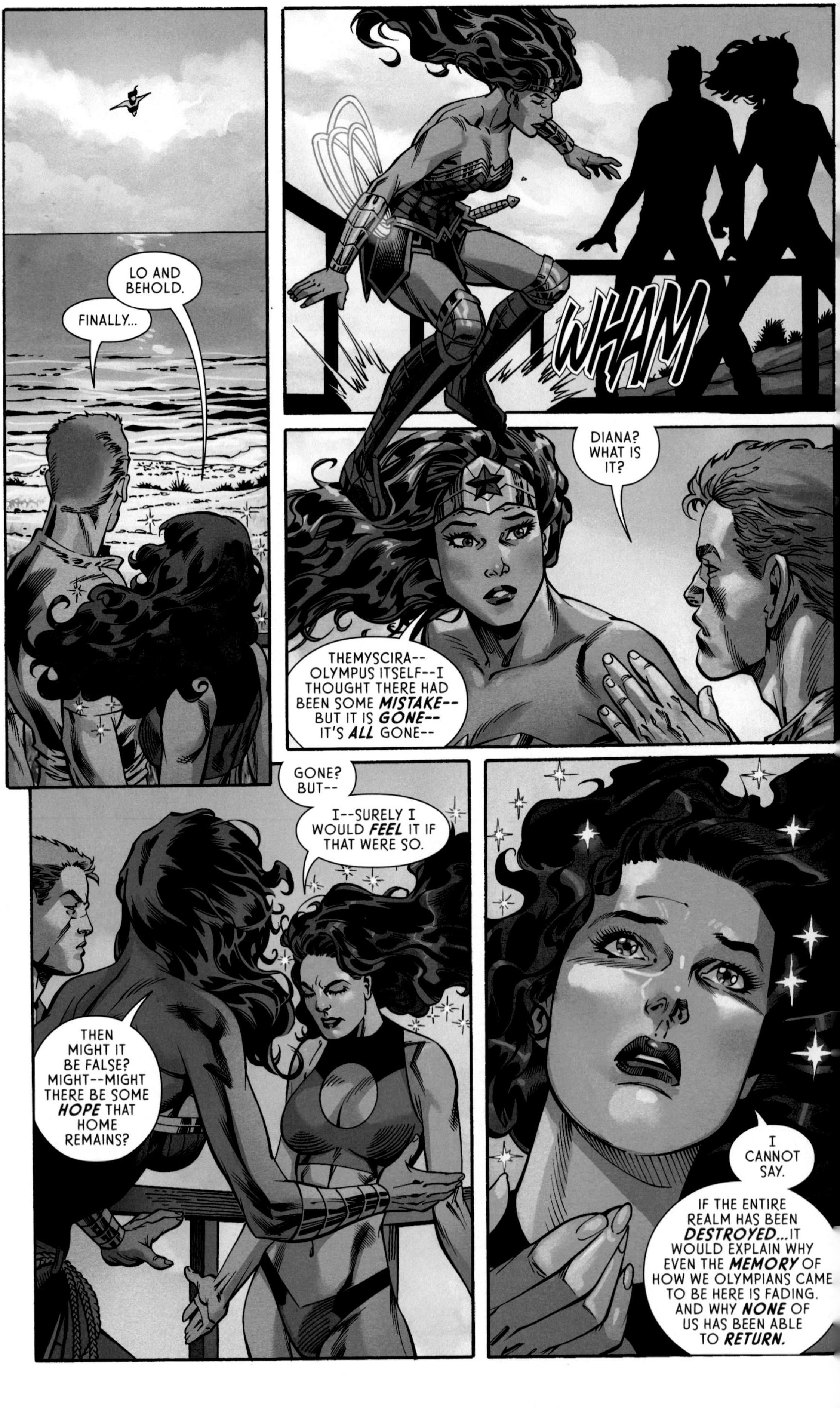

FINALLY...
LO AND BEHOLD.
WHAM
DIANA? WHAT IS IT?
THEMYSCIRA-- OLYMPUS ITSELF--I THOUGHT THERE HAD BEEN SOME MISTAKE-- BUT IT IS GONE-- IT'S ALL GONE--
GONE? BUT--
I--SURELY I WOULD FEEL IT IF THAT WERE SO.
THEN MIGHT IT BE FALSE? MIGHT--MIGHT THERE BE SOME HOPE THAT HOME REMAINS?
I CANNOT SAY.
IF THE ENTIRE REALM HAS BEEN DESTROYED...IT WOULD EXPLAIN WHY EVEN THE MEMORY OF HOW WE OLYMPIANS CAME TO BE HERE IS FADING. AND WHY NONE OF US HAS BEEN ABLE TO RETURN.

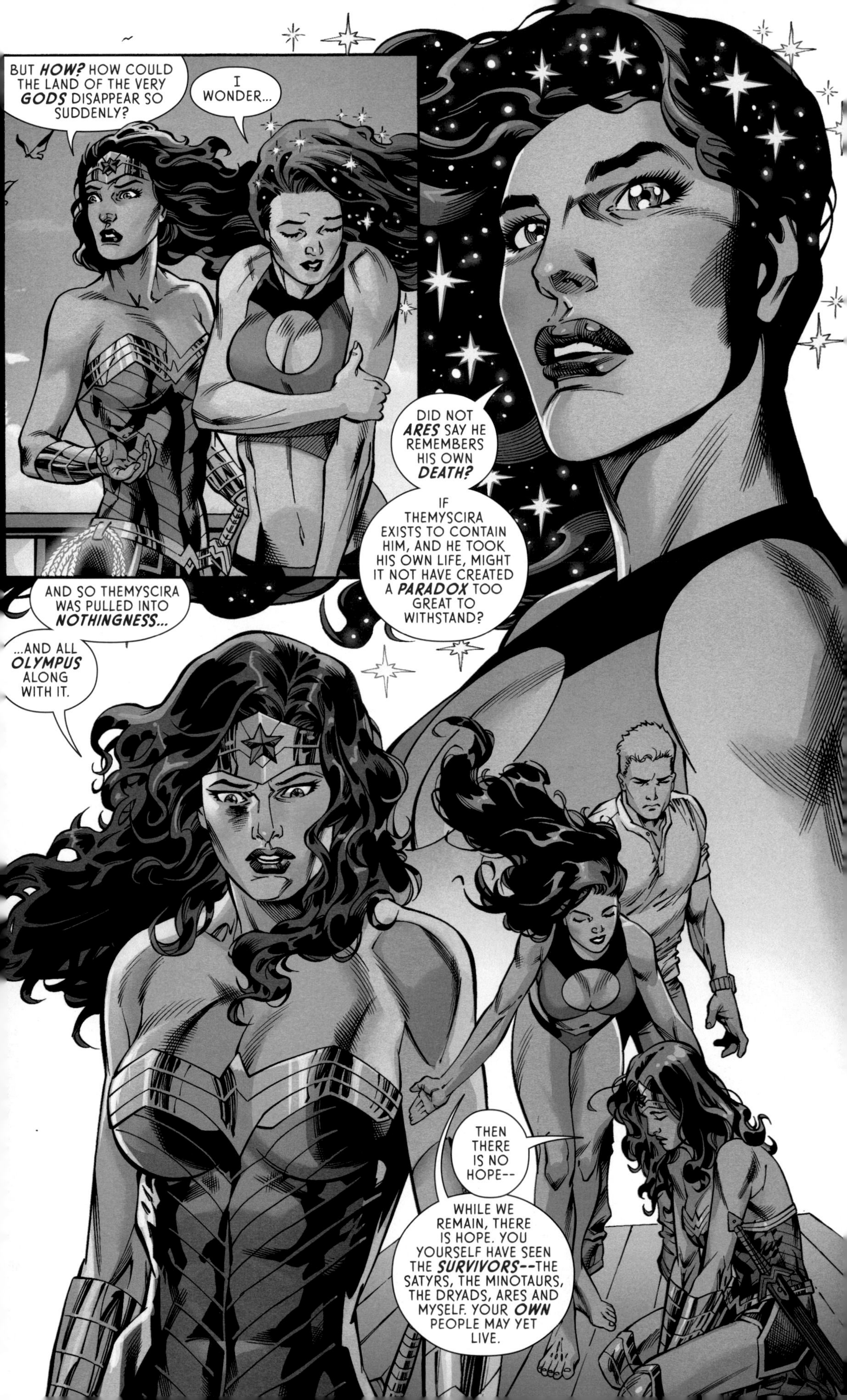
BUT **HOW?** HOW COULD THE LAND OF THE VERY **GODS** DISAPPEAR SO SUDDENLY?
I WONDER...
DID NOT **ARES** SAY HE REMEMBERS HIS OWN **DEATH?**
IF THEMYSCIRA EXISTS TO CONTAIN HIM, AND HE TOOK HIS OWN LIFE, MIGHT IT NOT HAVE CREATED A **PARADOX** TOO GREAT TO WITHSTAND?
AND SO THEMYSCIRA WAS PULLED INTO **NOTHINGNESS...**
...AND ALL **OLYMPUS** ALONG WITH IT.
THEN THERE IS NO HOPE--
WHILE WE REMAIN, THERE IS HOPE. YOU YOURSELF HAVE SEEN THE **SURVIVORS--**THE SATYRS, THE MINOTAURS, THE DRYADS, ARES AND MYSELF. YOUR **OWN** PEOPLE MAY YET LIVE.

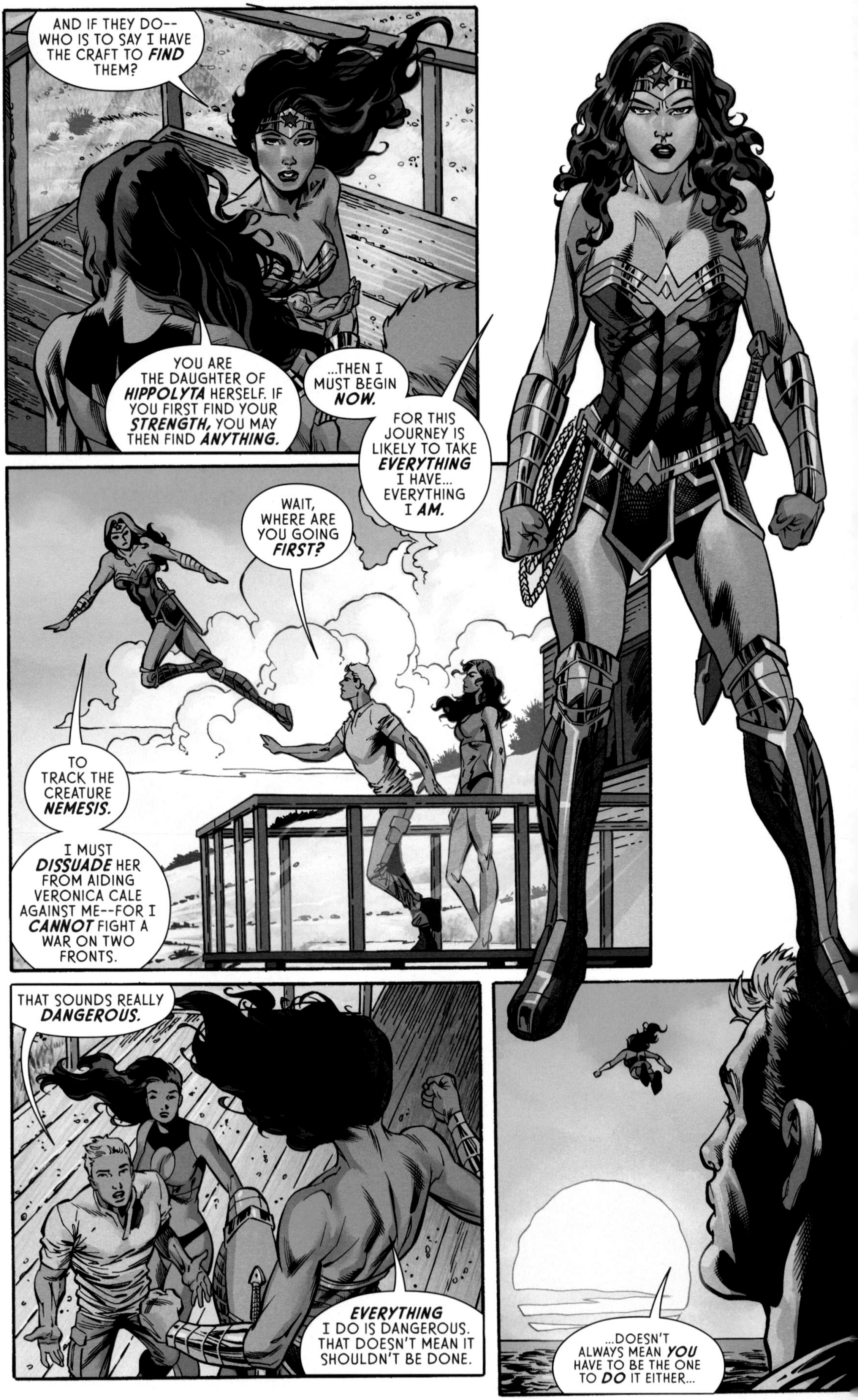
AND IF THEY DO-- WHO IS TO SAY I HAVE THE CRAFT TO FIND THEM?
YOU ARE THE DAUGHTER OF HIPPOLYTA HERSELF. IF YOU FIRST FIND YOUR STRENGTH, YOU MAY THEN FIND ANYTHING.
...THEN I MUST BEGIN NOW.
FOR THIS JOURNEY IS LIKELY TO TAKE EVERYTHING I HAVE... EVERYTHING I AM.
WAIT, WHERE ARE YOU GOING FIRST?
TO TRACK THE CREATURE NEMESIS.
I MUST DISSUADE HER FROM AIDING VERONICA CALE AGAINST ME--FOR I CANNOT FIGHT A WAR ON TWO FRONTS.
THAT SOUNDS REALLY DANGEROUS.
EVERYTHING I DO IS DANGEROUS. THAT DOESN'T MEAN IT SHOULDN'T BE DONE.
...DOESN'T ALWAYS MEAN YOU HAVE TO BE THE ONE TO DO IT EITHER...

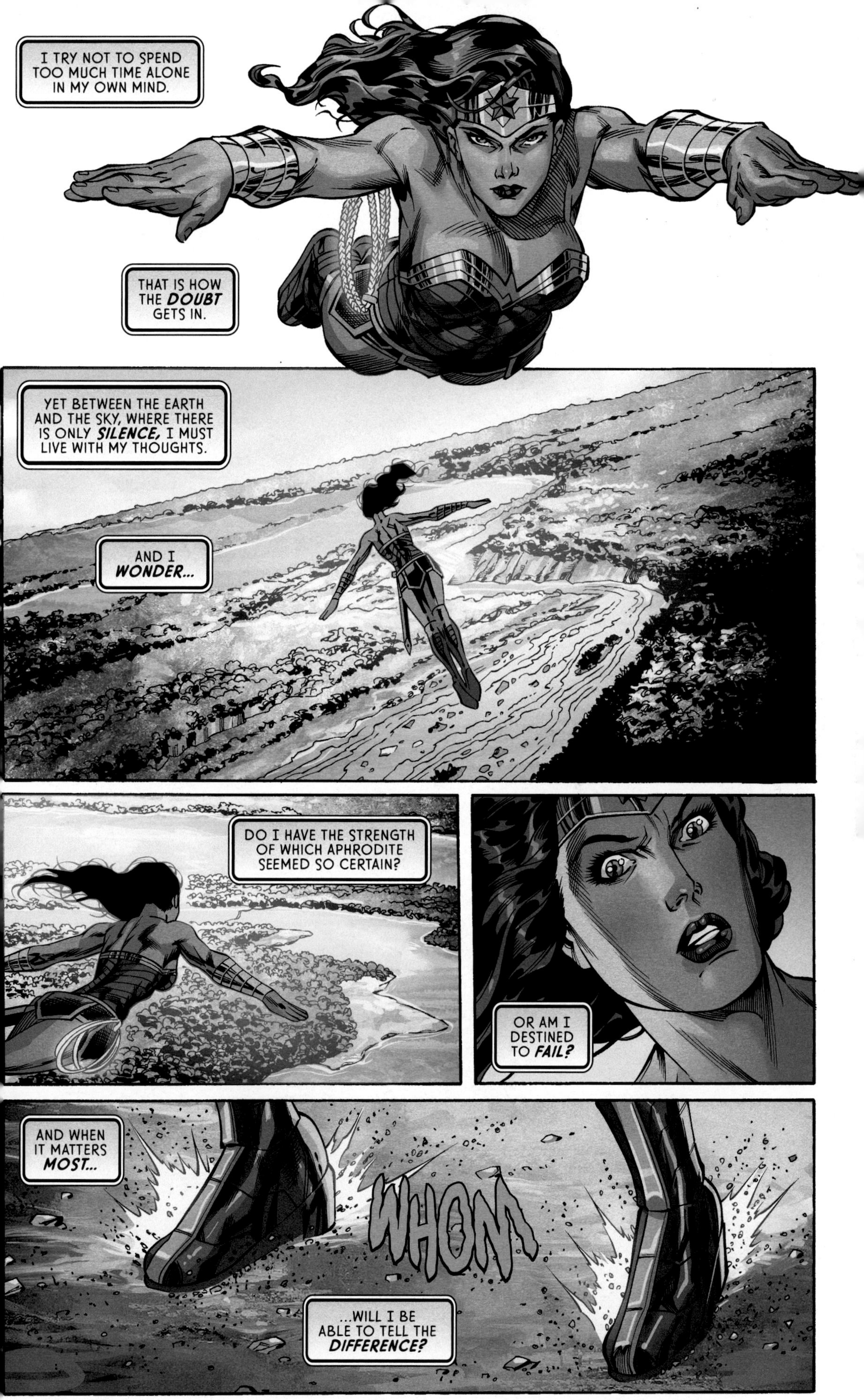
I TRY NOT TO SPEND TOO MUCH TIME ALONE IN MY OWN MIND.
THAT IS HOW THE DOUBT GETS IN.
YET BETWEEN THE EARTH AND THE SKY, WHERE THERE IS ONLY SILENCE, I MUST LIVE WITH MY THOUGHTS.
AND I WONDER...
DO I HAVE THE STRENGTH OF WHICH APHRODITE SEEMED SO CERTAIN?
OR AM I DESTINED TO FAIL?
AND WHEN IT MATTERS MOST...
WHOM
...WILL I BE ABLE TO TELL THE DIFFERENCE?

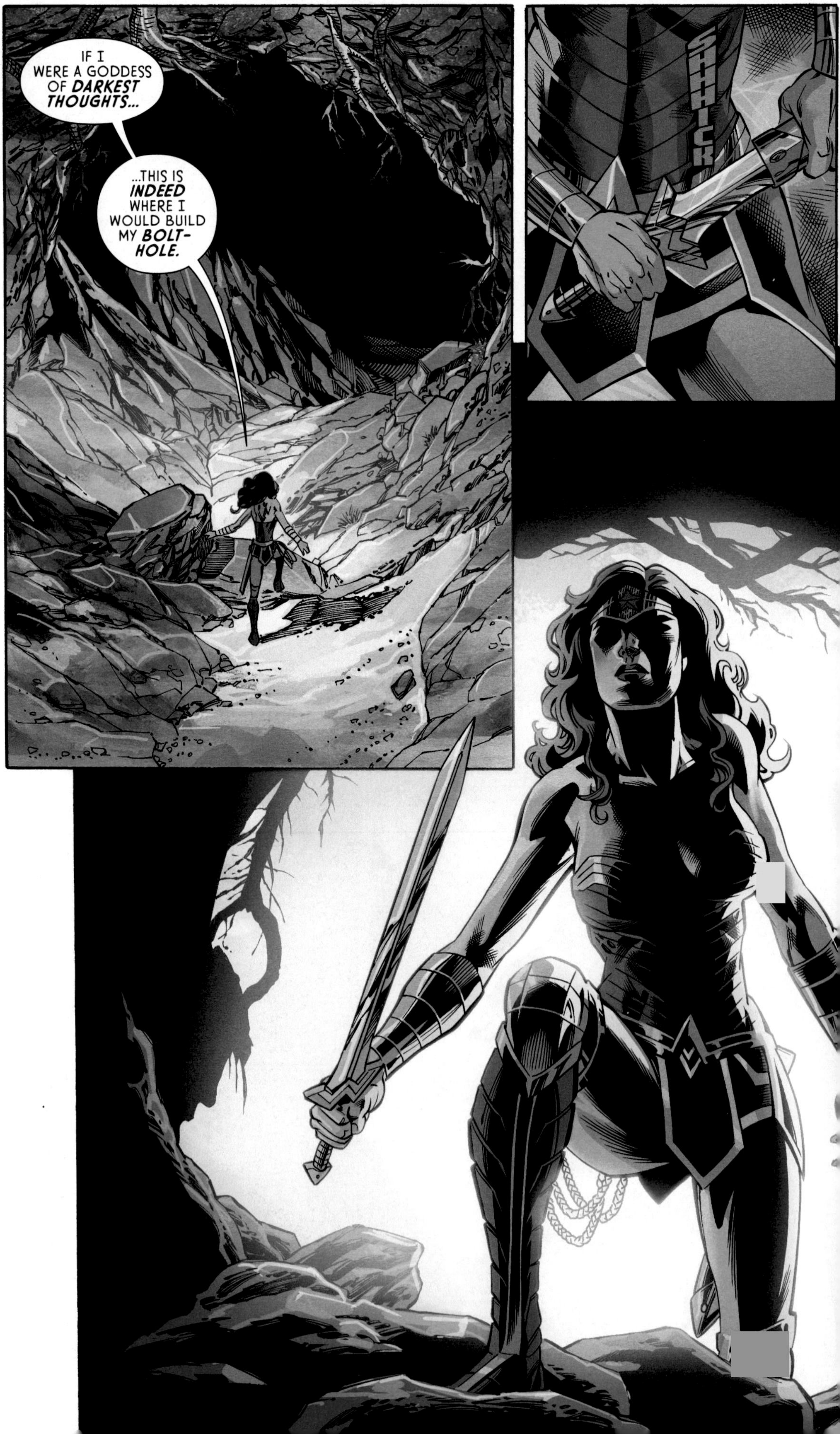
IF I WERE A GODDESS OF DARKEST THOUGHTS...
...THIS IS INDEED WHERE I WOULD BUILD MY BOLT-HOLE.
SHHICK

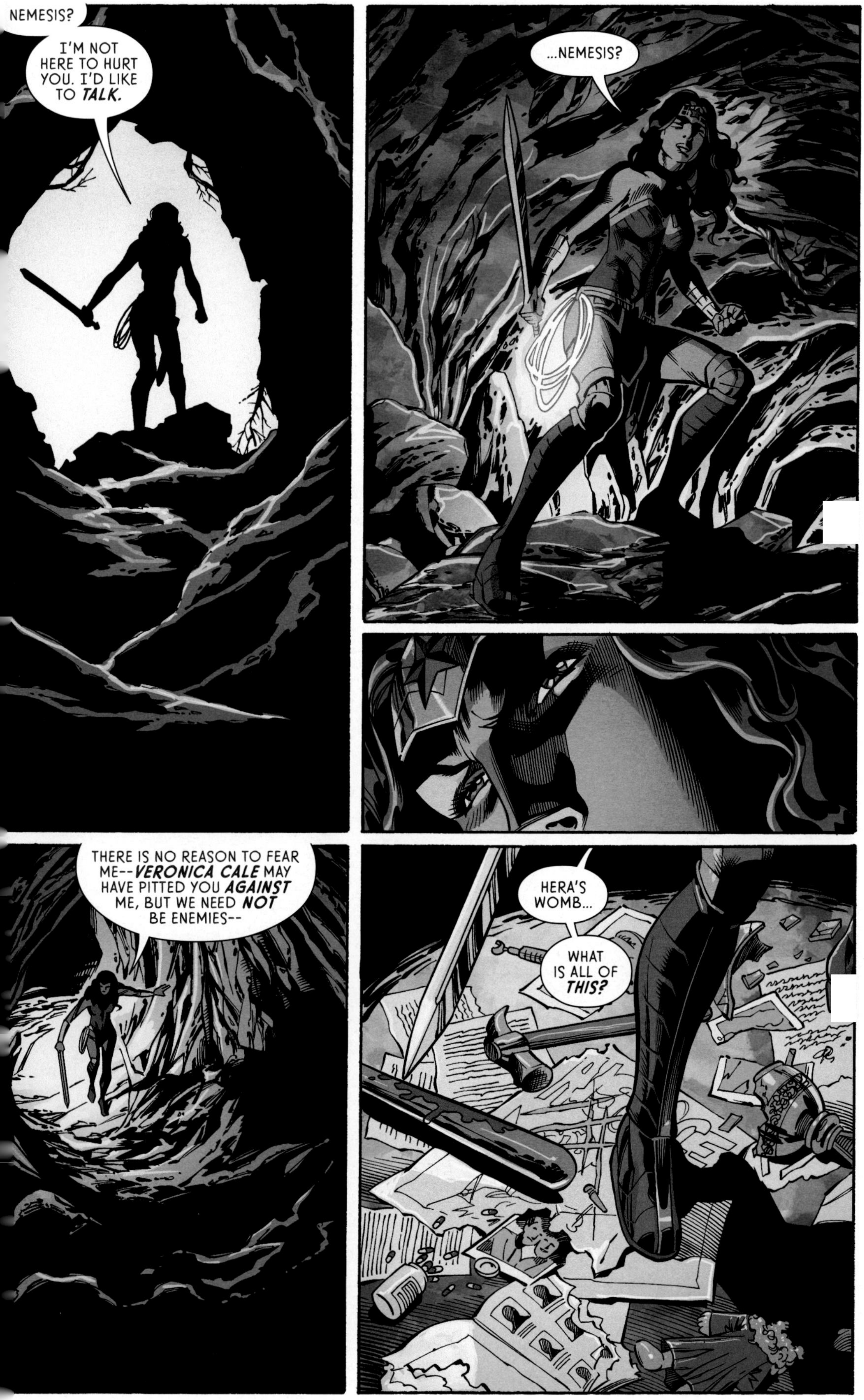
NEMESIS?
I'M NOT HERE TO HURT YOU. I'D LIKE TO TALK.
...NEMESIS?
THERE IS NO REASON TO FEAR ME--VERONICA CALE MAY HAVE PITTED YOU AGAINST ME, BUT WE NEED NOT BE ENEMIES--
HERA'S WOMB...
WHAT IS ALL OF THIS?

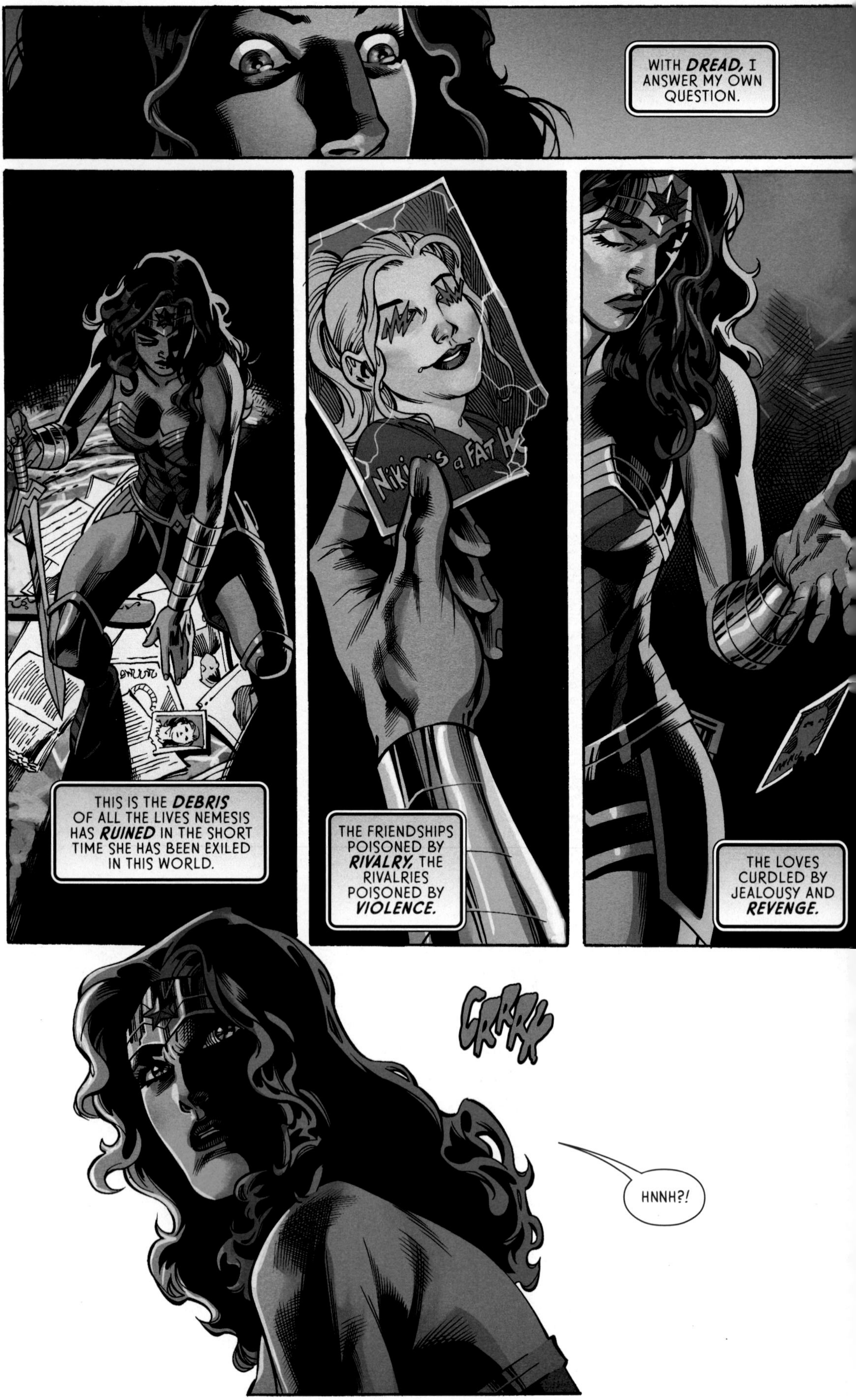
WITH DREAD, I ANSWER MY OWN QUESTION.
THIS IS THE DEBRIS OF ALL THE LIVES NEMESIS HAS RUINED IN THE SHORT TIME SHE HAS BEEN EXILED IN THIS WORLD.
THE FRIENDSHIPS POISONED BY RIVALRY, THE RIVALRIES POISONED BY VIOLENCE.
THE LOVES CURDLED BY JEALOUSY AND REVENGE.
CRRRK
HNNH?!

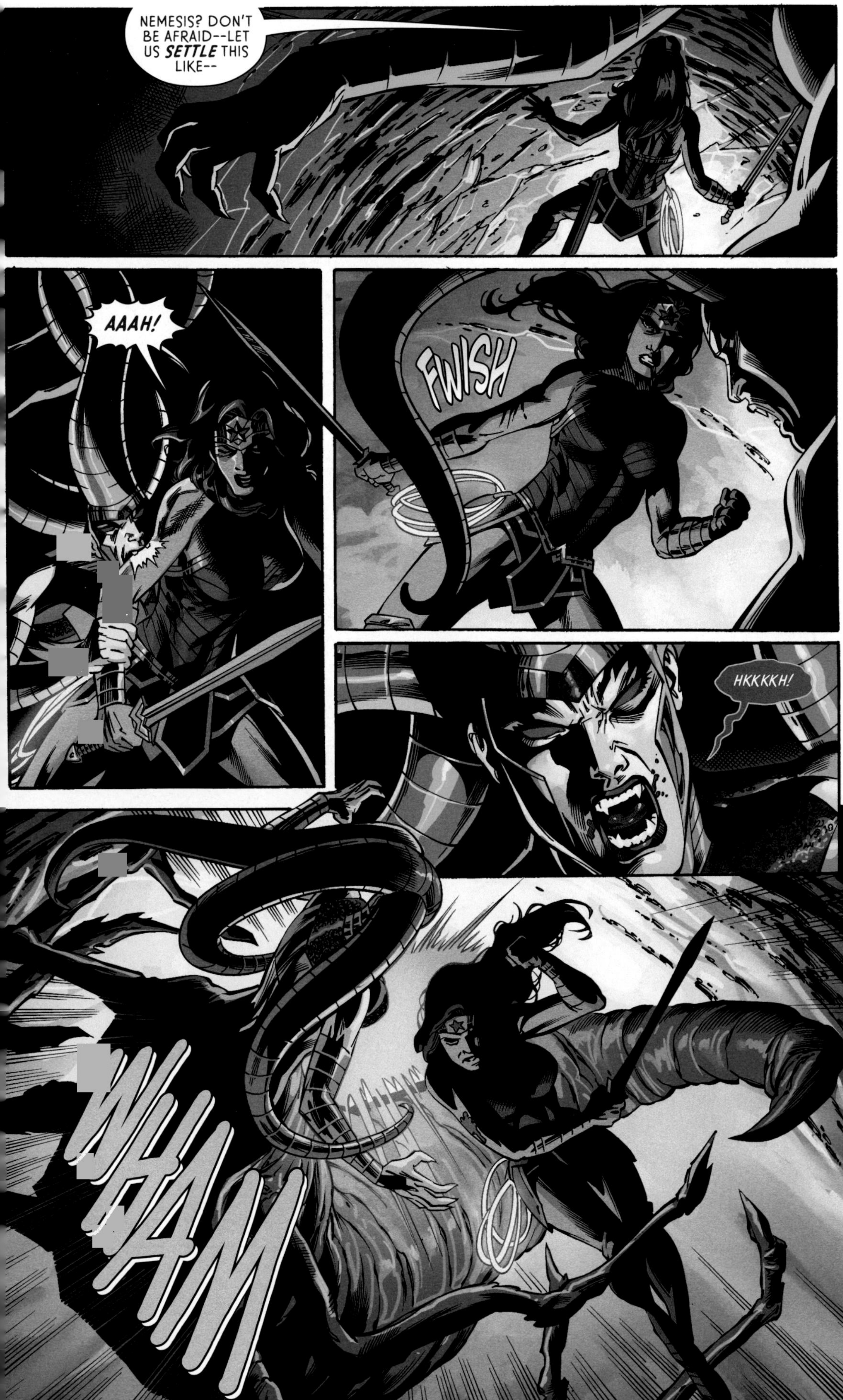
NEMESIS? DON'T BE AFRAID--LET US SETTLE THIS LIKE--
AAAH!
FWISH
HKKKKH!
WHAM

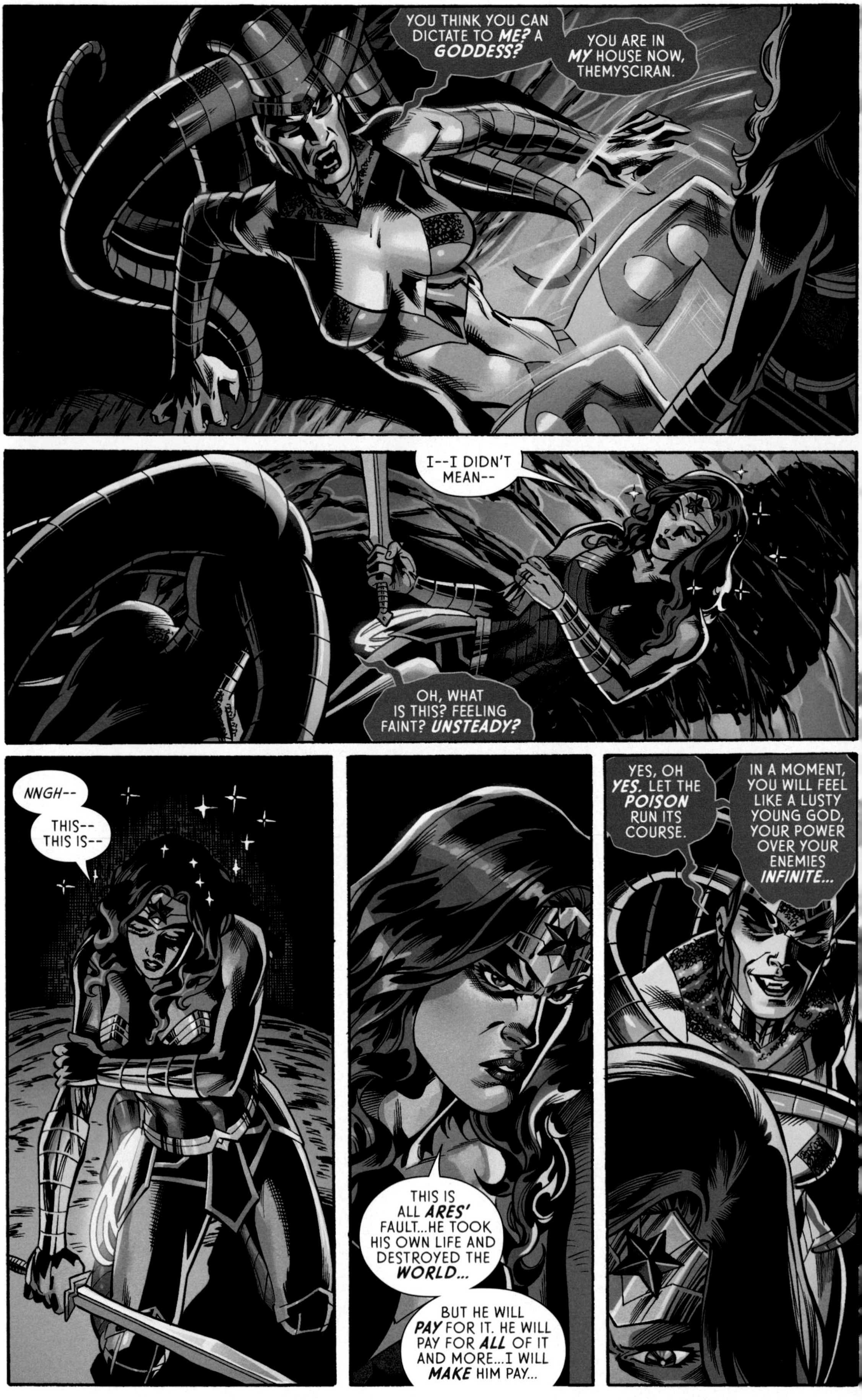
YOU THINK YOU CAN DICTATE TO *ME?* A *GODDESS?*
YOU ARE IN *MY* HOUSE NOW, THEMYSCIRAN.
I--I DIDN'T MEAN--
OH, WHAT IS THIS? FEELING FAINT? *UNSTEADY?*
NNGH--
THIS-- THIS IS--
THIS IS ALL *ARES'* FAULT...HE TOOK HIS OWN LIFE AND DESTROYED THE *WORLD...*
BUT HE WILL *PAY* FOR IT. HE WILL PAY FOR *ALL* OF IT AND MORE...I WILL *MAKE* HIM PAY...
YES, OH *YES.* LET THE *POISON* RUN ITS COURSE.
IN A MOMENT, YOU WILL FEEL LIKE A LUSTY YOUNG GOD, YOUR POWER OVER YOUR ENEMIES *INFINITE...*

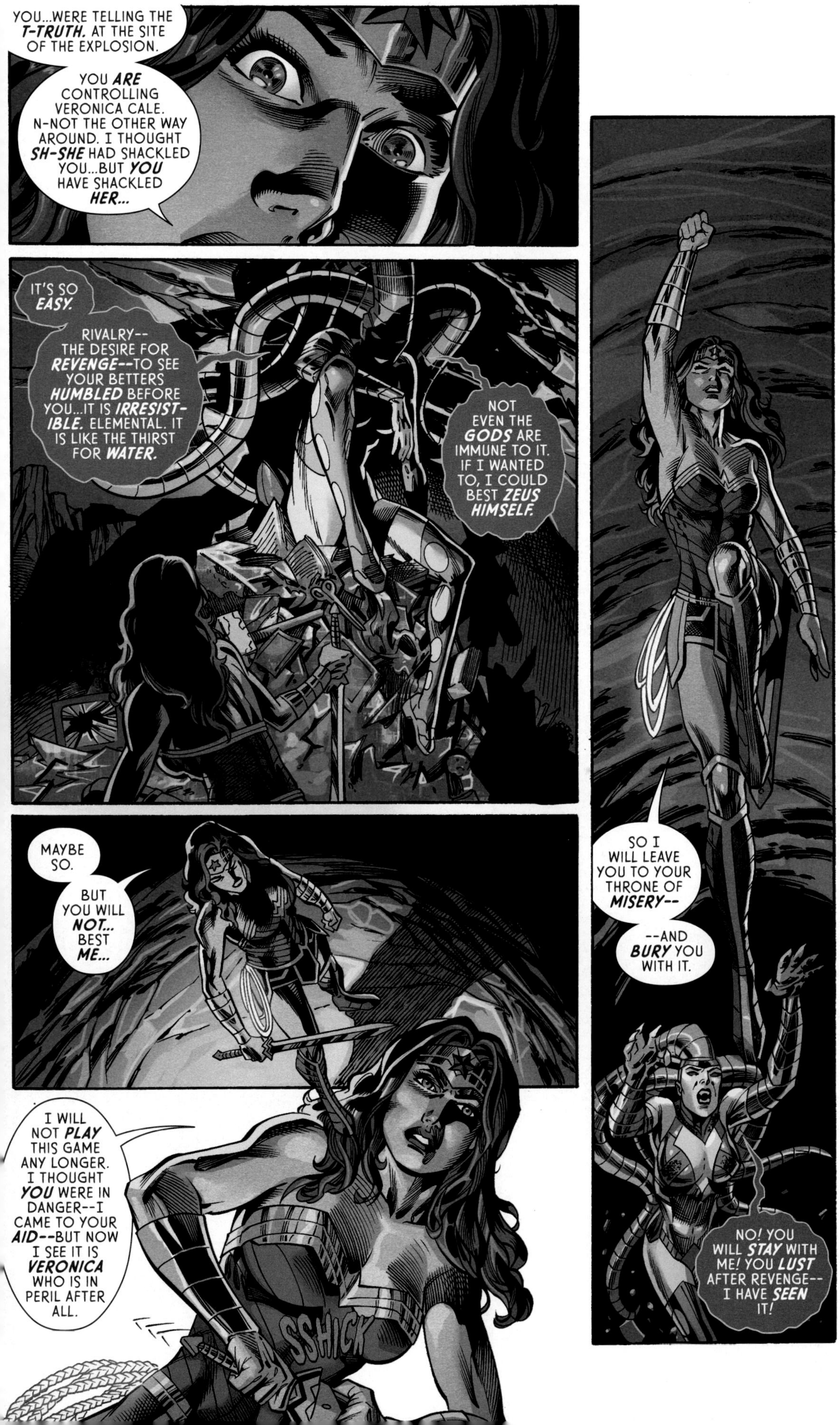
YOU...WERE TELLING THE T-TRUTH. AT THE SITE OF THE EXPLOSION.
YOU ARE CONTROLLING VERONICA CALE. N-NOT THE OTHER WAY AROUND. I THOUGHT SH-SHE HAD SHACKLED YOU...BUT YOU HAVE SHACKLED HER...
IT'S SO EASY.
RIVALRY-- THE DESIRE FOR REVENGE--TO SEE YOUR BETTERS HUMBLED BEFORE YOU...IT IS IRRESIST-IBLE. ELEMENTAL. IT IS LIKE THE THIRST FOR WATER.
NOT EVEN THE GODS ARE IMMUNE TO IT. IF I WANTED TO, I COULD BEST ZEUS HIMSELF.
MAYBE SO.
BUT YOU WILL NOT... BEST ME...
I WILL NOT PLAY THIS GAME ANY LONGER. I THOUGHT YOU WERE IN DANGER--I CAME TO YOUR AID--BUT NOW I SEE IT IS VERONICA WHO IS IN PERIL AFTER ALL.
SSHICK
SO I WILL LEAVE YOU TO YOUR THRONE OF MISERY--
--AND BURY YOU WITH IT.
NO! YOU WILL STAY WITH ME! YOU LUST AFTER REVENGE-- I HAVE SEEN IT!

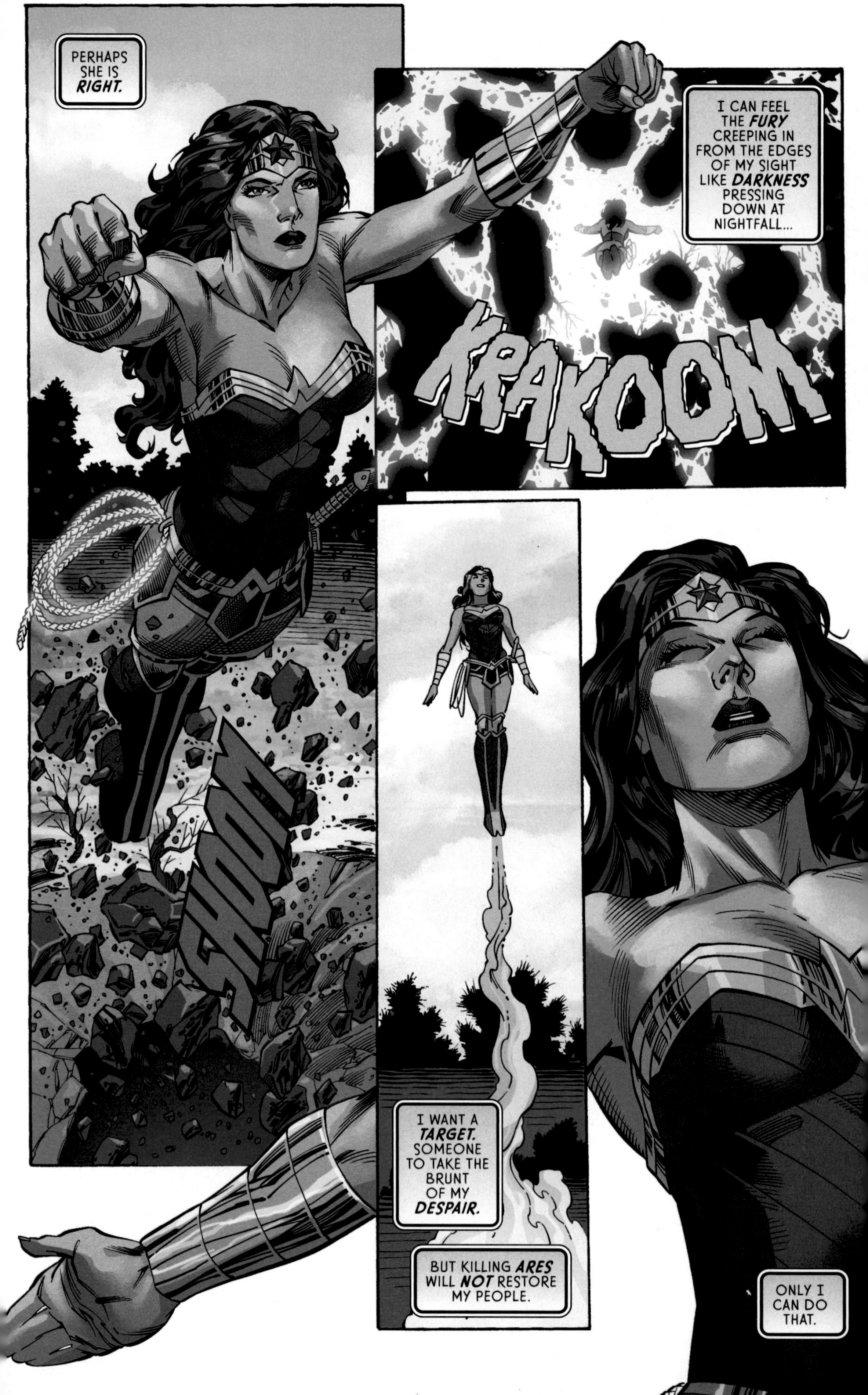

PERHAPS SHE IS *RIGHT.*
SHOOM
I CAN FEEL THE *FURY* CREEPING IN FROM THE EDGES OF MY SIGHT LIKE *DARKNESS* PRESSING DOWN AT NIGHTFALL...
KRAKOOM
I WANT A *TARGET.* SOMEONE TO TAKE THE BRUNT OF MY *DESPAIR.*
BUT KILLING *ARES* WILL *NOT* RESTORE MY PEOPLE.
ONLY I CAN DO THAT.

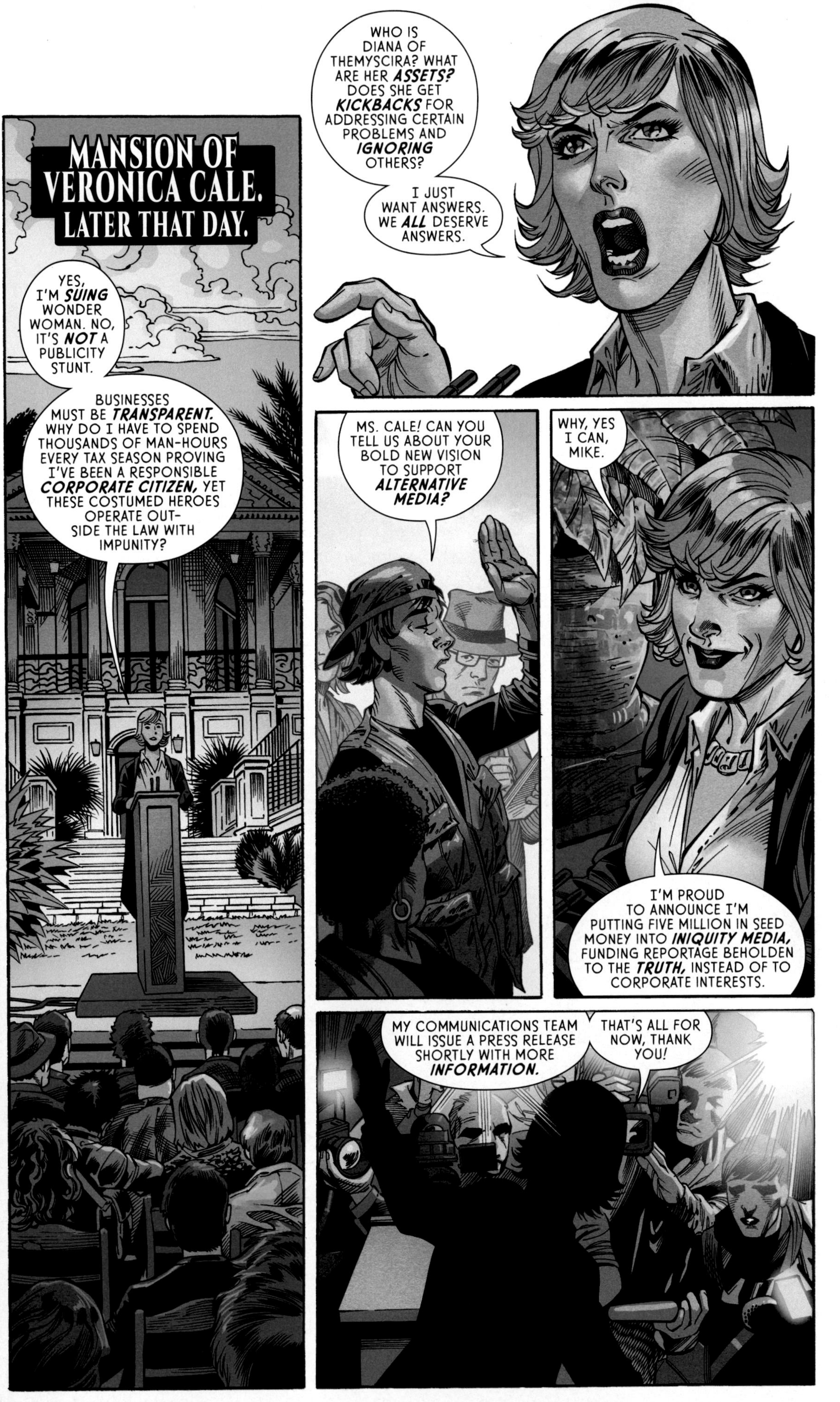
MANSION OF VERONICA CALE. LATER THAT DAY.
YES, I'M SUING WONDER WOMAN. NO, IT'S NOT A PUBLICITY STUNT.
BUSINESSES MUST BE TRANSPARENT. WHY DO I HAVE TO SPEND THOUSANDS OF MAN-HOURS EVERY TAX SEASON PROVING I'VE BEEN A RESPONSIBLE CORPORATE CITIZEN, YET THESE COSTUMED HEROES OPERATE OUTSIDE THE LAW WITH IMPUNITY?
WHO IS DIANA OF THEMYSCIRA? WHAT ARE HER ASSETS? DOES SHE GET KICKBACKS FOR ADDRESSING CERTAIN PROBLEMS AND IGNORING OTHERS?
I JUST WANT ANSWERS. WE ALL DESERVE ANSWERS.
MS. CALE! CAN YOU TELL US ABOUT YOUR BOLD NEW VISION TO SUPPORT ALTERNATIVE MEDIA?
WHY, YES I CAN, MIKE.
I'M PROUD TO ANNOUNCE I'M PUTTING FIVE MILLION IN SEED MONEY INTO INIQUITY MEDIA, FUNDING REPORTAGE BEHOLDEN TO THE TRUTH, INSTEAD OF TO CORPORATE INTERESTS.
MY COMMUNICATIONS TEAM WILL ISSUE A PRESS RELEASE SHORTLY WITH MORE INFORMATION.
THAT'S ALL FOR NOW, THANK YOU!

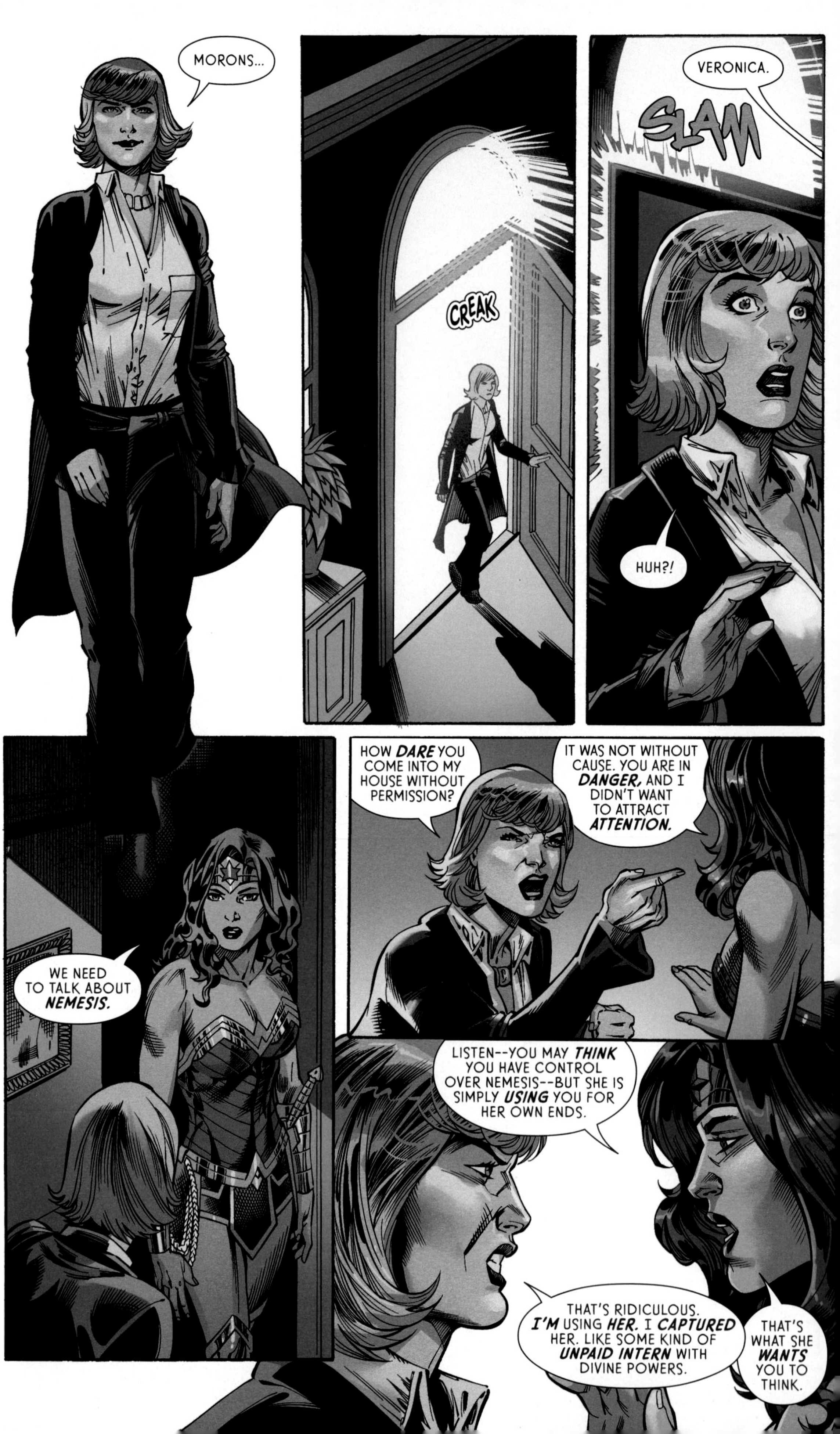
MORONS...
CREAK
VERONICA.
SLAM
HUH?!
WE NEED TO TALK ABOUT NEMESIS.
HOW DARE YOU COME INTO MY HOUSE WITHOUT PERMISSION?
IT WAS NOT WITHOUT CAUSE. YOU ARE IN DANGER, AND I DIDN'T WANT TO ATTRACT ATTENTION.
LISTEN--YOU MAY THINK YOU HAVE CONTROL OVER NEMESIS--BUT SHE IS SIMPLY USING YOU FOR HER OWN ENDS.
THAT'S RIDICULOUS. I'M USING HER. I CAPTURED HER. LIKE SOME KIND OF UNPAID INTERN WITH DIVINE POWERS.
THAT'S WHAT SHE WANTS YOU TO THINK.

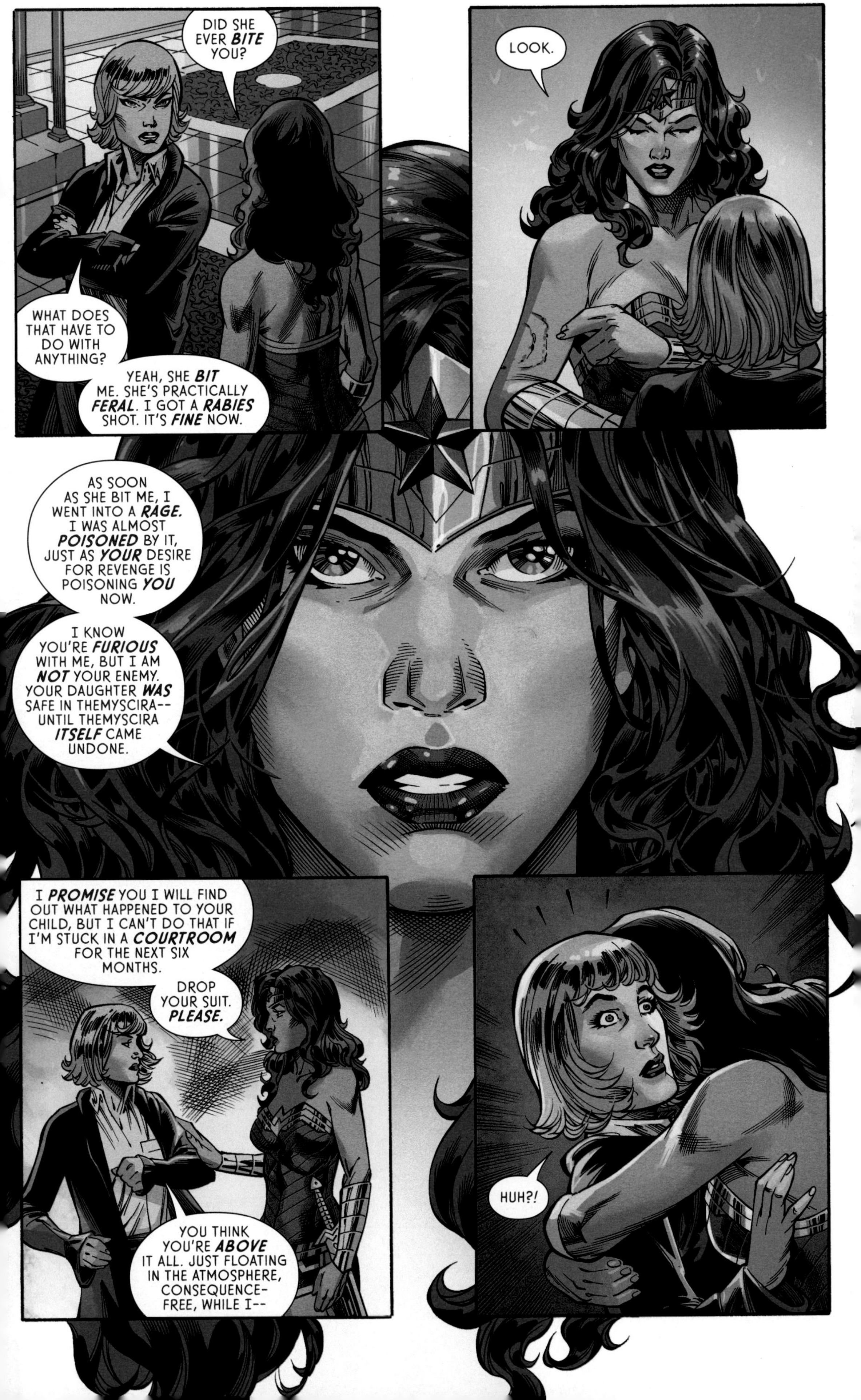
DID SHE EVER BITE YOU?
WHAT DOES THAT HAVE TO DO WITH ANYTHING?
YEAH, SHE BIT ME. SHE'S PRACTICALLY FERAL. I GOT A RABIES SHOT. IT'S FINE NOW.
LOOK.
AS SOON AS SHE BIT ME, I WENT INTO A RAGE. I WAS ALMOST POISONED BY IT, JUST AS YOUR DESIRE FOR REVENGE IS POISONING YOU NOW.
I KNOW YOU'RE FURIOUS WITH ME, BUT I AM NOT YOUR ENEMY. YOUR DAUGHTER WAS SAFE IN THEMYSCIRA-- UNTIL THEMYSCIRA ITSELF CAME UNDONE.
I PROMISE YOU I WILL FIND OUT WHAT HAPPENED TO YOUR CHILD, BUT I CAN'T DO THAT IF I'M STUCK IN A COURTROOM FOR THE NEXT SIX MONTHS.
DROP YOUR SUIT. PLEASE.
YOU THINK YOU'RE ABOVE IT ALL. JUST FLOATING IN THE ATMOSPHERE, CONSEQUENCE-FREE, WHILE I--
HUH?!

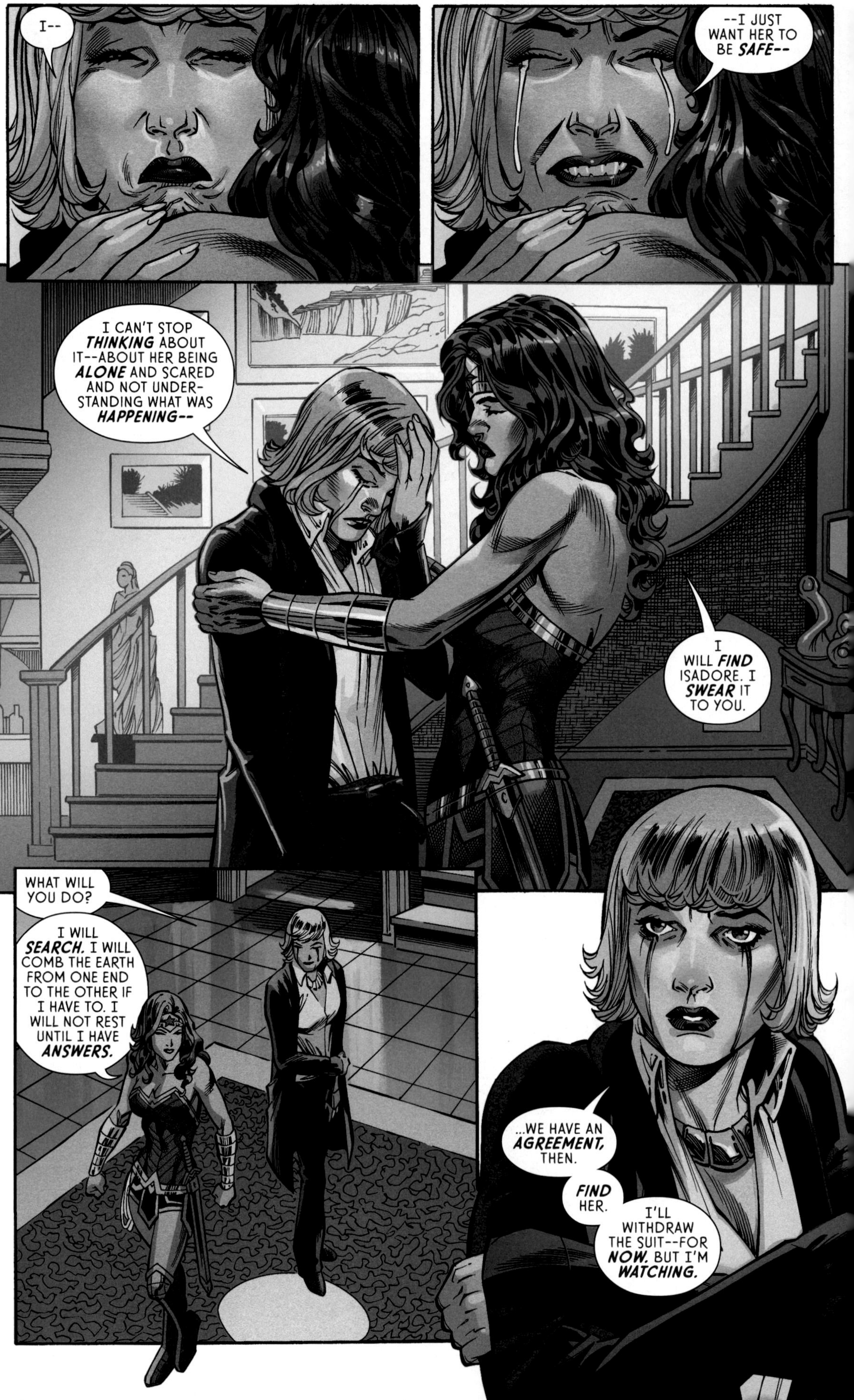
I--
--I JUST WANT HER TO BE *SAFE*--
I CAN'T STOP *THINKING* ABOUT IT--ABOUT HER BEING *ALONE* AND SCARED AND NOT UNDER-STANDING WHAT WAS *HAPPENING*--
I WILL *FIND* ISADORE. I *SWEAR* IT TO YOU.
WHAT WILL YOU DO?
I WILL *SEARCH.* I WILL COMB THE EARTH FROM ONE END TO THE OTHER IF I HAVE TO. I WILL NOT REST UNTIL I HAVE *ANSWERS.*
...WE HAVE AN *AGREEMENT,* THEN.
FIND HER.
I'LL WITHDRAW THE SUIT--FOR *NOW.* BUT I'M *WATCHING.*

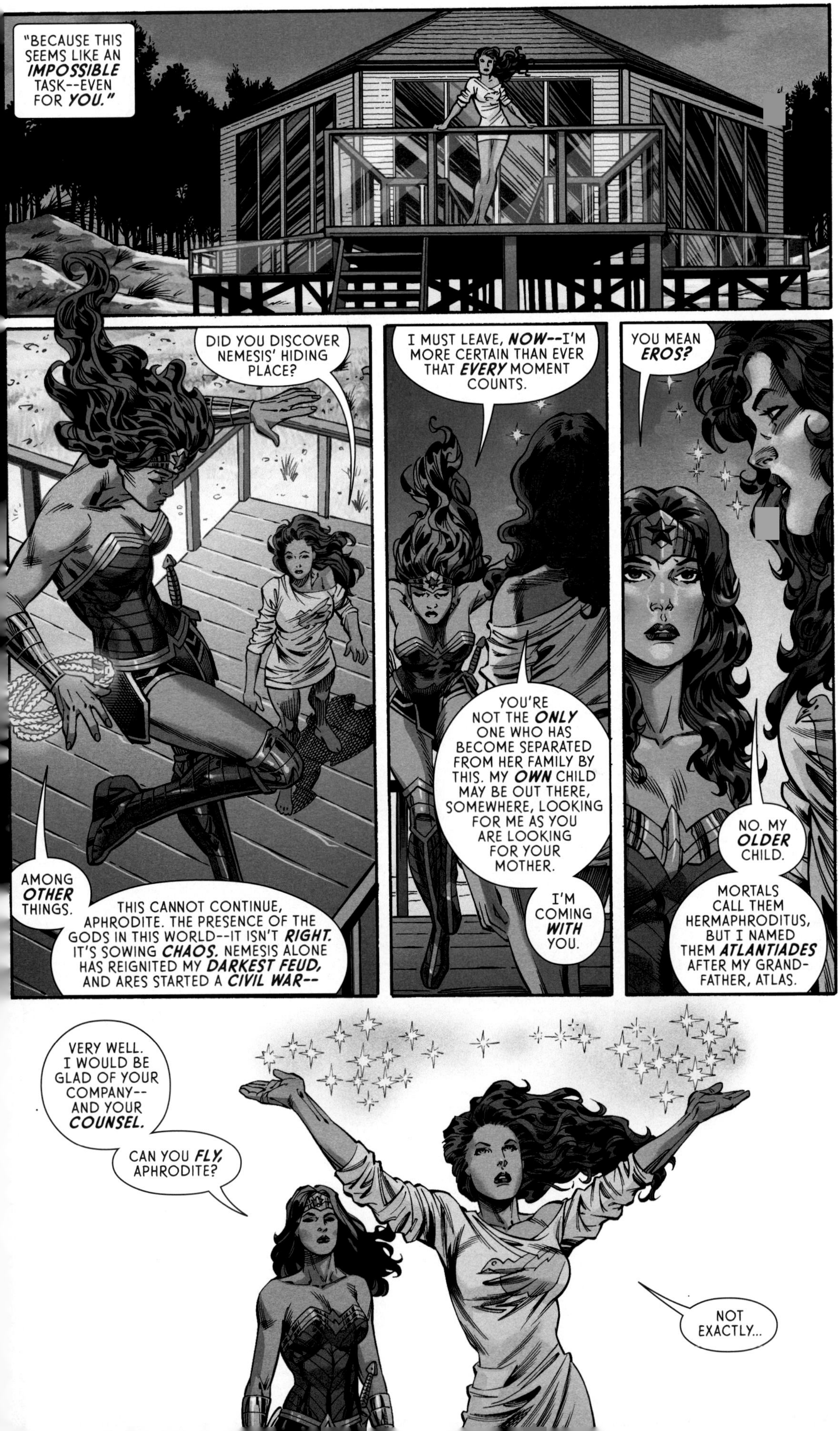
"BECAUSE THIS SEEMS LIKE AN IMPOSSIBLE TASK--EVEN FOR YOU."
DID YOU DISCOVER NEMESIS' HIDING PLACE?
AMONG OTHER THINGS.
THIS CANNOT CONTINUE, APHRODITE. THE PRESENCE OF THE GODS IN THIS WORLD--IT ISN'T RIGHT. IT'S SOWING CHAOS. NEMESIS ALONE HAS REIGNITED MY DARKEST FEUD, AND ARES STARTED A CIVIL WAR--
I MUST LEAVE, NOW--I'M MORE CERTAIN THAN EVER THAT EVERY MOMENT COUNTS.
YOU'RE NOT THE ONLY ONE WHO HAS BECOME SEPARATED FROM HER FAMILY BY THIS. MY OWN CHILD MAY BE OUT THERE, SOMEWHERE, LOOKING FOR ME AS YOU ARE LOOKING FOR YOUR MOTHER.
I'M COMING WITH YOU.
YOU MEAN EROS?
NO. MY OLDER CHILD.
MORTALS CALL THEM HERMAPHRODITUS, BUT I NAMED THEM ATLANTIADES AFTER MY GRAND-FATHER, ATLAS.
VERY WELL. I WOULD BE GLAD OF YOUR COMPANY--AND YOUR COUNSEL.
CAN YOU FLY, APHRODITE?
NOT EXACTLY...

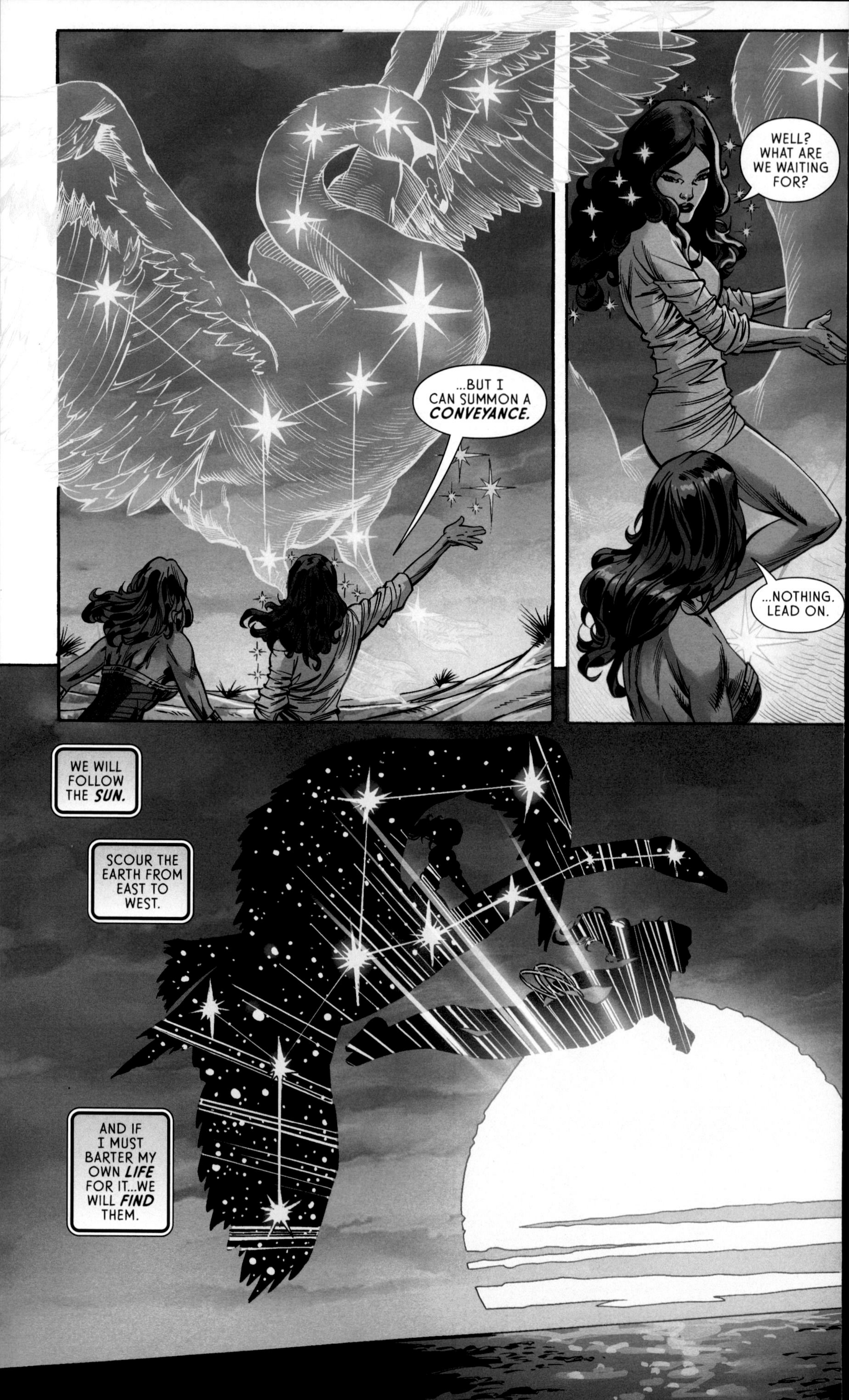
...BUT I
CAN SUMMON A
CONVEYANCE.
WELL?
WHAT ARE
WE WAITING
FOR?
...NOTHING.
LEAD ON.
WE WILL
FOLLOW
THE *SUN.*
SCOUR THE
EARTH FROM
EAST TO
WEST.
AND IF
I MUST
BARTER MY
OWN *LIFE*
FOR IT...WE
WILL *FIND*
THEM.

VARIANT COVER GALLERY

WONDER WOMAN #58 variant cover
by **JENNY FRISON**

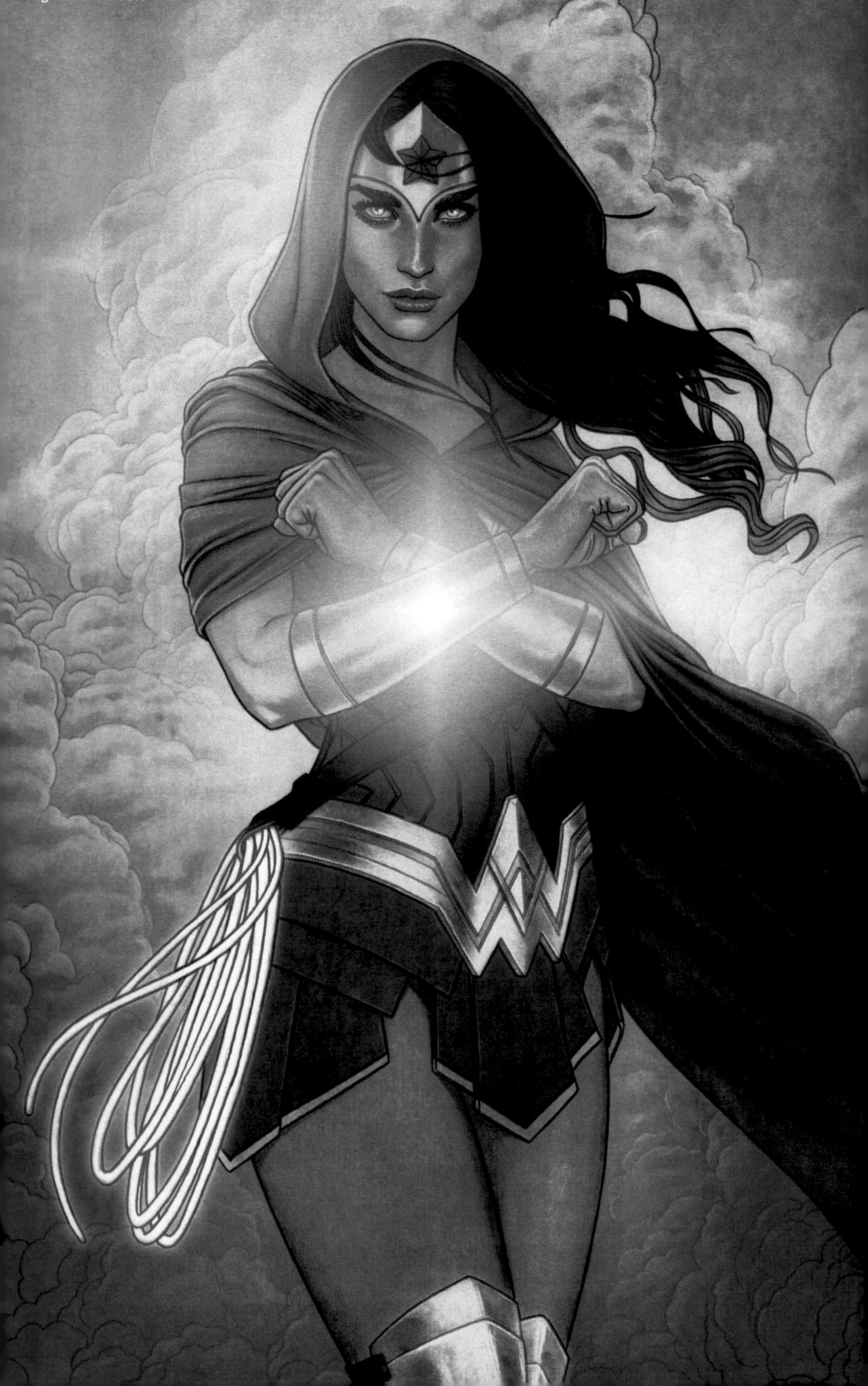

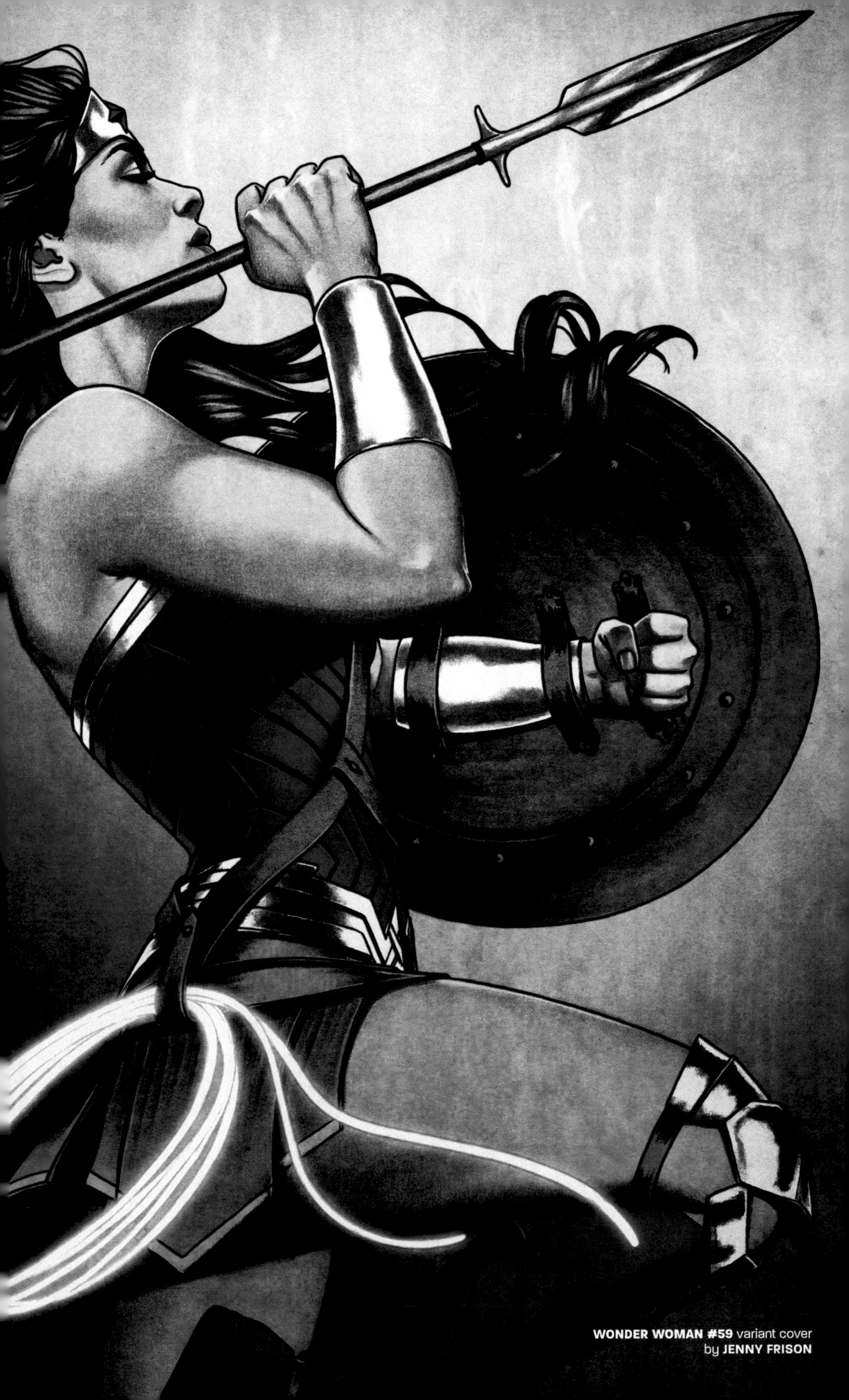

WONDER WOMAN #59 variant cover
by **JENNY FRISON**

WONDER WOMAN #60 variant cover
by **JENNY FRISON**

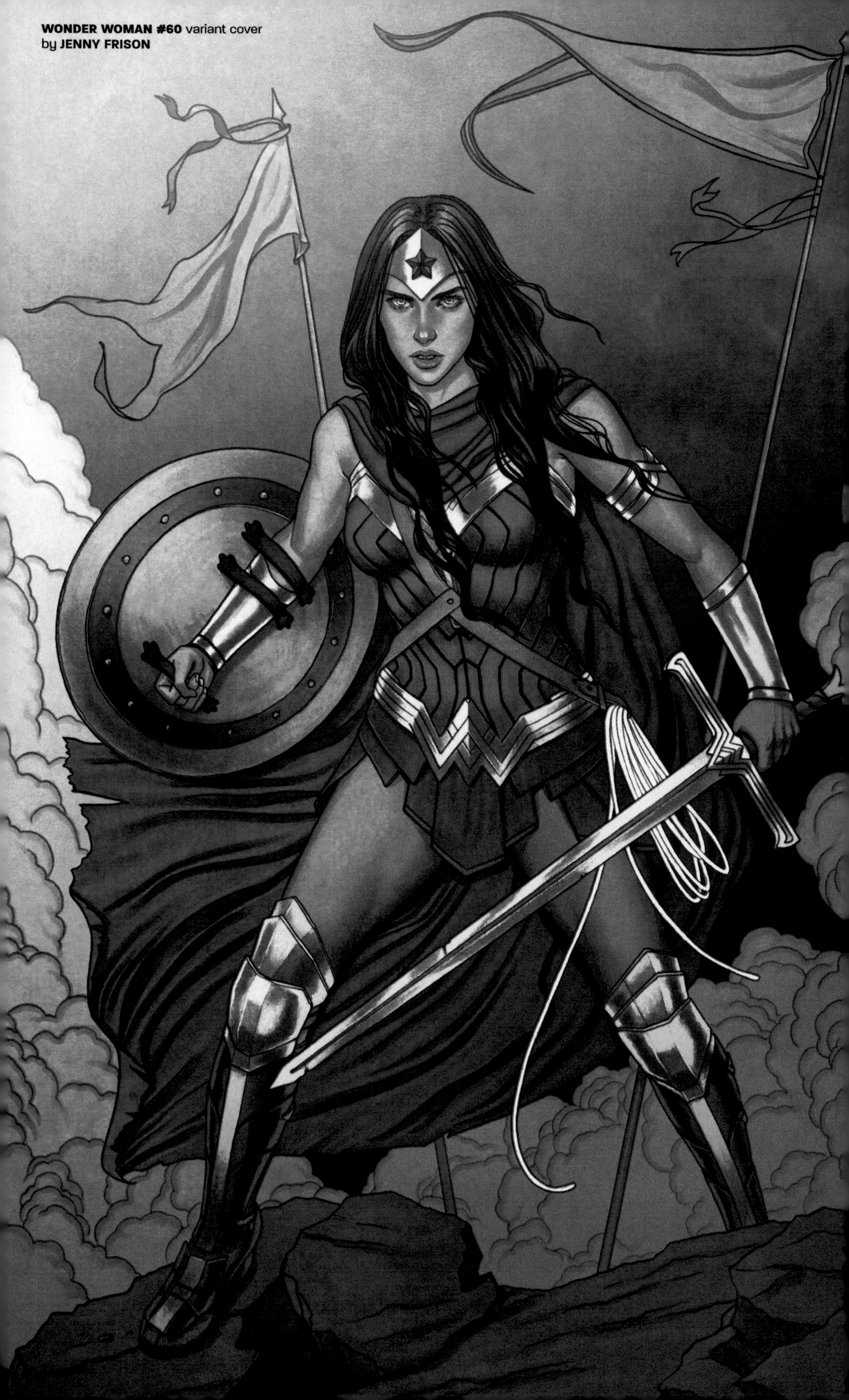

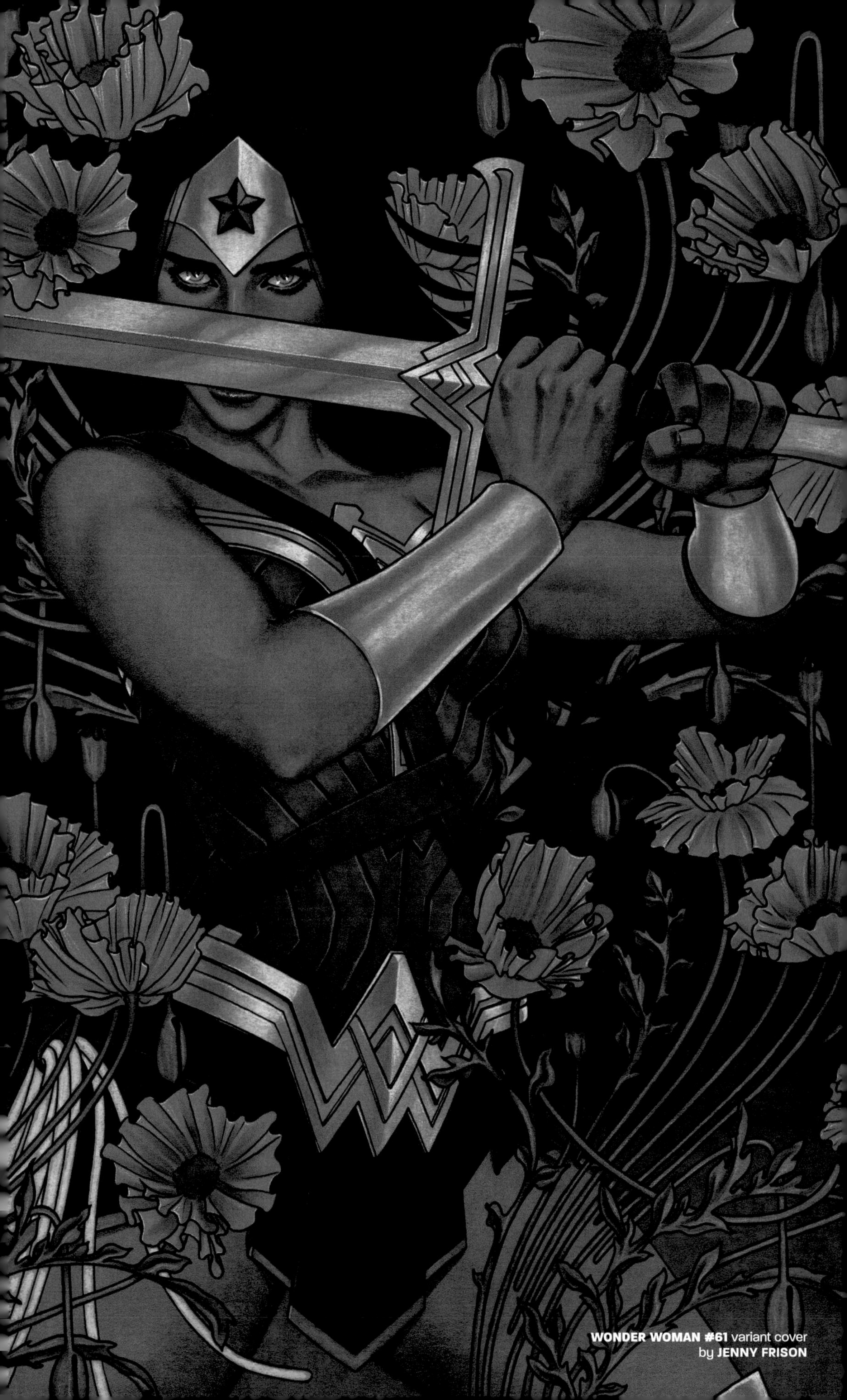

WONDER WOMAN #61 variant cover
by **JENNY FRISON**

WONDER WOMAN #62 variant cover
by **MATTEO SCALERA**

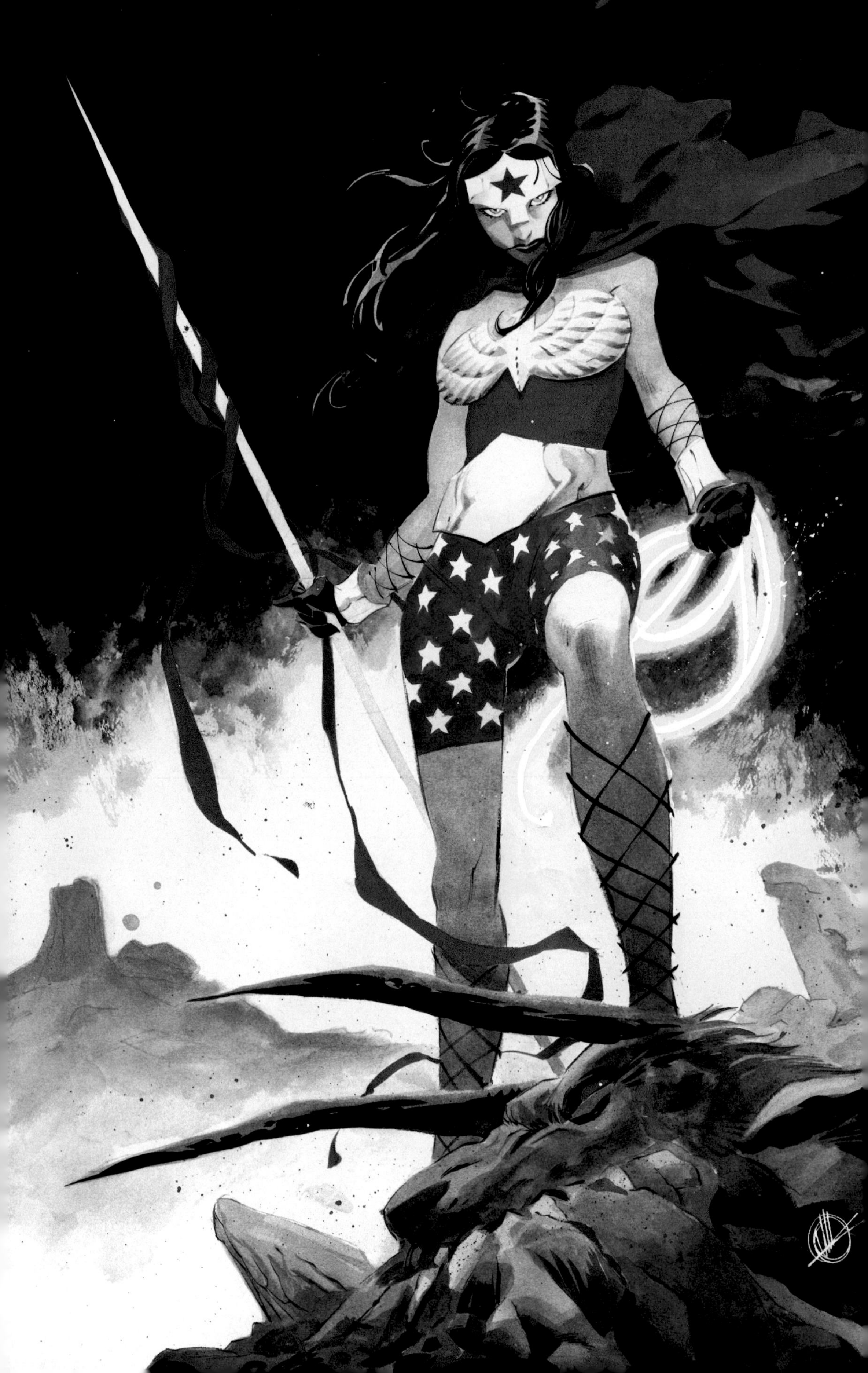

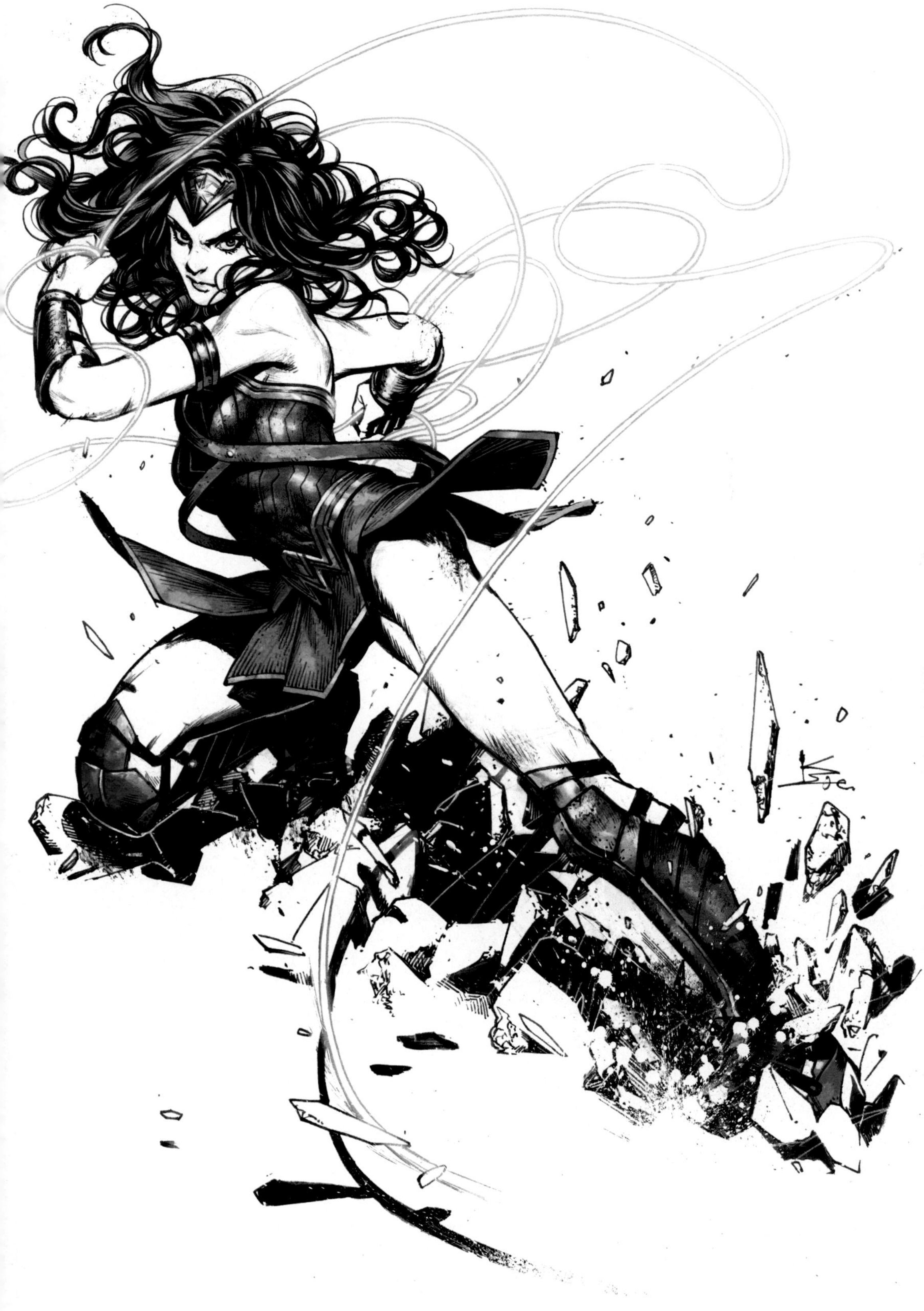

WONDER WOMAN #63 variant cover
by **KAMOME SHIRAHAMA**

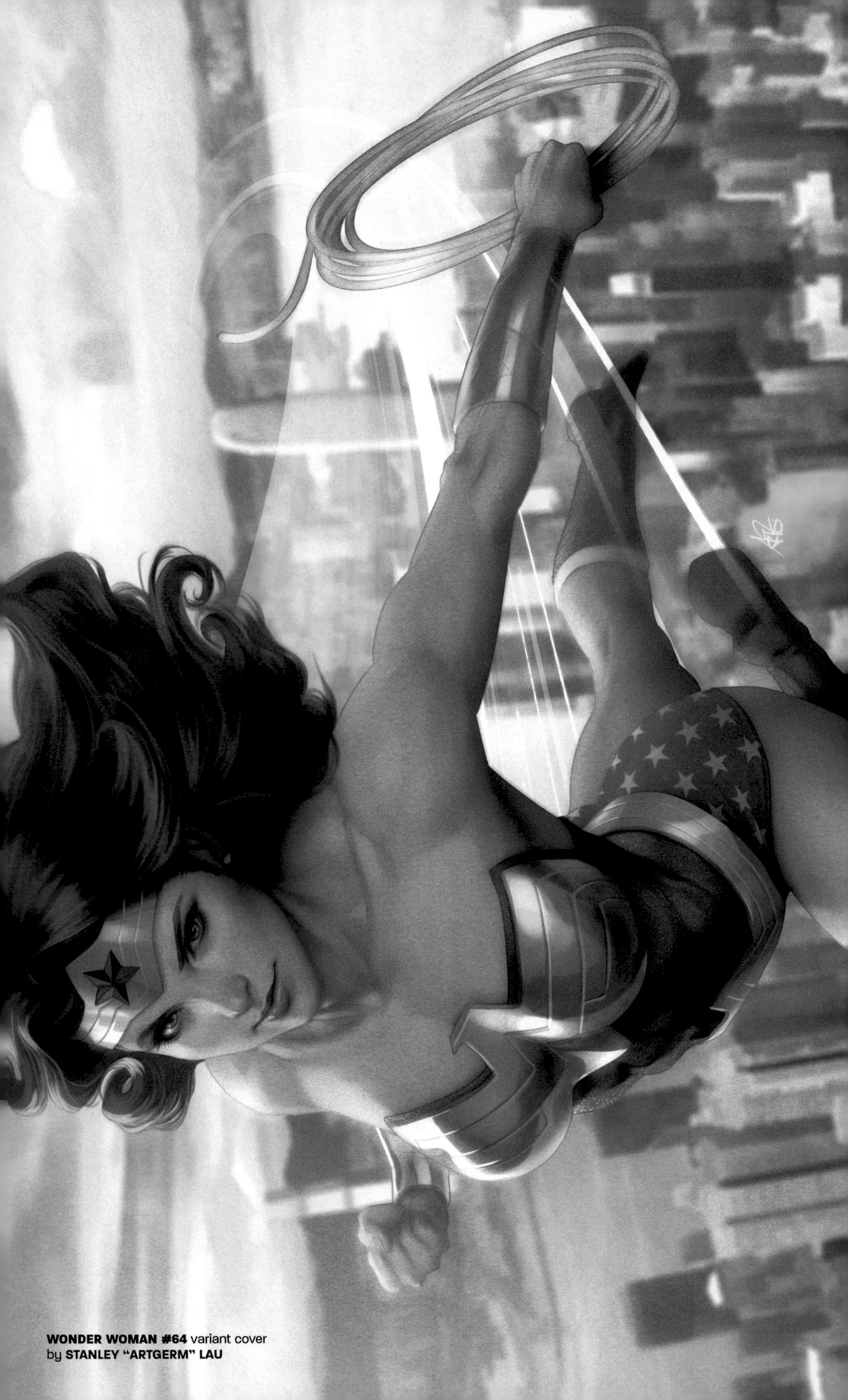

WONDER WOMAN #64 variant cover
by **STANLEY "ARTGERM" LAU**

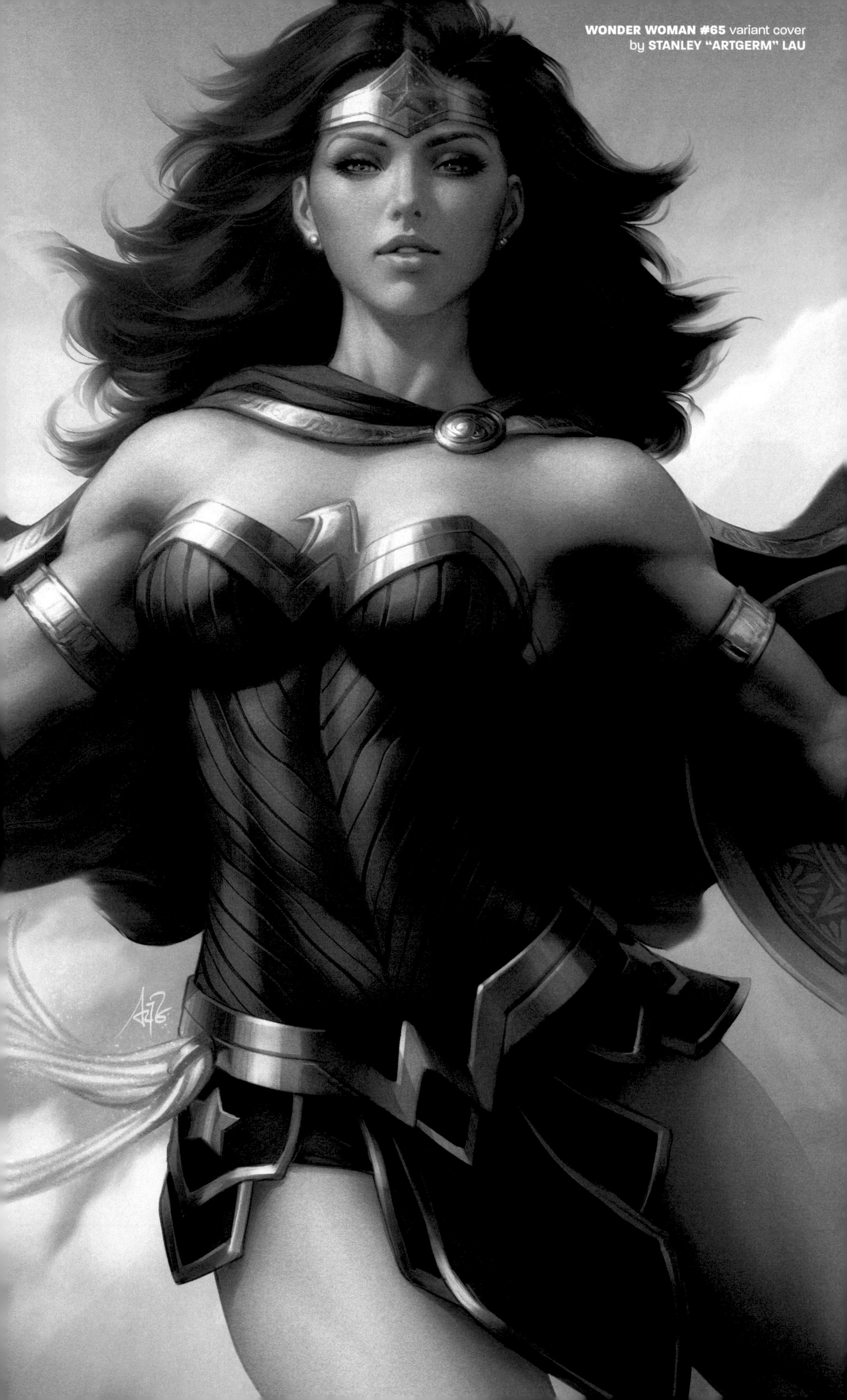

WONDER WOMAN #65 variant cover
by **STANLEY "ARTGERM" LAU**

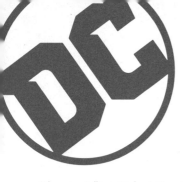

"Clear storytelling at its best. It's an intriguing concept and easy to grasp."
– THE NEW YORK TIMES

"Azzarello is rebuilding the mythology of Wonder Woman."
– CRAVE ONLINE

THE NEW YORK TIMES BESTSELLER
THE NEW 52!
WONDER WOMAN
"EXPECT A LOT MORE WONDER WOMAN FANS AFTER A FEW ISSUES OF THIS BOOK."
— USA TODAY
VOLUME 1 BLOOD
BRIAN AZZARELLO CLIFF CHIANG TONY AKINS

WONDER WOMAN
VOL. 1: BLOOD
BRIAN AZZARELLO
with CLIFF CHIANG

THE NEW YORK TIMES BEST-SELLING SERIES
THE NEW 52!
WONDER WOMAN
VOLUME 2 GUTS
BRIAN AZZARELLO CLIFF CHIANG TONY AKINS

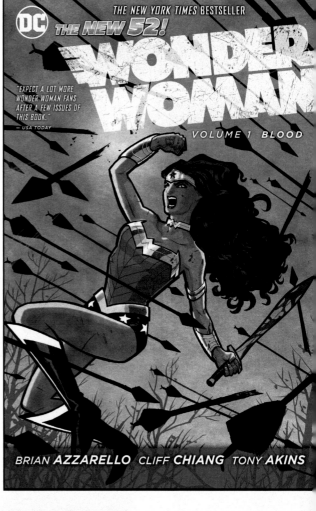

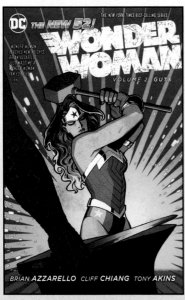

WONDER WOMAN VOL. 2: GUTS

THE NEW 52!
THE #1 NEW YORK TIMES BESTSELLING SERIES
WONDER WOMAN
VOLUME 3 IRON
BRIAN AZZARELLO CLIFF CHIANG

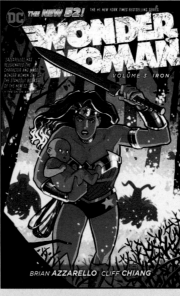

WONDER WOMAN VOL. 3: IRON

READ THE ENTIRE EPI

WONDER WOMAN VOL.
W

WONDER WOMAN VOL.
FLE

WONDER WOMAN VOL
BON

WONDER WOMAN VOL
WAR-TO

WONDER WOMAN VOL.
A TWIST OF FA

WONDER WOMAN VOL
RESURRECTI

Get more DC graphic novels wherever comics and books are sold!

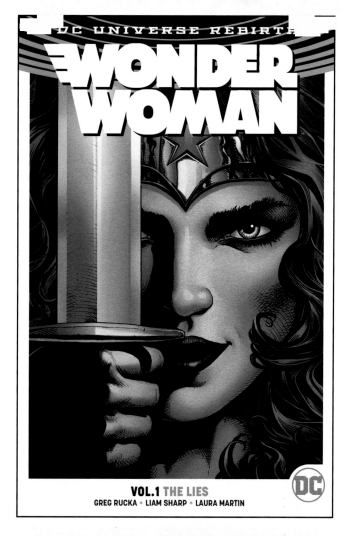

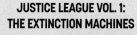

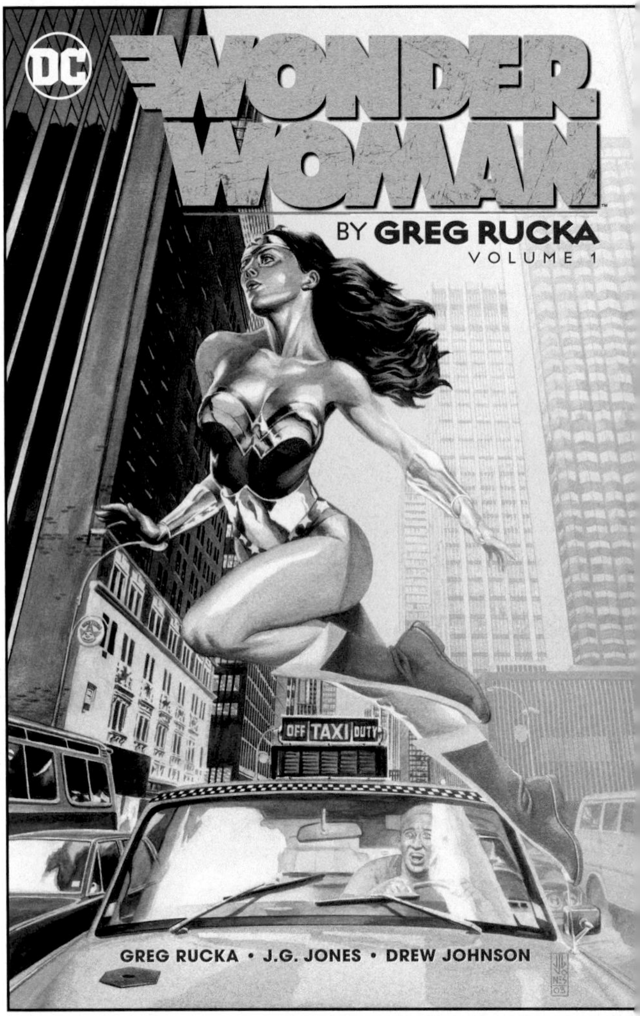
WONDER WOMAN
BY GREG RUCKA
VOLUME 1
OFF TAXI DUTY
GREG RUCKA • J.G. JONES • DREW JOHNSON

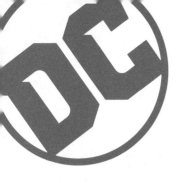

"One of the best writers for Wonder Woman in the modern era."
– NERDIST

WONDER WOMAN BY GREG RUCKA
with J.G. JONES & DREW JOHNSON

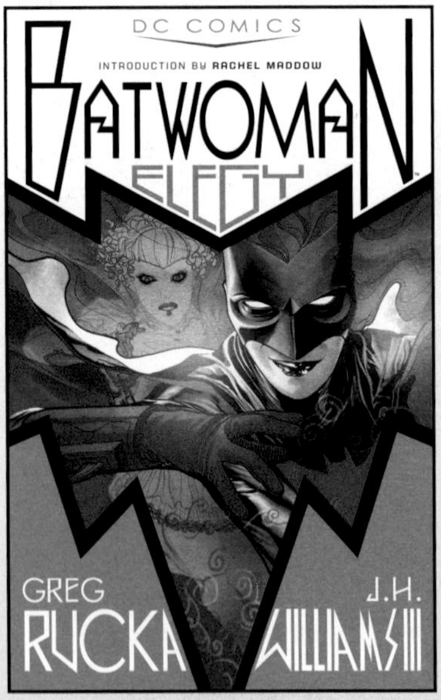
DC COMICS
INTRODUCTION BY RACHEL MADDOW
BATWOMAN
ELEGY
GREG RUCKA
J.H. WILLIAMS III

BATWOMAN: ELEGY with J.H. WILLIAMS III

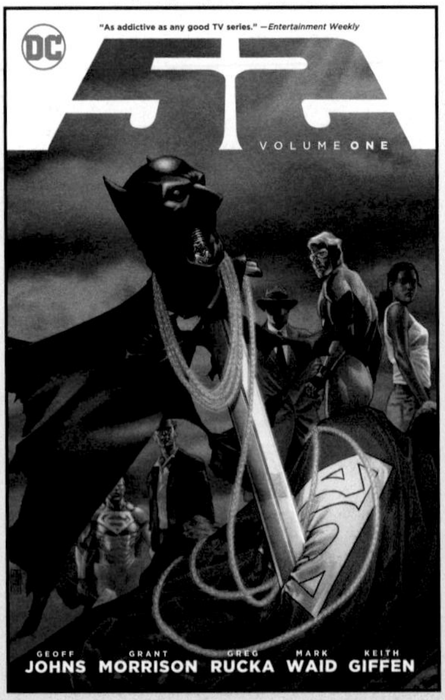
"As addictive as any good TV series." —Entertainment Weekly
52
VOLUME ONE
GEOFF JOHNS
GRANT MORRISON
GREG RUCKA
MARK WAID
KEITH GIFFEN

52 VOL. 1 with VARIOUS ARTISTS

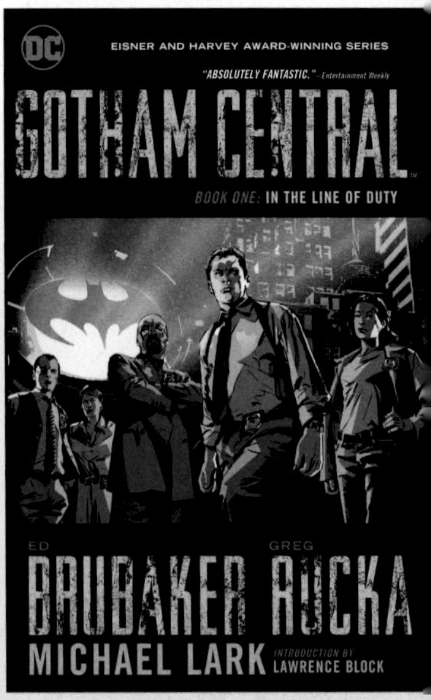
EISNER AND HARVEY AWARD-WINNING SERIES
"ABSOLUTELY FANTASTIC." –Entertainment Weekly
GOTHAM CENTRAL
BOOK ONE: IN THE LINE OF DUTY
ED BRUBAKER
GREG RUCKA
MICHAEL LARK
INTRODUCTION BY LAWRENCE BLOCK

GOTHAM CENTRAL BOOK ONE with ED BRUBAKER & MICHAEL LARK

Get more DC graphic novels wherever comics and books are sold!